Oh, That You Would Rend the Heavens and Come Down!

Oh, That You Would Rend the Heavens and Come Down!

The Eschatological Theology of Third Isaiah
(Isaiah 56–66)

Abraham Sung-Ho Oh

☙PICKWICK *Publications* · Eugene, Oregon

OH, THAT YOU WOULD REND THE HEAVENS AND COME DOWN!
The Eschatological Theology of Third Isaiah (Isaiah 56–66)

Pickwick Publications
An Imprint of Wipf and Stock Publishers
199 W. 8th Ave., Suite 3
Eugene, OR 97401

www.wipfandstock.com

ISBN 13: 978-1-62564-729-0

Cataloguing-in-Publication Data

Oh, Abraham Sung-Ho.

Oh, that you would rend the heavens and come down! : the eschatological theology of Third Isaiah (Isaiah 56–66)

xiv + 270 p. ; 23 cm. Includes bibliographical references.

ISBN 13: 978-1-62564-729-0

1. Bible. O.T. Isaiah—Criticism, interpretation, etc.. 2. Bible. Isaiah, LVI–LXVI—Criticism, interpretation, etc. 3. Eschatology—Biblical teaching.

BS1520.5 O44 2014

Manufactured in the U.S.A.

To the Holy Spirit,
who builds up and strengthens the church
through the Word and truth of God

Contents

Preface

This book is a lightly revised version of my Ph.D. dissertation. The title, *Oh, That You Would Rend the Heavens and Come Down! The Eschatological Theology of Third Isaiah (Isaiah 56–66)*, was originally that of the dissertation itself.

I give great thanks to my supervisors, Dr. Philip Jenson and Dr. Gordon Wenham. Dr. Jenson was my primary supervisor, who guided me from the beginning of my research. With his grateful aid and help, I upgraded to a Ph.D course and completed the dissertation. He has always been very kind to me and thorough in reading and commenting my writings. Because sometimes he has posited a different point of view from mine, I sometimes had difficulties, but eventually I was enabled to clarify my arguments through his critical insights. Through him, in the end, I have learned how to accept and continue a dialogue with someone who has different views, which is a great asset that I have gained from the life in the UK. Dr. Wenham has supervised me especially after Dr. Jenson has left for Ridley Hall, Cambridge. He was really kind and friendly. Due to Dr. Wenham's supervision, I was able to reset the overall structure of the dissertation. His comments were very useful, especially at the stage of completing the dissertation.

I also give thanks to my wife Hannah (Young-Ran Kim) and my children Paul (Jong-Wook) and Grace (Jee-Eun). My life with them in the UK is a real happiness, albeit as a stranger. Their love and prayer have continuously given strength and energy to me. Especially, every evening's prayer time with my wife has been precious as it spiritually sustained me. Although they also have experienced difficulties in the foreign land, all of us have had a beautiful time, which would have been impossible if we have continued to live just in Korea.

I have also to appreciate my co-workers and friends in the Bristol Korean Church. Kyounghoon Lee and his wife Hannah Kook and Jimin Rhee, members of the Praise and Worship Mission Team, were a great encouragement to me and to my church at the first stage of my ministry at the church. The church members, especially those who have attended the Friday prayer meeting, were great encouragement, too. In addition, I need to give thanks to many at the Trinity College as well as Shirehampton Baptist Church who are not mentioned by name.

I devote this book to the Holy Spirit so that He may use it for His work building up and strengthening Christ's church through the truth and the Word of God. Thanks and praises to the Lord as He has led me to study for a Ph.D. and provided all I needed while I was studying in a foreign country.

My prayer has always been that God's revival would come, not only to the Korean Church, but also to the churches in Bristol and the U.K. and in the whole world—"Oh, that You would rend the Heavens and come down!"

Abbreviations

1QIs^a	one of the original Dead Sea Scrolls for the Book of Isaiah

1QIs^a   one of the original Dead Sea Scrolls for the Book of Isaiah

ABD   *Anchor Bible Dictionary.* 6 vols. Edited by David Noel Freedman et al. New York: Doubleday, 1992.

BWANT   *Beiträge zur Wissenschaft vom Alten und Neuen Testament*

BZAW   Beihefte zur Zeitschrift für die alttestamentliche Wissenschaft

CBQ   *Catholic Biblical Quarterly*

ch   chapter

chs   chapters

CTJ   *Calvin Theological Journal*

DI   Second Isaiah

DNTB   *Dictionary of New Testament Background.* Edited by Craig Evans and Stanley Porter, 45–58. Downers Grove, IL: InterVarsity, 2000.

ESV   English Standard Version

IDB   *The Interpreter's Dictionary of the Bible.* 4 vols. Edited by George Arther Buttrick. Nashville: Abingdon, 1982.

IDBSup   *The Interpreter's Dictionary of the Bible Supplementary Volume.* Edited by Keith Crim. Nashville: Abingdon, 1984.

JBL   *Journal of Biblical Literature*

JETS   *Journal of Evangelical Theological Society*

JNES   Journal of Near Eastern Studies

JSNTSS   Journal for the Study of the Old Testament Supplement Series

JSOT   *Journal for the Study of the Old Testament*

JSOTSS	Journal for the Study of the Old Testament Supplement Series
KJV	King James Version
masc.	masculine
MT	Masoretic Text
NICOT	New International Commentary on the Old Testament
NIDOTTE	*New International Dictionary of the Old Testament Theology and Exegesis.* 5 vols. Edited by Willem A. VanGemeren. Grand Rapids: Zondervan, 1997.
n.d.	no date
n.p.	no page
NRSV	New Revised Standard Version
NT	New Testament
OT	Old Testament
OTL	Old Testament Library
PI	First Isaiah
pl.	plural
sg.	singular
Syr.	Syrian version
Targ.	Targums
TDIB	*Theological Dictionary for the Interpretation of the Bible.* Edited by Kevin Vanvoozer et al. Grand Rapids: Baker Academic, 2005.
TDOT	*Theological Dictionary of the Old Testament.* 15 vols. Edited by G. Johannes Botterwreck and Helmer Ringgren. Grand Rapids: Eerdmans, 1974–2006.
TI	Third Isaiah
TLOT	*Theological Lexicon of the Old Testament.* 3 vols. Edited by Ernest Jenni, with assistance from Claus Westermann, translated by Mark E. Biddle. Peabody, MA: Hendrickson, 1997.
TWOT	*Theological Wordbook of the Old Testament.* 2 vols. Edited by R. Laird Harris et al. Chicago: Moody, 1980.
v.	verse
VT	*Vetus Testamentum*

VTSup	Vetus Testamentum, Supplements
vv.	verses
WTJ	*Westminster Theological Journal*
ZAW	*Zeitschrift für die alttestamentliche Wissenschaft*

Chapter 1

Introduction

1.1 Introduction

Is there a coherent theology in Third Isaiah (TI)?[1] Volz says about TI, *"Tatsächlich sind die Unterschiede innerhalb der Abschnitte in zeitgeschichtlicher, stilistischer, geistiger und religiöser Hinsicht so groß, daß mir eine Einheitlichkeit der Persönlichkeit wie des Zeitraums ausgeschlossen erscheint."*[2] According to Volz, there is no integrated theology in TI as the segments of the text are distinct in terms of theology as well as authorship. On the other hand, Skinner writes, "the theology of the Trito-Isaianic prophecies has too little independence or originality to be made the subject of separate exposition. . . . The forms and imagery in which the longing for salvation is expressed are mostly borrowed from the older prophet [Second Isaiah]," implying the theological unity of Isaiah 40–66.[3] Childs goes even further,

1. TI (Trito-Isaiah) was originally the name given to the alleged prophet who is assumed to have written the section of Isaiah 56–66. However, since the hypothesis of multiple authorship of chs 56–66 has been raised, it came to refer to the writing itself. In these days, it may denote either or both of them according to the context of discussion. My usage of the term does not necessarily mean the alleged anonymous prophet as the issue of authorship does not form part of the primary concern of my study. First and Second Isaiah are abbreviated as PI (Proto-Isaiah) and DI (Deutero-Isaiah), respectively.

2. Volz 1932:199. "Really the differences within the segments are so great from a chronological, stylistic, spiritual, and religious point of view that the unity of the personality [i.e., author] as well as the period seems to me impossible." My translation.

3. Skinner 1898/1917:lxv. He (1898:xlv–lxvii) has worked out the unified theological

1

commenting, "[R]ather, it is essential to maintain them [the chapters of TI] as genuine prophecy that responds to the divine word, 'Thus says Yahweh,' an integral part of the larger prophetic book of Isaiah." Childs proposes the theological unity of the book of Isaiah.[4]

The diverse views on the theological unity of TI may reflect the fact that there are so many materials in TI—diverse in theological themes, concepts, motifs, and traditions. This theological diversity in TI materials has often been considered incompatible in a unified theology. The theological unity has also been disputed due to the alleged different historical situations and references in TI. But others have considered that these are not explicitly determined by internal evidence. Those who emphasize the canonical relation of TI to the rest of the book of Isaiah tend to see the theological unity of TI, although this also increases the complexity of theological discussions of TI. Judging by these different approaches, the problem is not just about the existence of diversity, but also the interpretation of the various materials.

In reality, theological unity may be seen either as the conclusion of theological study or as the assumption and starting point of it. As I have observed, no one has tried to investigate and demonstrate the theological unity of TI (or the book of Isaiah). Every scholar seems to assume the theological unity or disunity in accord with their preconceptions of the TI material. If I assume theological unity instead of disunity (see 1.2), my previous question may be changed: What would a coherent theology of TI look like?

This is what I am going to do in this dissertation—construct a coherent theology of TI. After an in-depth investigation of the methodologies for Old Testament theology, Hasel has suggested that the task of OT theology is to provide the "summary explanations and interpretations of the final form of the individual OT writings or blocks of writings."[5] Even though his study focused on OT theology in general, it is a useful articulation of what this dissertation is seeking to accomplish, a summary of the theology of TI, which to some extent may also be "a Biblical (or OT) theology in miniature."[6]

The question of coherent theology is followed by another question: how may such a coherent theology be constructed? The theological synthesis of a book, as Martens proposes, acknowledges the importance of accurate and detailed exegesis, but it is essentially a creative and imaginative

concepts of DI and TI.

4. Childs 2001:443. Also see Childs 1979:325–30. Childs has written his commentary (2001) based on this assumption.

5. Hasel 1989:93. However, this may be only one of the possible goals of OT theology.

6. Kraus 1992:12.

process which may not be reduced to exegesis.[7] I assume that a coherent theology is possible only on the assumption of the theological unity of TI. On the other hand, Hasel suggested a multiplex approach to the structure of OT theology and warned against adopting unified dogmatic categories or a single structuring concept, in order that the various themes, motifs, and concepts related to one another could "emerge in all their variety and richness."[8] So, any single approach to the theology of TI may be avoided. Consequently, a balance is needed between focusing on a coherent theology and taking into due consideration the diversity of TI materials to construct the theology of TI.

I propose that eschatology, as a general future hope of Israel, is the key to the theology of TI (though I am aware of Hasel's warning about a unified category). This is because eschatology is a comprehensive framework of theology, in which many themes may be incorporated more systematically than in the case of 'theology.' Thus, if TI is proved to be primarily eschatology, this will open up a full range of theological perspectives of TI, although some aspects of the 'theology of TI' may be excluded by such a systemization. So, it is important to identify the appropriate approach to the eschatology of TI not only to tackle the theological issues but also to present its main features.

In this chapter, I want firstly to survey the study of the theology of TI to justify my assumption that we need to see TI as a theological unity and that the theology of TI needs to be understood in relation, especially, to the rest of the book of Isaiah (1.2). The survey is also in order to suggest possible categories for the eschatology of TI. As an excursus, I also want to identify some eschatological issues in the theology of TI to set a guideline to the discussion about the eschatology of TI by defining several terminologies and to make some assumptions for its study (1.3). An outline of the structure of the dissertation as well as a conclusion will follow afterwards (1.4).

1.2 History of the Study of the Theology of TI in the Book of Isaiah

Traditionally, the book of Isaiah was considered a unity in terms of authorship, as implied in the Biblical passages,[9] even though the Isaianic author-

7. Martens 1996:224.

8. Hasel 1989:92–96.

9. There are evidences of Isaianic authorship (of the book) in Isa 1:1; 2:1; 8:1. In the New Testaments, DI and TI are also ascribed to Isaiah in Matt 3:3; and 4:14, 12:17–18; Luke 3:4; Acts 8:28; Rom 10:20; John 12:38–41 etc. Archer 1982:285–86. Also see Apocrypha (Sir 48:24) and Talmud (*Baba Bathra* 15a).

ship of the second part of the book (chs 40–66) was doubted by Ibn Ezra in the twelfth century AD.[10] Although critical scholars have separated TI from the rest of the book of Isaiah in terms of authorship and historical settings, there also has been a stream which has continuously tried to see the unity and challenge a sharp division. I am going to survey how TI relates to the rest of the book, especially to DI, in its theological aspect.

Reformers in the Pre-Critical Period[11]

While the Biblical interpretation of the Middle Ages relied on the leading of the church or the church fathers, the reformers in general based their interpretation on Scripture itself, insisting on historical, grammatical and literal interpretation.[12] Luther had noticed the change of the subject matter in ch 40 that may distinguish the two parts of the book, but did not propose a different authorship.[13] Calvin thought that the exilic situation is presupposed in chs 40–66 by the projection of the prophet Isaiah's mind into the future.[14] The assumption of the authorial unity implied the theological unity of the book.

Luther's interpretive principle of the Bible was Christological, which is evidenced in the Messianic and ecclesiastical interpretation of the book of Isaiah (not just TI). For him, the entire Bible is to teach and understand the Christ.[15] However, Luther's external theological control seems too simplistic to cover in particular the various theological themes which are not directly related to the theological core in TI. The point is that he was selectively mining TI since he had another interest in his theological interpretation.

For Calvin, the interpretive control shifts more to the Scripture itself, while Luther has a Christological focus.[16] His exegetical method, as he him-

---

10. Harrison 1969:765; Sekine 1989:3; Fitzgerald 2003:3–4.

11. The reformers may not represent the pre-critical period because of its relatively short period in the history of the church since Jesus Christ, but may be symbolic for the period especially in comparison with the critical period.

12. Grant 1984:92; Farrar 1886:325–27.

13. Childs 2004:193.

14. Smart 1967:15.

15. Childs 2004:198–204; Grant 1984:94. Luther (1527–30/1972:311 and 329) sees Isa 60 as a prophecy about the kingdom of the Christ (i.e., the church), relating "arise, shine" in 60:1 to Eph 5:14 and 8, and Isa 61:1 as that of the Christ as Jesus uses this verse to identify his own person in Luke 4:18. Isa 59:20–21 is also Messianic as Paul quotes it in Rom 11:26–27; 63:1 refers to the resurrection and ascension into heaven of the Christ. Luther 1527–30/1972: 306 and 352.

16. Grant 1984:96.

self summed it up, was to achieve "lucid brevity." He commented on each verse of a chapter to describe its plain sense as briefly as the text allows, while the thorough discussion of theological issues was reserved for his *Institutes* (1546).[17] His interpretation of a text is in the context of the entire Bible and, for him, the interpretation may be applied to the times of the interpreters.[18] Even though he never thought of 'theology of TI' separately, the theological enterprise of TI for him is directly associated with that of the entire Bible (especially the New Testament).

In conclusion, for these two pivotal figures of the Reformation, TI is part, not only of the book of Isaiah, but also of the entire Bible, from which theological discussion may develop. They contributed to Biblical scholarship in that they insisted on the grammatical, historical, and literary interpretation of the text, rejecting church authority as the interpretive key of the Scripture. As Childs rightly commented, these two scholars did not make a clear distinction between the exegesis of the text based on the original historical situation, and the theological development based on the context of the interpreter's theological understanding.[19] The category that Calvin adopted in *the Institutes* is too comprehensive for our purpose as it is directed at the theological systemization of the entire Bible.

Source Criticism

The first serious challenge to the unity of the book of Isaiah came in the eighteenth century. Döderlein (1775) and Eichhorn (1780–83) suggested that the second part of the book is to be ascribed to another author in the Babylonian exile, because of the differences in historical settings, style, and

17. Steinmetz 1982:158. Calvin is evaluated to have made a balance between his two precursors Bucer and Melanchthon to setup his methodology.

18. The 'redemption' in ch 59:19–20 may have double entendre in that it may refer for the Jews to the deliverance from the Babylonia and for the Christians to the salvation of Christ (Calvin 1550:800). While 60:1 is associated with the church and 61:1 with the Christ himself, in 63:1 the prophet speaks simply of YHWH contrary to Luther (Calvin 1550:804, 817, and 834). The "metaphor" of 'the new heaven(s) and earth' (65:17) denotes not only the restoration of the church of God after the return from Babylon but also the salvation as has been manifested in the advent of the Christ and will have been fulfilled in the last resurrection (Calvin 1550:864). Calvin here seems to intend that the church does not necessarily refer to the New Testament church but to the universal church that covers both the New Testament and the Old Testament periods.

19. It may be noted that the entire canon is legitimately the context, if the Biblical theology is at issue (Childs 2004:203), as sometimes it has been emphasized that the OT theology is "part of the larger whole" (Hasel 1989:95).

language, and theological concepts.[20] Theological distinctions that brought the authorial distinction of the two parts (chs 1–39 vs. chs 40–66) included the emphasis on divine majesty in the first part vs. that of YHWH's unique-ness and eternity in the second part. While other deities are recognized in the first part although they are subject to YHWH [the Lord], their very existence is denied in the second part of the book. Other differences were the remnant concept as the faithful left in Jerusalem vs. that as the exiled and returned, and the Messianic king in chs 1–39 replaced by the Servant of YHWH in chs 40–66.[21] This view soon dominated the majority of scholars. However, are those theological differences so distinct that they cannot be integrated in a unified theology at a more comprehensive level? The lack of interest in explaining such a view reflects the turn to the historical that was a key movement in general culture and scholarship of the time.

The authorial unity of the book was further challenged by Duhm, whose commentary on the book of Isaiah (1892) is regarded as an epoch-making contribution to TI research.[22] Duhm identified three anonymous authors in chs 40–66, who are responsible for chs 40–55 (excluding the Servant Songs), the Servant Songs (as Duhm named them),[23] and chs 56–66 respectively. The first is the fruits of Second Isaiah (DI), who worked in Lebanon or Phoenicia around 540 BC. TI worked in Jerusalem shortly be-fore the advent of Ezra and Nehemiah (i.e., a contemporary of Malachi).[24] Although Duhm had questioned the Babylonian setting of DI, the contrasts of Babylon vs. Jerusalem and exile vs. return in the two sections (DI vs. TI) became the common understanding among critical scholars thereafter due to Duhm's precursors (see above).[25] For Duhm, TI echoes the themes of the destruction as a past event and the future glory of Jerusalem in DI. In addition, the same editor not only put DI and TI together but also inserted several passages in DI and TI.[26] So DI and TI have some continuity. But, although he maintained the authorial unity of TI, which reflected the post-exilic Jewish community in Jerusalem, the possibility of disintegration in the authorial, literary, and theological unity of TI was latent. This is because

20. Childs 1979:316–17.

21. Driver 1913:242; Harrison 1969:775.

22. Sekine 1989:4.

23. The Servant Songs are as follows: (1) 42:1–4; (2) 49:1–6; (3) 50:4–9; and (4) 52:13—53:12. Duhm 1892:xviii.

24. Duhm 1892:xiii; Hanson 1975:33.

25. Smart 1967:16; Schramm 1995:22. The critical precursors such as Döderlein and Eichhorn had seen the prophet DI was in Babylon, as discussed above.

26. Duhm 1892:xiii, xviii. Later additions by the same redactor are 42:5–7; 44:9–20; 46:6–8; something in ch 48; 50:10–11; 52:3–6; 58.13–14; 59:5–8; and 66.23–24.

smaller units were continually identified and considered later redactional passages. Duhm held that chs 60–62 are continuous with the surrounding chapters in linguistic, stylistic, and theological respects, a surprising view from someone who had separated the Servant Songs from the context of DI.[27]

Duhm did not attempt a systematic theology of TI. His approach undermines the possibility of a comprehensive theological treatment because of its fragmentation of the subject matter that might be the basis for such a treatment. Duhm's aim was to distinguish authentic and inauthentic texts. Most would now regard this as strained, particularly in the way that the Servant Songs were isolated from their context.[28] Clements described the weakness of his approach as a "too hasty dismissal of so much material as unimportant or irrelevant."[29] However, despite the critical pitfalls in theological synthesis, his influence was crucial in that critical scholars who adopted a historical approach (whether source criticism or redaction criticism) tended to accept a sharp break between DI and TI.[30]

While Duhm's one-author hypothesis of TI has been maintained by a number of scholars,[31] it was challenged by others.[32] The literary unity of TI begins to disintegrate with Skinner, who argued that because of the diversity of subject-matter and the variegated standpoints, the text of TI cannot be from the same historical situation or be regarded as the work of a single author.[33] Even though the authorial unity of chs 40–66 was challenged by Skinner, he affirmed the theological continuity of DI and TI.[34] He discussed

27. Duhm 1892:xviii. In his position, Duhm stands against Cheyne and Kuenen.

28. Clements 1976:55; Skinner 1898:xlix and 258–63.

29. Clements 1976:55. This is partly because, according to Smart (1967:17), Duhm cannot accept that the passages that speak of redemption in purely spiritual ways (i.e., salvation achieved by the suffering and death of the Servant) may be compatible with the passages that describe salvation presented in the political and material terms (e.g., national restoration by Cyrus and the transformation of the world). Also see Skinner's view on this.

30. Maass 1967:157.

31. Such as Elliger (1928), Pfeiffer (1941), McCullough (1948), and Kessler (1960), et al. For McCullough (1948:36), TI precedes DI in date. Sekine 1989:11, 13, and 14; Pfeiffer 1941/1966:458; McCullough 1948:27, 30; Kessler 1956.

32. Such as Skinner (1898/1917) and Volz (1932:197–201). Cheyne (1895:xxx–xxxiii) and Skinner (1898:xv–xxxi) also support the multiple authorship of TI, although Cheyne maintained the literary unity of chs 56–66. See also Sekine 1989:4, 6, 10.

33. Skinner 1898:xxxi and xlv.

34. Skinner 1898:xlv–lxvii. However, for him (1898:xx–xxi), the theological difference of chs 1–39 and chs 40–66 signifies the different authorships. It includes the view of God, the concept of remnant, mission and destiny of Israel, Messianic king vs. the Servant.

the theology of chs 40–66 (DI and TI) under the categories of salvation, YHWH, Israel as the Servant of YHWH, and Israel and the nations.[35]

The concept of salvation includes both external reality of salvation of Israel and Israel's internal renewal. The former will be the restoration of the nation which includes the returning of YHWH to Zion, guidance and protection of the redeemed people by YHWH, and the change of the wilderness to the paradisiacal garden. The latter is the spiritual restoration of the people, which is portrayed especially as the re-establishment of the relation between YHWH and His people through the people's repentance.[36]

The view of God is also similar in DI and TI. YHWH is the Creator of the universe and the true and only God, to whom any other gods are not comparable. God is transcendent and immanent and is thus both exalted on high and related to the world. The portrait of YHWH as shepherd and warrior is also shared by both DI and TI.[37]

The mission of Israel as the Servant of YHWH is consistent in these chapters in that she is *"elect for the sake of mankind."*[38] He considered that "to some extent, the two views of the Servant—the national and the individual—tend to coalesce in the fulfilment contemplated by the prophet."[39] So, the character of the Servant of YHWH remains the same in two fundamental affirmations about YHWH, that is, he is elected by YHWH and commissioned for His service. Israel is called to be an instrument for the execution of the divine purpose of world-wide salvation. The concept of the Servant of YHWH is applied to the concept of the New Israel which is composed of servants.[40]

The Gentiles are not excluded from salvation although the nations are to serve Israel, since the redemption of Israel consequently implies the universal salvation for all the nations. The understanding of salvation of the nations (and Israel as well) in TI may be different in emphasis from that in DI in that salvation in TI may be less idealistic and more materialistic than in DI, but this does not mean negation of the salvation of the nations since the concept of salvation has a moral and spiritual dimension in TI as well as in DI.[41]

35. Skinner 1898:lxv–lxvii.
36. Skinner 1898:xlvi–l.
37. Skinner 1898:l–lv.
38. Skinner 1898:lvi. Italics his.
39. Skinner 1898:lxii.
40. Skinner 1898:lv–lxvi.
41. Skinner 1898:lxiii–lxv.

Consequently, the theology of TI is "of too little independence or originality" compared with that of DI, although immediate salvation and the Servant figure are distinct in DI.[42] Even though Skinner's theological discussion is more weighted on DI, the categories for his theology based on the main characters may provide insight into the theology of TI. However, in this work more theological themes need to be identified for the eschatological theology. It is suggestive that for Skinner salvation in DI and TI included both a physical return and the spiritual reformation of the people and also the portrait of YHWH as shepherd and warrior is common to both DI and TI. This is because there is a coherent idea of salvation and its eschatological fulfilment in chs 40–66. Although Skinner was interested in an integrated theology of TI and its themes and conceptions such as the future salvation and restoration of Jerusalem, he did not think of them in terms of the unifying category of eschatology. However, his theological themes such as salvation, the restoration of Zion, judgment and salvation of the nations etc., may be incorporated into a broader category of eschatological theology as a coherent whole.[43]

While Skinner maintained the theological unity of DI and TI despite assuming different authors thereof, Volz rejected the theological unity of TI and argued for multiple authors.[44] Volz considered that the historical, stylistic, and theological disparities were so great even in a single pericope that the unity of TI was impossible. For him, the fundamental differences in the view of God in TI make the theological (as well as the authorial) unity of TI absolutely impossible. The cruel portrait of YHWH in 63:1–6 is incompatible with the portrait of YHWH who dwells with the contrite and lowly spirit in 57:14–21.[45] A unified theology or authorship is also impossible because the people are treated sometimes as a closed whole (63:7—64:11[12]) and sometimes as separated groups. There is a separation of the pious people from the apostates in Jacob (59:20) and thus there are two cultic groups—the old YHWH-faithful and the new mystic and syncretistic groups (65:3–5). Other incompatibilities include the contrasts between the people who lament the destruction of Jerusalem and the Temple (63:7—64:11) and those who complain against the evil officers (56:9–12); between the people who want the internal construction of the community (56:1–8) and those who have no internal problems but hope for salvation (chs 60 and 62); and between the people who are like prostitutes (57:6–13), those who

---

42. Skinner 1898:lxv, lxvi.

43. Skinner 1898:xlvi–lxvi.

44. Sekene 1989:10; Schramm 1995:14.

45. Volz 1932:199.

are contrite pleasing God (59:9–14), and those who are fasting to please God (58:1–5). The objection to the construction of the Temple (66:1–2) and the lament over the Temple (63:18) or the praises on the precious stones of the sanctuary (60:9, 17) can also not form a consistent theology.[46] As for the nations, the idea of the nations as instruments to serve the glory of Zion and that of the Gentiles who are converted and accepted to the community may not comprise a unity.[47] Volz's understanding of the concept of salvation in TI is material wellbeing.[48] The break between 63:1–6 and 63:7—64:11[12] is further evidence of disunity of TI.[49] For Volz, different theological views indicate different authors. However, other writers discern in these seeming contradictory portraits of YHWH and the people a rich theology that is coherent at a higher or deeper level.

Volz also sees a sharp break between the theology of DI and TI.[50] For him, TI is based on an entirely different foundation from DI. While DI focuses on the glory of YHWH, TI emphasizes the glory of Jerusalem. DI always refers to the whole nation of Israel, although the sense of Israel is sometimes reinterpreted to denote a spiritual nature. But TI does not mention the people or Israel as a whole, but always as a special group within the whole, which is faithful to YHWH.[51] Although he admits "cultic universalism" in TI, it is distinct from the "absolutely free universalism" of DI (45:22–25) because it is not eschatological as it will be realized in the near future in this world (56:7).[52] The concept of salvation in TI is different from that in DI as it is described as more materialistic and external. The nations are just spectators of the salvation and glory of Jerusalem (56:1–6 are excluded in this aspect), and do not participate in the salvation, while the salvation of DI is universal. As for eschatology, while everything is connected to the eschatological hope in DI, eschatology in TI is related only to part of the text.[53] For Volz, because TI does not reflect a unified theology or

---

46. Volz 1932:199.

47. Volz 1932:199.

48. Volz 1932:197.

49. Volz 1932:198.

50. Volz 1932 and Zimmerli 1950/1963.

51. Volz 1932:197–98. 63:7—64:11[12] are excluded in this evaluation. This becomes a self-contradiction.

52. Volz 1932:207. The cultic universalism may be defined as a view that all the nations will participate in the Jewish YHWH-cult; the (free) universalism as a vision that all the nations will (also) be saved.

53. Although the words of DI recur in TI as literal quotations, their meaning is sometimes distorted in TI. The quotation of 40:3 in 57:14 is eschatologically understood, signifying the removal of obstacles hindering the arrival of salvation, as it

authorship, its eschatology does not form a coherent and consistent whole.[54] So, for Volz, the literary and theological break between chapters 55 and 56 is undoubted.[55]

Meanwhile, another movement in the critical study of TI has been a suspicion of the division of chs 56–66 from chs 40–55.[56] König (1926) found no case for the division because of the common theme of comfort in the two parts.[57] Torrey (1928) rejected the long-standing "Babylonian setting" assumption, because for him the "Cyrus" and "Babylon-Chaldea" passages such as 45:1, 44:28, 43:14, 48:14, and 48:20 were "interpolation."[58] Thus, he was able to argue for the unity of Isa 40–55 and 56–66 (including chs 34–35), because theories of TI generally assume a change of historical setting. The discrepancy in the subject matter of the two blocks is not great enough to undermine literary unity.[59] He worked out his theological approach to these parts, arguing, inter alia, that the Messianic figure of the Suffering Servant in DI is still present in the passages in TI such as chs 62, 61, and 63:7ff. and that the seemingly contradictory attitudes towards the foreign nations, i.e., very hostile on the one hand and sharing the salvation on the other hand, may be harmoniously understood in the two parts, by delineating a new line between the people of YHWH and His enemies.[60] Glahn (1934) also supported the unity of chs 40–66, though in a slightly different way from Torrey, because he believes DI wrote both Isa 40:1—56:8 and 56:9—66:24 in Babylonia and Jerusalem, respectively.[61] For Kissane (1943), the whole of chapters 40–66 were composed by a single mind and thus presented a unity, as the alleged distinct and independent fragments actually show a logical sequence in view of the thought of the book.[62] Even though Kissane

suggests a reading in the framework of tradition (Volz 1932:217–218). The portrait of YHWH armed with divine armor in 59:17, which has a connection to the Divine Warrior tradition in 42:13 and 52:10, refers to the eschatological coming of YHWH, while the promise of the 'spirit' in 59:21 is apocalyptic (Volz 1932:238, 240). The references to the cosmic bodies in 60:19–20, the New Heavens and Earth in 65:17–25, the sudden birth of the God's people in 66:7–9, and the eternal judgment of the sinners in 66:24 are apocalyptic, too.

54. Volz 1932:241, 281, 296, 297, 300.
55. Volz 1932:197–98.
56. Sekine 1989:9.
57. König 1926:536–49.
58. Torrey 1928:38–52.
59. Torrey 1928:7–8.
60. Torrey 1928:112–26, and 140.
61. Glahn 1934:118–78; Sekine 1989:9. According to Sekine (1989:10 and 13), The Glahn's thesis is repeated in Fisher 1939 and Penna 1958.
62. Kissane 1943:v–vi, xlvi–lxi. For him, chs 40–66 and chs 1–39 are a unity not

regarded the theology of chs 1–39 as continuous with chs 40–66,[63] he does not try to systemize the theology of TI (or, DI-TI), but just summarizes the message of each block of the text.[64] Torrey's position was followed by Smart (1967), who may be a precursor of the canonical approach (see below). In these discussions we can see theology, rather than history, coming more to the fore in the discussion of the character of TI.

In summary, because of the multiplication of sources, theological discussion of TI has been thin or extremely selective; theological interests have been subordinate to historical concerns. The history of source criticism of TI has focused on the closely related issues of the unity, authorship, historical setting, and dating, so it is a story of fissile debate between one-author and multiple-author hypotheses.[65] Some have followed Duhm's hypotheses for authorial and theological unity but others have challenged his one-author and unity hypothesis. A few have even pursued the unity of the DI and TI and so have fundamentally questioned Duhm's hypotheses. With Duhm, however, a firm break was made between chs 55 and 56, involving a geographical shift from Babylonia to Palestine and a temporal transition from exilic to post-exilic times. Theological discussion has generally been associated with DI rather than TI (or at best the relation between the two), mainly owing to the focus on historical matters. The conclusions of historical-critical investigation have proved sensitive to the subjective assumptions and opinions of scholars.[66] Because such historical approaches fragment the text, there is relatively little consideration of the significance of the canonical literary context. As Childs comments, this approach is "so concentrating on a level behind the text as to miss the text's own theological witness."[67] Occasionally, the external presumption of the Babylonia/Palestine and ex-

---

only in the theological aspect but also in the authorial one, in that the ideas of chs 40–66 are Isaiah's even though the compiler of the whole book may be his anonymous disciple, who might have modernized the master's idea. His categories for exegesis of TI are: the sins of Israel (56:9—59:21), the new Zion (60:1—63:6), and the purpose of exile (or, apostates and faithful) (63:7—66:24).

63. Kissane 1943:lvi–lxi.

64. Kissane 1943:xxxii–xxxiii and xlii–xlvi. He categorized theological ideas of chs 1–39 as corruption (religious and ethical abuses), chastisement (the Day of YHWH, YHWH's agent Assyria, ruin of Judah, and the remnant), and restoration (conversion, restoration, the Messiah and His kingdom, and overthrow of Assyria). Kissane 1941:xxxviii–xlvii.

65. Sekine 1989:24; Schramm 1995:11. Brief history of the study of TI is presented especially in Maass 1967:151–63; Harrison 1969:765–95; Hanson 1975:32–46; Sekine 1989:3–27; Schramm 1995:11–52; Smith 1995:1–6; Fitzgerald 2003:1–34.

66. Smith 1995:30.

67. Childs 2001:101.

ile/post-exile split tends to suffocate the theological synthesis of the text's message. Theological similarities and continuities are neglected due to giving priorities to the alleged time and place. Even though there have been some attempts to pay more attention to theological issues, it is still the case that source-critical issues have attracted more attention. A more coherent and complex theology may be possible if attention is focused on the text as a complex unity, rather than the disparate sources behind the text. On the other hand, it is for fortunate that there has been another stream that has continuously doubted the historical assumption of the general scholarship and insisted on the authorial or theological unity of chs 40–66 or the book of Isaiah.

Redaction-Criticism

Redaction-historical approach, focusing on how variegated materials came to reach the present form of TI, has dominated TI research more recently. While this approach shares the historical concerns with the previous approach, it is distinct in that it focuses more on the final form of the text. This approach often identifies authorial voices as authors or redactors.[68] If the common layers of pieces according to authors and dates are identified, the critics arrange them chronologically or discuss how and why they are put together to reach the present form. This approach often maintains a break between DI and TI, but their relation to the rest of Isaiah is of increasing interest.

According to Koenen, there are three models of this redactional approach: the unity hypothesis, the fragment hypothesis, and the supplementary hypothesis.[69] The first assumes a single authorship of TI, but with some later additions or emendations of the text. The second supposes that TI is made up of a series of independent units from different authors at different times, which were then collected to form the present text. The third assumes a core layer that grew through addition and a reworking process over time. The unity and supplement hypotheses tend to emphasize theological continuity, while the fragmentary hypothesis tends to highlight the diversity of the material.

68. This approach characteristically adopts the concept of redactor/compiler rather than author, although the concept has been suggested already in the source-critical approach.

69. Koenen 1990:1–7. The unity hypothesis is represented by Bonnard (1972); fragment hypothesis by Pauritsch, Whybray (1981), Sekine, and Koenen, Emmerson; and supplement hypothesis by Westermann, Vermeylen, Steck, Beuken, and Lau. According to Smith (1995:7), Koenen is included in the group of fragment hypothesis.

Although, for Pauritsch (1971),[70] TI displays no original unity, the unity of the redactional intention is still acknowledged, as presented in the introductory passage of 56:1–8.[71] Even though he admits that there is no "Trito-Isaianic theology" in that TI has not tried systematically to treat the religious ideas of the time, he briefly elaborates a more or less systematic approach to the theology of TI mainly in terms of 'the images of God,' 'condition of man,' and 'nature of faith.' For him, God is a God of promise/future hope and of the covenant; humanity is in darkness and without hope; faith arises from hope through prayer. The theology of TI is similar to that of DI and is deuteronomistic and eschatological in nature. Even though his analysis is brief (since theology is not the primary focus of his study), he affirms the theological unity of the message(s) of TI.[72] His eschatology, although not systematized, includes topics such as final judgment theophany (ch 66), cleansing the people (ch 59), glorious divine appearance, and the New Heavens and Earth (chs 65, 66).[73] Apocalyptic color is added at several places (63:1–6; 65:25; 66:24).[74] If theological rather than redactional unity is assumed, these theological concepts and eschatological (or apocalyptic) ideas may form a coherent eschatology at a higher level as they pervade the whole TI.

Some attempt to incorporate theology as a way of overcoming the limits of historical approaches. Sekine (1989)[75] adopts thirteen theological concepts to supplement the traditional redaction-critical methodology. These are used as criteria for determining the similarity and discrepancy of the pericopes, thus aiding a judgment about authorship.[76] However, Sekine's

70. According to Sekine (1989:18), Pauritsch set a new stage of the redaction-critical study of TI with his 1971 writing, because he thoroughly applies the literary-, form- or Gattung-critical methodology to the investigation of the units of the text.

71. For him (1971:219–26), TI texts come from several authors who lived at the end of 6C BC. See also McKenzie 1971:489. For Emmerson (1992:58 and 15–20), too, TI should be ascribed to the multiple authorships due to the inner inconsistency of the material, even though TI may be arranged in a logical way to show a symmetrical structure.

72. Pauritsch 1971: 226–41.

73. Pauritsch 1971:223, 221, 230, 231.

74. Pauritsch 1971:222, 223, 224.

75. The starting point of the study of Sekine (1989:25) is the assumption that chs 56 and 66 are the redactional layers and chs 60–62 are to be ascribed to the prophet TI. He (1989:27) assumes the multiple authors hypothesis in advance as is typical in the fragmentation model. Consequently, not only chs 60–62 but also 57:14–19; 65:16b–23, 25; and 66:7–16 are the work of TI (Sekine 1989:68–104, 182).

76. Sekine 1989:26 and 183–216. The complete list of the theological concepts is: salvation, grace, blessing, covenant, justice (righteousness), holiness, sovereignty, God, sin, good/evil, the nations, history, and eschatology. The last two concepts are not

theological concepts are not only subordinate to his historical interests, but they also fail to address the theology of TI as a whole. His theological concepts are also extremely specific. While Elliger suggests a theological correspondence and thus the authorial unity of 57:4, 58:1 and 59:20 because of פשע, Sekine argues that the occurrences in singular and in plural may reflect different sources.[77] If the theological unity of TI is assumed, these differences would enrich rather than limit the theological discussion of פשע. For him, chs 60–62, 65:16b–23, 25 and 66:7–16 have no reference to faith in God, rebellion against God, or seeking God, while 59:15b–21; 65:1, 24; 66:5–6, 17, 18–24 often mention the relation between YHWH and the people, so the two groups of the text belong to different authors and theologies. In 56:3, עם refers to the group of people in which there is no distinction between the Gentile proselytes and the Israelites (this implies universal salvation), while it refers to the whole of Israel, who are exclusively saved in 63:7–64:11[12] (63:7, 8, 14; 64:8[9]). It also denotes the people under judgment in 58:1. So the different senses of עם indicate different sources.[78] The conceptual differences in the nations (ה[גוים], ה[עמים]) indicate authorial differences.[79] In addition, salvation, which forms the central theme of chs 60–62, is particularistic and thus relates to Israel alone (60:16b), and is concrete and materialistic (60:1–16a, 17a, 18a, 19–20).[80] Conversely, salvation in 59:15b–21 is universalistic and includes the salvation of the nations (59:19a), which implies a different authorship or editorial hand in the passage.[81] For the same reason, Sekine ascribes 56:6–8 and 66:17–24 to the redactor, who is universalistic. As a rule, for Sekine different theological concepts are due to the different authorship, resulting in fragmentation. However, Sekine's theological approach may provide a possibility of integration in theology, so a coherent eschatology.[82]

---

directly applied to the pericopes, as there are no Hebrew equivalents. He separately discusses the concept of community. Sekine 1989:234–37.

77. Sekine 1989:249.

78. Sekine 1989:206.

79. The peoples (ה(גוים)) are neither saved (60:3, 5; 62:2) nor judged (60:10) in chs 60–62. But they are positively mentioned (i.e., salvation) in 66:18–20 and negatively (i.e., judgment) in 64:1. So the different use of ה(גוים) may determine sources as well. The peoples (ה(עמים)) are also neutral (i.e., subject to neither salvation nor judgment) in chs 60–62 (61:9; 62:10), while they are positive in 56:7 and negative in 63:3, 6.

80. Sekine 1989:188.

81. Sekine 1989:189.

82. If we admit that salvation and praise are the fundamental concepts of the nature of the saved community (as implied in 60:18b; see 4.3), the distinct above-mentioned two concepts of salvation may be integrated. This may be justified, as salvation and praise are contrast to violence as well as ruin and destruction, which are judgment due

Sekine considers that the eschatology of TI is apocalyptic. For him, the Divine Warrior Hymn in 59:15b–21 presents apocalyptic eschatology, but it lacks interest in the earth and portrayal of the change of nature, contrary to chs 60–62. So the passage shows a different stage of development from that of ch 60–62, which is at the same stage of development as 65:17–25, portraying cosmic change.[83] Because of his assumption of the theological as well as authorial differences in TI texts, Sekine, like Hanson, considers that TI displays a wide spectrum of apocalyptic eschatology.

In brief, although Sekine adopts a theological scheme in his redactional approach to TI, he thinks that a redactor might include contradictory sources and not be bound by a concern for unity. So, for him, a unified theology is impossible. However, if ways are found to integrate his distinct theological concepts, his work may point to a coherent eschatological theology.

Koenen (1990) points out that the fundamental limitation of the redactional approach is the subjectivity in deciding redactional matters.[84] To minimize the subjectivity of the methodology, he proposes not only three theological criteria for deciding different authors, but also three verification criteria.[85] However, the application of these criteria does not add up to a harmonized theology of the whole text. Although Koenen considers that the theology of TI is primarily eschatology (as the title of his monograph implies), his theology is not integrated because his redactional presumption divides the material in TI into two main groups, i.e., the works of TI and those of redactors. Theology is subordinated to redactional analysis.[86]

---

to the sins. Where Sekine finds an apparent theological and authorial difference, an attempt to harmonize the different theology at a higher level may facilitate a coherent overall theology.

83. Sekine 1989:211, 213. Although he usually follows Hanson, he differs at several points. While Hanson excludes 60:19–20 as an interpolation, Sekine keeps them. Both scholars see the verses as reflecting the radical transformation of nature and so apocalyptic.

84. He (1990:7–8) considers that the task of his redactional study is two fold: to decide which texts belong to one/same author and which texts to different authors; and to determine when, where, and from whom the individual layers were written with what theological intention.

85. Koenen 1990:7–8. Koenen's three criteria are content tensions; linguistic and stylistic differences; and discrepancy in the historical and spiritual-historical context. To affirm the same author in the two texts, there should be no tensions and differences (congruence criterion). The authorial agreement of the texts is to be based on what are already known as typical of an author (significance criterion). Even the significant parallelism may not form a single authorship as it may result from, e.g., the same historical situation or theological tradition (explication criterion).

86. Koenen 1990:215–40.

Koenen sees the entire theology of TI as eschatology, although his eschatology is to be understood in relation to the ethics of the people. For him, TI is the precursor of apocalyptic eschatology. He identified a negative view of the present world order—darkness, misery, and need, etc.—as a characteristic of apocalyptic. The portrait of the New Jerusalem in the future and that of the New Heavens and Earth (65:17) are also apocalyptic, since they exist in a new dimension entirely different from the present world order. In addition, the antithetical confrontation between the present and the future, such as 'no more will be x, but y' (60:18; 62:4, 8; 65:19, 20) and 'instead of x, it becomes y' (60:15, 17; 61:3), may be considered apocalyptic. Furthermore, an imminent eschatological expectation and quick beginning of salvation (62:1) may also be apocalyptic.[87] However, his eschatological theology of TI is fragmented because he treats the works of TI and redactors separately.[88] Although he sees an apocalyptic eschatology in TI, Koenen fails to construct a comprehensive and integrated theology, in part because of his redactional interest but also because of his acceptance of a radical social division.[89]

Meanwhile, sometimes there also has been an attempt to pursue the redactional integrity of the book of Isaiah as a whole. Ackroyd (1978; 1982) argues for the unity of the book of Isaiah with the assumption that chs 1–12 are connected to the rest of the book. For him, the "Holy One of Israel" is a link that connects the two parts (and even chs 56–66) and 9:6–9 is connected to 65:25.[90] Clements (1982; 1985) also argues for the unity of the book as a whole from the redactional perspective, even though there is more than one author for the book.[91] He shows the continuity between chs 1–39 and chs 40–66 because of the common themes of blindness/deafness and divine election.[92] Also for Sweeney (1998), the book of Isaiah is unity, TI functioning as a conclusion to the whole book.[93] Thus, chs 56–66 also present the goal of the book, i.e., to persuade the people to join the re-established covenant community of YHWH. For Rendtorff (1993), the book of Isaiah is a redactional unity, with chs 40–55 being the actual core of the redactional development, even though this view is peculiar from other scholars.[94] For

87. Koenen 1990:220–21.
88. Koenen 1990:224–29.
89. Koenen follows Hanson in the view of the social division of the TI community.
90. Ackroyd 1978:16–48.
91. Clements 1982:120.
92. Clements 1985:100–101.
93. Sweeney 1988a:88–89.
94. Rendtorff 1993a:167.

Williamson (1994), the book of Isaiah may be a redactional unity.[95] DI, being influenced by PI, is responsible for the edition of PI plus DI corpus, which TI has been developed from the combined PI and DI corpus by another editor who is responsible for the whole book. This movement has challenged the general trend of the redactional approach dividing the book into sections according to the historical or theological assumptions.

To be brief, redactional research on TI has been characterized more by divergence than consensus. The results range from the unity of the whole book of Isaiah, via unity and single authorship of TI, one main author and multiple redactors, to many authors and several redactors. There seem to be the two reasons for this. First, TI provides insufficient evidence for specific historical events or situations, so determining stages of the text is extremely subjective. Even the redactional critics are sceptical of their results: "[I]t may be that anything approaching a precise dating of this material will forever remain an impossibility."[96] Smith asks, "how much does the development (or, difference) of theology determine the differences of the author or date?"[97] Differences in style, language, and theological notions cannot determine date and authorship because even in one author such diversity can happen, especially if composition takes place over an extended period. Second, redactional research seems highly dependent on the critic's theological understanding. A critic's presupposed theology often determines the allocation of a passage to a particular date or author.[98]

From a theological perspective, as Smith points out, this approach characteristically emphasizes the incoherence and diversity of the pericopes, although some have attempted to explore the redactional/theological unity of TI or a larger corpus.[99] This approach assumes that Isa 56–66 is composed

95. Williamson 1994:20–21; 240–41.

96. Schramm 1995:52.

97. Smith 1995:147.

98. We can see this, for example, in the interpretation of the speaker in 61:1–3. Redaction critics typically identify an authorial/redactional figure. Yet Vermeylen (1977–78:471–89) does not find a prophetic figure; rather it is the community of the faithful that speaks (also see Smith 1995:23). For Emmerson (1992:75–78), it is TI that speaks not only in 61:1–3 but also in 62:1 and 6–7. For Hanson (1975/79:65–69), 61:1–3 is a reiteration of the earlier message spoken by the visionary group, it being either an individual or a group. Smith (1995:24 and 25) is confusing, because he says that the "I" in the passage is "most likely" TI, the author of chs 60–62, but also that 61:1–4 is "more likely" to refer to the Jerusalem community. These divergent views suggest that redaction-criticism is highly dependent on subjective assumption rather than on objective methodology.

99. Although the historical approach has theological concerns in TI, 'historical' concerns are still dominant as is typical in case of Whybray (1981:38–43). He considers that the community of TI confronts with the major three theological problems: (1) the

of diverse materials from multiple authors located in a wide time span.[100] The more sources are suggested, the thinner theology becomes. However, the theological concern in this approach is valuable. Sometimes theological considerations as well as other synchronic aspects are incorporated into the methodology more systematically to supplement the weaknesses of the redactional approach.[101] But the fundamental weakness is this: the critics tend to subordinate theological concerns to historical ones. When redactional critics have tried to elaborate the theology of TI, the results have not been satisfactory. According to Seitz, the lack of theological development in this approach is due to the absence of an agreed reconstruction. At best, theology in this approach is a theology through redactional intentionality, based on a redactional reconstruction.[102] The redactional approach does not bring theology as a center in the theological discussion of the final form of the text. If the literary and theological unity 'at some level' of the text is assumed, then theology may be the central interest of theological enterprise.

Canonical Approach and Its Precursors

There has been another movement in the critical study of TI condemning the separation of chs 56–66 from chs 40–55.[103] While the redactional approach may focus on the final form of the text with a historical interest, the canonical approach emphasizes the theological unity of the final form.[104]

---

relationship of the returned exiles to the people already resident in Palestine; (2) the huge gap between the real situation of the Palestine and the glorious promises of DI; and (3) the disputes about the rebuilding of the Temple in Jerusalem. His approach belongs to the fragmentation hypothesis.

100. Smith 1995:3. Especially fragmentation hypothesis tends to emphasize theological diversity, as in Grace Emmerson, who considers that such theological differences are based on different authorship. For her (1992:55–56), the ritualistic and ethical charges against the leaders and the people in chs 56, 57, and 58 cannot be congruent with the promises of unconditional salvation in chs 60–62 and the generous attitude towards the Gentiles in chs 56 and 66 cannot stand side by side with the gloomy report of the annihilation of the nations in 63:3–6. For her (1992:35–37, 40), even though DI and TI, being situated in the exilic and postexilic periods, respectively, have much of similarity in themes and forms of expression, TI is distinctive in the shifts of theological meaning. For the rejection of this view, see 2.2.

101. For example, Sekine—theological methodology; Koenen—theological methodology; Smith—rhetorical methodology; and Hanson and Schramm—sociological methodology, etc.

102. Seitz 2001:541.

103. Sekine 1989:9.

104. The term 'canonical approach' is suggested by Childs as highlighting the synchronic view of the final form of the Bible as well as the normative role of the canon in

Smart may be understood as a precursor of the canonical approach, since he explored the present form of the text not from a diachronic approach but from a synchronic perspective. Contrary to the previous interpreters, who have read the book based on the predetermined historical situation, he suggests a new reading: "to begin the exposition with the fewest possible assumptions, to read ch 40 as though we knew nothing of the prophet except what he himself tells us in the text of the chapter, then to read ch 41 in the light of what we have learned in ch 40, ch 42 in the light of chs 40 and 41, and so on throughout the twenty-eight[*sic.*] chapters."[105] This implies that the passages are to be understood primarily in the literary context of the book. Following Torrey (1928), Smart thought that chs 35 and 40–66 were a unity (see above). So, for him, the discrepancy in the subject matter of the two blocks (40–55, 56–66) is not great enough to undermine literary unity.[106] Nor were the references to Babylon and Chaldea in 43:14, 48:14 and 20 proofs of the prophet's residence thereof.[107] The Babylon residence of the prophet DI was hardly convincing, because the prophet's address to the exile did not require him to be among the exiles in Babylonia. But the prophecy was spoken not to the local community but to the widely dispersed people in the four corners of the earth. As the title of his monograph implies, Smart paid more attention to the theological aspects than previous scholars.[108] For him, the theology of these chapters of "DI" (chs 35 and 40–66) is "eschatological." The prophet was "projecting himself into the future to describe vividly the anticipated events," in that the nature of the salvific hope of the chapters is a future intervention of YHWH in the history of Israel and of the world.[109] In these discussions we can see theology, rather than history, coming more to the fore in the discussion of the character of TI.

Smart's approach has been recently supported by Childs' (1979; 2001) canonical approach and also by Seitz (1992; 2001).[110] Childs (1979) suggests

the faith community, as the predominating historical approach may not do justice with the literary point of view. Childs 1979:51, 65; Barton 1984:79.

105. Smart 1967:9. Torrey may be included in this category, because he (1928:53) assumes that the twenty-seven chapters of Isa 40–66 are written down by DI in their present order.

106. Torrey 1928:7–8.

107. Smart 1967:20–22. Smart (1967:18) did not commit himself to the "interpolation theory," unlike Torrey. So, for him (1967:9), it is not necessary to delete the Cyrus and Babylon-Chaldea passages as did Torrey.

108. See Smart 1967:18–19. For example, he sees the "highway" in 40:3 is not the physical road from Babylonia to Jerusalem, but an element of theophany, through which YHWH returns to His people. Smart 1967:22.

109. Smart 1967:37–39.

110. Seitz 1992:502.

that the canonical approach concerns primarily the final form of the text itself. Its aim is not to reconstruct a history of religious development but to investigate the religious text in relation to its role within the historical community of faith in ancient Israel.[111] This approach may share with historical critical methods an interest in doing justice to the integrity of the text, but differs from them in that it interprets the texts in consideration of their theological authority in the faith community. It also focuses on the theological shape of the canonical text rather than on a historical reconstruction.[112]

For Childs, Isa 40–66 (and thus Isa 56–66 as well) should be understood ultimately not against the historical background of Babylonian exile but against the canonical setting that the present form of the book of Isaiah provides.[113] This is also supported by the fact that there are no specific references to the historical context, no superscription, no date formulae, etc., in these chapters (the historical background is 'subordinated').[114] He understands the relation between the first and second half of the book through the scheme of prophecy-fulfillment, as indicated by the contrast between the "former things" and "latter things."[115] TI is dependent on DI and there is no radical tension at all between the two from the canonical perspective. Thus, TI should be interpreted primarily in the canonical context of the book of Isaiah.[116] He rejects Zimmerli's hypothesis that TI was spiritualized from DI.[117] Even though he did not elaborate the independent theology of TI, his commentary presents theological insights that might be the basis for a systematic theology of TI.

Seitz (2001) says that the conventional separation of chs 40–66 from the first part causes contradictory and conflicting views of origins, arrangement, editing, and integrity of the chapters.[118] He argues that the entire corpus of the book of Isaiah should be treated as a single volume in relation to other prophets in the canon.[119] He supports Childs' view that the historical setting of chs 40–66 is not clearly reflected within the context of the larger part of the book. These chapters work without necessarily foregrounding

111. Childs 1979:73.

112. Childs 1979:74.

113. Although he does not explicitly deny the multiple authorship of the book of Isaiah, historical matters are not primary concern for him.

114. Childs 1979:325–27.

115. Childs 1979:328.

116. Childs 1979:333–34.

117. Childs 2001:442.

118. Seitz 2001:311.

119. Seitz 2001:313.

their socio-historical background as the historical scholars intend to do. The mention of Cyrus in 45:1 is not intended to inform us of the text's precise dating, but rather it functions as a typology of "second pharaoh" in the "second exodus" theme. The text and the knowledge of Cyrus do not necessarily suggest that the author or audience were in Babylonia. Indeed, the audience is regarded as being dispersed over the whole earth. From the point of view of the literature, as Duhm noted, the perspective is Jerusalem-oriented, since 52:11 (48:20[*sic.*]) denotes Babylon as "there."[120] For him, a Zion-orientation is the text's intention, so an overemphasis on an exilic historical setting is a misinterpretation. In addition, a division of the book according to an alleged geographical setting is inappropriate.[121] As for authorship, he argues for the single authorship of the book of Isaiah, not necessarily in terms of a historical figure, but in terms of the authorized voice of the literature. The servants in TI are the disciples of the Servant of DI. They are actually responsible for the authorial voice in TI as well as being successors of the Servant in various ways. Since the servants firstly appear in ch 54, TI starts there and not in ch 56.[122]

In summary, the canonical approach sees the TI text against the context of the book and the canon as received (*tradiert*) in the faith community. It presupposes the theological unity and sometimes even the authorial unity of the book. It has an inclination to downplay the alleged historical setting in chs 40–55 and in chs 56–66. The theological rather than historical viewpoint becomes central, as the literary and theological unity is secured in the text of the canon.

Conclusion

Because source critics have tried to identify the sources and separated TI from DI due to the alleged geographical and historical setting, they have fragmented the text and have only been able to set out a thin theology. In redactional studies, there has never been an agreed redactional process, which makes a thick theology impossible. Although theological factors have sometimes been considered, the historical and redactional interest has still dominated theological concern. As a counter to this stream, some scholars

120. Here, Seitz distinguishes the actual setting of the author and the literary or imaginary setting that is presented in the text. We need to appreciate the latter rather than the former for the sake of interpretation of the text as the text presents. Seitz seems to confuse 52:11 with 48:20, as 52:11 reads, "סורו סורו צאו משם."

121. Seitz 2001:315–16.

122. Seitz 2001:316–21.

have assumed the unity of the second part of the book, and challenged a sharp break between DI and TI. It is especially canonical theologians that assume the theological unity of chs 40–66 (and the book of Isaiah). They see the text primarily in the context of the canon, and thus historical concerns are subordinated to theological interests. A theological continuity between DI and TI will be assumed for the study of TI in this dissertation, which may bring a possible construction of a deeper eschatological theology.

What is meant by such an eschatological theology is our next concern.

1.3 Excursus: Eschatological Setting of the Study

I have surveyed the history of the interpretation of TI in the book of Isaiah in the previous section to show that TI needs to be seen in the canonical context of the book and that it is reasonable to assume the theological unity of TI and the book. I have also proposed that the theology of TI is eschatology. In this excursus, several important terms used in the book will be defined by identifying eschatological and apocalyptic issues in general in the OT. They include eschatology, apocalyptic, and mythical. This section also sets out assumptions for the eschatological study of TI. Mythical thinking is at work in the concepts and the development of both eschatology and apocalyptic.

The term 'eschatology' at first signified in systematic theology the doctrine of the "last things," especially for an individual.[123] In OT research it may refer to the idea of the *end* of history (or the universe) in a narrower sense. But in a broader sense it signifies the general future hope as presented in, e.g., the prophecies of the OT.[124] The definition of eschatology has been related to other issues such as its existence before the prophets and the source of eschatology. It is also related to the definition of apocalyptic as well as the relation between history and eschatology.

Gressmann in *Der Ursprung der israelitisch-jüdischen Eschatologie* argued for the pre-prophetic existence of OT eschatology, considering that the prophetic pattern of the alternating doom and salvation and curse and blessing originated from Babylonian thought.[125] However, Mowinckel rejected his view, because it is difficult to find evidence of eschatological

---

123. Fiorenza 1984:271.

124. Jenni 1982:126.

125. Gressmann 1905:250–59. Sellin (1912) also acknowledged the pre-prophetic eschatology, although he rejected Gressmann's Babylonian influence, since for him OT eschatology originated from the message of Moses.

prophecies in Babylonia and Assyria.[126] Mowinckel argued that the question of the existence of eschatology in the prophetic books should not be confused with that of the authenticity of the eschatological sayings.[127] For him, such eschatological phrases as 'at the end of the days' were inserted at later times,[128] and thus there is no eschatology in or before the prophetic books.[129] Eschatology should be distinguished strictly from the "future hope" and is about the last things, the end of the present world order and the creation of a new order.[130] He looked for a possible source of eschatology in cultic thought.[131] Although there is an element of "hope" in the election and covenant tradition of Israel, which he called "natural, buoyant optimism," it is different in nature from what is called "eschatology," which is of a universal and cosmic character. "Eschatology" arises directly from the hope of national restoration, and thus presupposes the destruction of the nation. There is a crevasse between traditional hope and eschatological hope. The post-exilic cult, rather than the element of future hope in earlier traditions, provided the matrix for eschatology.[132] The "Day of YHWH" was originally a reference to the day of cultic festival and was later eschatologized when it lost the realistic connection with the world.[133] Thus, in Mowinckel eschatology is a new element to the traditional hope about the future.

However, according to Clements, Mowinckel's view of eschatology, being understood as about the end of the world and the inauguration of a new world order through universal disruption, reflects a narrow definition.[134] For Clements, eschatology in a broader sense is related to the Biblical idea of God's purpose in history: eschatology is Israel's hope based on the faith of YHWH, who has elected, and covenanted with, Israel. This hope has two features as its foundation. First, YHWH's purpose has a universal scope and is centered on the covenantal relationship. Second, His purpose is realized in the arena of history.[135] Vriezen as well considers that eschatology should not be limited to the dramatic cosmic change of the universe. The expression

126. Mowinckel 1959:126–27, 129.

127. Mowinckel 1959:130.

128. Mowinckel 1959:131.

129. Mowinckel 1959:130.

130. Mowinckel 1959:125. His view of definition of eschatology is "apocalyptic," as will be discussed later.

131. Mowinckel 1959:125–54.

132. Mowinckel 1959:133–34.

133. Mowinckel 1959 150.

134. Clements 1965:104.

135. Clements 1965:104–5. Clements personally adopts a broader sense.

אחרית הימים signifies not only the last days, but also the general future, and "things to come" do not distinguish between the future as the limit of the personal horizon and the absolute future in a modern sense.[136] Those who define the term "eschatology" broadly generally accept the presence of a pre-prophetic eschatology.[137] Those who tend to define eschatology more narrowly generally do not accept a pre-prophetic eschatology. Therefore, the question of dating eschatology is linked very closely to its definition, whether it is pre-prophetic or not, and whether it is broader or narrower. I prefer the broader definition, since not only is this generally accepted but there also is a strong doubt about the radical discontinuity between the post-exilic hope of national restoration and the traditional hope of Israel in her election and covenant.[138]

Mowinckel's view of the source of eschatology may be challenged as well. Firstly, contrary to his argument for a post-exilic cultic origin, cultic theology dates back to the early monarchic period, as he concedes.[139] If cultic theology reflects or projects eschatology, then it indicates a pre-prophetic origin of eschatology. Secondly, his understanding of the cultic elements does not seem persuasive, and thus his conception of "myth" is also questionable. In the New Year's Festival (*the festival of YHWH's enthronement* is his term), the coming of YHWH, His combat, His victory, and even His enthronement are dramatized.[140] These motifs are "mythical" elements, which re-enact the primordial creational events.[141] In the "myth," which *theologizes* the change of the seasons, the Deity battles against chaos and death, wins the victory, and is enthroned as a divine king. The victory and enthronement of YHWH in fact refers to the new season overcoming the old, which ensures prosperity of the community in the next year and brings confirmation that YHWH will not abandon Israel and will rule her forever, which constitutes eschatology.[142] But in the theologizing of the change of the nature, Mowinckel seems to confuse between the theological reference

136. Vriezen 1953:202.

137. Vriezen, Jenni, and Linblom, etc., are included in this category. Jenni 1982:127–28.

138. Contrary to Mowinckel (1959:125), Vriezen (1953:202), Clements (1965:104), and Reventlow (1997:170) adopt the broader definition.

139. Mowinckel 1959:139.

140. Mowinckel 1959:140. Through, for example, the procession of the Ark, and the proclamation יהיה מלך, etc.

141. Mowinckel 1959:143.

142. Mowinckel 1959:139–43. While in Canaanite myth, the change of the seasons is a symbolism of the divine struggle, in Mowinckel, the battle and victory of YHWH is a symbolism of the change of the seasons.

and the vehicle of the myth. For him, "myth" is a metaphor theologizing the natural phenomenon. However, we understand that the enthronement or victory of YHWH in the cultic drama is a re-enactment of the past event and refers to the divine action in the heavenly realm, which defines "myth" (see below). For example, the future divine salvation is portrayed as the new exodus, i.e., the re-application of the exodus in 51:9–12. The mythical description of YHWH in 59:15b–21 is understood as divine action in the heavenly realm.

Alternatively, von Rad in his *Old Testament Theology* considers that the driving motive of eschatology derives from the very nature of the view of time and history of Israel, which has been formed by the experience of God since the early stages of Israel. Israel always knew only time as containing events. For Israel, time is linear, and history is controlled by the Deity. Time/history is thus inherently "eschatological," in a sense that it moves towards the ultimate fulfilment.[143] In the prophets, a new element of the perspective of the world history was added and an orientation towards the future was even more emphasized, to accelerate eschatologization.[144] For von Rad, the ideological center of (prophetic) eschatology is the Day of YHWH, the climax of which is the coming of YHWH in person.[145] The Day of YHWH is the day of the battle of YHWH and His victory, as it has been shaped against the background tradition of the Holy War.[146] By this, it is evident that von Rad, suggesting implicitly a wider view of eschatology, sees the source of eschatology in the past tradition of YHWH's people, whether it is the Holy War tradition, or more broadly the view of history moulded by divine salvation in the past. However, the role of mythical materials in the formation of eschatology does not seem to be fully considered. For example, the description of the divine action of eschatological salvation in 59:15b–21 is not only a re-application of the past Divine Warrior tradition, but it also develops the actions of YHWH in the heavenly realm, which reflects mythical thinking (see below).

Cross attempts to combine von Rad (*Heilsgeschichte* school) and Mowinckel (Myth and Ritual school) in his understanding of OT eschatology, trying to show that cultic tradition, formed in the period of the kings, and

143. von Rad 1965:100–101, 106.

144. von Rad 1965:112–13.

145. von Rad 1965:119.

146. von Rad 1965:119–24. Von Rad has found the Holy War traditions in Judg 7 (cf. Isa 9:4), 2 Sam 5 (cf. Isa 28:21), 1 Sam 7:10, Josh 10:11, Exod 14 & 15, etc. It is strange for him not to try to elaborate the concept of the Day of YHWH starting with, and based on, these passages. He just started from the prophetic passages. See von Rad 1959:97–108.

the older Holy War tradition, a heritage of tribal amphictyony, do not conflict with each other. Mythical elements have been included together with historical elements in the covenant renewal cult in the earlier stage of Israel, which re-enacted the exodus and conquest events.[147] The Day of YHWH is at the same time both the day of victory of YHWH in holy warfare and the day of enthronement in YHWH's festival.[148] Cross' idea forms an enhanced basis for the understanding of eschatology in that it combines the two distinct elements—myth and salvation history. However, his elaborations do not solve the problem of the role of the cult in relation to eschatology, in part because he reiterates the tension between Gressmann's view of foreign influence of eschatology and Sellin's view of indigenous eschatology in that in his view of the cult, Israel has *shared* the Canaanite myth and *theology*.[149] But this is highly questionable because the polytheistic references in Canaanite myth were not accepted in Israel, although the mythical way of thinking (i.e., references to the heavenly/spirit realm) may be shared. So, although the issue of the source of eschatology requires further evaluation of the roles of the cult, myth, and creation theology,[150] Cross' integration may not be successful.

Von Rad's attempt to find out the source of eschatology in tradition has been modified or extended recently by Petersen. He argues that OT eschatology developed from a complex set of traditions, i.e., traditions of the promises to the patriarchs, David-Zion tradition, and Sinai tradition. These provided expectations which are essential elements of eschatology, although the 587 BCE fall of Jerusalem may have functioned as the catalyst to form a fully fledged eschatology. Patriarchal promises about the land and progeny, and becoming a great nation, provide a certain *expectation* for the identity and existence of Israel. The Davidic Covenant of a continuous reign of the Davidic line in 2 Sam 7 is linked not only to the patriarchal promise tradition but also to the notion of king on the throne and to that of Zion the Davidic city, in which the Deity also dwells. This tradition of the Davidic Covenant also produced the *expectation* of a future blessing of a secure Israel that the Davidic king rules. These expectations included both historical and cultic elements. The Sinai Covenant tradition inherently bears a *future orientation*, as it returns blessings or curses in the future according to the future

147. Cross 1966:12–13.

148. Cross 1966:30.

149. Cross 1966:21.

150. See Nickelsburg 1992; Aune 1992; Smith 1993; Clements 1965; Whitley 1963, etc.

obedience or disobedience of the covenant people.[151] For him, prophecies, in which the Davidic tradition and the Sinai Covenant are fused, present prophetic eschatology.[152] If this kind of future-oriented expectation, which is based on past traditions, is to be included in the category of eschatology, this must be in a broader sense, which in turn suggests a pre-prophetic, as well as prophetic, dating of eschatology. Peterson's understanding clarifies that a time element involved with the promise-fulfilment scheme is essential in the development of eschatology. However, the role of mythical language and thinking, crucial in the development of eschatology, is missing or neglected in his understanding, as it is in von Rad. For example, he does not acknowledge that the divine action of creation is repeated in the eschatological vision as in Isaiah 65:17.

In summary, issues of the definition, dating, and source of eschatology are related to each other. A broader definition is preferable, based on the purpose and salvific actions of YHWH in history. It has been observed that the religious traditions of Israel have eschatologizing momentum. Especially the covenant traditions including patriarchal promises provide the expectation for the future. The promise-fulfilment scheme is the pivotal element for the development of eschatology. The role of mythical thinking that the transcendental YHWH is working in history and that the divine action in the heavenly realm is re-applied in the eschatological future has not been appropriately considered as possible a matrix from which eschatology develops.

The role of mythical thinking is more clearly exhibited in the concept of apocalyptic, which is the next issue for our discussion. The term 'apocalyptic' originally refers to the theological/literary features of the Jewish apocalypses in late Judaism.[153] Because apocalyptic usually addresses Israel's future hope, eschatology in the broader sense includes the theology of apocalyptic literature, i.e., apocalyptic eschatology, as a particular form of eschatology.[154] The definition of apocalyptic [or, apocalypse] is related to the understanding of its major features. Authors may differ in the theological implications of the term apocalyptic, partly because they have different

---

151. Petersen 1992:576–77. He does not suggest these three sources are exclusive to each other.

152. Petersen 1992:577.

153. Hanson 1984:29–30; Allen 1990:15; von Rad 1965:301. According to Travis (1979:54), it is widely accepted that "the designation 'apocalyptic' may properly be given to the Biblical book of Daniel, sixteen non-canonical books and a large number of the Qumran scrolls."

154. Vriezen 1953:202; Clements 1965:105; von Rad 1965:301.

interests and views on the core characteristics of apocalypses.[155] Theological positions about the issues of apocalyptic are dependent on each other. Before defining the term, therefore, we need to review the two major views on the source or origin of apocalyptic.[156]

Seitz, following von Rad, considers that apocalyptic originated from the wisdom tradition.[157] For Seitz, the eternal realities are "manifested through a revelation (apocalypse)" to those who have wisdom and the sacred texts to comprehend the eternal realities. So, for him, apocalyptic is defined as what is "*interpreted truly*" to disclose the eternal realities as an "appeal to the past (word of God) for the purpose of disclosing revelatory truth in the present."[158] So it is more related to the "exegetical" or interpretive process of the past word of God as exemplified in the new creation account in 65:20–23 or the citation of 11:6 in 65:25, than to a set of the theological features of a certain genre (the apocalypses). Thus, for him, prophetic eschatology and apocalyptic eschatology are not distinguished in terms of theology, but only in their mode of revelation. While prophecy is an inspired address, apocalypse is a wise interpretation of the inspired texts.[159] For him, the social location of TI's prophecy is found within the cult, as the prophets progressively preached in the context of Israel's cult in the postexilic period.[160]

Seitz's idea of the re-application of the previous revelation of divine plan as the new revelation of the future divine salvation illuminates the eschatological/apocalyptic development, suggesting mythical thinking at

155. Wright (1992:280–82) suggests two main characteristics of apocalyptic: the disclosure of the secrets of the eternal reality (esotericism) and the cataclysmic change of the universe (cosmic dimension of the vision). Aune et al. (Aune, Geddert, and Evans 2000:48) suggest eight features of apocalyptic. According to Travis (1979:58–60), apocalyptic is generally understood as having the four (alleged) general features such as a clear distinction between the present, which is evil, and the coming world; the imminence of the end of the world; pessimism about the present world; and predetermined course of history. However, he argues that, of the four, the last two are not necessarily characteristics of apocalyptic.

156. There may be another view of origin, i.e., a view of the Babylonian origin. But the main ideas of this will be rejected later, so this view is not discussed at this stage. See Russel 1964:19.

157. Seitz 1999:74–76; von Rad 1965a:301–8.

158. Italics his. As it were, the 'apocalyptic' denotes the involvement with "the disclosure of truth with reference to prior testimony in texts or tradition or teaching."

159. Seitz 1999:74–76.

160. The cultic use of TI as well as PI/DI may be suggested because TI is included in the larger corpus of the book of Isaiah, the materials from DI and PI are included in TI, and similar languages and expressions of DI and TI are included in the Psalter. Seitz 1992:504.

work. However, his proposal for a cultic location of apocalyptic hardly supports the view of wisdom tradition as its origin. Rather, mythical thinking is more appropriate as a direct source of apocalyptic than the cult itself, although the latter may be the major locus for the former. The proclamation of divine action may have developed and continuously been re-applied to the life of Israel in the thought of the prophets and the addressees of the proclamation even outside the cult. Besides, it may be difficult to distinguish between the materials in the canon as direct revelations in the past and those as re-applications of the past words to the present. In addition, it is questionable to identify 'mantic wisdom,' by which eternal reality is revealed, e.g., when Joseph and Daniel have interpreted dreams, and the 'proverbial wisdom' of the sages.[161] Furthermore, contrary to von Rad, an apocalyptic view of history is not necessarily pessimistic and deterministic, as Travis observes.[162] In relation to determinism, von Rad comments, "God sees events twice. In the first instance he sees them in their primeval, predetermined state and then once again when they have appeared in history 'in their time.'"[163] This may also suggest mythical thinking since the protological event is applicable to history at multiple times (see below).

For Hanson, on the contrary, apocalyptic developed from the prophetic tradition.[164] Hanson defines apocalyptic as the disclosure (usually esoteric in nature) of the cosmic vision of the sovereign salvific will of YHWH. In this disclosure, "the visionaries have largely ceased to translate [their visions] into instrumentality due to a pessimistic view of reality growing out of the bleak post-exilic conditions within which those associated with the visionaries found themselves."[165] For him, there is an essential continuity

161. Aune, Geddert, and Evans 2000:48.

162. Travis 1979:58–60. See below for the discussion of dualism.

163. Von Rad 1972/75:265. He (1972/75:273) adds, "this act of revelation is a non-recurring one; it lies at the beginning and concerns the whole of history right through to its eschatological conclusion. . . . [T]he end erupts abruptly into a world of history which is growing darker and darker, and the benefits of salvation which have long been pre-existent in the heavenly world—'until time comes to an end'—(Son of Man, the New Jerusalem) makes their appearance."

164. Hanson 1975:6 ; Carroll 1982:48; Aune 1992:595. For him (1975:6), "[T]he apocalyptic literature of the second century and after is the result of a long development reaching back to pre-exilic times and beyond, and not the new baby of second-century foreign parents." Travis (1979:61) argues for the theological continuity between prophecies and apocalyptic, contrary to von Rad, who rejects the connection between apocalyptic and prophecies.

165. Hanson 1975:11. Aune, Geddert, and Evans (2000:47) summarized Hanson's apocalyptic features as: (1) esoteric disclosure of the secrets of the universe to the chosen, (2) cosmic scope of the divine action, (3) disconnectedness with plain history (no translation into plain history) of the vision, (4) pessimistic view of history, and (5) 'the

between prophetic and apocalyptic eschatology in that both are revelation originally from YHWH. Hanson's term "apocalyptic eschatology" in contrast to "prophetic eschatology" facilitates "both elements of continuity and change in the development."[166] Prophets unfold the divine plans as displayed in the divine council and announce them to the nation; visionaries disclose the cosmic vision of the salvation of sovereign YHWH.[167] However, while the prophets translate the plans of divine council into the terms of plain history (e.g., real politics of the nations and human instrumentality), the visionaries [i.e., apocalypticists] do not.[168]

For Hanson, the eschatological message of TI (early apocalyptic) has a strong connection with that of DI (proto-apocalyptic), especially in chs 60–62, but it is not limited to the message of DI.[169] TI's apocalyptic eschatology developed due to the sociological struggle between hierocratic priests and the prophetic visionary group in 'the gloomy post-exilic situation.'[170] As the prophetic group lost their political hegemony in the community, being defeated by the hierocratic priests, they ceased to translate their cosmic vision into the plain language that portrays history.[171]

For Hanson, DI adopted (Israel's version of) the conflict myth, which inaugurates the apocalyptic development (so, 'proto-apocalyptic'). The mythical element in DI represents the cosmic dimension of the divine actions, "which had been absent in prophecy."[172] Hanson considers that the original home of the Divine Warrior Hymn (59:15b–20) was "the cosmic realm of myth."[173] The hymn reflects mythical thinking, celebrating the work of YHWH in the past, but becomes eschatologized to present the divine work in the future.[174] By the adoption of the hymn, prophetic eschatology was transformed into apocalyptic eschatology, becoming detached from plain history and universalized to cover the nations as well as Israel and even to embrace the entire cosmos.[175] "The influence of myth, with its

---

bleak post-exilic conditions.'

166. Hanson 1975:10.

167. Hanson 1975:11.

168. Hanson 1975:11.

169. In this, Hanson follows G. von Rad, although for von Rad (1965:279–81) TI is not apocalyptic.

170. Hanson 1984:32.

171. Hanson 1975:11.

172. Hanson 1975:126–27.

173. Hanson 1975:118, 126.

174. Hanson 1975:124–25.

175. Hanson 1975:126.

dualistic imagery of a conflict between the warrior god and the insurgent foe, ultimately would lead to a picture of judgment in apocalyptic eschatology which construed the enemy increasingly in terms of absolute evil."[176]

Hanson's view needs to be appreciated for several points. He acknowledges the "mythopoeic" or mythical elements, i.e., the realities in the heavenly realm in both prophecies and apocalyptic. He recognizes the literary function of the Divine Warrior Hymn. Childs criticizes Hanson's "the history of religion's approach," commenting that "such a concern for historical origins does not aid greatly in understanding the passage according to its literary function in chapter 59."[177] However, in my judgment the Divine Warrior Hymn is understood as presenting a prophetic description of the divine (apocalyptic) revelation of the heavenly realities, and not as history. Hanson detects the heavenly realm and the two-tier world-picture as reflected in the hymn, which is the basis for the mythical thinking. Mythical thinking may be defined as a way of thinking that takes into consideration realities and activities in the heavenly realm based on a two-tier-world picture.[178] The vision of YHWH's salvific action in the heavenly realm is expected with certainty to be realized ultimately in historical reality. Often the reality in the heavenly realm, e.g., YHWH's victory over the mythical monster, is applied in the historical world at multiple times. Due to his understanding of the hymn he considers that the divine actions involve a cosmic dimension.

However, Hanson's idea that prophecy and apocalyptic have introduced mythical thinking and the cosmic dimension by the adoption of mythical materials needs to be reconsidered. For him, the adoption of the conflict myth by DI is a "new" movement, assuming that mythopoeic thinking belongs to the (royal) cult alone.[179] However, mythical materials have been ever present not only in the cultic message, but since ancient times

176. Hanson 1975:207.

177. Childs 2001:489.

178. For the sense of myth, we accept the Levenson's conception in that myth is the symbols expressed in the timeless languages although myth is originally from the protological time (the ultimate past) while apocalyptic languages are not necessarily protological (Levenson 1985:102). See below in the main text.

179. Hanson understands that although Israel's ancient literature reflects mythopoeic thought, prophetic religion lacks the mythical elements, and it is in the royal theology of the Jerusalem court that the ancient myth and ritual pattern was combined with "the archaic league tradition of the ritual conquest." Here, Hanson tends to put prophets essentially against the royal cult of Jerusalem, since the latter keep the mythical vision untranslated into historicality, while the former do this. However, it is suspicious whether the ancient mythical element and the theology of the royal cult are sharply separated from the Deuteronomistic History. Mythical materials are included in Exod 15, Judg 5, and Josh 10 as well as in the royal cult or prophecies, presenting the heavenly realm as related to the earthly realm.

in Israel as witnessed by the Song of the Sea (Exod 15:1b–18), as he concedes.[180] The mythical materials express a mythopoeic thinking in Israel's religion. But, it is not by the introduction of a mythical element (such as the Divine Warrior Hymn) but by mythopoeic thinking that the eschatology of DI and TI develops, although the two are closely related. Mythical material is part of mythopoeic thinking; mythopoeic thinking is not brought about by the introduction of mythical material. This is because the divine actions of creation and exodus and other salvation actions of YHWH are already mythical. It is strange that only the prophets avoid mythical thinking, while others (such as the ancient people, those who had cult, and post-exilic visionaries) have a mythopoeic mind. The prophets also frequently refer to the heavenly realm. Furthermore, Hanson's assumption on the sociological struggle in the post-exilic situation is not clearly supported by the text of TI (see 5.2).[181] In addition to this, the assumption of pessimism is also rejected by Travis (see below).

Keeping in mind the two views of apocalyptic, I define "apocalyptic" as "the heavenly languages ('mythical patterns' is Seitz's term[182]) revealing the eternal realities, often involving the (cataclysmic) cosmic vision of the last things."[183] In this definition, three main theological features of apocalyptic may be suggested: (1) the apocalyptic or mythical representation of the eternal realities; (2) apocalyptic duality (distinction between the present age and the age to come) and the consequent discontinuity with the present world; and (3) the cosmic scope of the vision, i.e., cataclysmic change of the universe.

180. For Hanson, while DI has maintained the tension between cosmic dimension of YHWH's action and the historical reality, TI could not so do and focused on the cosmic dimension of the divine action without relating it to the history. But the disconnectedness widened in apocalyptic should not be over-emphasized. It should be thought of in connection with the mythical thinking in common in both DI and TI. Both prophecy and apocalyptic develop by the mythopoeic thought of Israel—although DI and TI may have different emphases.

181. His methodology that borrowed from Max Weber is questionable. Hanson 1975:20–21; Childs 2001:444; Seitz 2001:525. Hanson's view of 'the bleak post-exilic conditions' as the origin of the apocalyptic in TI may be unwarranted because the historical conditions are not the primary concern of the TI text and this may be an *eis-egesis* in the interpretation of TI.

182. Seitz 1999:74.

183. For the distinction between apocalypse, apocalyptic (eschatology), and apocalypticism, see Hanson 1975:8–12.

Apocalyptic or Mythical Representation[184]

Hanson considers that apocalyptic language may refer to transcendental realities in the heavenly realm, while some consider the language as metaphor of the historical reality. For the cosmic scope in apocalyptic visions, Hanson understands cosmic imageries as 'literal' since the new heaven and earth replace the old ones and eschatological judgment involves the whole creation.[185] Here, "literal" means "straightforward descriptions of heavenly reality," as Wright observed.[186] For Hanson, mythical languages refer to the heavenly realm as in the Divine Warrior Hymn (59:15b–21), and apocalyptic is also mythical. However, Wright argues that a "'literalist' reading" of this change of the universe is not warranted in Jewish thought, if this includes the destruction of the universe.

For Wright, apocalyptic language such as the cataclysmic change of the universe is metaphorical and refers to events within history,[187] although he recognizes the possibility of metaphysical representation of such language.[188] For him, some of the apocalyptic visions are concerning the heavenly realm itself, as "intended to be taken 'literally,' that is, as straightforward description of heavenly reality."[189] For him, "the heavenly and the earthly realm belong closely with one another," and apocalyptic language "sometimes make[s] use of the metaphysical correspondence between the earthly and the heavenly."[190] However, for him, within the Jewish worldview of the first century, the real end of the space-time universe is not known.[191] Thus, "when they used what we might call cosmic imagery to describe the coming new age, such language cannot be read in a crassly literalistic way without doing it great violence."[192] Wright's understanding of the heavenly realm is very limited, since 'heaven' is "God's dimension of present reality" alone.[193] He

184. That is, representation in the heavenly realm. 'Metaphysical representation' is Wright's (1992:290) term.

185. Hanson 1975:155, 207.

186. Wright 1992:284.

187. Wright 1992:280–85. According to him, "apocalyptic language uses complex and highly coloured metaphors in order to describe one event in terms of another, thus bringing out the perceived 'meaning' of the first."

188. Wright 1992:284, 290.

189. Wright 1992:284.

190. Wright 1992:291.

191. Wright 1992:285.

192. Wright 1992:284–85. For him, literal reading of the cosmic imageries is as if historians would understand the metaphorical language 'earth-shattering event' referring to the fall of the Berlin Wall as a real earthquake several centuries later.

193. Wright 1999b:13; n.d.:9.

does not consider that the apocalyptic language in Dan 7 and Mark 13 may go beyond the historical and literary contexts to refer to the ultimate future or heavenly aspect.[194] So, he tends to downplay the transcendental aspects of the apocalyptic language. For Wright, "the [cosmic] events, including the ones that were expected to come as the climax of YHWH's restoration of Israel, remained within (what we think of as) the this-worldly ambit."[195] Thus, for him, apocalyptic is about the historical world and is to be understood as metaphor and the cataclysmic imagery has "nothing to do with the world itself coming to an end."[196] For Wright, the 'literalist reading' of the change [i.e., the end and recreation] of the universe "belongs closely together" with a moral/theological duality. That is a radical dualism, which incorporates three kinds of dualities: "the distinction between the creator and the world (theological/cosmological duality is his term), the distinction between the physical and the non-physical world (cosmological duality is his term), and the distinction between good and evil (moral duality is his term)."[197] I doubt, however, whether a literalist understanding of apocalyptic language necessarily "belongs closely together" with these three dualities, since the destruction of the universe does not necessarily require an inherently evil universe (see below).

Wright's understanding of the apocalyptic languages is to some extent dependent on Caird's view of myth and mythical thinking/representation. For Caird, providing Wright with a theoretical background about the metaphoric understanding of the apocalyptic/mythical languages, "myths are stories about the past which embody and express a people's traditional culture."[198] For Caird, myth is the universal instinctive center of reference or the universal type of the stories or events or places or persons. So, myth is "emblematic," and he emphasizes the literary function of mythology (Myth[L] [literary] is his term).[199] It is a specialized kind of metaphor, which has a historical referent. "It tells a story about the past, but only in order to say something about the present and the future. It has a literal referent in the characters and events of the vehicle story, but its tenor referent is the situation of the user and his audience."[200] He does not consider the "vehicle story"

194. Wright 1999a:265.

195. Wright 1992:285.

196. Wright (1992:285) supports Caird, Glasson, and Borg rather than Schweitzer on the matter of apocalyptic representation.

197. Wright 1992:285.

198. Caird 1980:220.

199. Caird 1980:223.

200. Caird 1980:224.

to form a self-sustained world, whether a thought world or spirit/heavenly world (these two being closely related). For him, the mythical language in Isa 51:9–11 and Col 2:15 refers to the events of the exodus and the cross, which happened in real history. These passages represent the conviction that God is Lord of history.[201]

Caird's understanding of mythical representation may however be challenged. First, Caird does not seem to acknowledge the spiritual world or heavenly realm.[202] He tends to neglect or misunderstand the existence of spiritual beings.[203] Second, Caird does not appear to pay attention to the nature of the "vehicle story," but only to its literary function. Although, as Caird observed, mythological language or God-talk may point to reciprocal

201. Caird 1980:209, 213.

202. Caird 1980:213, 224. For Caird (1980: 224), to understand the tenor of the myth as a transcendental reference is allegorization. The 'powers and authorities' in Col 2:15 are personifications of the structures of the political, social, and religious power. In Col 2:15 or Isa 51:9–11, the idea that mythological language may be involved in the 'spirit world' and thus to interpret the verses into (or, in the framework of) the 'spirit world' (in his term) is 'nonsense,' for him. However, we also need to take notice of the 'so-called' vehicle, which does not belong to this world. Only after the literal under-standing of the myth (vehicle is his term) as a literary complex that refers to the things in the mythological world (as he accepts that myth has a "literal referent in the char-acters and events of the vehicle story"), can we come to understand the sense (tenor is his term) of the mythology in the narrative, which tells about the historical world. The two-tired world-view (i.e., heavenly world vs. earthly world) has been justified as the Biblical thought, as Wright (1992:252–59) already assumes in his theological/ontologi-cal (theological/ cosmological is our term) duality.

203. Caird 1980:238, 213, 238–39, 241–42. (1) For Caird (1980:238), demons are not realities, but ones which occur only in the fantasies, although he admits that they occur in the gospel narratives. (2) Caird (1980:213) considers the 'powers and authori-ties' in Col 2:15 as the *personifications* of the political, social and religious structures of power, because mythologicalL language has (only) a historical referent. The term per-sonification implies that the powers and authorities are this-worldly realities. They do not tell anything above the historical world, for him. (3) In understanding the powers, authorities, sovereignties, thrones and lordships in Pauline letters, he (1980:238–39) concedes that Paul's idea is in line with Deut 32:17, in which demons are associated with the pagan religion. He admits that "these terms denote 'heavenly beings,' which represent the power structures of the old world order." But what he means by 'heavenly beings' is not certain. They are different from demons but only *represent* earthly reali-ties. It is not entirely obvious why and how demons and the heavenly beings are differ-ent in Caird's categorization. (4) Caird (1980: 241–42) accepts that Paul's claim that the law was ordained through angels in Gal 3:19 is linked to Deut 33:2, in which YHWH comes with myriads of 'holy ones.' But, for him, these 'angels of Sinai' are "the symbols of a derivative and provisional authority, and are therefore in the same category as the sons of God who preside over the destinies of other nations." The "spiritual beings" (in his term) *stand for* the political, social, economic and religious structures of power. For him, however, the spiritual beings do not belong to the spiritual realm, but are *immanent* within the physical world.

interaction with the human or natural world (in a metaphoric way),[204] they are basically understood to describe their own world, i.e., a mythological world (as directly related to the thought world of the vehicle story), which is distinct from this world, before they are applied to the historical events of this world in the narrative.[205] In this understanding, contrary to Caird, the relation between myth and the present is not linear (at the same level) but direct, not horizontal but vertical, as timeless time is linked directly with every moment of historical time. Myth primarily belongs to the heavenly realm. Third, Caird does not accept that Biblical man has "the mythopoeic mind", i.e., mythical thinking, because mythopoeic/mythical thinking is so primitive that it had already disappeared before the earliest document of the OT was written.[206]

Levenson, however, has observed that there is in both the OT and the NT language that requires "mythical" thinking.[207] His view is that mythical language refers primarily to the realities in the heavenly realm, although these are in turn connected to the earthly realities. For him, myth is defined as the protological events that happened in mythical time (i.e., timelessly) and carry the continuing relevance in every moment of history (Myth[P] [protological] after Caird's terminology).[208] In this definition, myth is a legitimate theological way of understanding the world that does not belong to this world: the other world or heavenly world.[209] While myths[L] (for Caird)

204. Caird 1980:177–78.

205. See below, for the sense of 'myth.'

206. Caird 1980:193, 197.

207. Levenson 1985:102–10. According to Levenson (1985:105, 106), the reference to David in Ezek 34:23 requires a mythical thinking as it does not fit the historical thinking of David's death (1 Kgs 2:10). The Biblical statement that 'YHWH' built the Temple 'before' the election of David in Ps 78:69–70 may be contradictory to the historical facts that 'Solomon' has built the Temple 'after' David's death (1 Kgs 6:1) and thus displays the deeper meaning of the poet in his mythical thinking. For Levenson, historians' perspective and mythical perspective are coexistent in the Hebrew Bible. Caird (1980:210) also admits that Isa 51:9–11 and Col 2:15 reflect the language of myth. In Isa 51:9–11, "[T]he prophet declares his conviction that this initial cosmic victory over the forces of chaos, darkness and evil was repeated at the exodus, when the waters of the sea were cut in two to provide Israel with a path to safety . . . ." The mythological language in Col 2:15 signifies "God (or Christ) won a victory over the cosmic powers."

208. Levenson 1985:103; Childs 1962:20. For the various meanings of myth, see Caird 1980:220–23. Myth[P] in Caird's term is Myth (Pragmatic), which is different from Myth (Protological) above.

209. According to Caird (1980:219), Bultmann argues in effect that mythology is 'theological use of metaphor.' As it were, myth is theological language or 'God-talk', i.e., any sentence containing the word 'God' is myth (Myth[T] (theological) in Caird's term). "Mythology is the use of imagery to express the otherworldly in terms of this world and the divine in terms of human life, the other side in terms of this side." (Quotation

are stories about *the past*, myth[P] (for Levenson) concerns the *protological* events.[210] By definition, myth[L] is inherently confined within this world and history, because it is formed from, and functions to describe, the historical world (the past and the present/future, respectively). However, the tense of myth[P] is not the past, according to Levenson, but timeless time, which is different from historical time but still closely related to it.[211] Levenson seems to balance representation of the apocalyptic in the heavenly realm and its earthly counterpart.

If we follow Caird's view of apocalyptic representation, then we are forced to follow the view that there is no 'real' cataclysmic change of the universe that the apocalyptic language (cf. 65:17, 25) refers to.[212] Besides, we are liable to reject the heavenly realm, or at least to neglect the ultimate future aspect of heavenly language (as Wright does in Mark 13), because the language (either prophetic or apocalyptic) refers only to historical realities as metaphor. In fact, Wright suggests that the first-century Jewish world-view does not support such a 'literalist' reading of the apocalyptic language, because the Jews only longed for the imminent restoration in the historical arena. But it is not certain whether the OT and the first-century Jewish world-view really exclude the literal view of (destruction and) recreation. The Biblical texts often seem to suggest far-reaching visions that are not necessarily confined to the immediate historical and literary contexts (see 5.3 on 65:17–25). I will assume that there is a heavenly world which is related to this earthly world,[213] and some language may refer to it (so Wright). But I also assume that the heavenly language may involve the ultimate future beyond the historical context (pace Wright). While (Wright and) Caird tend(s) to neglect the mythical representation, Hanson concedes that apocalyptic may refer to the heavenly realm, so

originally from Bultmann 19xx:16). Considering this, myth[P] and myth[T] are identified if we limit our primary concern on the mythology of the OT since Levenson in fact does not think that the term mythical is necessarily related to the protological (i.e., creational) events as in the above examples, because mythical time does not distinguish between the past, the present, and the future (Childs 1962:74). (Creation myth of the ANE has no way to validate the 'content'/theology of mythology in ANE while mythology in the OT is authentic for the purpose of OT theology.)

210. Caird 1980:220.

211. Caird 1980:220. Also see Childs 1962:74.

212. Wright (1992:299, 300; 1999:265; 2007:107, 133–34) tends to share this view. Although in places he (2007:116, 173, 175) mentions "the renewal of the entire cosmos," or "a great act of new creation," or even "a new heaven and a new earth," these phrases do not imply the destruction of the universe, but something dramatic in this physical world, so eventually metaphoric.

213. How they are related precisely to each other may be beyond this dissertation.

the cosmic imagery of apocalyptic may be 'literal.'[214] So, I accept Hanson and Levenson's view of mythical representation of the 'heavenly' languages, based on the two-tier-world picture, assuming that the 'heavenly' language not only is divine perspective of the present reality but also may have an ultimate realization in the future.

Apocalyptic Duality of the Two Ages

Traditionally, apocalyptic has been considered to be influenced by the radical Persian dualism, having a pessimistic view of history. For Hanson, in apocalyptic, the world to come is totally distinct from the present world as the present world order is so evil that it will be entirely destroyed.[215] However, Hanson's dualistic understanding of apocalyptic and the 'pessimistic view of history' (these two are closely related) may be over-emphasized. For Wright, Jewish apocalyptic does not include a moral/cosmological dualism.[216] Travis also persuasively argues that the apocalyptic view of history is not necessarily pessimistic because there was a positive view of history, especially in earlier apocalypses such as Daniel. The negative view of history reflects the desperate circumstances of their particular periods, and the saving actions of God are recognized in the past as well as in the future.[217] Although the last two scholars recognize a distinction between the present age and the eschatological time (this may be called 'eschatological [or apocalyptic] duality'), they do not consider that apocalypses presume a radical dualism. For them, the present world is not *inherently* evil.[218] The apocalyptic view of history is not

214. For the sense of 'literal,' see above on page 33.

215. Hanson 1975:158.

216. Wright 1992:297. The moral/cosmological dualism (cosmological dualism is his term) is a distinction between the Platonic good world and the physical evil world as related to ethical quality. For him, neither included in the Jewish apocalyptic are the moral/anthropological dualism (distinction between good soul and evil body; anthropological dualism in his term) and moral/theological dualism (distinction between a good god and a bad god; theological/moral dualism in his term), which, together with moral/cosmological dualism, form the proper sense of '(radical) dualism.'

217. Travis 1979:58–61.

218. (Radical) dualism is the view that moral quality is inherently associated with the structure of the universe (moral/cosmological duality is my term), so that the physical world is *inherently* evil and has to be destroyed while the heavenly world (or the Platonic universe) is *inherently* good. The destruction of the universe and the death of the human body do not necessarily imply that the universe and human body are inherently evil in Biblical thinking. Human body is not inherently evil in Biblical thinking but needs to be resurrected (or recreated) after all, because it became to involve sinfulness *a posteriori* but not inherently. Likewise, although the universe and materials are not ontologically evil, they need to be recreated with the cataclysmic change if they are

necessarily ontologically pessimistic (so Travis), although an apocalyptic text may still have an eschatological/apocalyptic duality.[219] Thus the influence of the ancient Iranian Zoroastrianism is not compelling and I do not assume apocalyptic a moral/cosmological duality (i.e., dualism).[220]

The apocalyptic duality forms a discontinuity between the two worlds, as often the coming world is presented as the New Heavens and the New Earth. Apocalyptic also has theological/cosmological duality (a distinction between the heavenly world and the earthly world; theological/ontological is Wright's term), which is distinguished from a moral/cosmological dualism, which implies that the two worlds are inherently involved with moral quality.

Cosmic Scope

Since Hanson assumes a two-tier-world picture (i.e., heavenly/cosmic realm vs. earthly world) and the mythical/apocalyptic representation, he takes a 'literalist' reading of the cosmic vision.[221] If we accept the mythical representation of apocalyptic, the cosmic change of the universe is 'literal' [i.e., a straightforward description] based on the dual-world picture. Although prophetic eschatology also has an eschatological duality, which is characterized by the discontinuity between the two ages before and after the start of eschatological era, in apocalyptic eschatology this discontinuity becomes extended to the cosmic level.

In summary, I suggest by apocalyptic three outstanding features: (1) apocalyptic representation (i.e., mythical representation) refers in a more or less direct way to the heavenly realm, which is ultimately related to the earthly realm, (2) apocalyptic/eschatological duality is characterized by discontinuity between the apocalyptic world (i.e., world to come) and the present world (i.e., history), and (3) a cosmic scope of vision is often involved. Apocalyptic representation requires an understanding of a two-tier-world view.

a posteriori associated with the evil as the earth is cursed by the Fall (Gen 3:18; Rom 8:18–25). If the 'negative view of reality' does not involve the cosmological implication, then it does not distinguish apocalyptic from prophecies.

219. I do not assume that eschatological duality does necessarily involve with (moral/cosmological) dualism, which is the term implying that the present world is ontologically evil. Duality is distinguished from dualism, the former being a feature of the universe, while the latter being an ideology to see the universe.

220. Wright 1992:297.

221. Hanson 1975:134. It appears that Wright also admits a two-tiered world picture judging by his terminology 'theological/ontological duality' (theological/cosmological is my term), which distinguishes between the heavenly world and the earthly world, although he differs in the view of linguistic usage of apocalyptic representation from Hanson.

As regards the relation between the present and the eschaton (eschatological future) or between history and eschatology, the final issue of eschatology and apocalyptic, there are several views that differ from Mowinckel's. However, scholars do not always distinguish between the horizontal or temporal aspect of eschatology (eschatology[H]) and the vertical or spatial aspect of eschatology (eschatology[V]). This distinction is facilitated by mythical thinking. There is a clear break in Mowinckel between history and eschatology/the eschaton or between this world and the world to come (Model A; discontinuity in terms of timeline), since eschatology (eschatology[H]) is to bring a new world order by the end of the present.[222] For Clements (Model B), however, YHWH's purpose, which leads to eschatology, is fulfilled in the arena of history.[223] So Eschatology (eschatology[H]) and history are continuous.[224] However, because discontinuity is not part of this understanding, it does not fully explain the divine action that makes history eschatology not only in the process of time (horizontally) but also here and now (vertically). For example, he who responds to the invitation of eschatological salvation in 56:1 joins the eschatological salvation here and now.

For Schunck (Model C=A+B), Israel's thought does not distinguish between internal-temporal (*innerzeitlich*) and final-temporal (*endzeitlich*) actions, which suggests continuity between the present and the eschaton (Model B). He considers that, for the prophets, there is a critical break only between what is now and what is to come, which may display some discontinuity between history and eschatology (eschatology[H]; Model A). The one is to be destroyed; the other has not even the slightest continuation of the present, which forms proper eschatology, as the word אחרית presents.[225]

---

222. Mowinckel 1959:154. Whitley (1963:202) also follows Mowinckel in arguing that the new world order is essentially different from the present world order.

223. Clements 1965:104–5.

224. For Uffenheimer (1997:209–11), too, there is continuity between history and eschatology (eschatology[H]) in both DI and TI. The actual events at present are interpreted in view of, and related to, eschatology in DI and TI. The eschatological expectation of the coming of the nations to Zion is understood as a real historical event in 60:5–22 and 61:5–9. The land of Israel is understood as an eschatological reward in 58:14. He (1997:200–217) tries to categorize four types of eschatology: (1) eschatology as the imminent continuation of contemporaneous history; (2) the detachment of eschatology from history; (3) the eschatological interpretation of current events; (4) eschatological activism. But it is not certain whether these four form distinct stages of a development or whether these four are different aspects of a consistent eschatology. For Freedman (1960:153), too, history and eschatology are not distinguished as eschatology is the result of history and history is the background of eschatology. History contains eschatological elements in that salvific divine intention is realized in history. So for him, history is eschatological (continuity).

225. Schunck 1964:320. He follows Boman (1952:109) in the view of time in Israel.

Eschatology includes not only the non-historical final phase (eschatology$^{(H)}$) but also history. However, the break resides with the judgment of God, which creates things completely new.[226] So Schunk notes some discontinuity, although he admits continuity between history and eschatology$^{(H)}$.[227] So, "discontinuity (former/new) is embedded in continuity."[228] However, according to Oswalt (1981), the God of the prophets both works immanently in the cosmos and is transcendental, above and beyond it, at the same time. The promise of salvation will be fulfilled within the framework of human experience, but which goes far beyond it as well. Prophecies are projected into a wider plane to form eschatology.[229] Therefore, a more nuanced elaboration for the continuity/discontinuity between history and eschatology may be possible by the introduction of mythical thinking.

Model A   history _____   _____ eschatology$^{(H)}$

Model B   history _____   _____ eschatology$^{(H)}$

Model C   history _____   _____ eschatology$^{(H)}$

           eschatology$^{(V)}$ _____
Model D   history _____   _____ eschatology$^{(H)}$

           eschatology$^{(V)}$ _____   eschatology$^{(V)}$=eschatology$^{(H')}$
Model E
           history _____   _____ eschatology$^{(H)}$

Figure. Eschatological Models

So, he seems to put a break between the present and the combined future and eschatology. But he replaces the word final-temporal (*endzeitlich*) with extra-temporal (*außerzeitlich/außergeschichtlich, transzendental*) in his later article (Schunck 1974:119).

226. Schunck 1974:119–120. See note above. "*Wo der Bruch mit dem bisherigen, unter Gottes Gericht stehenden sündigen Sein vollzogen wurde und ein ganz neues Sein nach Gottes Willen und in Gemeinschaft mit ihm begonnen wurde, da ist das Eschaton bereits da, dort steht der betreffende Mensch bereits im Eschaton.*" ["Where the break with the present sinful being standing under God's judgment was carried out and quite a new being has begun by God's will in the community, then the eschaton is already there, and there the person in question stands already in the eschaton." (My translation).]

227. Lindblom (1952:58) emphasizes continuity and discontinuity of historical world in understanding eschatology.

228. Leene 1997:228, 231.

229. Oswalt 1981:293–94.

For Vriezen (Model D), there is no fundamental distinction between the general future and the eschatological future (eschatology[H]). The Hebrew אחרית הימים refers both to the future in the prophet's horizon (i.e., near future) and the last days in the eschatological sense (i.e., eschaton, or distant or ultimate future).[230] For Vriezen, the new thing, i.e., eschatology, is "*the* renewing act of *the* historical drama" (italics his). Even though it takes place within the framework of history, it changes the world into something definitely different.[231] However, he considers that there is a sharp break between history and supra-history (i.e., eschatology[V]) rather than between the present and the future and thus that there is continuity between prophecy and apocalyptic.[232] For Vriezen, the eschatological salvific expectation will be achieved in "an absolutely decisive new situation in the world," as Jerusalem will be the center of interest, bearing universal and supra-natural features in 65:15–25 and 66:5–24. So for him eschatology is "historical and at the same time suprahistorical" and the eschatological renewal "takes place within the framework of history but is caused by forces that transcend history, so that what is coming is a new order of things in which the glory and the Spirit of God (Is. xi) reveals itself."[233] Here, mythical thinking may be detected that needs to be developed. Vriezen's conception requires a distinction between horizontal and vertical aspects of eschatology, the latter especially being called suprahistory or eschatology[V]. However, Vriezen's view seems to lack a sufficient emphasis on the introduction of an entirely new element in the history, as what is to come indicates in Schunck, which makes history and eschatology distinct. I suggest that in mythical thinking, a supra-natural description of reality (eschatology[V]), which is discontinuous with history, is realized in reality (eschatology[H]), although this eschaton is in continuation of history. This brings a discontinuity between history and eschatology[H] as well as continuity (eschatology[H]) (Model E).

In conclusion, there is both continuity and discontinuity between history and eschatology. A distinction between vertical and horizontal aspects is needed to describe eschatology. Mythical thinking is needed to understand eschatology.

---

230. Vriezen 1953:202.

231. Vriezen 1953:218.

232. Vriezen 1953:224, 219. As it were, Vriezen sees that the future and the eschaton (i.e., eschatology[H]) are continuous (in terms of [the process of] time) while history and eschatology (eschatology[V]) are discontinuous (in terms of the quality of time). History includes the past, the present, and the future.

233. Vrizen 1953:218–19, 222.

Methodology in Approaching Eschatological Issues

In the study of eschatological theology, many issues are cross-linked to each other. This is why tackling a particular issue in isolation cannot be a complete solution. A position on one issue influences the position on other issues. Scholars are often influenced by their own content and beliefs. What they assume is often what they discover in the texts. For example, their own metaphysical pre-understanding of the world (i.e., world-view) influences their understanding of Israel's view of time and history, which in turn influences their understanding of eschatology, which then fits into, and supports, their assumption. Therefore, we need to be very careful not to impose our metaphysics or theology upon the Biblical texts.

We need to adopt a holistic approach to understand the eschatological issues in relation to other theological concepts and thoughts in TI. As Nickelsburg has suggested, because of this variety in eschatological issues, we need to focus on a particular text, i.e., TI in our case, in order to obtain an integrated solution.[234]

In order to investigate the eschatology of TI, I select four particular themes and the passages that correspond to them: the covenant (56:1–8), the coming of YHWH (59:15b–21), Zion (60:1–22), and the New Heavens and the New Earth (65:13–25). These four themes/texts are considered to epitomize the 'story' of the eschatological plan of YHWH in TI. Other themes and issues may be included in these categories.

Conclusion

Eschatology is understood broadly as the future hope of Israel. Its investigation is our aim, in particular in TI. Prophetic eschatology refers to the eschatology of the prophets. Apocalyptic eschatology refers to eschatology in apocalyptic literature or eschatology of theological features thereof. Apocalyptic is considered to have three particular theological features: apocalyptic/mythical representation, eschatological/apocalyptic duality and discontinuity, and cosmic scope of the vision. We have seen that eschatological issues are interrelated not only to each other but also to the wider framework of theology and metaphysical assumptions as well. So we need a holistic approach to deal with all the eschatological issues and focus on a particular (section of a) book, i.e., in our case TI, rather than tackling each issue individually.

234. Nickelsburg 1992:592.

1.4 Conclusion and the Plan of this Book

This book attempts to sketch a systematic and integrated theology of TI on the assumption of theological unity, as required by the survey of the study of the theology of TI. According to the survey, largely due to the fragmentation of text and theology, it has proved difficult to construct an eschatological theology through a historical methodology. This is mainly because of an excessive interest in historical matters, which may not be pivotal for theological construction of the text. But on the basis of a theological unity as assumed in a canonical approach, the alleged historical diversity of DI and TI can be otherwise viewed and there emerges the possibility of constructing a coherent theology. This theological perspective also invites a reading of TI in the context of the previous parts of Isaiah.

I have assumed that eschatology is at the heart of a unified theology of TI. So I want to explore the nature of eschatology (i.e., eschatological theology) as presented in TI. This includes the relationships between the covenant, the coming of YHWH, Zion, and the New Heavens and the New Earth. The continuity and discontinuity between past/present and future and between history and eschatology also emerges at various points in the study of the eschatology of TI. An eschatological approach also allows the integration of other key theological themes such as salvation and judgment, justice and righteousness, and cult, as well as key characters such as Israel, the nations, and the Messianic figure. These topics and themes cannot be pursued exhaustively but will be described in the framework of the theological interpretation of several key texts.

Chapter 2 as an exposition of Isa 56:1–8 tries to show that the covenant concept is pivotal in understanding the eschatology of TI. Chapter 3 exposits Isa 59:15b–21 and shows that the coming of YHWH is the decisive eschatological event (as it inaugurates eschatology), through which YHWH not only cleanses Israel but also judges the nations to form the new people of YHWH and bring about the eschatological era. Chapter 4, the study of Isa 60, portrays Zion, the eschatological temple-city, to which the nations/kings flow, and the eschatological people of YHWH, being formed from the nations as well as Israel. Investigating 65:13–25, chapter 5 presents the New Heavens and the New Earth, in which the New Jerusalem is restored. Chapter 6 will summarize the key themes that recur in the exegetical sections.

Chapter 2

The Covenant as Eschatological Framework (56:1–8)

2.1 Introduction

In chapter 1, I surveyed the study of the theology of TI especially in relation to the study of the theology of the book of Isaiah. The survey has shown that while previous historical approaches to the theology of TI tend to fragment the theology as well as the text of TI, a canonical approach tends to see the literary as well as the theological unity of TI and the whole book of Isaiah. While ultimately TI cannot be interpreted apart from the rest of the book of Isaiah, its theology is sufficiently rich for it to comprise the focus of this dissertation.

In connection with the purpose and assumptions of this study, Isaiah 56:1–8 is chosen as the first passage to tackle, not only because the passage introduces the TI corpus, but also because it presents one of the most important themes of TI—the covenant theme. This chapter argues that the covenant concept is the key theme of 56:1–8 and that it forms the framework of the eschatology of TI, even though it is not presented in a systematic way in the text of TI. To this end, I will discuss the significance of 56:1–8 in its canonical context—not only in continuity with the preceding chapters of the book, but also in relation to other parts of TI (2.2). I will then discuss a theological interpretation of the passage, not only to grasp the eschatological vision presented in the passage but also to see the relations between the theological themes (2.3).

2.2 Isa 56:1–8 in the Book of Isaiah

Why is this passage considered an introduction to the TI text? There is new-ness in 56:1–8, but also a continuity with the previous parts of the book of Isaiah, and the traditional view of the newness of 56:1–8 is sometimes overemphasized. On the one hand, 56:1–8 recapitulates the eschatological theology of DI and also relates to the eschatological vision of PI. On the other hand, it presents an overview of the eschatological vision in TI. So, 56:1–8 can be considered the prologue of TI.

According to Whybray, "the tone of this passage is strikingly different from that of chapters 40–55."[1] His evidence for this statement is threefold: firstly, the passage deals with "particular problems arising within the Jewish community" in the post-exilic era—the problems presuppose an entirely different historical situation from that of chs 40–55; secondly, this passage is not the work of DI, in the light of "the uneven literary character";[2] thirdly, the words of DI are "here used in quite a new sense," as a "re-interpretation" of the DI's message(s) is characteristic of TI.[3]

The presupposition of a post-exilic situation in Palestine in 56:1–8 is based, on the one hand, on the geographical assumption of the audience of DI (especially in ch 55), and, on the other hand, on the reference to the Temple (56:5, My house, My wall; 56:7, My Holy Mountain, My house, [My] house of prayer [x2]) and several ritual activities (56:7; burnt offering, sacrifices, and my altar) that are normally carried out in the reconstructed Temple.[4] The audience of ch 55 is considered to be in Babylon according to

1. Whybray 1981:196.

2. Whybray 1981:196. He follows Michel (1966:220–25) in this view. For Skinner (1898:xxx–xxxi), "inferiority of style" forms a characteristic of TI in general compared to DI.

3. Whybray 1981:196. According to Skinner (1898:xiv), "there is a distinct break at the end of ch. lv," following Duhm's hypothesis. He similarly presented three evidences for this view (1898:xxix–xxxi): (1) historical allusions in chs 56–66 assume a post-exilic situation; (2) modification of theological viewpoints; (3) phraseological inferiority of TI to DI.

4. Volz 1932:202. For Skinner (1898:xxix–xxx), the historical allusions to the post-exilic situations of TI include: (1) reference to the existing Temple (56:7; 60:7; 62:9; 65:2; 66:6)—but this does not necessarily attest its real existence since the text does not aim to portray the historical situation (see below in the main text), (2) partial gathering of the exiled Israelites (56:8; cf. 57:19; 60:4, 8; 66:20)—but this is understood otherwise as I will discuss in the main text, (3) social condition of injustice (58:3–6, 9; 59:3–4, 13–15)—this is not necessarily post-exilic; it could also be pre-exilic, (4) split of the community—DI and PI also have the trace of the divide of the community, (5) idola-trous practices—these are not necessarily post-exilic; continuity with DI is sufficient, (6) delayed salvation—there is no reference to the actual return of the people from the exile. So Skinner's allegation of post-exilic situation is rejected.

55:12–13, while the people addressed in ch 56 are in Palestine.[5] However, a change of the historical situation may not be warranted.

Contrary to Whybray, the geographical location of the audience in chs 40–55 may not be Babylon as discussed in 1.2. The exodus imagery or תצאו (55:12–13) does not necessarily suggest the generally accepted Babylonian context. The charge "go out from *there* (צאו משם)" in 52:11 implies that the real geographical situation of the audience or reader is different from the geographical setting that is assumed in the narrative (Babylon). As for (the existence of) the Temple and the ritual activities in it, Whybray suggested that "groups of exiles have now returned to Palestine, and regular worship has been re-instituted. The Temple has been rebuilt, or at least its rebuilding is projected."[6] Thus, Whybray inferred that the passage treats individual problems of the post-exilic community of proselytes and eunuchs—whether or not they are accepted by the cultic community (56:3–7). For Volz, these problems come to the fore especially in the annual feast in which Diaspora Jews come to the Jerusalem Temple, since the returned Diaspora Jews have different views on the proselytes and eunuchs from the people of the Jerusalem community.[7] This assumption of the historical situation begins to function as a hermeneutical key to the passage. For Volz, joining to YHWH (56:3, 6) is the cultic link to Him. The memorial and name that are given to the foreign (and eunuch) covenant-holders (56:5) are not subject to spiritual interpretation but reflect a real cultic practice. Keeping the covenant and the Sabbath of the converted in 56:6 is not eschatological but just evidence of their participation in the Jewish faith community. Although 56:7 reveals the centrality of the Jerusalem Temple in the world (in this sense it presents cultic universalism[8]), the 'house of prayer for all nations' cannot be eschatological, but refers only to the present time. The phrase 'who gathers the dispersed of Israel' in 56:8 originated from eschatological language, but displays the post-exilic community order. Consequently, the whole passage is entirely dominated by a historical perspective.[9]

However, although the passage includes references to the Temple and ritual activities, a historical reconstruction based on them is not warranted by the narrative and is thus external to the text. Childs commented that

5. Rendtorff 1993c:185–86.

6. Whybray 1981:196.

7. Volz 1932:203. Pauritsch (1971:250) tries to reconstruct the historical situation in a more nuanced way. Sehmsdorf (1972), Donner (1985), Lau (1994), Duhm (1892) also tried to reconstruct one.

8. Cultic universalism may be defined as "a view that all the nations will participate in the Jewish YHWH-cult"—it is different from the universalism of DI.

9. Volz 1932:202–6.

"Whybray's interpretation, which has largely become a consensus, is derived from a prior assumption that a new subsequent historical situation is being addressed."[10] Furthermore, the presumption of the post-exilic *Sitz-im-Leben* of the passage distorts the overall interpretation of the passage. 56:1–2 is tied only loosely to the rest of the passage and thus is an editorial comment (Volz). Also 56:8 is considered originally a separate oracle (Whybray).[11] However, if we assume the unity of the passage in the context of the present form of the text (as I have discussed in chapter 1) and do not bring the historical setting into the center of the interpretation, 56:1–2 is not to be set aside as editorial insertions but gives a clue to interpret the whole of the passage.

As Volz admits, the righteousness/salvation pair (56:1) has a connection to 51:5 and 46:13, which implies that the whole passage is understood in the context of the eschatological expectation of DI. Thus the imminent divine righteousness and salvation in the two DI verses metonymically stand for the eschatological divine works in DI (see below).[12] The idiom in 56:8, eschatological language as Volz admits,[13] also supports interpreting the passage in the eschatological context, forming an *inclusio* together with 56:1–2. Thus the passage is not primarily about the individual problems of the historical community at that time, but lies on the eschatological horizon, being detached from the allegedly post-exilic *Sitz-im-Leben* of the text. A literary reading makes the textual (i.e., literary) level the primary context for the interpretation of the passage, and justifies an eschatological interpretation rather than a historical interpretation. Thus, not only cultic activities such as keeping the covenant and the Sabbath (56:2, 4, 6) and offering sacrifices (56:7), but also the monument and the name (56:5) may be understood as eschatological. The Holy Mountain and the Temple/My altar (56:7) can also be eschatological. In addition, Skinner's idea that the 'already gathered' (people) suggests a post-exilic situation is unconvincing (see 2.3).

Therefore, the alleged newness of the historical context of the passage is at least minimized by the theory of no geographical shift of the audience in between chs 55 and 56.[14] The cultic language (temple, sacrifice, Sabbath, law, etc.) is a new emphasis compared with the concerns of DI, but this does not reflect a new historical situation of the passage. It is a (new) way to

10. Childs 2001:453.

11. Volz 1932:203; Whybray 1981:199.

12. Volz 1932:204. Also see Whybray 1981:196. Divine salvation and righteousness are near both in DI (51:5 and 46:13) and in TI (56:1) (see below).

13. The phrase has a connection to 11:12, which is in the eschatological context in PI.

14. Seitz 2001:472; Childs 2001:453. See further chapter 1.

express the eschatological vision of TI (and DI) (see 2.3). So, it also shows continuity in terms of a bigger idea of eschatology/theology.

As for Whybray's second point of the newness of 56:1–8, scholarly reconstruction for the authorship/redactorship of the passage has never reached consensus. For Volz, 56:1–2 is considered an editorial comment due to his historical presuppositions (see above). For Sekine, 56:1–5aα and 5bα belong to an author, while 56:5aβ, 5bβ, and 6–8 are ascribed to an editor who worked later because he judges that "better than children" is theologically an over-estimation (5aβ) and because "will not be cut off" is unnecessary for the sentence's unity (5bβ).[15] For Lau, 56:1 is the heading of the TI collection and 56:8 is a secondary supplement (because "scattered of Israel" is not mentioned before and the theme of "collection" appears new).[16] However, for Smith, 56:1–8 forms a unity, because 56:1 and 8 exhibit an *inclusio*, referring to the intervention of YHWH, and because of the repetitions of the key words such as עשה, שמר, and שבת.[17] Therefore, the alleged "uneven literary character" of the passage is not convincing since it primarily depends on the reader's theological judgment/pre-understanding or his assumption about the background historical situation. As I have argued in chapter 1 (Introduction), the assumption of the unity of 56:1–8 is reasonable, as also Smith has shown. Furthermore, although Skinner argues that the inferior style of TI shows different authorship, this is a highly subjective argument.[18]

Thirdly, the idea that new senses to DI's message are introduced in 56:1–8 seems to be an overestimation, as it is based on the scholars' historical pre-understanding. According to Whybray, 56:1b כי־קרובה ישועתי לבוא וצדקתי להגלות) is "virtually a quotation" of 46:13, but it is a re-interpretation. While צדקה in 56:1b (and 46:13) signifies deliverance, in 56:1a it denotes righteousness, a quite different meaning. Thus, for him, "[T]he Deutero-Isaianic note of expectancy of an imminent divine act of deliverance has been lost." This is because "the author has contrived to imply that salvation is to be achieved through the perfecting of human behaviour within the Jewish community."[19] However, whether the concept of imminent divine salvation (צדקה; 56:1b) has been cancelled in order to allow humans to achieve righteousness (צדקה; 56:1a) is not certain (see 2.3), as קרוב is maintained in 56:1b.

Rendtorff also recognized the newness of 56:1. He admits two different senses of צדקה in 56:1a and in 56:1b because it lies in different contexts. The

---

15. Sekine 1989:35, 182. He follows Pauritsch (1971:36, 40) for 56:5aβ and 5bβ.

16. Lau 1994:262, 278. His idea will be rejected later.

17. Smith 1995:51–54.

18. Skinner 1898:xxx–xxxi.

19. Whybray 1981:196–97.

subject of the verb is different in those two half-verses, and the words have different parallels (משפט in 56:1a; ישועה in 56:1b). While the צדקה/משפט (righteousness/justice) pair occurs frequently in PI, emphasizing צדקה as a human response, the ישועה/צדקה (righteousness/salvation) pair occurs frequently in DI, emphasizing צדקה as divine character and act of salvation. So, for him, newness occurs in 56:1 in that "[A]t no earlier point in the book of Isaiah do we find a verse or even a paragraph in which these two different aspects of צדקה are combined in this way."[20] Thus, for him, 56:1 is a "deliberate beginning of something new," although at the same time it establishes a deliberate continuity with PI and DI.[21]

However, although the formal appearance of the two pairs (righteousness/justice, righteousness/salvation) in one verse in 56:1 is new, this should not be emphasized too much because צדקה refers to the reciprocal relationship between YHWH and Israel even in the pre-exilic period. It is "a term that established the grounds for a harmonious relationship between parties in accordance with mutual obligations of just behaviour" (see below).[22] Besides, there sometimes are cases in which divine salvation and human response (or, requirement) are closely interconnected as in 46:12–13 (see 2.3 on 56:1). Furthermore, occurrence of two different senses in one verse does not necessarily suggest significant theological differences between DI and TI, but can be understood as a strategy to present a theological concept at a higher level.[23]

If Whybray's (and also Rendtorff's) suggestion of newness in 56:1–8 is minimized as I have shown, then what is the canonical function of 56:1–8?[24] Once the priority of historical understanding is reserved, 56:1–8 is continuous with chs 54 and 55, as well as linked with 66:15–24 and the rest of TI, in the literary and theological point of view (see 2.3).[25]

20. Rendtorff 1993c:183.

21. Rendtorff 1993c:184–85.

22. Childs 2001:455–56.

23. See 2.3, for the relation between 56:1a and 56:1b, which contain (allegedly) two different senses—the two different parallels of צדקה in a verse may suggest a deeper theology.

24. There are three views on the understanding of the canonical function of 56:1–8, according to Beuken (1989c:19): (1) as an introduction to TI (Polan); (2) as a bridge between DI and TI (Beuken); and (3) as a literary composite of different authors (historical critics). The first view sees that 56:1–8 reflect the post-exilic situation and form together with 66:15–24 an envelope structure in TI. The second view considers that PI, DI, and TI are not three independent writings but have strong correlation and TI is the continuation of the other two. The third view does not see the passage as a unity, but a mixed of original words and later additions. Beuken (1989a:37) prefers the second one.

25. Even for Duhm (1892:380), TI has possibly written his writings "only as an

According to Grace Emmerson, the text of TI forms a concentric structure and especially chs 56 (vv. 1–8) and 66 (vv. 18–24) correspond to each
other in that they have common themes such as the Temple and the offering
of sacrifice, and an open attitude to outsiders, including the nations.[26] This
notable correspondence signifies for her that these two sections are a deliberate framework for TI.[27] However, her view that 56:1–8 and 66:18–19, 21
tell that "foreigners are admitted to the covenant community on equal terms
with native-born Jews" is not convincing, although admittedly the two passages have common themes and thus share the higher level of theology in
terms of the covenant. Not only 56:1–8 but also 66:15–24 are in the context
of eschatology,[28] and not subordinate to the historical interpretation, so the
eschatological covenant is the common theme of the two passages.[29]

Furthermore, 56:1–8 is closely related to chs 54–55,[30] which are centered on the covenant theme (see 2.3).[31] Albeit implicitly, eschatological
salvation is promised (54:1–3, 7–8, 13–14; 55:12–13), affirmed (54:9–10;
55:3–5), and offered (55:1–3, 6–7), as it is related to the covenant in chs 54–

---

appendix to DI" or at least the intention in 56:1–8 goes back to DI, so in theological
aspect TI is based on DI.

26. Emmerson (1992:12) repeats the first view of Beuken's category. Also see Westermann, Beuken, Steck.

27. Emmerson 1992:19–20. For various suggestions for the concentric structure of
TI, see O'Connell 1994:216–18.

28. If we assume the unity of chapter 66 (especially, 66:15–24), then 66:15–16
(theophanic text) and 66:22–24 (the New Heavens and Earth) form context of the eschatological interpretation of 66:15–24.

29. Emmerson 1992:66. See further in 2.3.

30. Although ch 55 has usually been considered to be a conclusion of DI (Skinner
1898:xiv; Melugin 1976:87), this has been challenged. According to Melugin (1976:87),
55:6–13 as the epilogue of DI corresponds to the beginning of DI (40:1–11): Parallels
include the theme of the returning of merciful YHWH (55:6–7; 40:11), the promise
of exodus from captivity (55:12–13; 40:3–4), the assertion of the radical differences
between YHWH and humanity (55:8–9; 40:6–8), and the reliability of the word of
YHWH (55:10–11; 40:6–8). However, Seitz (2001:472–73) finds a better concluding
passage of DI is 52:7–12, because (1) chs 55 and 56 are closely related (see the main
text) and (2) chs 54–55 are similar to TI in terms of language and style. He sees that the
role of the servants ("servant followers of the servant" is his term), the pivotal theme of
TI, has been initiated by the death of the servant at ch 53. He recognizes that the inner-
community conflict, which has been usually argued as peculiar to TI, has been already
present in DI (chs 40–53), and suggests that it becomes starker by the death of the
Servant. So, there is no great time gap between DI and TI, and the stories about or by
the servant followers of the Servant starts at ch 54. According to O'Connell (1994:219,
221–222), TI starts at 55:1 because 55:1—56:8, which is corresponding to the concluding chs 65–66, forms a "pattern of triadic repetition." To pinpoint the exact beginning
of TI is beyond the scope of this dissertation.

31. Melugin 1976:174.

55. According to Seitz, chs 54–55 and ch 56 are closely associated in terms of several key themes such as the covenant (55:3; 56:4; cf. 54:10), gathering of the nations to Israel (55:5; 56:6), two contrasting feasts (55; 56:9–12), and reference to servants (54:17; 56:6). Eschatological salvation is reaffirmed in 56:1. Thus, 56:1–8 and chs 54–55 share the theme of the covenant, the pivotal theme in this section that is related to eschatological salvation.

56:1–8 is also connected to the rest of TI. 56:1–8 is linked to 59:15b–21 in terms of the covenant theme (59:21). The *inclusio* of the covenant in 56:4, 6 and 59:21 suggests that the covenant theme is the interpretive key of chs 56–59.[32] The eschatological salvation is delayed and the covenant is breached due to the sin of the people in 56:7—59:15a (especially, 58:1; 59:1–2). 56:1–8 is also connected to 61:1–9 by means of the covenant theme (61:8) and thus further to chs 60–62.[33] In the unit of chs 60–62, too, eschatological salvation is achieved because the covenant is restored by the coming of YHWH in 59:21 and salvation is declared to come in 62:11. As I shall show later, in 63:7—64:11[12] the covenant theme (63:8–9, 16; 64:7[8]; see 2.3) is pivotal, though this is implicit. The communal lament (63:7—64:11[12]) implies that the covenantal relation is breached. As a general summary, my view is that 56:1–8 lies in the narrative as continuation of ch 55. 56:1–8 is to be understood in the context of chapters 54–55, which is centered on the covenant theme, and is connected to the rest of TI by an important theme.

In conclusion: with respect to the formal appearance of the key terminology and the usage of the ritual language, a change begins in 56:1–8. 56:1–8 recapitulates the overall eschatological message of DI. The passage foreshadows the eschatological message of the rest of TI including the concluding section, i.e., chs 65–66 (as I shall show in 2.3). So, 56:1–8 functions as an introduction to TI, although the continuity between 56:1–8 and chs 54–55 is more significant than the discontinuity.

2.3 Theological Interpretation of the Text

Accepting that 56:1–8 continues DI's eschatological vision and projects it into TI, this section will show, through a brief theological exposition of the text, that the key message is the universal expansion of eschatological salvation and that the covenant concept incorporates the various themes of the eschatology of TI. Theological themes such as justice, righteousness, salvation, the Sabbath, covenant, Holy Mountain (Zion), and the Temple will be expounded, albeit not systematically.

32. Childs 2001:490.

33. Chs 60–62 form a unity, with ch 61 being the axis of the chapters. See 4.2.

<table>
<tr><td>1 Thus says YHWH:</td><td>כה אמר יהוה</td></tr>
<tr><td>"Keep justice, and do righteousness,</td><td>שמרו משפט ועשו צדקה</td></tr>
<tr><td>for soon My salvation will come,</td><td>כי־קרובה ישועתי לבוא</td></tr>
<tr><td>and My deliverance be revealed."[34]</td><td>וצדקתי להגלות:</td></tr>
</table>

This verse sets the passage in the context of the eschatological expectation of the previous parts of the book (especially DI). It demands a proper reaction of the people in accordance with that expectation. The eschatological expectation is presented concisely as 'salvation' (ישושה) and 'deliverance' (צדקה) of YHWH in 56:1b, which are imminent (קרוב). Verse 1a requests the people to keep justice (משפט) and to do righteousness (צדקה). Above all, we need to investigate the sense of צדקה, after elaborating the intertextual references.

56:1b summarizes the imminent expectation of eschatological salvation in DI. As many commentators have observed,[35] 56:1b quotes 46:12–13 and 51:5–6(8). In 46:13 and 51:5 as well as in 56:1b, the divine salvation (ישועה) and righteousness (צדקה) in parallel are 'imminent' (קרוב).[36] Chapter 45:8, in which צדקה and ישע (salvation) are commanded to be brought forth by YHWH, may also exist behind the second half-verse. In 46:13, YHWH promises that He is going to bring soon His צדקה and that His salvation will not be delayed.[37] The certainty and imminence of deliverance of Israel from her oppressor, which is symbolized as Babylon, is emphasized in this verse.[38] In 51:5–6, the divine salvation is "drawing near speedily" and has already gone forth, so it is on the way; the purpose of YHWH the Creator is not to be thwarted by his ephemeral creatures.[39] This imminence of the divine salvation in DI is kept also in 56:1, as the word קרובה indicates.[40] Some commentators find an allusion to קרוב in 55:6.[41] In this verse, YHWH is near. According to Beuken, the eschatological expectation of DI may be summarized as the fact that YHWH comes to Zion (40:10; 52:8) and that

34. Biblical passages are by private translation based on ESV if not specified.

35. Whybray 1981:196; Koenen 1990:13; Childs 2001:456.

36. Although 46:13 adopts תשועה instead of ישועה and 51:5 צדק and ישע instead of צדקה and ישועה, there seem to be no substantial differences between ישועה (fem.), תשועה (fem.) and ישע (masc.) and between צדק (masc.) and צדקה (fem.). Also see below.

37. Muilenburg 1954:543.

38. Whybray 1981:117.

39. Whybray 1981:156.

40. There is no need to assume a change of implied readers between chs 40–55 and chs 56–66, contrary to Laato (1998:171). See 2.2.

41. Koenen 1990:13; Lau 1994:263.

salvation is near (46:13; 51:5; 55:5).[42] If this is the case, 56:1b is actually a summary of the eschatological expectation of DI, being taken as a background of TI's message, since the salvation of YHWH will come *soon* (56:1b; 62:11) and YHWH comes in TI (59:19–20; 63:19b[64:1]; 66:15).[43] Consequently, the eschatological expectation of 56:1–8 (and TI, in fact) is based on that of DI, that is, the eschatology of TI is fundamentally a continuation of that of DI. This is not only because TI quotes and reuses the DI's message, but also because there is a narrative continuity especially between chs 54–55 and 56:1–8.[44] However, human obligation is emphasized in 56:1–8, compared with the *Vorlage* in DI.

What does צדקה mean in 56:1b and 56:1a, then? While the primary nuance of צדקה in 56:1b is divine salvation as in 59:16, 17 and 63:1, it is human behavior in 56:1a as in 57:1; 58:2; 60:17; 64:4–5 (see 2.2): two different meanings of a word in different contexts—is that all? Isn't this an intentional device to deliver a deeper theology?

צדקה (of YHWH) in 56:1b forms a hendiadys with salvation, so the sense of צדקה (of YHWH) is virtually equivalent to the salvation of YHWH, as is typical in DI, especially in the quoted verses. Divine righteousness is not only an attribute of YHWH but also his righteous acts—He displays the righteous laws and standards in accordance with His righteousness, and then judges rightly in conformity with His righteous character as well as those standards.[45] Then, to which does this divine righteousness refer in 56:1b— attribute or action? Considering that "salvation comes" is a theophanic text, the divine צדקה may signify an attribute of YHWH or rather YHWH himself, as His צדקה may be a metonym for YHWH. However, the only

---

42. Beuken 1989c:37.

43. The subject "coming of YHWH" will be discussed separately in chapter 3.

44. Childs 2001:453, 456; Seitz 2001:485; Lau 1994:264. According to Beuken (1989c:37), while YHWH comes to Zion, in TI, he lives in Zion and with the people, and he also collects the nations there, forming a just society (57:13; 15; 19; 58:2f., 12, 14; ch 60; 61:3f.; ch 62; ch 64; 65:1f., 11, 18, 21–25; 66:18–23). There is no mention of the Temple in DI, while TI uses בית to denote it. Nevertheless, there is no antagonism between the two eschatology, difference being movement of the interest. I will discuss more about the continuity and discontinuity between the eschatological expectations of DI and TI later in the main text.

45. Stigers 1980, TWOT (2):752–54; Johnson 2003, TDOT (12):243, 250. In 41:2; 42:6; and 45:13, the *act* of YHWH is righteous (צדק) in the sense that it is with a view to achieving, or has power to achieve, His righteous purpose. (For Muilenburg [1954:449], צדק signifies "successful completion" in 41:2.) In 41:10, צדק (i.e., right hand of my righteousness) signifies the righteous saving act of YHWH (Stigers 1980, TWOT [2]:754). In 45:23, צדקה דבר means the word of YHWH, which has power to fulfil the divine purpose of YHWH (צדקה in 45:24 has the same meaning).

other place that צדקה is involved with the verb גלה is Ps 98:2,[46] in which the divine צדקה is the salvific work of YHWH. Although both attribute and salvific action of YHWH may be possible for צדקה in 56:1b, the latter seems better. To conclude, righteousness in 56:1b is divine, signifying salvation or deliverance of YHWH.

What then does (the human) צדקה denote in 56:1a, in which צדקה and משפט are in parallel? Human righteousness appears frequently as a parallel to justice (משפט) as in 1:21, 27; 5:7; and 16:5, and as a hendiadys with justice in 9:6[7] and 33:5.[47] In general, the basic connotation of the root צדק is conformity with an ethical standard.[48] Righteousness in humans denotes the acts and lives—physical and mental—in accordance with values and norms, which are given by the commands of God in the case of Israel in the covenantal framework.[49] So a righteous person tries to establish the peace and prosperity of the community in regard to others, not only his own. To decide the meaning of the parallel pair,[50] we need to ask: what do '(to) keep justice (שמר משפט)' and '(to) do righteousness (עשה צדקה)' mean in 56:1a? To 'do righteousness' (עשה צדקה) appears elsewhere only in 58:2,[51] in which the phrase is parallel with "not to abandon justice [ordinance] of their God (משפט אלהיו)" and "to ask for ordinances of righteousness (משפטי־צדק)." Contrary to Box, this verse does not suggest any reference to the actual ritual in the Temple, since the context of the verse is everyday life and relationship

46. The verb גלה is piel in Ps 98:2, while niphal in 56:1b.

47. A complete list of righteousness/justice parallel is: 1:21, 27; 5:7, 16; 9:6[7]; 16:5; 28:17; 32:1, 16; 33:5 in PI. It appears in 56:1; 59:9, and 14 in TI. Righteousness is parallel to אמונה (or, אמן) in 11:5 and 1:26. The typical meaning of שפט may be in forensic and legal context, although the basic meaning is not necessarily confined to judicial decision making, although the basic meaning of שפט is 'to decide, judge,' 'to rule, govern,' 'to decide between,' and 'to decide juristically.' The "ma-noun," משפט, may refer to the act of judgment, various aspects of legal process (court, case, laws, etc), or the legal verdict itself. According to Johnson, the ma-noun may denote the place of action, the action, the result of action, and the means of the action etc. Liedke 1997, TLOT (3):1393; Enns 1997, NIDOTTE (2):1142; Johnson 1998, TDOT (12):87; Schultz 1997b, NIDOTTE (4):838–839.

48. I follow Stigers (1980, TDOT [2]:752), who does not differentiate the meanings of צדק and צדקה in an actual fact.

49. The human righteousness is character of צדיק in 5:23 and 26:7. It may signify the way of behaviors of the righteous as in 33:15. It is also the character and behavior of the community as in 1:26; 26:2; and 33:5. So human righteousness is a very broad and higher concept that covers individual and society, physical and mental aspects in humans.

50. I assume that the parallel pair signifies what both משפט and צדקה signify in common as a higher and broader concept, because the two words complements to each other to form a coherent concept.

51. In Ps 106:3, both עשה צדקה and שמר משפט come together.

with YHWH rather than ritual itself.[52] The 'ordinances of righteousness' has a parallel in Ps 119:7, 62, and 106,[53] in which they signify the statutes of the Torah. So, 'to do righteousness' may signify keeping the statutes of Torah, as associated with seeking justice [ordinances] of YHWH. For Alexander, משפט is virtually equivalent to the Torah since they are parallel in 42:4 and 51:4.[54] This is reinforced by the thesis that "to keep justice (שמר משפט)" may not be different from "to keep my judgments (שמר משפטי)" and/or that the combination of "to keep justice" and "to do righteousness" may be equivalent to "to do/keep justice and righteousness." שמר משפטי and עשה משפט וצדקה are Deuteronomistic.[55] So, "to keep justice" and "to do righteousness" are to achieve the Deuteronomistic ideal, which YHWH required of the people through the covenant order as substantiated in the Torah.

This is reinforced by the fact that not only משפט in a broader sense but also משפט וצדקה as a hendiadys refer to the covenant order. According to Williamson, the hendiadic pair of 'justice and righteousness' broadly refers to the social justice, "often entailing notions of equality and freedom."[56] Its maintenance is entrusted to the kings and other leaders of society as is the case of the ideal king in 9:6[7] and 11:4–5.[57] It is thus considered as a quality of the ideal society, as in 1:21 and 5:7 the parallel pair of justice and righteousness signifies the ideal of the past. Besides, in a broader sense משפט may refer to social justice, which is not limited to the legal sense, but includes merciful consideration of the powerless such as orphans, widows and the poor.[58]

Both 'keeping justice' and 'doing righteousness' signify observing the covenantal order, although the two may have primarily different meanings, as they lie in parallel to form a higher concept. Delitzsch also considers

52. Odeberg 1931:138; Muilenburg 1954:678.

53. Odeberg 1931:138.

54. Alexander 1846b:334.

55. Koenen 1990:13–14; Odeberg 1931:33–34. שמר משפטי occurs in Lev 18:5, 26; 19:37; 20:22; 25:18; Deut 5:1; 7:11, 12; 8:11; 11:1, 32; 12:1; 26:16, 17; 30:16; 1 Kgs 2:3; 8:58; 9:4; 2 Kgs 17:37; 2 Chr 7:17; 33:8; Neh 1:7; 10:30; Ps 106:3; 119:106; Ezek 11:20; 18:9; 20:19; 36:27; cf. Lev 18:4, עשה משפטי. The phrase עשה משפט וצדקה occurs in Gen 18:9; 2 Sam 8:15, 1 Kgs 10:9, 1 Chr 18:14, 2 Chr 9:8; Ps 99:4; Prob 21:3; Jer 9:23[24]; 22:3; 22:15; 23:15; 33:15; Ezek 18:5; 18:19, 21, 27; 33:14, 16, 19; 45:9. cf. Deut 33:21, צדקת יהוה עשה ומשפטיו ; Ps 103:6, משפטים ומשפטים עשה צדקת יהוה (YHWH is the subject); in Gen 18:9 and Prob 21:3, עשה: צדקה ומשפט; in Jer 9:23[24], עשה חסד משפט וצדקה.

56. Williamson 2006:135–36; Weinfeld 1992:228–46.

57. The Messianic Davidic king is symbolized as a shoot in 11:1. Clements 1980a:121–122.

58. So, what the hendiadic pair signifies justice alone can signify. Johnson 1998, TDOT (12):91; Schultz 1997b, NIDOTTE (4):844.

that 56:1 presents the objective standard of covenantal relationship, and that justice, righteousness, and salvation are understood in the framework of the covenantal relationship.[59] To conclude, righteousness in 56:1a is a human norm of the life of the people, as conditioned by the covenantal order.

How then are 56:1a and 56:1b related to each other, and what is the relation between human action and divine salvation? Kraus interprets כי as "because (*denn, weil*)" and not as "so that (*damit*)": "Keep justice and practice righteousness, *because* my salvation is near to come. . ."[60] For him, "the conjugational כי, which connects the warning call with the announcement of the nearness of salvation, is understood as not conditional but causal."[61] The increasing nearness of salvation is the reason and the motive for a change—renewal of life in view of the coming eschatological salvation. For him, 60:1 is understood in the same way: "By the coming light of YHWH, here the life is able to become clear and bright."[62] But he considers that the possibility of conditional understanding is not to be entirely denied, although he denies Duhm's concept of work righteousness (*Werkgerechtigkeit*), because there is a movement between 46:13 and 56:1.[63] Especially in ch 58 he considers that a conditional understanding is operating.[64] Childs sees the relation between the response of the people and the saving action of YHWH is "not conditional but causal: do righteousness [so] that deliverance will come."[65] Although Kraus and Childs use the same term 'causal,' they differ in understanding the direction of cause and effect between human response and (divine) salvation. However, Koenen understands כי-sentence as apodosis, but he also denies Zigler's apodosistic interpretation "keep righteousness . . . , so that (*damit*) salvation comes . . . ." Koenen perceives that the salvation comes only to the righteous (57.20f.), only to the repentant (59.20), or only to the servants of YHWH (65.8ff.). So, "[B]ecause salvation will soon come, one should behave in such a way that one can participate in it. One should practice justice, not 'so that salvation enters,' but 'so that one wins part of it.'"[66]

59. Delitzsch 1873:360–61.

60. "*Wahret das Recht, übt Gerechtigkeit, denn mein Heil ist nahe dem Eintreffen und meine Gerechtigkeit ihrer Offenbarung.*" Lau (1994:265) follows this interpretation.

61. "*Das konjunktionelle* כי*, das die Mahnung mit der Ankündigung der Heilsnähe verbindet, ist nicht konditional, sondern kausal zu verstehen.*"

62. "*Vom kommenden Lichte Jahwes her das Leben hell und klar zu werden vermag.*"

63. Duhm 1892:380.

64. Kraus 1966:327–29.

65. Childs 2001:456.

66. Koenen 1990:14–15. "*Weil das Heil bald kommen wird, soll man sich so verhalten, daß man an ihm partizipiert Man soll also Gerechtigkeit üben,* »*nicht, damit das*

We can support Koenen's view of the selectivity in salvific realization, although it is not certain why Koenen rejects Zigler, because they are both apodosistic. The selectivity can be evidenced in the light of the preceding context (chs 54–55), which offers salvation in connection with the covenant concept.[67] In the light of chs 54–55, the speech of 56:1 is addressed to everybody, to the sinners as well as to the righteous, as in the prophetic invitation(s) in 55:1–3 and 6–7, and even to the nations as in 55:4–5.[68] Those who respond to this invitation will benefit by salvation (as is promised that "your soul may live"; 55:3), join the covenantal order that is promised to David (55:3), and be entitled to the divine forgiveness and restoration of the relationship between them and YHWH (55:7). Those who do not respond to this invitation will be excluded from that blessing. Chs 54–55 seem to suggest that the offer of salvation may be extended even to the nations. For the new Davidic king is promised as a leader and commander of the nations. YHWH promises that He will summon the nations and they will hasten to the future Davidic king. In 56:1b, too, the salvation is offered not only to Israelites but also to non-Israelites, as we shall see in 56:3. In both chs 54–55 and 56:1–8, salvation is imminent (קרוב; 55:6 and 56:1). Only those who obey the prophetic command in 56:1a, either Jews or the nations, will benefit from the prophetic promise in 56:1b.

However, Koenen's rejection of Kraus is not entirely convincing, because the realization of salvation in each individual is conditional on his response to the eschatological invitation. Kraus's observation has some measure of truth in this sense. If we ask whether it is conditional that those addressed will receive salvation, then we may answer positively, because the unrighteous will not enjoy the salvation that is offered while those who respond to the charge of 56:1a may be able to join it. The people have to obey the prophetic charge so that they may benefit from the salvation that has already been predicted.[69]

However, the dependence of the achievement of salvation upon human response does not necessarily mean that human behaviour may *automatically* (i.e., without divine salvific and gracious work) decide the achievement of divine salvation. This may be why Koenen rightly rejects Kraus. It is because salvation is offered in advance by YHWH and YHWH alone that the people who respond to the offer can enjoy it. So Duhm's concept of

---

Heil eintrete, sondern damit man an ihm Teil gewinne«."

67. As I have shown before, 56:1–8 is to be understood in the context of chs 54–55.

68. For Kissane (1943:208), 56:1–2 is virtually a repetition of 55:6–7.

69. Childs and Zigler's interpretation may be understood in this sense, if the coming salvation in their interpretation is intended to signify the actual achievement of it by the individual.

work righteousness is denied. The obedience or disobedience of the people to the prophetic charge cannot bring divine salvation. This has already been proclaimed to come regardless of the human behavior. Even if the people do not respond to the prophetic charge to keep justice, salvation and judgment will still come, because the offer of salvation has been made already in DI (salvation and judgment are not to be separated but are two sides of a coin; see chapter 3) and as promised YHWH will perform salvation (and judgment).[70]

At this stage, it becomes evident that three different senses of "salvation" need to be recognized in 56:1b: (1) salvation as an offer of salvation; (2) salvation as a divine act; and (3) salvation as realized in the people. The phrase "salvation comes" is theophanic language, and signifies that YHWH who saves is coming or YHWH is coming to save.[71] Although the offer of salvation of DI is reaffirmed—and fulfilled in some sense—in 56:1b, this half-verse is still a promise that requires a response by the people. It includes warning and invitation, so the former sense of salvation is signified by 56:1b. Then, which is signified by the salvation in 56:1b—act of salvation (verb) or result of salvific action (noun)? On the one hand, the prophetic charge to keep justice as an invitation/admonition to join the divine salvation is 'because of the offer.' On the other hand, gaining salvation by any individual depends on a response to the prophetic charge. However, the latter is due to the divine action.

Then, is the human response which achieves justice and righteousness in the human realm understood as the divine process to carry out His saving work in the divine realm? If 56:1b is an offer of salvation, which requests 56:1a, and if the fulfilment of 56:1a results in the realization of salvation in 56:1b (if the two theses are the case), then the answer is probably yes. The divine action to save and the human response to achieve justice and righteousness are simultaneous.[72] The saving acts of YHWH are realized in the people who achieve justice and righteousness; salvation is what the individuals achieve through their obedience. This signifies that the restoration of the covenant order, which is expressed as keeping justice and doing righteousness, is understood as eschatological salvation, as discussed before. This is also evidenced by intertexts. The association of שׁמר and the

---

70. 56:1 may be called a warning in negative sense, although Childs (2001:454) doubts it, because anyone who does not respond to the prophetic charge will be excluded to the salvific benefit. But invitation may be better for its title in positive sense.

71. Schnutenhaus 1964:14–19.

72. The divine and human spheres together are involved in the salvation of the people.

singular משפט appears elsewhere only in Hos 12:7[6] and Ps 106:3.[73] In Hos 12:7[6], to keep lovingkindness and justice (חסד ומשפט שמר) is understood as the response of the people to show that they return to YHWH and as the condition in which they can wait for Him, i.e., His salvation. So, in this verse, to keep justice is understood in the context of restoration of the relationship between YHWH and the people. In Ps 106:3, שמר משפט and עשה צדקה are associated in him who is to be blessed and is entitled to the divine salvation (Ps 106:4). So, the restoration of the covenant by keeping justice and doing righteousness results in the *achievement* of divine salvation by individuals, which is expressed as the restoration of the covenantal relation with YHWH. This will be verified again (see 2.3). So the two apparently different things (the saving act [verb] and the state of being saved [noun]) are denoted by one word "salvation," as a Hebrew word often does not distinguish between the behavior (verb) and the result of it (noun). The third sense of salvation (noun) may be displayed as a human quality since it is achieved by the people in them.

To sum up, the relation between human response and the offer of divine salvation is both causal and conditional: that is, because (divine act of) salvation comes, they are required to respond to it (cf. Kraus), but only the one who obeys the command achieves the realization of the offer. It is because of the announcement and promise of the imminent salvation that the response of justice and righteousness of the people is invited. Without the offer of salvation in 56:1b, justice and righteousness as human work in 56:1a are not entitled to divine salvation. However, the relation between human response and the realization of salvation in them is conditional. The realization of the offer of salvation in individuals is dependent on human obedience. Human response and divine act of saving co-operate to produce salvation in people, although the divine initiative is always first.

If the state of salvation in 56:1b is identified with the achievement of justice and righteousness in 56:1a, then what is the logic of צדקה which is found both in 56:1b and in 56:1a? It seems that צדקה is used intentionally to suggest our thesis that the divine saving act and the human achievement of justice and righteousness work together in the people. The same word צדקה is applied to the human sphere in 56:1a and to the divine sphere in 56:1b at the same time. The divine righteousness as a divine salvific work and the human righteousness as a human achievement coincide, being realized in the saved people.

This is also the case of משפט, which may be applied not only to humans but also to YHWH. The pair justice/righteousness seems to refer both

73. Lau 1994:263.

to the divine salvation and human actions as evidenced in 59:9–15. (1) In 59:8, 15, justice is evidently human. (2) The מִשְׁפָּט of YHWH may signify His attribute and behavior.[74] According to Schultz, the מִשְׁפָּט of YHWH may signify His universal rule based on His universal authority or sovereignty, the principle with which He rules the universe. It may also signify the act of judgment or the result of judgment, which may be either positive (to the righteous) or negative (to the guilty).[75] As far as justice belongs to YHWH, it denotes salvation. Therefore, even though justice in 59:11 may not have the divine subject, it signifies salvation since it is coupled with salvation in 59:11. So the justice/salvation pair in 59:11 probably refers to the divine saving work, since they are hoped for by the people as they are to come from YHWH, and since justice is parallel to salvation. (3) The salvation/righteousness pair refers without doubt to the divine saving work in 59:16 and 17.[76] (4) Justice/righteousness in 59:9a may be salvation since it is parallel to justice/salvation in 59:11 due to נקוה ל in parallel in 59:9b and 59:11. Oswalt states, "the concepts are tilted more toward the salvific in this verse [59:9],"[77] which is possible especially due to the following phrase "we hope for" in 59:9b. But, on the other hand, justice/righteousness in 59:9a may also signify human aspect, since 59:10 describes human behavior. The justice/righteousness in 59:9a may also connote the human achievement of justice and righteousness because the justice in 59:9 is continuous with that of 59:8 and it is part of the confession of the sinful state, as the conjunction עַל־כֵּן indicates.[78] (5) The justice/righteousness in 59:14 more probably also refers to the human aspect because it is also confession. This may be reinforced by the justice which follows in 59:15b. Consequently, the canonical

74. It signifies punitive judgment of YHWH in 4:4 and 34:5 (Williamson 2006:100–101). It is divine quality in 5:16. There is a dispute about whether justice and righteousness in 5:16 are divine or human. While Moberly (2001:xx) considers that they are human mainly because those in 5:7 are human as YHWH sought them in the people of Israel and because of the contextual continuity, Williamson (2006:375–76) rejects his view, although he admits ambiguity in deciding between them, because נקדש displays that it will be done by "his own justice and righteousness." Since the text of 5:13–17 contrasts the human abasement of Israel owing to the exilic judgment on them and the exaltation of YHWH, the justice/righteousness can not be a characteristic of the people. Sweeney 1996:124–125; Skinner 1898:40.

75. Schultz 1997b, NIDOTTE (4):843; Liedke 1997, TLOT (3):1397–98; Schultz 1997c, NIDOTTE (4):219.

76. Whybray 1981:227; Muilenburg 1954:694.

77. Oswalt 1998:519. See also Whybray 1981:223 and 225.

78. This inference may never be absolute, as Oswalt comments. As for Smart, justice and righteousness are synonyms for salvation. But, this seems strained especially because of 59:14 that reached scholarly consensus as human virtues. Skinner 1898:191; Whybray 1981:225; Smart 1967:255.

distribution of the word pairs seems to suggest that the justice of the community that they have to construct is actually the consequence of divine salvation if the unity of the passage is assumed. Thus it is natural to think that divine salvation is realized among people in the earthly realm.[79] On the other hand, it is also probable that the salvation/righteousness pair primarily refers to the divine salvation, but also signifies the righteous social order that is achieved by the divine salvation.[80]

Therefore, it is plausible that justice/righteousness may simultaneously refer to both the divine work of salvation and the human ethical and religious response. Motyer comments that the restoration has two sides, objective divine redemption and subjective human-responding life, although the emphasis may differ according to the context.[81] So Beuken opines that justice and righteousness in 56:1 is not only a human commitment but also a divine gift.[82]

In conclusion, TI's eschatology is based on that of DI, although the verbs associated with salvation are different in DI (יצא; 51:5) and TI (בוא; 56:1b).[83] The aspect of human obedience of the eschatological promise is emphasized in TI more than in DI (although this aspect is also not foreign to DI).[84] Justice and righteousness as part of human obedience (56:1a) signify the restoration of the covenantal order and may be inseparable from salvation (56:1b). The state of salvation will be brought about by YHWH's salvific work, but is the consequence of human response.

79. The word distribution at issue is:

Justice	59:8	A
Justice/righteousness	59:9	B (=A')
Justice/salvation	59:11	C (=B')
Justice/righteousness	59:14	B (=A')
Justice	59:15b	A
Salvation/righteousness	59:16	C'
Righteousness/salvation	59:17	C"

80. This argument does not necessarily mean that the divine work and human behavior are confused. They are distinct, but complementary and co-operating in achieving and fulfilling salvation and justice in the community because they belong to different categories (divine and human). However, it may imply that whichever aspect is dominant in a specific text, the other aspect should not be neglected as they are complementary.

81. Motyer 1993:51.

82. Beuken 1989c:21.

83. Beuken 1989a:22. The often-held argument that TI cancel DI is rejected.

84. Childs 2001:456.

2 Blessed is the man who does this,	אשרי אנוש יעשה־זאת
and the son of man who holds it fast,	ובן־אדם יחזיק בה
who keeps the Sabbath, not profaning it,	שמר שבת מחללו
and keeps his hand from doing any evil.	ושמר ידו מעשות כל־רע:

In this verse, the human obedience of 56:1 is re-charged, dividing people into two groups and bringing eschatological salvation beyond the nation. This verse is considered as a continuation of 56:1 because of the chiastic relation of the key verbs such as עשה and שמר in 56:1a and 56:2a.[85] So, זאת refers back to 56:1 (especially 56:1a), and בה refers to זאת.[86] So, as Whybray commented, "the verse sets out the meaning of the admonition in verse 1a in specific terms."[87] Therefore, שמר משפט and עשה צדקה explicate keeping the Sabbath and refraining from any evil, or vice versa.

The beginning אשרי may be related to 30:18, the only other occurrence in Isaiah, where the prophet encourages the people to patiently trust in YHWH, who will deliver them from the oppressor Assyria.[88] In this verse, YHWH is called God of משפט. For Clements, since משפט means "good order," the verse implies that "God will eventually be gracious to those who have repented and are looking to him for a renewed life and nation."[89] So אשרי may be connected to the divine salvation expressed in terms of the divine משפט as well as the grace and compassion of YHWH. In 56:2, the people are encouraged to be obedient by אשרי.[90] The obedient will enjoy משפט, צדקה, and ישועה (56:1) as in 30:18.

Not only the prophetic charge in 56:1a but also אשרי in 56:2 tends to divide the people into two categories, obedient and disobedient. This

---

85. Beuken 1989c:22; Park 2003:62. 56:1a, עשה צדקה, שמר משפט; 56:2a, עשה זאת, שמר שבת. In 56:2b, עשה and שמר are once more repeated. Contrary to Koenen (1990:11, 15), who sees a break in 56:1 since it is a heading.

86. Delitzsch (1873:361) considers that זאת and בה refer to what follows as in Ps 7:4[3], but this is not convincing. In Ps 7:4[3], there is no antecedent and in what follows there is an indication for appositive אם, which is repeated. But, in 56:2, two nouns (בן־אדם, אנוש) and two participles (שמר, x2) are appositive as entitled to blessing. So, it is strange זאת and בה refer to the two participles. However, because one who is blessed is the one who does what is in v. 1 (i.e., to keep justice and to do righteousness) and two participles of שמר expounds who is blessed, זאת and בה eventually can designate the actions of two participles, as Whybray (1981:197) suggested זאת and בה refer both backwardly and forwardly, which is ultimately correct in content, but wrong in formal grammar.

87. Whybray 1981:197.

88. Brown 1997:572. אשרי is not necessarily an influence of wisdom literature. Whybray 1981:197.

89. Clements 1980a:250.

90. Brown 1997:250.

division is eschatological in nature, as is typical in prophetic speech.[91] For Koenen, he who is אשרי is representative of the righteous in 57:2.[92] For him, 56:2 is a programmatic verse, parallel to 57:1–2 and 57:20–21 in that in those passages the contrast between the righteous and the wicked is stark, and their deeds and the consequences of their deeds are described.[93] Those passages are structural features indicating that 56:2—57:21 is a unit.[94] In this context, he who is אשרי refers to the righteous in the unit. However, the contrast between the righteous and the wicked is surely implicit, although Koenen claims for the explicit contrast in 56:2 and 57:20–21. Chapters 56:9—57:21 (as well as 56:1–8) as a whole show such a contrast, which is characteristic not only throughout TI but also in the whole book of Isaiah.[95] Therefore we can still claim that the existence of the wicked or the disobedient lies behind the text of 56:1–2 as Koenen observed. This prefigures the divide in the community in TI as a whole (see 5.2).

Then, what does שמר שבת mean?[96] For Whybray, although it originated in ancient Israel, the Sabbath is a "distinguishing mark of the Jews" only from the exilic era.[97] For Westermann, "the real point which the admonition wants to make is that the only real indication of whether a man truly holds to 'justice and righteousness,' whether he is truly devout, is strict observance of the Sabbath." It is a "badge denoting membership of the community that worshipped Yahweh."[98] However, such a sociological understanding is dubious, because the literary context of keeping the Sabbath is eschatological (see 2.2), so the issue becomes what the practice of keeping the Sabbath signifies in the eschatological sense. Observance of the Sabbath, like keeping justice and righteousness, means an observance of the covenantal order. A wider theological concept or eschatology is the primary level of the narrative representation. The phrase שמר שבת has several links to the laws (Exod

91. Here, 'eschatological' signifies that by the coming of YHWH who saved and judges, the people are divided into the two categories (see chapter 3). For the selectivity of the recipients of salvation, see 56:1.

92. Koenen 1990:22.

93. Koenen 1990:15, 23. He sees this as the influence of wisdom tradition.

94. Koenen 1990:27.

95. This is not necessarily an influence of wisdom tradition, contrary to Koenen. Koenen's argument may be biased possibly by his assumption that he set apart 56:1 as a heading.

96. שמר שבת occurs elsewhere in the OT: Exod 31:13, 14, 16; Lev 19:3, 30; 26:2; Deut 5:12. In Leviticus, it is plural form, elsewhere singular.

97. Whybray 1981:197; Westermann 1969:310. For Westermann, "[D]uring the exile the Sabbath had become a badge denoting membership of the community that worshipped Yahweh."

98. Westermann 1969:310.

31:13–14, 16; Lev 19:3, 30; 26:2; Deut 5:12). First, the Sabbath is "a Mosaic institution so far as its legal appointments were concerned," since it is the fourth Commandment (Deut 5:12; cf. Exod 20:8; Lev 19:31).[99] It is closely related to the Temple/sanctuary or Temple cult (Ezek 22:8; 23:38; 46:1–3).[100] So it is understood in the covenantal framework. Keeping the Sabbath signifies the observance of the law as a key component of the Deuteronomic law (Exod 31:13; Lev 19:3; Deut 5:12) that maintains the covenantal order and is thus a "touchstone of loyalty to YHWH."[101] Second, the Sabbath is a "ceremonial copy of the Sabbath of creation" (Exod 31:13–17), as a regular rest day, when work stops (58:13–14; Exod 23:12; 34:21).[102] It is an eternal sign between YHWH and the people of Israel that YHWH made heaven and earth in six days and on the seventh day he rested (שבת) and was refreshed (Exod 31:17). The observance of the Sabbath is considered a "perpetual covenant" (Exod 31:16) and the Sabbath is a sign between YHWH and the people (Exod 31:13), by which YHWH sanctifies Israel.[103] The Sabbath is holy to YHWH and it is a time of holiness (58:13).[104] Third, the Sabbath (לעשות את־יום השבת) is the memorial of the redemption by the exodus (Deut 5:15).[105] As the Sabbath is the rest of the creation and signifies the rest of the redemption (i.e., the exodus) in the Promised Land, it prefigures the eternal rest. This is supported by TI. In 58:13–14, the eschatological blessing is conditional on keeping Sabbath. This conditional promise is parallel to the conditional promises of 58:8–9 and 10b–12, which are eschatological. The phrase הרכבתיך על־במותי ארץ in 58:14 refers back to Deut 32:13a, which signifies "the conquest and the invincibility of the people of God in their

---

99. Delitzsch 1873:393; Hasel 1992:852.

100. Park 2003:161; 175, 177–78.

101. Hasel 1992:852; Koenen 1990:24. Cited from Greenberg 1983:367.

102. Delitzsch 1873:393; Park 2003:161.

103. Hasel 1992:852.

104. According to Park (2003:165–67), the concept of (the preservation of) Sabbath is unable to be separated with the concept of holiness (Exod 31:13; Gen 2:3) and the glory of YHWH (Exod 16:10).

105. Focusing on the ultimate ends of the Sabbath, Alexander (1846b:335) considers that Sabbath is not merely a ceremonial which is restricted to the Temple as part of Mosaic institutions (contra Gesenius), but recognition and profession of YHWH (1) as "the omnipotent Creator of the universe (Exod 20:11; 31:17)," (2) as "the sanctifier of his people, not in the technical or theological sense, but as denoting him by whom they had been set apart as a peculiar people (Exod 31:13; Ezek 20:12)," and (3) as "the Saviour of this chosen people from the bondage of Egypt (Deut 5:15)"—the Sabbath is commanded to keep in order that the people remember YHWH as the redeemer of the people from Egypt. Hasel (1992:851–52) also pointed out the tree points.

possession of the land."[106] והאכלתיך נחלת יעקב אביך refers to Deut 32:13b and 9, in which the phrase denotes the abundant provision of YHWH in the Promised Land.[107] In 66:23, on every eschatological Sabbath, YHWH is worshiped by all flesh, i.e., all the people of the nations including Israel. Thus, the Sabbath is an eschatological concept—keeping Sabbath deserves the eschatological blessing.

Furthermore, the phrase "to hold it fast" (יחזיק בה; 56:2) refers back to justice and righteousness in 56:1a. It affirms that keeping justice and righteousness is equivalent to walking in the covenant as חזק is associated with ברית in 56:4 and 6. The phrase שמר ידו מעשות כל־רע alludes to the Deuteronomistic formula עשה הרע בעיני יהוה,[108] challenging the people who depart from YHWH and the covenantal relation with him (see chapter 3). They are to keep from doing evil in order to remain within the valid covenantal framework. Thus, Sabbath-keeping is the decisive requirement for the maintenance of the covenant order.[109]

In summary, the Sabbath is not just a ritual, but its observance is a means of testing faithfulness to YHWH in the covenant order. Consequently, keeping the Sabbath is understood as one of the key indications of keeping justice and doing righteousness, as it refers to maintaining covenantal order in order to keep right relation with YHWH as His people.

As has been observed, אנש and בן־אדם may refer to 51:12.[110] If this is the case, the comfort of YHWH, which is offered to Israel (in 40:1 as one of the main themes of DI) and confirmed in 51:12–13, is extended universally in 56:2, to anyone (בן־אדם, אנש)—either Israelites or the people of the nations (see below)—who meets the requirements of 56:2. This is a development of the universalism of DI—all nations will be saved (45:22, 49:6).[111] For Beuken, אנש and אדם signify the aspect of humanity that is created, contingent, weak, and threatened. So, the link with 51:12 tells that frail people can be blessed by "sticking to the equitable way of life."[112] In the cited text, for Whybray, YHWH, Creator (51:13) and Redeemer (51:9–10),

106. Craigie 1976:381; Beuken 1989a:120–21. "I will make you ride on the heights of the earth."

107. In Dt, Jacob is the inheritance of YHWH; in ch 58, the land is the inheritance of Jacob. "I will feed you with the heritage of Jacob your father."

108. Koenen 1990:24. The formula appears in: Num 32:13; Deut 4:25; 9:8; 13:12; 1 Kgs 14:22; 16:25, 30; 2 Kgs 13:11; 14:24; 15:18; 23:32, 37; 24:9, 19; 2 Chr 3:22; (Isa 65:12, ותעשו הרע בעיני); Jer 52:5.

109. Beuken 1989c:36; Lau 1994:267.

110. Koenen 1990:24; Beuken 1989c:23–24.

111. Beuken 1989c:23–24.

112. Beuken 1989c:23–24.

refutes the charge of inactivity of YHWH (51:9) and charges in reply that "it is not he who has forgotten his people (cf. 49:14), but they who have forgotten him (emphasis his)."[113] So, Israel and the nations do not stand at different positions in that any individual is invited and can receive the blessing by their response.

To conclude, the concept of (keeping) justice and righteousness (56:1a) is explicated as the concept of (keeping) the Sabbath, the key of the covenantal relationship between YHWH and His people. Keeping the Sabbath as an eschatological request tests people and divides them into two groups—obedient and disobedient. The universalism of DI develops in 56:2, blessing being open to any human beyond the community.

3 Let not the foreigner	ואל־יאמר בן־הנכר
who has joined himself to YHWH say,	הנלוה אל־יהוה לאמר
"YHWH will surely separate	הבדל יבדילני יהוה
me from His people";	מעל עמו
and let not the eunuch say,	ואל־יאמר הסריס
"Behold, I am a dry tree."	הן אני עץ יבש: ס

The universalism of salvation in 56:2 develops in 56:3–7. In regard to 56:3–7, there have been attempts to reconstruct the historical situation behind the text, but no consensus has been reached yet (see 2.2). A literary reading suggests that the eschatological context is the primary level of the passage.

Donner considers that 56:3–7 is about the admission of non-Israelites and eunuchs to the Temple community of Jerusalem.[114] For him, the historical situation of the passage fits the Jerusalem community at the time of Nehemiah and Ezra.[115] The post-exilic community tried to cleanse itself according to the community law of Deut 23:2–9[1–8], part of the Torah of YHWH, from which situation the complaints in 56:3 arise.[116] The prophet cancels Deut 23:2–9[1–8] "in the name of YHWH" in 56:3–7, although Deuteronomy had achieved canonical validity.[117] By this abrogation, the blood community changes into the confessional community.[118]

---

113. Whybray 1981:160.

114. Donner 1985:81.

115. Donner 1985:82. He (1985:83–84) considers that Neh 9:1–2; 10:29–32; 13:1–3; Ezra 9:1–2; and 10:11 provide the historical background.

116. Donner 1985:84.

117. Donner 1985:87. He (1983:91) calls it "topical abrogation." For Koenen (1990:30) and Delitzsch (1873:362), the present prophecy cancels the stipulation of the law in Deut 23:2–9[1–8].

118. Donner 1985:87.

The question is however whether there are clear links between Isa 56:3–7 and Deut 23:2–9[1–8] and between 56:3–7 and the historical situation of Ezra and Nehemiah. Deut 23:2–9[1–8] does not refer to "foreigners" (בן־הנכר) unlike 56:1–7, but specifically Ammonites and Moabites (23:4[3]), and Edomites and Egyptians (23:8–9[7–8]). While 56:3–7 concerns eunuchs (סריסים), Deut 23:2[1] speaks of "one whose testicles are crushed or whose male organ is cut-off" (פצוע־דכא וכרות שפכה). For Donner, however, it is "topical abrogation" and "the abrogating text does not literally quote the abrogated text."[119] For Lau, however, abrogation is valid only when an old text is replaced by the new text with a new revelation, but Deuteronomic community law has the status of Holy Scripture, even for Donner.[120] The fact that Donner considers this a unique canonical abrogation makes his case shaky.

For Lau, too, 56:3–7 deals with the cultic integration of eunuchs and proselytes into Israel.[121] However, for him, the two texts (56:3–7 and Deut 23:2–9[1–8]) do not deal with the same problem.[122] For Lau, the castrated (סריסים) in 57:3–7, who do not appear in Deut 23:2–4, "belong to Israel in so far as they serve as king's slaves," while those whose testicles are crushed and whose male organs are cut-off in Deut 23:2[1] may refer to "foreign fathers of a family who mutilated themselves in the course of a ritual castration (possibly an indication of Canaanite fertility cult)." Deut 23:3–9[2–8] successively treats hybrids (ממזר) and foreigners of a certain condition. The castrated (סריסים) are not so because of cultic mutilation, but may be tormented or punished prisoners of war. סריס may be childless royal officers.[123] The Israelite or non-Israelite סריסים are not considered as the mutilated in Deut 23:2[1], so are not excluded by the Deuteronomic community law.[124] As for the foreigners, too, Deut 23:3f. mentions definite nationalities (including hybrids), and not "foreigners" (בן־הנכר) in general, so does not directly contradict 56:3.[125]

However, for Lau, the rigorous group misunderstood the community law in Deut 23:2–9[1–8], thinking that foreigners and eunuchs are identified with the people mentioned in Deut 23:2–9[1–8], which reflects fears of

119. Donner 1985:94.

120. Lau 1994:270.

121. Lau 1994:278.

122. Lau 1994:268–72.

123. Lau 1994:270.

124. Lau 1994:268–69.

125. For Beuken (1989c:24), הנכר means foreigner that is ethnically different from Israelites. בן־הנכר is not one who has foreign fathers, but just a foreigner.

the two classes.[126] So, for him, Ezra and Nehemiah texts are the background of 56:3–7.[127] Eunuchs are not mentioned in Ezra and Nehemiah because they are considered by the rigorist view to be excluded from the blessing of God as they are childless.[128] For him, the prophetic Torah of 56:3–7 is against the rigorist view about the community law in Deut 23:2–9[1–8].[129]

However, Lau's assumption of the rigoristic group of the community, who misinterpreted the Torah, lacks evidence. Contrary to Lau, the non-existence of סריסים in Ezra and Nehemiah may indicate that there is no link between the two texts, and this link has been found by the presumption of the same historical situation rather than from the textual evidence. Further-more, for Beuken, סריס probably means the physically castrated. Although it can designate a courtier or a military commander, there is no hint of a court either in a foreign country or in Jerusalem.[130]

The link with the historical situation of Ezra/Nehemiah or with Deut 23:2–9[1–8] is questionable, since there is no evidence for a significant role played by the eunuchs and foreigners.[131] The cited speech may not be a real complaint, but a rhetorical device. A specific historical situation does not come to the fore in the passage. The reference to the complaint alone cannot be definite evidence for or against the historical reality behind the com-plaint, although it may not deny the mimetical/analogical anchorage of this passage in the historical arena. It needs to be considered that 56:3–7 has an eschatological context (i.e., 56:1 and 8) and the speaker develops his speech on the basis of these assumed complaints with a view to universal widening of the salvation invitation.

As Beuken pointed out, it is not a matter of community order because the framework 56:1 and 8 suggests an eschatological understanding of the text.[132] Considering the link between chs 55 and 56, TI is portraying a uni-versal salvation which is accessible to everybody (55:1–5) who returns from his way (55:7) to YHWH.[133] For Beuken, the foreigner and eunuch are "ran-dom cases" for illustration. For him, there is a thematic link between the foreigner and the unknown people who want to rush to Israel in 55:5 and between the eunuch who considers himself a dried tree and the thirsty who

126. Lau 1994:269.
127. Lau 1994:269, 272.
128. Lau 1994:272.
129. Lau 1994:272.
130. Beuken 1989c:24.
131. Beuken 1989c:26.
132. Muilenburg
133. Beuken 1989c:26.

are invited to come to water in 55:1–3. He who responds to the invitation of
55:1–3 is one who joins himself to YHWH in 56:3 when YHWH reveals his
righteousness (56:1).[134]

Skinner thinks that the two *complaints* of foreigners and eunuchs in
56:3 are "the main subject of the oracle":[135] "YHWH will surely separate me
from his people" and "Behold, I am a dry tree." It is certain that 56:3 treats
the issue of inclusion or exclusion into the people of YHWH. However
this is not a cultic community in the historical sense but the eschatological
people. Cultic universalism, as in Westermann and Volz, is to be rejected
(see below).[136] Joining to YHWH is explained in 56:6.

In conclusion, 56:3 sets possible complaints within the narrative in
order to develop and exemplify the universalism raised in 56:2. The text
(56:3–7) alone has insufficient evidence to reconstruct the historical situation or to link the situation with other texts in the OT.

4 For thus says YHWH: "To the eunuchs who keep My Sabbaths, who choose the things that please Me and hold fast My covenant,"	כי־כה אמר יהוה לסריסים אשר ישמרו את־שבתותי ובחרו באשר חפצתי ומחזיקים בבריתי:

In this verse and the following, a divine promise is proclaimed against
the (assumed) fears of the eunuchs. There are three criteria for them to
join the eschatological salvation: (1) keeping my Sabbath, (2) choosing
what pleases YHWH, and (3) holding fast to the covenant with YHWH.
For Childs, these criteria resemble a life under the Torah and function as
tangible expression of the Mosaic covenant.[137]

The three criteria do not seem to signify different things, but to be
three different expressions of one thing because (1) the three do not form
a complete categorical list of one thing, (2) the narrative has been operating within the bigger idea of justice/righteousness or the covenant, and
(3) Sabbath-keeping may be a central requirement for the covenant. "What
pleases Me" (חפצתי) in 56:4a has a link in 55:11 (חפצתי) and possibly in
53:10 (חפץ יהוה).[138] For Beuken, "what pleases Me" (חפצתי) links between
the two themes of exodus (55:13) and entrance into the house of YHWH
(56:6–8).[139] In ch 55, it is the divine word that accomplishes what pleases Me

134. Beuken 1989c:27. See 2.2 and 56:4 below.

135. Skinner 1898:163.

136. Westermann 1969:163.

137. Childs 2001:458.

138. Beuken 1989a:29; Motyer 1993:466. The link with 53:10 will be discussed in
56:6 in connection with the servants.

139. Beuken 1989:29.

(עשה את־אשר חפצתי), while it is those (the eunuchs) who enter eschatological salvation in ch 56 that choose what pleases Me (בחרו באשר חפצתי). The
link of חפצתי in 56:4 with 53:10 may suggest that two common themes of
chapters 55 and 56 (repentance and entering Temple mount) are based on
the work of the Servant, in whose hand the pleasure of YHWH (חפץ יהוה)
will prosper (53:10). The exodus imagery as the eschatological portrait of DI
presents the message of forgiveness (repentance) and new thing (i.e., new
creation).

The efficacious divine word is the agent of the new creation in ch 55
(55:12–13),[140] while the obedience (possibly, through repentance/conver-
sion) of the eunuchs is effectively recognized as gaining a memorial and
a name which is everlasting and the right to enter the Holy Mountain of
YHWH in ch 56.[141] However, the phrase does not only bring the theme
of exodus from ch 55 into ch 56. For Motyer, ch 55 is a "well-constructed
unity" and "pivots on the call to repent (55:6–7)." So, the effectiveness of the
divine word accomplishes the call to repent (this is חפצתי) in the one who
responds to the invitations (55:1–3, 6–7).[142] This is exactly what the phrase
wants to emphasize in 56:4, because the real commitment of a eunuch to
YHWH deserves the eschatological salvific benefits, regardless of his physical conditions.

Then, what is the concept of the covenant? According to a recent study
by Park, the covenant is not to be understood as a "contract" from two
equivalent contracting parties.[143] For him, the concept of ברית is "one-sided
declaration of intention," as the Hebrew word is interpreted as "self-obligation" (or, oath, law, or promise).[144] For Park, the covenant in 56:4 and 6 as
well as in the whole book of Isaiah is linked with the covenants of Abraham
(Gen 17; cf. Gen 15) and Noah (Gen 9), since these belong to the priestly
documents.[145] As for the Abrahamic Covenant in Gen 15 and 17, ברית is not

140. The exodus imagery not only presents a picture where the mountains and hills
join the triumphant chorus for the wondrous new exodus in 55:12, but also displays the
transformation of the desert (i.e., recreation) in 55:13. Muilenburg 1954:651.

141. Motyer 1993:452.

142. Motyer 1993:452, 457–458.

143. For Park (2003:112), the idea of mutual contract is absolutely foreign to the
Hebrew Bible as a "description of the relation between God and human."

144. Park (2003:112) follows Kutsch (1994:339–352), who interprets it obligation
or regulation, Crüsemann (1994:21–38), who comments that "the most reflected covenant theology of the OT . . . is very far from any contract idea," and Perlitt (1986), who
argues that ברית is "for theological reasons in no case a (mutual) alliance (pactum)
between God and human."

145. Park 2003:114–15. The Abrahamic ברית appears in Gen 15:18 and Gen 17:2, 4,
7 (x2), 9, 10, 11, 13 (x2), 14, 19 (x2), 21.

at all in either chapter about a "contract between the two equal parties." It is just a "self-obligation of YHWH," since in Gen 15 it is only YHWH who passes through the lane between animal pieces. In Gen 12:1–3, too, it is the promise of YHWH that grants the land, offspring, and the blessing, which are effective not only for the whole nation but also for the whole of humanity. In Gen 17, too, for him, ברית is in no way about "a contract with mutual partners."[146] For Park, the phrase חזק בריתי refers to the self-obligation of YHWH, and not to the human obligation.[147] While he has a doubt whether 56:1–8 means by ברית יהוה an affiliation to the new cult community, he suggests that ברית (because it is related to the Abrahamic Covenant) does not refer to the "demand of the circumcision as a human obligation," but to the "self-obligation of YHWH and His promise," although "circumcision of the heart" is an important theme in the book of Isaiah (29:13; 32:6; 44:18; 46:12; 51:6–7) for the salvation and judgment of YHWH.[148]

However, Park tends to over-emphasize YHWH's unconditional commitment in the Abrahamic Covenant. He neglects the conditionality of the Abrahamic Covenant, although he recognizes that the human response of "faith" in Gen 15:6 corresponds to the self-obligation of YHWH.[149] He also admits that ברית is associated with the human obligation of circumcision in Gen 17:10–14.[150] Furthermore, in 17:1 Abraham is ordered to "*walk* before YHWH" and "to *be* perfect." Even in Gen 12:1–3, Abraham is commanded to *go* and *be* a blessing, which requires human obedience. For him, "*die Problematik der menschlichen Verpflichtung der Beschneidung keine Rolle bezüglich der ewigen Selbstverpflichtung Jhwhs spielt, Gott für Israel und für die ganze Völker bzw. die ganze Menschheit zu werden*," but this is not convincing.[151] Although YHWH's commitment is emphasized in the Abrahamic Covenant, human obligation or, rather, response is not to be neglected. So, the Abrahamic Covenant is relational between YHWH and Abraham (and his descendants).

As for the Noachic Covenant in Gen 9, Park considers that the concept of ברית covers only the self-obligation of YHWH, since both the rainbow, the everlasting sign of the covenant, and creation, which is covered in the

---

146. Park 2003:116–18.

147. Park 2003:120.

148. Park 2003:120–22.

149. Park 2003:116.

150. Park 2003:119.

151. Park 2003:119. "The problems of the human obligation of circumcision play no role in regard to the everlasting self-obligation of YHWH to become a God of Israel and for all the nations or the whole of humanity." (My translation).

covenant, belong exclusively to YHWH.[152] However, this is very question-able because, as he recognizes, the bans on eating blood of living beings (Gen 9:4–5) and of homicide (Gen 9:6) are included in the framework of the Noachic Covenant. In addition the creation command that is given to Adam in Gen 1:22 and 28 is repeated in Gen 9:1 to Noah and his family. Park becomes clearly self-contradictory in claiming both the obligations of YHWH and the people at the same time:

> Im Sinne des Bezugs auf den Noahbund beinhaltet der Ausdruck חזק בריתי in Jes 56 einerseits den Glauben an die Selbstverpfli-chtung Jhwhs für die Bewahrung der ganzen Schöpfungswelt, zu der auch die Völker gehören, sowie andererseits die soziale Aufgabe der Menschen zum Recht und Gerechtigkeit gegen Blutvergießen Unschuldiger.[153]

The main fault in Park's analysis is that he neglects that the various tra-ditions of the covenant concept (Noachic, Abrahamic, Mosaic, and Davidic Covenants) are incorporated into a unified or an over-arching concept in the nearer context and in TI as a whole, forming a consistent eschatological hope of Israel in TI.

It is against the context of chs 54–55 that the covenant in 56:4, 6 is to be understood. According to Melugin, chs 54–55 hinge on the theme of the covenant, as he comments, "indeed, it [the covenant theme] is so promi-nent that it serves as a theological principle of organization instead of a purely mechanical means of association," although chs 54–55 are somewhat "*loosely* organized" (italics his).[154] In 54:1–6, the covenantal relation be-tween YHWH and His people is portrayed with marriage imagery—Zion's sons will be numerous and her seed will inherit the nations (54:1–3), since she once was deserted and ashamed but will be restored by her husband redeemer YHWH (54:4–6). Isaiah 54:7–10, which is an announcement of salvation, is linked to the previous passage by עזב (54:6//54:7) and גאל (54:5//54:8).[155] So in this passage, the language of covenant (חסד, 54:8, 10; ברית, 54:10; and the reference to Noah, 54:9) is related to the language of

152. Park 2003:125.

153. Park 2003:131. "In relation to the Noah covenant the expression חזק בריתי in Isaiah 56 contains on the one hand faith in the self-obligation of YHWH for the pres-ervation of the whole creation world to which also the nations belong, as well as, on the other hand, the social duty of the people for righteousness and justice for the bloodshed of the innocent." (My translation). Park's statement evidences the "mutual" understand-ing of the covenant concept, which may evidence his self-contradiction.

154. Melugin 1976:174.

155. The parallel between "says your redeemer YHWH" in 54:8 and "says your God" in 54:6 may be another link.

marriage.[156] The broken (marriage) relation (i.e., covenantal relation) will be restored since YHWH promises it by an appeal to the terms of the Noachic Covenant. 54:11–17 is related to the covenant language of 54:10 (ברית שלומי) by the term שלום in 54:13.[157] 55:1–5 displays the dominance of the covenant people over the nations by the language of the Davidic covenant, 55:4–5 reaffirming "the expectation of 54:3 that 'your seed will inherit the nations.'" For Melugin, the "*eternal* sign that will not be *cut off* (italics his)" in 55:13 relates to the settlement (כרת) of the "eternal covenant" in 55:3, and 55:6–7 is "prophetic imitation of priestly Torah."[158] In these two chapters, which are integrated by the covenant theme as the dominant connector, various traditions are brought up to form a portrait of the promise of divine salvation. This promise includes the "permanence of the settlement" of the Noachic Covenant (54:9–10) and the supremacy of the covenant people in the Davidic Covenant (55:3–5). It also includes the numerous descendants of a barren woman (this reminds us of Sarah) in the Abrahamic Covenant, who will inherit the nations (54:1–3),[159] and the restoration of the broken relationship of the Mosaic Covenant (55:6–7). These are all incorporated in chs 54–55 to present the eschatological promise of salvation. The theme of the covenant in 56:4, 6 develops in this context. The covenant in 56:1–8 refers primarily to the Mosaic Covenant, but this is understood within the context of its close relation to other covenants.

There are only two places in which ברית occurs elsewhere in TI: 59:21 and 61:8. The covenant in 59:21 is above all Mosaic, because the covenant has been broken due to the sins of the people in 56:9—57:13 and 58:1—59:15a (see 6.2). However, it may also be in line with the traditions of the Noachic and Abrahamic Covenants since ואני זאת בריתי is in the priestly style and alludes to both covenants in Gen 9:9 and 17:4. עד-עולם may have a strong overtone of Gen 9 (vv. 9, 12) and Gen 17 (vv. 7, 8, 13, 19).[160] If this is the case, it is natural that the author of 59:21 (or, 59:15b–21) may think of an overarching concept of the covenant, which covers Mosaic, Noachic, and Abrahamic Covenants, because the restoration of the Mosaic Covenant is related to the continuation of the Noachic and Abrahamic Covenants. The enforcement of the Mosaic covenant by the coming of YHWH does not

---

156. Melugin 1976:173. For him, 54:7–10 is a formal unit.

157. Melugin 1976:174.

158. Melugin 1976:174, 172.

159. Motyer (1993:445) comments, "[T]he picture of Sarah, the barren woman who was to bear the miracle child and become the mother of a family more numerous than the stars, provides background (Gen 11:30; 16:1; Isa 51:2)."

160. Torrey 1928:424; Whybray 1981:228; and Delitzsch 1873:408.

mean abandoning the Noachic and Abrahamic covenants but keeping them (see chapter 3).[161]

The everlasting covenant in 61:8 has been deemed to be dependent on 55:3, in which the everlasting covenant is associated with the Davidic Covenant.[162] 61:9 is reminiscent of Gen 12:2, so the covenant in 61:8 may be understood as the fulfilment of the Abrahamic promise.[163] So the Davidic and Abrahamic covenants are closely related here.

The covenant formula in 63:8 (ויהי ל—ל—), which is found in Lev 26:12 and Deut 29:13, may be further evidence for the continuous concept of the covenant.[164] According to Rendtorff, the covenant formula is closely related to the covenant, as it was initially given to Abraham and later re-established with Moses.[165] The formula is used usually to denote a relationship (see Gen 20:12; 24:67; 28:21; Exod 2:10; 15:2; Num 36:11), just as the covenant formula Lev 26:12–13 implies that the exodus event has achieved the intention of YHWH to make Israel His people. Deut 29:13 confirms that this intention of YHWH harks back to the promises to the patriarchs Abraham, Isaac, and Jacob. Thus the promises to the patriarchs are achieved by making Israel the people of YHWH through the covenant. In brief, the covenant formula in 63:8 affirms that Israel has been in a covenantal relationship with YHWH. These remarks reinforce the continuity between the different covenant traditions.

The covenant concept is thus a term defining a relationship between YHWH and His people, rather than a one-sided "self-obligation of YHWH." So covenant may be defined as a framework for the mutual (covenantal) relationship between the parties that are covenanted (i.e., between YHWH and His people). This reciprocal relationship does not necessarily mean that the two parties are equal in their burden of duty—in fact that of YHWH is infinite because of his passion for the covenantal order, especially as

161. If we find a parallel of this verse in Jer 31, this may suggest a continuous relation between the covenant tradition and the new covenant.

162. Whybray 1981:244.

163. Whybray 1981:244.

164. "And He became their Savior" (ויהי להם למושיע) (63:8b) may be a quotation of Exod 15:2 because of ויהי־לי לישועה (Delitzsch 1873:452). According to Rendtorff's (1998:13) categorization, 63:8 belongs to the C group of the formula, which has two elements defining both parties of the covenant. 'My people' and '(My) sons/children' are the first part of the covenant formula; "And He became their Savior" (ויהי להם למושיע) (63:8b) is another half of the formula. The covenant formula may also be reminiscent of Exod 6:7, as this is the first occurrence of the C-type formula.

165. Rendtorff 1998:43–46. The continuity between Abrahamic and Mosaic Covenants, as is evidenced, e.g., in Exod 3:7–14; 6:2–5, is also supported by McConville (1997:749).

in 54:9–10 and 55:1–3 (see ch 3). The aspect of human obligation of the covenant is disclosed in the fact that, as I have already discussed, covenant in this passage is understood to be achieved by keeping justice and doing righteousness (56:1). Keeping Sabbath (56:2) is another criterion of the covenant. If the three criteria joining the eschatological salvation in 56:4 are understood as appositives, keeping from all evils (56:2) and doing what pleases YHWH (56:4) are understood as principal requirements for the covenant.[166]

The covenant is for Beuken the "whole of the obligations which YHWH imposed" and is represented by the Sabbath (Exod 31:12–16).[167] To keep the covenant of YHWH is equivalent to obeying the voice of YHWH and continuing as the treasured possession (סגלה) of YHWH among the nations (Exod 19:5). Its core principles include keeping the statutes, judgements, and commandments (מצוה, משפט, חקה) of YHWH (Lev 26:15; Deut 33:9). It is represented by the keeping the Torah (Isa 24:5; Hos 8:1; Ps 78:10) and remembering YHWH (Ps 44:18[17]). The Davidic sons who keep the covenant of YHWH will sit upon the throne forever (Ps 132:12).

In conclusion, 56:4 presents the three criteria for the eunuchs to join the eschatological salvation. In fact, they converge into the keeping of the covenant, since keeping the Sabbath and choosing what pleases YHWH are understood as requirements for the covenant. The covenant is the mutual relationship between YHWH and His people, in which several traditions are incorporated.

5 I will give in My house	ונתתי להם בביתי
and within My walls a monument and a name	ובחומתי יד ושם
better than sons and daughters;	טוב מבנים ומבנות
I will give them an everlasting name	שם עולם אתן־לו
that shall not be cut off.	אשר לא יכרת: ס

This verse promises blessing to those (eunuchs) who meet the three criteria in 56:4: 'a monument and a name' and 'an everlasting name.'

"My house" refers to the Temple (56:7; 60:7; 64:11; 66:1, 20). Temple as בית יהוה or בית אלהים in the eschatological context has a connection in 2:2–4 (see 56:7). This terminology is new in TI compared with DI.

---

166. Park (2003:69) comments: "[S]ocial justice, the Sabbath, the covenant, cult and eschatology are not separated from each other in 56:1–8, but are closely intertwined with each other." However, the Sabbath and cult have primarily an eschatologized sense and are not limited in contemporary practice (that is, the Sabbath and Temple cult are language for expressing eschatology) due to the eschatological framework of the passage.

167. Beuken 1989:27.

Scholars consider that the wall (חומה) refers to the Temple wall (Whybray, Koenen, Skinner, and Duhm)[168] or, figuratively, the divine presence (Motyer) or dwelling (Alexander).[169] Others argue for the city wall (Jerome)[170] or, as its figurative meaning, the place of protection (Beuken).[171] Temple wall may be an easy interpretation, because it could be another expression of the preceding ביתי with a view to emphasis. However, חומה as Temple wall occurs only in Ezek 40:5 and 42:20 in the OT, while חומה as city wall frequently occurs in TI (60:10, 18 and 62:6) as well as elsewhere in the OT.[172] Furthermore, it seems unlikely that the same material object is referred to twice in succession. Alternatively, בביתי ובחומתי may be a hendiadys suggesting a figurative sense for two physically different things. So חומה better signifies the Jerusalem wall (Jerusalem as an eschatological place) or rather its figurative meaning, the protected community of YHWH (60:18).[173] This interpretation is made more likely by the fact that the Temple Zion and the city Zion (the people in the New Jerusalem) are integrated in the eschatological portrait (see 56:8 and chapter 4). Not only in the (eschatological) Temple, but also in the (eschatological) community, blessing is given, although these two are integrated into one in the eschatological vision.

For Delitzsch, יד and שם are closely related to form a hendiadys, being qualified by "better than children." יד means a memorial as in 2 Sam 18:18; 1 Sam 15:12; and Ezek 21:24,[174] although יד originally means a place (Deut 2:17; Deut 23:13; Jer 6:3).[175] His conception of יד expresses recognition in the community. Robinson, however, argues that יד means possession, share, or portion. He rejects 'monument,' because he believes that the context of the phrase is the inheritance in the Promised Land and that monument does not fit the context.[176] This view is developed by Beuken, for whom יד ושם is a hendiadys, where יד signifies a concrete monument as in Absalom's monu-

---

168. Whybray 1981:198; Koenen 1990:32; Skinner 1898:166; Duhm 1892:382.

169. Motyer 1993:466; Alexander 1846b:336.

170. Alexander 1846b:336.

171. Beuken 1989a:28.

172. See 26:1 and 49:16 in PI and DI (Zech 2:9[5]; Ps 122:7).

173. Although Beuken (1989a:28) considers that 'My wall' is 'place of protection' based on 26:1; 49:16; 60:10, 18; Zech 2:9; and Ps 122:7, it is strange for him to think of it as the Temple wall. He unnecessarily tries to find the meaning of יד ושם only in the Temple.

174. Delitzsch 1873:362.

175. יד is interpreted as place in: LXX, Tg, Vg, Syr. In the OT, יד as place: Deut 2:37; Deut 23:13; Jer 6:3.

176. Robinson 1975:282–283. For him, the 'name' in 56:5 is the "sustained life in the promised land."

ment (2 Sam 18:18), but figuratively, a place or share (2 Sam 19:44).[177] For Beuken, it is an assigned place in the Temple where one stays and serves. The promise to the castrated is motivated by Temple piety—to dwell in the Temple is better than earthly wealth (Ps 23:6; 34:9). So the one who has place and name in the Temple is similar to the Levites, who have no other inheritance in Israel than YHWH.[178]

For Lau, however, 'monument' is acceptable, while 'place' or 'portion' is not.[179] Because there is no mention of יד in 56:5b, יד is senseful only in conjunction with name. Since eunuchs lack progeny, they are promised the preservation of their name instead, so יד is about the continuation of name.[180] This is evidenced by the fact that יד ושם is parallel to זרעכם ושמכם (66:22), both of which signify eternal continuation.[181]

For Seitz, יד is a "euphemism for 'penis'" and the name is a development of the theme in 55:13.[182] The everlasting name (שם עולם), which will not be eradicated (לא יכרת) in 56:5, has a link with 55:13 (ליהוה לשם לאות עולם), in which the name and eternal sign will not be eradicated (לא יכרת).[183] This everlasting name has a link to 48:19.[184] In 48:19, the future salvation of YHWH is expressed as a new thing. It is portrayed with exodus imagery (48:20–21). In this context, 'the name that will not be cut off' suggests a fulfilment of the Abrahamic promise of descendants like the sand. So the everlasting name signifies an inclusion in the eschatological community as a descendant of Abraham. Seitz's suggestion that יד is a euphemism is possible, because of the link with 66:22, in which progeny is involved.

My judgment is that the first context of יד (ושם) is בביתי ובחומתי—not only in the Temple but also in the city. So יד may signify a place, portion, or share in the eschatological salvation. However, as in 56:5b, יד ושם carries the implication of continuation or eternity. This is evidenced by the intertextual links with 55:13, as Seitz observed, and with 66:22. In relation to the link with 55:13, יד may be the equivalent of the sign (אות), since יד ושם, which is eternal, corresponds to the "name and eternal sign" (לשם לאות עולם) in

---

177. Beuken 1989c:28. Also see Gen 35:4; 1 Sam 24:12; 2 Kgs 11:7; Jer 6:3, for the sense of share.

178. Beuken 1989c:28. Num 18:20; Deut 10:9; Josh 13:14.

179. Lau 1994:273–74.

180. Lau 1994:274.

181. Koenen 1990:29.

182. Seitz 2001:485.

183. Beuken 1989c:29.

184. Beuken 1989c:30; Lau 1994:275.

55:13. So 'eternal' in 56:5 is a quality not only of the name but also, implicitly, of יד. The link with 66:22 may relate יד to progeny.

In conclusion, eunuchs who meet the requirements are promised that they may join in the eschatological salvation. The phrase יד ושם ultimately signifies this eschatological blessing, containing the qualities of continuation and share.

6 And the foreigners who join themselves to YHWH,	ובני הנכר הנלוים על־יהוה
to minister to Him, to love the name of YHWH,	לשרתו ולאהבה את־שם יהוה
and to be His servants,	להיות לו לעבדים
everyone who keeps the Sabbath and does not profane it,	כל־שמר שבת מחללו
and holds fast My covenant;	ומחזיקים בבריתי:

This verse sets three criteria by which anyone (represented by foreigners) can benefit from the eschatological salvation of 56:7. The three participles (הנלוים, כל־שמר, ומחזיקים) correspond to the three demands on the eunuchs in 56:4. So 56:6–7 repeats the same pattern of 56:4–5: a qualification and a promise.[185]

What is "joining to YHWH" (הנלוים על־יהוה)? For Skinner, joining signifies becoming a proselyte by accepting the symbols of Jewish nationality (circumcision, etc.).[186] However Muilenburg rejects this view.[187] Joining to YHWH is not a real practice but has an eschatological sense. As Beuken observed, the following three infinitives (להיות, לאהבה, לשרתו) explain joining to YHWH: ministering to Him, loving the name of YHWH, and being His servants.[188] For Koenen, there is a word play between joining (נלוים) in 56:6 and the Levites (ללוים) of 66:21.[189] If this is the case, it may imply that anyone who becomes one of the people of YHWH in the eschatological era can serve YHWH as (priests and) Levites do.

The phrase שרת יהוה may signify the cultic activity of the foreigners in 56:6,[190] since the term שרת often refers to a priestly service in the Temple (Exod 29:30; 30:20; 35:19; 39:1; cf. Isa 60:7, 10; 61:6).[191] However, in the context of 56:1–8, actual cultic practice may not be the primary reference. According to Beuken it is not understood as cultic service in 56:6 or 61:6, but merely as access to the house of YHWH. Because of the eschatological con-

185. Muilenburg 1954:658.
186. Skinner 1898:164–65.
187. Muilenburg 1954:658.
188. Beuken 1989c:30.
189. Koenen 1990:29.
190. Koenen 1990:29.
191. Muilenburg 1954:658.

text שרת does not indicate any concrete cultic task.[192] In Deut 10:12, serving YHWH (לעבד את־יהוה) is parallel to fearing YHWH (ליראה את־יהוה), walking in the way of YHWH (ללכת בכל־דרכיו), and loving YHWH (לאהבה אתו), implying that it signifies walking within and remaining faithful to the covenant, not necessarily cultic service.[193] In the Deuteronomic concept, the practice and privilege of the Levites in Israel are the way to explain the place and role of the people of Israel among the nations. What Levites are to the lay Israelites is what Israelites are to the nations. So serving YHWH is not necessarily a cultic activity, because it may apply to people in general and signify the faithful life of the people to YHWH.

To love the name of YHWH, for Childs, is a re-application of the older (Deuteronomic and Deuteronomistic) tradition of YHWH and His people in covenantal relationship (Deut 7:9; 13:4[3] etc).[194] In Deut 7:9 loving YHWH is equivalent to keeping His commandments, both of which are essential for the covenantal faithfulness of the people for YHWH. In Deut 13:4[3], it is the general indication of the faithfulness of the people to YHWH. So, loving the name of YHWH signifies covenantal allegiance to YHWH as in the Deuteronomistic literature.[195]

Becoming a servant is applied to the whole of Israel (Lev 25:55) and to the cultic community (Ps 135:1).[196] The relational formula —ל—ל expresses the relation with YHWH of the people as servants (Deut 10:12; 11:13; Josh 22:5—in these verses עבד is used as a verbal form). The servants in 63:17 are the covenant people, who are pleading for YHWH to come in the darkness. In chs 65–66, they are the eschatological people of YHWH, who enjoy the eschatological blessing. The servants will be spared in TI (65:8) to be recipients of the eschatological salvation (66:14; 65:13–15), inheriting the land [literally, mountains] of Judah (65:9). The servants, members of the new Zion, will be righteous because the eschatological Zion will have righteousness as its characteristic (60:21; 60:3, 10, 11; 62:1, 2). They are in the covenantal relationship with YHWH in Zion and are righteous (See chapter 4).

The 'servant(s)' has a special meaning in TI especially in relation to DI.[197] The 'righteous' (צדיק) Suffering Servant in the fourth Servant Song in DI will make many 'righteous' (צדק; 53:11). The servants will be given

192. Beuken 1989c:30.

193. Also in Deut 11:13 and Josh 22:5, serving YHWH is used as synonymous to loving YHWH (the two terms are in parallel).

194. Childs 2001:459; Koenen 1990:30.

195. Beuken 1989c:30.

196. Beuken 1989c:31.

197. Beuken 1989c:31.

righteousness (צדקה) and will inherit (נחלה) in 54:17, which is the only occurrence of the plural form of עבד in DI, and after that only the plural form appears in TI. Therefore, the concept of servants suggests that the eschatological salvation of DI is fulfilled in TI and the membership of the eschatological community is effected by the death of the Suffering Servant.[198]

The other two criteria (keeping Sabbath and holding fast the covenant) for entrance into eschatological salvation appear in apposition to "joining to YHWH." This also shows that joining to YHWH is the condition of the covenantal relationship with YHWH in the eschatological salvation.[199]

In conclusion, the three-fold criteria for foreigners to enter the eschatological salvation are presented in 56.6. But they are in fact summarized as one: entering the covenantal relationship with YHWH.

7 these I will bring to My Holy Mountain,	והביאותים אל־הר קדשי
and make them joyful in My house of prayer;	ושמחתים בבית תפלתי
their burnt offerings and their sacrifices	עולתיהם וזבחיהם
will be accepted on My altar;	לרצון על־מזבחי
for My house shall be called	כי ביתי בית־תפלה
a house of prayer for all peoples.	יקרא לכל־העמים:

To the foreigners who meet the three criteria of the preceding verse, three promises are given: (1) they will be brought to the Holy Mountain; (2) they will be made joyful in the house of prayer; and (3) their burnt offerings and their sacrifices will be accepted on the altar. These promises suggest that the foreigners will have the same cultic relationship as between YHWH and His people. The cultic language is understood as eschatological as discussed above.[200]

The foreigners who meet these requirements are brought to the Holy Mountain. This Holy Mountain is the eschatological paradise in 65:25 and is identified with the eschatological Jerusalem in 66:20.[201] So, the qualified foreigners (and eunuchs) will join the eschatological community in covenantal relationship with YHWH.

For Seitz, Isaiah's vision of the flow of the nations into Zion and their learning Torah in 2:2–3 is fulfilled in 54:1—56:8.[202] 55:5 is also the precursor of the gathering of the nations. In 54:13 the children of Zion learn the

198. Beuken 1989c:31; Beuken 1990:67–87.

199. The nature of the "joining" the people of YHWH will be expounded in chapters 3 and 4.

200. Muilenburg 1954:658.

201. Koenen 1990:29. In terms of the phrase "My Holy Mountain," 56:7 is linked to 66:20.

202. Seitz 2001:485. See 56:5, for the Temple as expressed as 'My house,' referring back to 2:2–3.

Torah. The people of the nations are brought to My Holy Mountain in 56:7. The Holy Mountain is the eschatological Zion, which incorporates the city and Temple. In 2:2–4, the mountain of (the house of) YHWH is synonymously interchanged with the Temple of YHWH and these are identified with Zion and Jerusalem and the teaching and Torah of YHWH come from there. So in the eschatological vision Zion as the name of the city (Jerusalem), and Zion as the name of the Temple (mountain) are coalesced. In PI, Zion is sometimes the name of the city of Jerusalem (1:8; 2:3; 3:16–17; 4:3–4; 10:24; 12:6; 30:19; 31:9; 33:5, 14, 20; 34:8; 35:10; 37:22, 32) and sometimes it refers to the Temple mountain (2:3; 4:5; 8:18; 10:12, 32; 18:7; 24:23; 29:8; 31:4). In 10:32, הר ב(י)(ת־ציון is parallel to גבעת ירושלם, so Zion is characterized as both the Temple mountain and the city of Jerusalem. In DI and TI Zion always refers to Jerusalem, whether it is the historical city (40:9; 51:3; 64:9[10]) or the redeemed community (51:11; 52:8; 59:20). However in 66:20 Jerusalem is identified with the Holy Mountain. Here, the nations will bring the offspring [brethren] of Israel to the Holy Mountain.

Qualified foreigners are made joyful in "My house of prayer." "My house of prayer" is unique in expression in the OT but is reminiscent of the dedicatory prayer of Solomon in the Temple (1 Kgs 8:41–43), which includes the prayer for the foreigners.[203] However, not only Solomon's prayer but also the prosperity of Davidic and Solomonic times may be background for the text, alluding to the eschatological vision of restoration. This prefigures the eschatological wealth as well as the service of kings in 60:4–9, as modelled by the visit of the Queen of Sheba in 1 Kgs 10.[204] Joy (שמח) relates to the cultic festivals of Israel in connection to the Temple (Lev 23:40; Num 10:10; Deut 12:12; 27:7).[205] In Jer 31:13 maidens and young men and old will rejoice since YHWH will ransom and redeem Jacob (31:11). The foreigners attending the eschatological festival will rejoice, because they are fully incorporated into the eschatological salvation.

"Their burnt offerings and their sacrifices will be accepted on My altar." TI's vision develops that of PI, where Egyptians will offer sacrifice (19:19–20) to YHWH. "In that day there will be an altar to YHWH in the midst of the land of Egypt, and a pillar to YHWH at its border (19:19)."[206] In 19:20 YHWH will send a saviour to deliver the Egyptians, when they cry out to Him because of oppressors. This reciprocal relationship may be considered a covenantal relationship, although 19:19–20 lacks a covenantal

203. Delitzsch 1873:363; Beuken 1989c:32.
204. Dumbrell 1977:39–40.
205. Beuken 1989c:32; Muilenburg 1954:658.
206. Beuken 1989c:33.

formula.[207] The worship of YHWH extends to the foreigners in 56:7, while in 19:19–20 Egyptians will worship YHWH.[208] So, the cultic language indicates not just the worship of YHWH but also a covenantal relationship by which YHWH guarantees protection and salvation to the foreigners.

In the 'house of prayer for all nations,' the emphasis lies on the 'all nations' (כל־העמים) and not on the prayer.[209] All nations will enjoy salvation in the Temple, since they are fully accepted as the people of YHWH. עמים is adopted for the universal salvation (i.e., salvation of the nations in addition to Israel) in DI and is reaffirmed here (45:22; 49:6; 51:4–5).[210]

In conclusion, qualified eunuchs and foreigners will enjoy the eschatological Zion in full covenantal relationship with YHWH.

8 The Lord YHWH,	נאם אדני יהוה
who gathers the outcasts of Israel, declares,	מקבץ נדחי ישראל
"I will gather yet others to him besides those already gathered."	עוד אקבץ עליו לנקבציו:

This verse announces the promise of YHWH to gather His people from the nations, joining the eschatological framework of the passage with 56:1. For Muilenburg, the verse is connected to "these I will bring" in 56:7a.[211] The verb קבץ with YHWH as a subject appears only in the prologue (56:8) and the epilogue (66:18), expressing YHWH's gathering of Israel and the nations.[212]

In DI, YHWH will gather His people as a shepherd gathers his flock (40:11). He will gather Israel and her offspring from the east and the west (43:5; 54:7).[213] In DI, the gathering may have two senses: physical (i.e., gathering the people from exile) and spiritual (or, covenantal;, i.e., restoration of the relation between YHWH and the people who had broken it before).

---

207. According to Alexander (1846a:359, 361), the language of 19:19 is "borrowed from the Mosaic or rather from the patriarchal institutions," and that of 19:20 has an "allusion to the frequent statement in the book of Judges, that the people cried to God, and he raised them up deliverers who saved them from their oppressors (Judg 2:16; 3:9, etc)." For Wildberger (1997:276), "the author of the present passage envisions some type of re-enactment of the deliverance from Egypt," since צעק (Exod 5:8, 15; 8:8, etc) is the "technical term when the 'saviour' Moses stands in the stead of Israel and 'cries' to Yahweh."

208. Childs (2001:144–145) considers that the worship of Egypt and Assyria (19:23) together with Israel resonate with the assembly of the nations in 2:2–4.

209. Beuken 1989c:33; Lau 1994:277.

210. Beuken 1989c:34.

211. Muilenburg 1954:659.

212. Beuken 1989c:34; Koenen 1990:29.

213. Beuken 1989c:34.

Association of the two verbs קבץ and נדח is Deuteronomistic (Deut 30:4) and Isaianic (11:12).[214] The pilgrimage of the nations to the Holy Mountain is inspired by 11:12, in which the gathering of the banished of Israel from the four corners of the world is promised, being associated with the Davidic monarch (11:10).[215] This banishment and restoration of the exiles is understood as the punishment and forgiveness of YHWH for his people within the framework of the covenant as described in the stipulation of the covenantal enforcement in Deut 30:4.[216] So, 56:8 is fulfilment of both the Davidic and Mosaic Covenants.[217]

What do the 'others' and 'those already gathered' mean? Those working from a historical perspective may understand the latter by adding 'from exile', and the former as the rest of the scattered people of Israel plus the nations. For Skinner, the verse is one of the post-exilic indicators, as a partial gathering of the scattered Israel has already taken place.[218] But this is not compelling, because there is continuity of the audience between DI and TI. This is evidenced by the fact that there is a divide of the community in PI-DI as well as TI, and the people are fallen into idolatry both in TI and DI. Canonically, however, in 54:7, the barren woman Zion is promised that her descendents will be gathered. In 55:5, the nations whom David does not know are summoned and hastily run to him. 56:8 is a repetition [reaffirmation] of these schemes of gathering—those of the scattered descendents of Israel and the nations.[219] In this understanding, the actual return of the exiles is not guaranteed by the text.

In conclusion, YHWH declares that He will gather the scattered of Israel and the nations in the eschatological era. This is a re-affirmation of the expansion of the eschatological salvation to the nations.

2.4 Summary and Conclusion

This chapter has argued that the covenant concept is not merely a key theme of 56:1–8. It forms the framework of the eschatology of TI, although it is

214. Koenen 1990:31. YHWH gathers the banished of Israel in Deut 30:4; Neh 1:9; Isa 11:12; 56:8; Jer 23:3; 29:14; 32:37; Mic 4:6; and 3:19.

215. Lau 1994:278.

216. 56:8 has a connection to Deut 30:4 in terms of קבץ and נדח.

217. Lau (1994:278) considers that 11:12 (אסף) is behind 56:8 as a model text due to the theme of collection of scattered Israel.

218. Skinner 1898:163–64, 167.

219. Pace Lau (1994:278), who considers that 56:8 is a secondary addition because there is no reference to the collection of the scattered Israel before. Beuken (1989a:35) considers that 'to him' signifies Israel.

not presented in a systematic way in the text of TI. The covenant concept incorporates the major themes of TI such as justice, righteousness, (keeping) the Sabbath, and salvation. The covenant is the mutual relationship between YHWH and the people. The covenantal bond to YHWH is the key to the eschatological salvation. In TI, different covenant traditions form an integrated concept of the covenant.

56:1–8 may be the prologue of TI, but it does not show an absolute break with the preceding chapter(s)—more continuity is recognized between eschatology of the two parts of the book than discontinuity. The passage bridges TI and DI (and sometimes connects with PI as well). It fits into an eschatological context, in which the eschatological vision of DI is summarized and used as a basis of the eschatological portrait not only of this passage, but also of TI as a whole. So there is continuity between the eschatology of the two parts of the book.

According to the eschatological expectation transferred from DI, justice and righteousness are required to join the eschatological salvation. The (human) justice and righteousness are understood to be the pivotal elements of the covenantal order. Compared to DI, human response is emphasized in TI. However human justice and righteousness are considered to be achieved by the divine action of salvation. So the divine and human acts co-exist in an individual's salvation.

Keeping the Sabbath, which expounds keeping justice and doing righteousness, is the fundamental requirement for the covenantal order in the relationship with YHWH. Due to the "eschatological window" enveloping the passage (56:1, 8), the cultic language, such as burnt offering and sacrifice as well as (keeping) the Sabbath, is to be understood in the eschatological sense, that is, it may not necessarily refer to actual cultic activities, but signifies the eschatological implication of those activities.

The key message of the passage is the expansion of eschatological salvation. It is open wide even to the eunuchs and foreigners if only they meet the requirements. The requirements are eventually a covenantal bond to YHWH for both eunuchs and foreigners. Although different language is adopted, the two illustrations repeat the same pattern: eschatological salvation is given to those who commit to the covenant with YHWH. The qualified eunuchs (in fact, anyone who is qualified) are promised an eternal name and share/memorial in the eschatological salvation. The qualified foreigners (in fact, anyone who is qualified) are entitled to enter the Holy Mountain of YHWH, i.e., the eschatological Zion, in full covenantal relationship with Him.

YHWH affirms His intention to gather His people from the scattered Israel and the nations as well. By this, it is clear that the eschatological salvation is open wide to everybody, whether Israel or from the nations.

Chapter 3

The Coming of YHWH (59:15b–21)

3.1 Introduction

In chapter 2, I have shown that the covenant concept is pivotal in the eschatology of TI. As the governing theme of 56:1–8 it incorporates the themes of the passage. As the introductory section of TI, 56:1–8 bridges between TI and DI. The key message of 56:1–8 is the expansion of eschatological salvation even to foreigners and eunuchs (i.e., a universal salvation), provided they commit to the covenantal bond to YHWH. Even the people of Israel are required to keep justice and do righteousness to be entitled to the eschatological salvation which is imminent, since their obedience anticipates the restoration of the covenant. The qualified individuals are promised not only an eternal name and a share of the eschatological salvation, but also entry to the Holy Mountain of YHWH, the eschatological Zion. The covenant as understood in TI is an integrated concept of the covenant traditions in ancient Israel.

In connection with the previous chapter, I now try to show that the coming of YHWH, another crucial element of the eschatology of TI, fulfils the eschatological expectation of 56:1–8, initiating the eschatological era and exacting eschatological judgment and salvation. The consequences of this coming relate first of all to Israel, but it will also affect the whole world. The coming of YHWH is also accompanied by an intermediate figure (a Servant figure or envoy). To this end, 59:15b–21 is chosen because it is a typical theophanic text which portrays the coming of YHWH in TI, but 63:1–6, the structural counterpart of 59:15b–21 in the text of TI, is also considered. Although there are several other theophanic texts in TI such as 66:15–16 (or 66:15–24) and 63:19b—64:2, not only is 59:15b–21 more detailed and comprehensive, but from a structural point of view it also clearly shows the transition between the present state (chs 58–59) and the future state of Zion (ch 60). In 59:15b–21, YHWH is coming to fulfil the promises and expectations of 56:1–8 (see 3.2). I will discuss the significance of 59:15b–21 in the whole of TI especially focusing on the intertextual relations between the passage and the rest of TI (3.2), and elaborate on the theological interpretation of the passage verse by verse (3.3). In an excursus, I will investigate 61:1–3 as identifying the Messianic figure suggested in 59:15b–21 (3.4).

3.2 Isa 59:15b–21 in TI

This section tries to show that the coming of YHWH is in order to deal with the sins of the people and to restore the covenant. I will show that 59:15b–21 is related to the immediate context and especially with 63:1–6, its structural counterpart in TI. The coming of YHWH is a crucial event in the eschatological enterprise of TI as the controlling theme of the passage (also see 3.3).

A. 59:15b–21 in the Preceding Contexts (chs 59, 58–59, 56–59)

For what purpose is YHWH to come in 59:15b–21 as displayed in the preceding contexts? This section has sometimes been separated from the rest of the chapter. For Budde, it deals with the destruction of the nations while the sin of the people in Israel has been challenged in the preceding context.[1] For Whybray, the presupposed situations in 59:1–8, 59:9–15a, and 59:15b–21 are very different from each other so that the whole chapter cannot be deemed a (liturgical) unity.[2] However, the three sections of the chapter are widely accepted to be closely connected logically with each other:[3] in the first section (59:1–8), the people are charged with their sins; in the second (59:9–15a),

1. Koenen 1990:67.
2. Whybray 1991:220. He sees that the difference in the situations in the first two sections and the third section is much greater than that between the first two sections.
3. Seitz 2001:498 and 500; Muilenburg 1954:686; Koenen 1990:60; and Childs 2001:486. The widely accepted structure of the chapter is the division: 59:1–8 (accusation of sin; 59:1–4 + 59:5–8); 59:9–15a (confession of sin; 59:9–11 + 59:12–15a); and 59:15b–21[or, 20] (intervention of YHWH; 59:15b–18 + 59:19–21[or, 20]), each section having a subsection. Oswalt (1998:518 and 525) proposes one more division in 59:12. 59:21 is considered interpretive epilogue by Childs (2001:486). Beuken (1989a:124) considers 59:21 as a separated section, forming a four-section structure.

al intervention.[5]

Furthermore, it has been argued that chs 58–59 form a single extended unit: the phrase "those who turn from transgression (פשע) in (the house of) Jacob" in 59:20 has a parallel in 58:1 (פשעם ולבית יעקב חטאתם), forming an enveloping structure in chs 58–59—both chapters are centered on the sin of the people.[6] For Seitz, the key words such as justice and righteousness (58:2, 8; 59:4, 8–9, 11, 14, 17) link the two chapters 58 and 59.[7] The light metaphor of salvation also links the two chapters in 58:8, 10 and 59:9–10.[8] So, in the view of chs 58–59, YHWH comes to restore justice by dealing with the sins of the people.

In addition, 59:15b–21 fulfils the promise(s) in 56:1–8. Four observations support this: (1) theophany in 59:15b–21 is prefigured by the coming of salvation in 56:1b (קרובה ישועתי לבוא). The coming of divine salvation is theophanic language. So, 56:1–8 and 59:15b–21 relate to each other as promise and fulfilment of the eschatological salvation, which is achieved by the coming of YHWH. (2) The keyword pair ישועה/צדקה (59:16, 17//56:1b) occurs in the both passages uniquely in TI (Also take note of the pair justice/righteousness in parallel between the two chapters—59:9, 14//56:1a).[9] In 56:1–8, the people are urged to do justice and righteousness as the divine salvation and righteousness is to come soon, while in 59:15b–21 justice

---

4. Childs 2001:486; Hanson 1975:120.

5. Kendall 1984:391–405 (especially, 402–5).

6. Childs 2001:485; Steck 1991:177, 182; Skinner 1960:186.

7. Seitz 2001:498.

8. Koenen 1990:64–65.

9. Although the word pair may also be related to 61:10 (ישע צדקה), 62:1 (ישועה צדק), and 63:1 (ישע צדקה hiphil), or 64:5 (ישע צדק niphal).

and righteousness are restored by the coming of YHWH, because Israel has failed to keep justice and righteousness in 59:1–15a (especially 59:9 and 14; in fact, in 56:9—59:15a). This is the motive for the divine intervention in 59:15b–21. (3) The covenant (59:21//56:4, 6) is parallel. So, the covenant in 56:1–8 and 59:15b–21, forming an *inclusio* of chs 56–59, must be an interpretive key of the section.[10] (4) The name of YHWH (59:19//56:6) is also parallel in both texts.[11] While those who love the name of YHWH are promised eschatological salvation in ch 56, the name of YHWH is feared by the new people of YHWH in ch 59. Therefore, since these four elements are crucial to the eschatological message of both passages, as Polan suggested, 59:15b–21 and 56:1–8 are linked "both structurally and thematically" with each other.[12]

The structural link between 56:1–8 and 59:15b–21 suggests that the rest of the section chs 56–59 (i.e., 56:9—57:21 and 58:1—59:15a) should be understood in the light of the two passages (so Childs). 56:1–8 announces the coming salvation and requires the observation of justice and righteousness, which are key elements of the covenantal order. 56:9—57:21 addresses the inability of the leaders in Israel to do justice and righteousness because of their sins, while 58:1—59:15a deals with the failure of the general people.[13] So, the covenant is broken because of the sins of the people. In 59:15b–21, YHWH thus comes and restores the covenant, as well as justice and righteousness.[14]

In brief, in view of the preceding contexts, YHWH comes in 59:15b–21 to restore the covenant as well as justice and righteousness by dealing with the sins of the people. 59:15b–21 is not unrelated to the preceding contexts—rather, chs 56–59 display a creatively devised structure, centered on the themes such as salvation (coming of YHWH), justice and righteousness, as well as the covenant.

---

10. Childs 2001:490.

11. יהוה שם also occurs at 60:9 in TI.

12. Polan 1986:315.

13. Steck 1991:177.

14. Childs 2001:485; Oswalt 1998:512, 527. Oswalt suggests the structure of chs 56–59 as follows: "The repetition of the call to righteousness (56:1–8; 58:1–14), the description of Israel's inability to do righteousness (56:9—57:13; 59:1–15a), and the announcement of the delivering power of God (57:14–21; 59:15b–21) lead to this climactic point."

B. 59:15b–21 in Relation to the Following Contexts (chs 60–62, 63:1–6)

For Volz, although 59:15b–21 is an eschatological passage, it is unrelated to chs 60–62, another eschatological passage, because it is theocentric and describes the coming of YHWH the Warrior, while chs 60 and 62 (for him, these two chapters form unity, without ch 61) are Zion-centric and do not portray the Day of YHWH but rather the day of Jerusalem.[15] Although, for Volz, 63:1–6 is eschatological like chs 60–62, the image of a dreadful wine-presser in the passage is not compatible with the YHWH who is portrayed as showing tender love to the broken-hearted and granting salvation in chs 60–62.[16] For Westermann, too, 63:1–6 is discontinuous with chs 60–62, which is generally agreed, according to Smith,[17] because the two sections have a different theology of the nations and their fortune, and because 63:1–6 has an apocalyptic nature, which is different from chs 60–62.[18] In the latter, even the nations are saved, albeit as the servants of Israel, while in the former they are judged and annihilated. These conceptions in the two sections are not compatible.[19] So, for Westermann, the two sections have different authors.[20] As a result, for those who see mainly theological differences, like Volz and Westermann, although every unit of 59:15b—63:6 may be eschatological, the two sections do not form a harmonious eschatology as a whole.

However, assumption of unity leads to a more consistent theology. If the unity of chs 60–62 is assumed contrary to Volz (see chapters 1 and 4), not only chs 60–62 but also the larger section of 59:15b—63:6 may represent the deeper theology of TI. This may be evidenced by the relations especially between 59:15b–21; chs 60–62; and 63:1–6.

Firstly, 59:15b–21 and 63:1–6 present a single theophanic event (in the heavenly realm), forming a literary framework for chs 60–62, as suggested by the literary links between 59:15b–21 and 63:1–6.[21] Both texts deal with

15. Volz 1932:239.

16. Volz 1932:199.

17. Smith 1995:43.

18. Ruszukowski 2000:48.

19. Westermann 1969:384. For Kissane (1943:255), too, 63:1–6 is not logically connected to the preceding and the following contexts, but to 59:15b–21. For Hanson (1975:204), 63:1–6 does not reflect the inner-community polemic, which may indicate, for him, the independence of the passage.

20. Westermann 1969:384; Lau 1994:282.

21. Muilenburg 1954:724; Hanson 1975:203; Whybray 1981:252; Seitz 2001:501; Beuken 1989a:246.

the divine intervention of the coming YHWH as warrior, involved with the theophanic verb בוא (59:19, 20; 63:1, 4). 63:5 is almost a repetition of 59:16. The phrase אין־איש also suggests a connection between 59:16 and 63:3. These verses display the singular intervention of YHWH in His coming.[22] Moreover, the garment (בגד) with which YHWH is equipped in 63:1 and 59:17 may also link the two passages: while YHWH puts on the garment of vengeance in ch 59, in 63:1–3 the garment is blood-stained. Both texts are about vengeance (נקם) in 63:4 and 59:17: the coming of YHWH in 63:4 is the year of vengeance, while vengeance is YHWH's armor in 59:17. In both texts, salvation (59:16–17//63:1) and redemption (59:20//63:4) are involved with the theophany as well. YHWH is motivated by wrath (חמה) in both texts (63:3, 5, 6//59:18). In short, YHWH the Divine Warrior is engaged in the war motivated by divine wrath to exact judgment with an ultimate view to salvation and redemption. Thus, two passages are closely related to each other, and this is why it has been argued that the two passages form a framework for the chs 60–62.[23]

Meanwhile, Vermeylen rejects the idea of 'literary framework,' although he also observes the common elements in the twin passages such as vengeance, redemption, salvation and righteousness as well as the garment of YHWH.[24] First, for him, chs 60–62 are not homogeneous or a closed whole. Thus, it is unnecessary for 63:1–6 to mark a closure of the chapters as an important landmark. Second, several theological differences between 59:15b–21 and 63:1–6 suggest that the latter reinterprets the former, so the two passages are not written at the same time, but 63:1–6 is the second reading of 59:15b–21.[25] For Vermeylen, there is a significant difference between 59:16 and 63:5, which are often considered as a literary link—while צדקה, which sustains YHWH, was associated with justice to be exercised in favour of the persecuted community in 59:16, it is '(re-)interpreted' in 63:5 in a punitive sense ("my own wrath sustained me").[26] The reason for clothing is also different in both places: while in 59:15b–21 it is for the salvation of Israel, in 63:1–6 it is to slaughter the nations—the enemies in 59:18 are identified with the nations in 63:3 and 6 by the interpretation of author. Besides, 63:1–6 shows no concern for the conversion of sinners contrary to 59:15b–21.[27]

---

22. Koenen 1990:84.

23. Muilenburg 1954:724; Koenen 1990:83; Fisher 1939:187–88.

24. Vermeylen 1978:469.

25. Vermeylen 1978:469.

26. Vermeylen 1978:469–70.

27. Vermeylen 1978:470.

However, the priority of chronological order of the passages has been disputed, and a consensus has not been reached yet.[28] For Ruszukowski, 63:1–6 is assumed and reinterpreted in 59:15b–21, since 63:1–6 is related to the external enemies, which is archaic, while in 59:15b–21, the enemies are more abstract and general 'enemies of YHWH.'[29] So, for him, "for typological reasons Isa 63:1–6 is still to be placed before 59:15b–21."[30] For Koenen, however, 59:15b–21 and 63:1–6 are written by the same hand.[31] A literal parallel is found between 59:16 and 63:5. The phrase אֵין־אִישׁ also provides a connection between 59:16 and 63:3. However, while in 59:16 there was no man/intervener, there was no helper/supporter in 63:6. YHWH is supported by his righteousness in ch 59, but by his wrath in ch 63. The garment is for vengeance in 59:17; it is blood-stained in 63:1–3. For him, these differences do not form a different date or authorship. But, while salvation is emphasized in 59:15b–21, the wrath of YHWH (חמה x3, אף x2) dominates 63:1–6.[32] For Koenen, the coming of salvation is achieved by the final theophany to Zion. The coming of YHWH is the fulfilment of the promise of imminent salvation in 56:1b, as בוא (56:1; 63:1) corresponds to 59:20. So, the theophany in 63:1–6 also fulfils the promise in 59:20 as well as in 56:1.[33] For Koenen, judgment is prepared in ch 59, while it is carried out in ch 63, because the sequence of the coming of YHWH may be judgment → coming of YHWH → salvation.[34]

In order to define the literary relationship between 59:15b–21 and 63:1–6, historical concerns can shed little light on the theological implications of the passages in the present form of the canon. Our concern is the canonical intention of the twin passages in the structure of TI, functioning as a framework for chapters 60–62, as often suggested.[35] If we admit that the coming of YHWH is for the dual purpose of salvation/reward and judgment/punishment, as we shall see in 3.3, and if we also assume a bigger,

---

28. 59:15b–21 is original for Vermeylen (1991:470, 489) and Volz (1932:263). For Duhm (1892:445), Westermann (1969:279), Whybray (1981:226), and Sekine (1989:145), 63:1–6 is older than 59:15b–21. See Koenen 1990:83. For Bonnard (1974:392), the two texts come from the same author, or two authors share the inspiration with each other. For Budde and Fisher, 59:15b–21 and 63:1–6 form a single unit. See Childs 2001:515; Pauritsch 1971:138; Koenen 1990:83.

29. Ruszukowski 2000:70.

30. Ruszukowski 2000:49.

31. Koenen 1990:84.

32. Koenen 1990:84.

33. Koenen 1990:85.

34. Koenen 1990:85.

35. Muilenburg 1954:724; Koenen 1990:84.

coherent theology that covers both salvation and judgment as intention(s) of the coming YHWH, then the alleged differences may not be present, the coming of YHWH being viewed as a coherent and consistent whole. Theological differences in the two passages do not necessarily suggest that the two passages are different events, but that they present different aspects of a single theophanic event. Vermeylen's observation of the heterogeneity of chs 60–62 does not necessarily negate the idea of framework, since the objection seems to be based on a fragmented understanding rather than on a more comprehensive theology. Chs 60–62 have often been argued as unity (see 4.2). In fact, as Beuken observed, 63:1 announces the achievement of the coming of YHWH in 59:20 (also Koenen), focusing on the terrifying aspects of the judgment of the coming YHWH. This judgment in 63:1 has already taken place in Edom. Thus, for Beuken, 63:1–6 is an event that should come before the glory of Zion, but now is told retrospectively.[36] This suggests that 59:15b–21 and 63:1–6 form a single and unified, but complex, description of the coming of YHWH. It has been generally suggested that the twin passages 59:15b–21 and 63:1–6 form a framework for the eschatological message of the core of TI, chs 60–62.[37]

Secondly, chs 60–62 (predominantly ch 60) are the consequence of the coming of YHWH in 59:15b–21, which is the eschatological divine action. This is because: (1) the coming of YHWH and His glory in 59:15b–21 recurs in 60:1–3—the one functioning as promise, the other as fulfilment. (2) The light metaphor in 59:9–10 is connected to that in 60:1–3.[38] The people of sin walk in darkness (חשך), gloom (אפלה) and twilight or night (נשף) (58:10; 59:9, 10). The people who are in the darkness at present hope for the light. This hope may be achieved in the future through the salvation brought by the coming of YHWH. According to Torrey, 59:1–15a, as darkness (judgment), is contrasted to ch 60, as light (salvation). For him, 59:9–10 have a literary connection with 58:10 in that they share the light-darkness contrast (אפלה-צהר, חשך-אור). Thus, the contrast in 58:10 prefigures the canonical structure of chs 59 and 60.[39] Violence and destruction (שד ושבר) are in their ways in 59:7, while they are no more within the border in 60:18.[40] They do not know the way of peace (שלום) in 59:8, while peace becomes their officers in 60:17. The glory of YHWH is promised to be revealed in 59:19

---

36. Beuken 1989a:248.

37. Beuken 1989a:246; Westermann 1969:296–308; Emmerson 1992:15–20.

38. Koenen 1990:71; Seitz 2001:504–5; Torrey 1928:439–40.

39. Torrey 1928:439–40.

40. שד ושבר uniquely occurs there in the OT, although שד והשבר in 51:19 may also be related.

and is proclaimed to have come in 60:1–2. The Redeemer will come to those who turn from their sins in Jacob in 59:20, while YHWH will be revealed as their Redeemer, the Mighty One of Israel, in 60:16.[41] If this is the case, the alleged theological discontinuity between chs 60–62 and ch 59 (for example, no words of condemnation of sins in chs 60–62[42] and the lack of the inner-community struggle in that section, which are dominant in chs 56–59 and 65–66) is not persuasive and does not suggest evidence of a different theology or authorship between the two sections. It rather reflects the canonical intention (the authorial meaning of the text in the canonical context) which emphasizes continuity of the bigger theology: due to the universal judgment of the coming YHWH in 59:15b–21, the new era has come in chs 60–62 and only the eschatologically saved people are described there (see 3.3). That is, the opponents and oppressors of the servants are removed by the judgment either within Israel or in the nations and do not enter the eschatological Zion, as discussed later (3.3).

Thirdly, the coming of YHWH in 63:1–6 also fulfils the promise of the coming in chs 60–62 (especially, ch 62) as the literary links are undeniable.[43] This is because: (1) the coming conqueror, being able to save in 63:1, revisits the theme of the coming of salvation which is announced in 62:11.[44] So the theophany in 63:1–6 is the fulfilment of the expectation in ch 62. (2) 63:4 affirms that redemption is to be achieved, as is anticipated in 62:12.[45] 63:4 also suggests that the divine work in 63:1–6 is the fulfilment of the day of vengeance in 61:2 (or vice versa).[46] (3) The theme of vindication (צדקה ; ישע) in 63:1 takes up from 62:1–2 (צדקה ; ישועה).[47] Salvation and righteousness are the controlling concepts of chs 60–62.[48] (4) 63:1 suggests that the sentries who are set in 62:6–7 are on duty to see the Redeemer come.[49] So the dialogue in 63:1–3 is between them.[50] (5) Furthermore, 63:1–6 extends the topic of vintage from 62:8–9.[51] For Koenen, only after the destruction of the

41. Ruszukowski 2000:61–62.

42. Whybray 1981:229; Smart 1967:256.

43. Koenen 1990:82; Smith 1995:43.

44. Beuken 1989a:248; Smith 1995:43. See 3.2.4, for the identification of the two.

45. Smith 1995:43.

46. Lau 1994:279; Muilenburg 1954:724; Koenen 1990:82. See 6.3.2.

47. Seitz 2001:518.

48. Koenen 1990:82, 83.

49. Westermann 1969:380; Seitz 2001:518.

50. Seitz 2001:518; Whybray 1981:252; Westermann 1969:380; Vermeylen 1977–78:490.

51. Vermeylen 1977–78:490.

enemy nations, can Israel have rest and enjoy the fruits prophesied in 62:8–9.[52] Therefore, although 63:1–6 lacks the description of salvation (in fact, this is implied in 63:1, 4), while chs 60–62 portray salvation in terms of the glory of Zion, the message of the passage is not alien to that of chs 60–62.[53] So, for Koenen, 63:1–6 was written in the light of chs 60–62.[54] For Beuken, chs 60–62 do not break the original link of 59:15b–21 and 63:1–6. Rather, 63:1–6 is related not only to 59:15b–21 but also to ch 62,[55] because the question, which the sentry asks to the coming one in 63:1, refers to both 59:18–20 and 62:11.[56]

With these observations, we may suggest that the twin theophanic passages (59:15b–21; 63:1–6) present a formal indication that chs 60–62 are an eschatological portrayal which is closely related to the coming of YHWH in 59:15b–21 and 63:1–6. Chapter 63:1–6 describes the coming of YHWH as already accomplished (this is retrospective), while in 59:15b–21 the coming is described as in the future (this is prospective).[57] As Koenen comments, the eschatological judgment prepared in 59:15b–21 is carried out in 63:1–6, the two forming a unified whole.[58] Thus, 59:15b–21 and 63:1–6 describe the one divine war of the coming YHWH from different perspectives. The twin theophanic passages form the background of chs 60–62, and the glorification of Zion in chs 60–62 is the result of the coming of YHWH in 59:15b–21 and 63:1–6.[59] The eschatological era comes in chs 60–62 only after the divine war in 59:15b–21 and 63:1–6. As Childs has argued, eschatological salvation has to be preceded by divine judgment.[60] The coming of YHWH (59:15b–21; 60:1–3; 62:11; 63:1–6) becomes the prerequisite of the glorification of Zion (chs 60–62), which is achieved only after the warlike judgment by the coming YHWH.

In conclusion, 59:15b–21 fulfills the eschatological expectation(s) of the preceding parts of TI (especially, 56:1–8),[61] and, together with 63:1–6,

52. Koenen 1990:83.

53. Oswalt 1998:594–95. Holmgren (1974:137–42) even contends for the unity of chs 60–62 and 63:1–6 in terms of authorship.

54. Koenen 1990:83.

55. Beuken 1989a:246.

56. Beuken 1989a:248.

57. Alexander 1846b:413; Beuken 1989a:247; Lau 1994:280.

58. Koenen 1990:85. Kissane (1943:255) sees that 63:1–6 forms a logical consequence of 59:15b–21 in that the latter describes YHWH prepares the war while the former portrays YHWH Who completes the war with victory.

59. In this reason, Kissane (1943:256) posits 63:1–6 just before ch 60.

60. Childs 2001:519. For Kissane (1943:256), 63:1–6 has to be put logically between 59:15b–21 and ch 60.

61. Polan 1986:315.

also forms a literary framework for the chapters 60–62 as has often been suggested.[62] 59:15b–21 is closely related not only to the introductory section 56:1–8 as well as 59:1–15a, but also to 63:1–6, the twin theophanic passage. It is also related to chs 56–59 and 60–62 as well, without interrupting the narrative continuity. In regard to the preceding context, the promise of the coming salvation is achieved, the inability of the people to observe justice and righteousness as required in 56:1–8 is overcome by the coming YHWH, and the admonition urging people to join the covenant in 56:1–8 is fulfilled in 59:15b–21. In relation to the following context, the coming of YHWH in 59:15b–21 results in the salvific era in chs 60–62; salvation as well as righteousness and justice expected in chs 60–62, are fulfilled by 63:1–6, which is a complementary section of the theophanic event of 59:15b–21. Only after the divine work in the theophanic event, is the eschatological vision of chs 60–62 realized.

3.3 Theological Interpretation of the Text

This section tries to show that an eschatological era opens with the decisive coming of YHWH, which is caused by the breach of the covenant due to the sins of the people. The coming YHWH carries out judgment as well as salvation, ultimately with a view to the restoration of the covenant. Not only the identification of the enemies that are to be punished, but also the scope of salvation of the coming YHWH will be elaborated. In the concept of the 'coming of YHWH,' the sending of an envoy of YHWH is included, who functions as a Messianic figure.

15b YHWH saw it, and it displeased him that there was no justice.	וירא יהוה וירע בעיניו כי־אין משפט:

This verse presents the divine reaction to the sinful state of the people and their responses to it in 59:1–15a (or, chs 56–59). Because there was no justice, YHWH was not pleased.

What motivates YHWH to come in 59:15b–21? YHWH's intervention in the passage is based on His decision to deal with the sins of the people according to His perception of the injustice in the community, as portrayed in 59:15b–16a, and His appraisal thereof. YHWH realized (ראה) that there was no justice in the community, and no man and intercessor (59:16), which was displeasing to Him (וירע בעיניו). The verb ראה in 59:15b and 16a expresses the cause/motive of theophany, as it denotes YHWH's

---

62. Muilenburg 1954:724; Koenen 1990:84.

recognition of the situation and connects sin with theophany.[63] Not only the conjunction ו but also מֹשֶׁפָּט, the absence of which YHWH saw, connect this verse to the previous passage (59:9–15a), which is characterized by the breach of the covenant (see 3.2).[64]

The coming intervention of YHWH is to enforce the covenant. It is noteworthy that the phrase וַיֵּרַע בְּעֵינָיו (be evil before YHWH; 59:15b) is the Deuteronomic evaluation formula (1:16; 65:12; 66:4; Deut 4:25; 9:18; 17:2; 31:29), which refers to the evils that give rise to the curses of the covenant tradition.[65] In the Deuteronomic verses, the formula refers to the breach of the Mosaic Covenant, including specifically the violation of the first Commandment.[66] This suggests that the divine evaluation of the injustice of Israel in 59:15b could be related to the Mosaic Covenant.

Furthermore, as discussed in 2.3, in/justice (מֹשֶׁפָּט) is the key concept in the sin of the people (59:4, 8, 9, 11, 14, 15; cf. 58:2), relating to the covenantal order. Justice here has a more nuanced human (and social) character, but as we have discussed in chapter 2, the moral order and divine salvation are closely related as justice (59:15) and righteousness (59:16) have a double-sided meaning—the lack of human justice causes YHWH to come to restore it by bringing his justice and salvation.[67] The divine intervention is due to the prospect of no self-improvement in Israel.[68]

YHWH's response is also a reaction to the response of the people to their sins. Since 59:15b–21 is closely related to the previous passage (59:9–15a), it is natural to think that YHWH's intervention responds to the lamentation and appeal of the people in 59:9–15a. As Kissane observed, the thought process of 59:15–16 is very similar to that of 57:17–19: iniquity/injustice → divine anger → divine perception → intervention for salvation (restoration, peace, and healing).[69] In addition, there are many parallel words in the

63. Westermann 1969:350, 352; Beuken 1989a:142.

64. Pauritsch 1971:92. The key words (justice/righteousness and salvation/justice) of 59:9–15a look back to 56:1–8, in which those words stand for the covenantal order (see chapter 2).

65. Koenen 1990:68.

66. Deut 4:25 (עָשָׂה הָרַע בְּעֵינֵי יהוה) is related to the first Commandment. In Deut 9:18 (לַעֲשׂוֹת הָרַע בְּעֵינֵי יהוה), the evil refers to the rebellion of making Golden Calf idol. In Deut 17:2 (יַעֲשֶׂה אֶת־הָרַע בְּעֵינֵי יהוה-אֱלֹהֶיךָ), it refers to the break of the Mosaic Covenant especially by the worship of idols. In Deut 31:29 (תַּעֲשׂוּ אֶת הָרַע בְּעֵינֵי יהוה), it also refers to the whole Covenant tradition which Moses established for Israel. Koenen 1990:74; Wildberger 1991:48–49.

67. Beuken 1989a:143.

68. Skinner 1960:192; Muilenburg 1954:694; Delitzsch 1873:403.

69. Kissane 1943:250.

two texts.[70] Thus, the text 57:14–21 (or, more specifically 57:17–19) may illuminate the divine perception and motivation for saving in 59:15b–21, that is, the intention of YHWH for intervention. There is no explanation of the process leading from divine perception to divine intervention in 57:18: As soon as He saw him (=? Zion), He promised to heal him. However, 57:15 suggests two aspects of divine motivation for action: His nature that He dwells with the contrite and lowly of spirit and His purpose to revive the spirit/heart (לב/רוח) of the lowly/contrite (דכא/שפל).[71] In this connection, it seems evident that mourning (57:18b) and the fruit of lips (57:19a), which follow repentance, are actually associated with divine motivation which should come in between the perception and the intervention in 57:18a. This may also be supported by the fact that YHWH as Redeemer (i.e., the saving response of YHWH) comes (only) to those who denounce sins in 59:20. In conclusion, the motivation of YHWH lies partly with His nature (holy but dwelling with the lowly) and partly with the responsive attitude of the people (mourning and contrition), which in turn reinforces that the divine intervention in 59:15b–21 is based on the repentance of the people in 59:9–15a, exactly as the canonical form has intimated.[72]

In conclusion, YHWH recognized the situation of the sinful people. It was actually a breach of the covenant, characterized by the lack of justice, which made YHWH furious. The people's penitent response (cf. 57:18b, 19a; 59:9–15a, 20) may be another motive for the coming YHWH to save them.

16 He saw that there was no man,	וירא כי־אין איש
and wondered that there was no one to intercede;	וישתומם כי אין מפגיע
then His own arm brought Him salvation,	ותושע לו זרעו
and His righteousness upheld Him.	וצדקתו היא סמכתהו:

This verse continues the perception and appraisal of YHWH in 59:15b that motivates Him to act—to save as well as to punish. YHWH sees that there was no man and no intercessor (59:16a) and relies on His own arm to bring salvation and righteousness (59:16b).

---

70. Parallel are: עון (iniquity, 57:17//59:2, 3, 4, 6, 7, 12), סתר (to hide, 57:17//59:2), הלך (to go/walk, 57:17//59:9), דרך (way, 57:14, 17//59:8), לב (heart, 57:15, 17//59:13), רעה (to see, 57:18//59:15, 16), שלום (peace, 57:19 (x2), 21//59:8 (x2)), and רחוק (far away, 57:19//59:14). Jones (1964:63) also has noticed of the divine perception in 57:18.

71. This is in fact a strong paradox since holiness implies distinctiveness.

72. According to Whybray, the promise of salvation (59:15b–21) is not logically in close connection with 59:1–15a. According to Koenen, Budde and Feldmann are in a sense supportive for Whybray in that they see 59:15b–20(21) as later addition. However, with Childs it is possible to interpret the chapter in its canonical form. Whybray 1981:220; Koenen 1990:67; Childs 2001:484–90.

Why does YHWH see that 'there was no man'—what does it mean? First, it may signify that there is no man who is able to solve the problem of injustice in Israel and thus divine intervention is required, charging the leaders of Israel.[73] Because there was no responsible and righteous leader (cf. 51:18), justice is missing. The image of man in this case may be warrior, as the word איש can occasionally signify (1 Sam 4:9 and 1 King 2:2).[74] Historical figures such as Cyrus and Nehemiah have been suggested as possible, but it cannot be proved, because the language of the passage is insufficient to connect with a historical situation.[75] Nevertheless, this interpretation is not entirely discounted, as both the leaders and the lay people have been accused in chs 56–59.

Second, it may signify that 'there is no righteous man at all' to emphasize the total corruption of Israel especially in regard to the preceding context. The idea may have an analogy in Jer 5:1, in which no one is upright at all, so that the punishment falls on the city (the situation is similar), because איש and משפט are parallel in Jer 5:1 and 59:15–16. This view contrasts human inability and divine power to intervene in the situation, as Bonnard interprets the phrase as "with his [=YHWH's] own power."[76] Although this interpretation takes into account the immediate preceding context, it does not refer to the parallel 'no intervener.' Nevertheless, this view cannot be wholly discarded.

Third, the '(no) man' may also signify the 'helper' or 'counselor' that may help YHWH. This would emphasize the sovereignty of YHWH in judgment as in creation in 40:12–14; 41:28; and 44:24.[77] For Whybray, the links with DI show YHWH alone created the universe without the help of other gods, demonstrating the "superiority of the monotheistic Israelite traditions of creation over those of other nations, especially those of Babylon."[78] For Beuken, creation is an archetype of the exodus and redemption, achievement

73. Herbert 1975:152.

74. The predominant imageries of man in the Bible that are related to the public life may be the warrior, king, shepherd, teacher/preacher, elder/leader, etc. See Ryken 1998:531 and 533.

75. Whybray 1981:226; Skinner 1960:192; Duhm 1892:404. Duhm (1892:404) suggests Cyrus, but Muilenburg (1954:694) rejects this view. While Skinner (1960:192) rejects Nehemiah, Whybray (1981:226) accepts it.

76. Bonnard 1972:392.

77. Beuken 1989a:251; Muilenburg 1954:694. The 41:28 is more probable in literal connectivity.

78. Whybray 1981:53–54, 70. 'No man' in DI context may be interrelated with the emphasis on the sovereignty of YHWH over the void idols (40:12–26, especially 40:18, 25). According to him, Marduk is unable to create the universe by himself, but only with the help of his father Ea.

of YHWH alone.[79] This is supported by another link of 'no man' in 50:2, in which the motif is related to the exodus theme.[80] For Westermann, too, the aloneness of YHWH reflects the mythical idea that YHWH struggles with the chaos monster (Ps 74:13–14; Isa 51:9)—in myth, the cosmic battle is between two persons alone.[81] However, an objection may be raised because there is no reference to the creation or exodus in the context, which is social and contemporary. But, the language of the divine actions in the passage is mythicalized referring to the heavenly realm, coming to be divorced from a specific historical event. Hanson calls the passage a Divine Warrior Hymn, although the theophany may ultimately be anchored in the historical realm (see 1.3). In short, the 'no man' refers to the 'aloneness of YHWH' in the heavenly realm. This view takes note of the literary connections with DI texts, which are understood in parallel with the mythical thinking, as the passage is known as the Divine Warrior Hymn (see 1.3).

Fourth, it may also foreshadow the concept of a mediator as a divine agent: this is based on the parallelism in the verse as well as literary links with DI.[82] In this case, the "man" is understood to be virtually interchangeable with the "מפגיע" (intercessor, intercession [or, intervention]; // "no man"). According to Seitz, "no man" refers to the work of the Servant (53:12, ולפשעים יפגיע) as the parallel פגע indicates.[83] This literary connection may be reinforced by the "arm" that is found not only in 59:16, but also in 53:1 and 52:10, in which the arm of YHWH is revealed in the work of the Servant.[84] It is parallel in both places (chs 53 and 59) that the problem is the sin(s) of the people. As scholars have noticed, the Servant bore the transgression of Israel in ch 53; the arm of YHWH takes charge of it to bring salvation and righteousness in ch 59, because there is no man or מפגיע. The contrasting link of "no man" with the Servant's work in DI may also be strengthened by the fact that the "no man" in 41:28 is related to the reason why YHWH gives in 41:27 the herald of good tidings (מבשר), who is identified with the Servant

79. Beuken 1989a:251.

80. For Beuken (1989a:143) and Childs (2001:485), ch 50 may be in the background of ch 59 because of 59:16//50:2 (no man) and 59:1–3//50:2 (sin and complaints).

81. Westermann 1969:382. Seitz (2001:520) also supports this idea of mythical origin, considering that the motif is "closely related to another DI's conception: God's sovereign incomparability, here extended to the martial sphere."

82. This idea may be found in Ezek 22:30. Take note of משפט in 22:29 (//ch 59), and the image may be similar to that of sentry in Isa 62.

83. Seitz 2001:502; Beuken 1989a:143. Jones (1964:63) and Oswalt (1998:528) also see the connection.

84. The divine arm motif appears in the book of Isaiah in 9:20; 17:5; 30:30; 33:2; 40:10, 11; 48:14; 51:5, 9; 52:10; 53:1; 59:16; 62:8; 63:5. In 44:12, idol's arm; in 63:12, Moses' arm.

in 42:1.[85] The comment on the absence of a mediator speaks of his necessity (the mediator is sent in 59:19–21; see below). Because of the absence of a mediator, YHWH has to rely on His own arm (59:16), which is revealed as (the work of) the Servant in the fourth Servant Song (52:13—53:12), who is identified in turn with the envoy sent in 59:19–21. In conclusion, not only "no man" but also "(no) intercessor" and the "divine arm" have recalled that YHWH has worked Himself in (the work of) the Servant by His own arm. This may suggest necessity of the role of the mediator/intercessor, but also that the role of the mediating figure here, if any, may be considered as the work of YHWH Himself (see 59:19–21). The apparent contradiction between 'no (other) man' (aloneness of YHWH) and the Servant figure who is sent on behalf of YHWH may show a tension between identification and differentiation of the figure with YHWH as is evidenced in the arm of YHWH, which signified the figure. In short, the aloneness of YHWH, which is revealed by the arm of YHWH, refers to the Servant in DI, who has intervened/interceded for the sake of the people's sins.

Do we have to choose one of the four understandings? None of these can be entirely rejected—rather, each has some measure of truth. Especially, the third and fourth interpretations are affirmed due to the intertextual links to DI, while the first two may fit the immediate context. This is the way how TI develops the message of DI.[86]

The words such as ראה, רעע בעיניו, and משפט that are used to describe the divine perception and evaluation in 59:15b–16 evidence the image of YHWH as Judge.[87] As Jones rightly pointed out, the image of the Warrior God, which is evidenced not only by the arm of YHWH but also by the armoury with which He equips Himself in 59:17, is mixed up with that of Judge in the passage.[88] YHWH is a Judge–Warrior who makes a judicial decision about the people in accordance with the observations and His character and, at the same time, who goes to battle to implement His decision. If we admit to Brettler's analysis about the metaphor of divine image of YHWH, He is King as the metaphors of judge and warrior are sub-metaphors of king—the metaphoric fields overlap but can cohere in the concept of king.[89]

85. Beuken 1989c:418.

86. TI takes the vision of DI and develops it by adding new elements or applying it to the new situation, i.e., the eschatological horizon, as in 56:1–8; 60:1–22; and 65:13–25.

87. Jones 1964:63.

88. Jones 1964:63. He suggested that the mixture of images is not unusual in the Biblical prophecies. Kissane (1943:250) also notices the image of judge. Also see Delitzsch 1873:404.

89. Brettler 1989:160.

YHWH as Judge acknowledged that no man is involved, so He relies on his own arm and righteousness. The parallel of divine salvation and righteousness refers back to 56:1b, in which eschatological salvation is announced. This implies that the coming of YHWH in this passage (59:15b–21) is in fact the fulfilment of the proclamation of the eschatological salvation in 56:1–8 (see 3.2).

In brief, YHWH's recognition and mention of 'no man' not only emphasizes the aloneness of YHWH in undertaking the eschatological task as revealed in the creation, but also foreshadows the intermediate figure, whose task is considered as YHWH's own, as part of His eschatological enterprise. The phrase refers back to the Suffering Servant in DI. The coming YHWH is the King, i.e., the Judge-Warrior.

17 He put on righteousness as a breastplate,	וילבש צדקה כשרין
and a helmet of salvation on His head;	וכובע ישועה בראשו
He put on garments of vengeance for clothing,	וילבש בגדי נקם תלבשת
and wrapped Himself in zeal as a cloak.	ויעט כמעיל קנאה:

In this verse, YHWH arms Himself with righteousness, salvation, vengeance, and zeal with a view to undertaking the eschatological task. This reveals the portrait of the coming YHWH as a Divine Warrior engaged in the battle.[90]

Where does the Divine Warrior imagery come from? The words in 59:17 such as breastplate (שרין), helmet (כובע), garments (בגד), clothing (תלבשת), and mantle (מעיל), as well as the arm of YHWH in 59:16, expand upon the imagery of YHWH as warrior—this may be an original, creative interpretation of the traditional undeveloped idea of God as a warrior.[91] The Divine Warrior image belongs to the Divine Warrior tradition, which is familiar in the book of Isaiah (12:1–6; 40:10; 42:13; 49:24–25; 52:10; 63:1–6; cf. Exod 15:3).[92] According to this tradition in Isaiah, the might and victory of YHWH are emphasized: YHWH is my strength, song, and salvation (12:2). He will come with might, with His arm ruling for Him—reward (שכר) and recompense (פעלה), i.e., the spoils of victory, are with Him

90. For Beuken (1989a:144), YHWH is preparing a battle.

91. It is widely agreed that this verse is the prototype of Eph 6:13–17. (Also see Wisd 5:17ff. and 1 Thess 5:8.) Oswalt 1998:528; Whybray 1981:227; Muilenburg 1954:695; Kissane 1943:250. According to Neufeld (1997:154), the mythological imagery of the Divine Warrior is recognized in ch 59, the tradition of which culminating in Eph 6:10–20.

92. Skinner 1960:193; Kissane 1943:241, 250; Whybray 1981:227; Westermann 1969:351; Muilenburg 1954:694; Beuken 1989a:144. VanGemeren (1990:454?) also includes 12:1–6. As for the divine zeal as a motivation of YHWH's salvation, see especially 9:6[7], 26:11, 37:32, 42:13, and 63:15. Motyer 1993:491.

(40:10).[93] He is Warrior (כאיש מלחמות), who has zeal (42:13). YHWH is mighty enough to save the people from the power of the enemy (49:24–25).[94] In 52:10, the holy arm of YHWH is disclosed before the nations, so that all the ends of the earth will see the salvation (i.e., victory) of YHWH. The Divine Warrior tradition or imagery is based on the exodus tradition, because 42:13 is linked with Exod 15:3 (איש מלחמה) and because the arm of YHWH (59:16) originates from the exodus tradition (Exod 15:16) and the old salvation formula "with strong hand and outstretched arm" (Deut 4:34; 5:15).[95] For Muilenburg, too, "The [Divine Warrior] imagery is related to the great conflict and triumph of the day of YHWH."[96] According to Jeremias, the purpose of the coming of YHWH as warrior has been changed in the book of Isaiah: to battle against the foreign nations (19:1), to free Israel (40:10–11, 42:13), and to fight against the wicked in Israel (59:15–19; 66:15–16).[97] However, within the overall theology of the book of Isaiah, this view cannot be maintained. Even in PI, YHWH rises and takes His place in court to judge the people of Israel due to their sins (3:14; 1:24–28; 29:1–4);[98] even in DI, the nations will also be saved (40:5; as we shall see in 4.3); in TI, YHWH will battle against the enemies in the nations, too (59:18; 63:3, 6; 66:15–16). Although there may be differences of emphasis from place to place (or, from time to time), the purpose of His coming has been coherent and consistent—He always fights against sin/sinners in His coming (1:28) as we shall see later (59:18).

What is the nature of the judgment at the coming of YHWH? Being prompted by the iniquities of the people, the divine judgment is retributive as evidenced in 59:17b–18—not only against the sinners, but also to the righteous. The coming of YHWH is (on) the day of vengeance (61:2; 63:4; so von Rad; see 1.3). YHWH intends to repay (שלם) the iniquities and repay the wicked individually (ושלמתי על־חיקם, 65:6). He will render recompense to his enemies (משלם גמול לאיביו, 66:6). In these verses, the punitive aspect of repayment is seemingly emphasized, but the positive side should not be neglected. Recompense also vindicates or rewards the righteous, because the keywords such as vengeance (נקם), recompense ((ה)גמול), and repay (שלם) imply both salvation and judgment as the actions of the coming YHWH. Although it was judged that there was no man doing righteousness

93. Whybray 1981:52.
94. Whybray 1981:147.
95. Pauritsch 1971:98.
96. Muilenburg 1954:695.
97. Jeremias 1984:898.
98. Roberts 1982a:107.

and justice, YHWH's salvation/redemption is given to the repentant (see 59:15b and 20).

(1) *Vengeance* (נקם).[99] As God of the covenant, YHWH may implement vengeance against not only the nations but also Israel (see below), aiming at the reconstruction of justice and the reinstallation of the covenant.[100] In 1:24, vengeance is on the Israelite ringleaders, called 'My enemies,' who corrupted the community (1:21–26), thus signifying punitive judgment on them (negative sense).[101] However, with the terminology 'day of vengeance' (61:2; 63:4; 34:8; cf. 35:4), divine vengeance is not only an exhibition of divine wrath on the nations (63:6; 34:2) but it saves Israel (or, His people) (63:1; 35:4) (positive sense).[102] The word thus is not necessarily negative: it may signify both judgment and salvation (positive sense) of Israel and the nations.

(2) *Recompense* ((גמול(ה).[103] Recompense ((גמול(ה), which is often used in conjunction with שלם, being rendered as repayment or requital, is the principle by which YHWH deals with the people in accordance with their deeds, whether they are the righteous or the wicked. It can be either a "manifestation of love" or a "manifestation of the wrath" of YHWH,[104] and thus mean not only punishment but also reward.[105] While in 59:18 and 66:6,

99. The word נקם (as nominal), tinted originally with a legal connotation, can be interpreted as vengeance, revenge, or requital. Vengeance is related to lawfulness, justice, and salvation, and thus, the divine vengeance may be defined as retributive administration of God with a view to maintenance of justice. These words do without any negative connotations such as cruelty, arbitrariness, and illegitimacy that the modern terms may have. This is primarily because the nuances change as the term is applied to YHWH.

100. The divine vengeance against the nations is usually because of unlimited lust of power (e.g., Isa 47:3) or because Israel's existence is threatened (e.g., Num 31:2, Deut 32:35). Breaking of the covenant by the people of Israel may also cause the divine vengeance on them (Lev 26:15). Sauer 1997b, TLOT (2):768; Peels 1997a, NIDOTTE (3):154–56.

101. Not only נקם is parallel in 1:24 and 59:17, the two words denoting enemy, i.e., צר and איב, also come both in 1:24 and 59:18. The word seems to carry mainly the negative sense in 47:3.

102. The concept of Israel transfers to that of the people of YHWH.

103. Recompense ((גמול(ה) is an accomplishment of one's own initiation as the verbal form גמל underlies the subsequent development of an action as in 3:9. Recompense ((גמול(ה) may be rendered as repayment or requital. The word is used often in conjunction with שלם. Sauer 1997a, TLOT (1):321; Carpenter 1997, NIDOTTE (1):872–73.

104. Sauer 1997a:321; Carpenter 1997:872–73; Delitzsch 1873:405. As Delitzsch (1873:405) commented, it can denote either "retribution as looked at from the side of God" or "forfeiture as regarded from the side of man." (In regard to the theological discussion about the divine perspective and human perspective of the retribution, further study will be needed.)

105. 59:18a contains both salvation of the people and judgment of the adversaries;

judgment is emphasized because the divine recompense is (told) to be imposed on the enemies (negative sense), in 35:4 the recompense will result in the salvation of Zion (positive sense).

(3) *Repayment* (שלם).[106] שלם with YHWH as its subject may mean, negatively, the retribution or the revenge of YHWH on Israel's sins or on the enemies and, positively, it can also mean reward or repayment for the good deeds of the people, as it takes 'comfort' as the object in 57:18.[107] The repayment of the enemies in 65:6 and 66:6 also brings vindication of the servants as well, the punishment of evil being accompanied by the vindication and salvation of the righteous as portrayed in 65:8–16 and in 66:7–14.[108] Positively, those who depart from their sins are "repaid" with redemption and the covenant (59:20, 21).

While vengeance is an activity which aims at the restoration of violated righteousness/justice relations within the community, zeal is the "inner drive of the holiness of God," by which YHWH maintains covenantal order.[109] While the divine קנאה in 63:15 is for Israel, in 59:17 it may be both 'for' those who depart from sin (59:20) and 'against' the enemies (59:18).[110] These two are not distinguished chronologically because judgment/ salvation/ punishment are done at the same time in the actions of the coming YHWH. The divine קנאה may support Him whether He exerts salvation or judgment on Israel and the nations. So, it, too, may have both a negative and a positive sense.[111]

59:18b emphasizes the aspect of judgment on the foes; and 59:18c does not seem to concern whether the islands will be saved or judged.

106. As the basic meaning of the word שלם is "to repay," it may mean the retribution or the revenge of YHWH on the Israel's sins or on the enemies and it can also mean reward or repayment to the good deeds of the people. According to Nel (1997, NIDOTTE [4]:130–31), the commonly known sense of שלום (peace, wholeness, soundness, or completeness) is one that is overemphasized. The verb, the most of Biblical instances of which having YHWH as its subject, can be used either positively or negatively.

107. Nel 1997, NIDOTTE (4):130–31.

108. For the positive and negative aspects of the repayment, see Sauer 1997a, TLOT (1):321; Carpenter 1997a, NIDOTTE (1):872–73.

109. Beuken 1989a:145; Muilenburg 1954:695.

110. For the identification of the enemies, see below.

111. The angry, fierce reaction of YHWH's קנאה against Israel is usually because of the infringement of the divine honor due to their idolatry or their breach of the covenant. This implies the negative sense of divine קנאה towards the people (and the positive sense of His קנאה toward His own honor). The divine קנאה against the nations is usually because Israel, the covenant partner of YHWH, is threatened in existence and security by her enemies. This implies that YHWH has a positive sense of קנאה toward His people because of His compassion and pity on them. Peels 1997b:938–39; Sauer 1997c, TLOT (3):1146–47.

The shift of tense from perfect in 59:15b–17 to imperfect in 59:18–20 seems to designate a change in the heavenly realm.[112] Even though Whybray has felt in the change of tense an impression of patchwork that the two passages are not originally a single composition, he eventually admitted a certain continuity of situation.[113] Muilenburg considers that the past tense is a prophetic perfect of certainty, which displays a certain future event.[114] According to Childs, however, the past tense means the action of YHWH in the past, which has been hidden but is now expressed for the first time, while 59:18 expresses the future execution of judgment.[115] For Beuken, the narrative tense is not prophetic perfect, which describes the future as if it has already happened, but it "recovers the past as example of what is to happen again."[116] It seems to me that since the Divine Warrior Hymn is heavenly language describing the heavenly realm and applicable both to the present/past and the future (see 1.3), the tense change presents only the relative order in logic or in 'time' of the heavenly realm. Although YHWH has acted in the heavenly realm (in his mind and action), the manifestation in history has not been fully complete. The action of YHWH as expressed 'past' in 59:15b–17 is not separated from that of 59:18–21 as expressed future since they form a single theophanic event, but the former precedes the latter in logic, or in time of the heavenly realm. However, even though the past tense is used, 59:15b–17 is, like 59:18–21, part of the future promise of divine action, responding to the present situation of the people in the earthly realm.

In summary, the divine judgment is the process of evaluating and judging the deeds of the people and repaying them according to their deeds, whether these bring punishment on the enemies or rewards for the repentant, as vengeance, recompense, and repayment imply.[117]

18 According to their deeds, so will He repay,	כעל גמלות כעל ישלם
wrath to His adversaries, repayment to His enemies;	חמה לצריו גמול לאיביו
to the coastlands He will render repayment.	לאיים גמול ישלם:

112. Also see above on 59:16.

113. Whybray 1981:225. Also see the previous discussion about the unity of the chapter.

114. Muilenburg 1954:694; Skinner 1960:192; Childs 2001:489.

115. Childs 2001:489; Lau 1994:218. For Lau (1994:220), v. 18 is at present.

116. Beuken 1989a:142. The future divine intervention is spoken in the confession of former salvation actions.

117. There seems no substantial difference of meanings of the three words apart from the special linguistic usages such as 'day of vengeance,' 'repay (שלם, usually in verbal form) wrath' and 'repay recompense (usually in noun),' etc.

This verse continues to present the nature of the judgment by the coming YHWH, as evidenced in the keywords such as repay (שלם) and recompense (גמול) as in vengeance (נקם) in 59:17.[118] YHWH repays to people according to their deeds and will make recompense to His enemies and coastlands.

The most important issue in this verse (59:18) will be this: who are the adversaries (צר) and enemies (איב) whom YHWH is going to bring into judgment by His coming in 59:15b–21? Because the word נקם can be applied to both Israel and the nations, and the word גמול to both the righteous and the wicked, it is difficult to decide who the enemies of YHWH are in 59:18, so scholars have not reached a conclusion. The fact that the community of Israel has been at issue in 58:1—59:15a may imply that (1) the enemies of YHWH are the wicked within the community; (2) the nations may be His enemies, because the recompense is directed to the coastlands (איים) (59:18). Other alternatives for the enemies of YHWH will be (3) both Israel and the nations, or, more precisely, (4) sin/sinner(s).

(1) Skinner has said, even though he admits the clause (59:18) itself identifies the adversaries with the coastlands, that this is a misunderstanding of the message of the passage, because the earlier part of the chapter has challenged the Jewish apostates, and no other verses in the context speak of a worldwide judgment. For him, because it is logically impossible that the Gentiles will be judged by the sins of Israel, the words are a gloss, as LXX omits them.[119] So because of the immediately previous context, the

---

118. Some scholars have considered this verse is corrupted because the LXX has a shorter form and Syr. and Targ. also have different texts. Whybray 1981:227; Odeberg 1931:193–94; Westermann 1969:351. Some scholars consider that the last three words are added later as an interpretive gloss, because the context has defined the enemies as those within Israel and not as external enemies, and 'isles' are the recipient of the message of the Servant in 49:1 rather than adversaries. Odeberg 1931:194; Whybray 1981:227; Kissane 1943:250; Muilenburg 1954:695. But, others have tried to interpret the coastlands as in the text, which is our purpose. See Seitz 2001:501; Westermann 1969:350. Anyway, actually these two views about the islands are closely related with the understanding of the enemies as the wicked within the community or as the external enemies (see below in the main text). Oswalt (1998:525) sees the second כעל lacks the object; however, according to Lau (1994:221), as the double כעל is understood as an idiom like כ ~ כ, the emendation is not needed. Motyer (1993:492) also sees that כעל functions as conjunction, while Muilenburg (1954:695) supports that it signifies "(even) now" as a temporal adverb. For Alexander (1846b:373), 'them' is assumed: "According to their deeds, according to them. . ." Even though the scholars do not reach a consensus, the general meaning of the verse is very clear as Oswalt (1998:529) and Odeberg (1931:194) suggested: "God will repay his foes; he will take vengeance on those who have opposed him."

119. Skinner 1960:193–94.

nations cannot be the enemy. For Westermann,[120] following Skinner, the previous context, having no mention of foes from without, is important in this matter. He considers that the traditional view of theophany, God's advent to save Israel and to destroy her enemies, is applied to the present situation, since 63:1–6, the *Vorlage* of 59:15b–21(20) in his view, presents the nations as the adversaries of YHWH. According to him, the language of 59:15b–21(20) ("obsolete language" is his term) speaks of the external adversaries, but actually the tenor of the language is telling about the internal foes. Whybray joins Westermann as he comments that it is very strange that the words borrowed from 63:1–6 are applied to a different situation.[121] While this view, identifying enemies as intra-community adversaries, takes due consideration of the previous context and thus the unity of ch 59, it has neglected the textual evidence of the verse itself. Actually, contrary to Skinner, not only 59:18, but also 59:19 mentions the worldwide effect of theophany. More importantly, this view does not take into proper consideration the context of the following ch 60.

(2) For Kissane, the adversaries are the international oppressors of Israel, and not the evildoers in Israel since other traditional passages, such as 40:5 and 52:10, picture YHWH as the Warrior against international enemies. Despite this view, for him, the coastlands (איים) in DI are not Israel's oppressors as they are urged to receive the message of the Servant in 49:1, which is peculiar.[122] Even though Muilenburg accepts that 59:20b may indicate the adversaries within Israel, he feels a stronger case may be made for international foes as suggested by 59:18c and 19.[123] While this view, advocating the foes from outside Israel, pays attention to the evidence of the passage and the traditional theological scheme, it does not interpret the passage in its larger context(s), either before or after.

(3) For Seitz, the language of divine judgment in 59:15b–21 (and 63:1–6 as well) have been, as in Westermann, traditionally applied to the external adversaries ("extramural" is his term) as in 1:24, 42:13, and 52:10. However, the language of originally "extramural" judgment is applied to the "intramural" injustice, since from the preceding context the domestic concern of injustice is involved at this point. Unlike Westermann, however, he has noticed that the consequence of the judgment extends to the whole

---

120. Westermann 1969:350.

121. Whybray 1981:226–27.

122. Kissane 1943:250–51. Schramm (1995:141) even argues that the coastlands refer not to foreigners, but to "those within the restoration community who do not turn away from transgression," based on intertextual relations with 1:24b, 27–28a, which seems to require precise evaluation.

123. Muilenburg 1954:695.

world, the so-called extramural range.[124] Smith agrees with Seitz, judging that traditional language is applied to the enemies of YHWH both in and outside of the community.[125] "Because Israel failed, there is no difference between Israel and the nations in terms of divine judgment."[126] As Delitzsch commented, "He hides the special judgment upon Israel in the general judgment upon the nations."[127] This view, supporting both inside and outside adversaries, has appropriate regard to the context (not only the previous, but also the following) and the textual evidence as well.[128] However, it is not so easy to explain why such an expansion occurs only in this passage, although this is parallel to the expansion of the eschatological salvation in 56:1–8.

(4) Oswalt argues that the enemy is sin, and the purport of the passage is that "God is going to defeat that foe to the ends of the earth." There is no reference to a special power country neighboring Israel that threatens her, while traditionally the Divine Warrior has been described as coming to defeat Israel's enemy countries as in Exod 17:8–13 and Josh 5:13–15. Nevertheless, Israel requires deliverance at this point as she is *defeated* not by any foreign armies, but rather by sin such as unrighteousness and injustice. The sin of the people [or, the sinful people], rather than the people (of Israel) themselves, has been at issue in chs 56–59.[129] First of all, this view, interpreting the adversary as sin, does not seem to contradict, like the third view, the preceding and the following context, in that it pays regard to the problem of evil within the community. It also provides a worldwide effect after removal of sin in the nations. This view (that YHWH fights against sin the enemy) may be challenged because the abstract 'sin' may not be intended by the text and because of the dominant semantic field of personal צר/איב, which does not seem to fit the abstract. However, the objection does not seem to be ab-

124. Seitz 2001:501.

125. Smith 1995:124.

126. Seitz 2001:501.

127. Delitzsch 1873:405–6. This view is also followed by Beuken (1989a:147), who comments: „Zij wil veilig stellen dat wanneer God aan zijn vijanden in Israël vergelding uitoefent, dit ook de volken wereldwijd zal treffen." ("They want to ensure that when God exercises revenge to His enemies in Israel, this also will apply to the nations around the world.") For Skinner (1960:194; 1915:28), the verse is connected back to 3:13, so "the idea must be that of general assize, in which Israel is judged first."

128. Koenen (1990:69), joining this view (pp. 66 and 72), notices the intertextual correlation between the passage and the following chapters.

129. Oswalt 1998:525–27. Here, Oswalt even uses the capital letter to denote (the) sin (that is, the monster Sin) as he believes that this is "the ultimate development of the Divine Warrior motif in the Bible." Herbert (1975:152) agrees with Oswalt, commenting "the enemies may be moral and spiritual evils," although without detail analysis.

solute, because (a) sometimes abstract concepts such as justice, righteousness, etc. have come to the fore in the text (e.g., 62:11), and (b) metaphorical
terms, which are dominant in ch 59, sometimes adopt personification of
such abstract concepts, as in "righteousness does not overtake us" (59:19),
"His righteousness upheld Him" (59:14), and "truth has stumbled" (59:14).
So, the author/redactor may conceive the abstract concept here. Or, rather,
it may be said that the enemies signify the sinners or the wicked (whether
they are within Israel or outside it), because the sin is closely related to the
person who carries it.[130] If this is the view of TI, it would be a *generalization*,
as this view would change the traditional scheme of Israel vs. the nations (as
the people of YHWH and the enemies of YHWH, respectively) into that of
the righteous vs. the wicked (as the new concept of people and the enemies
of YHWH, respectively).[131] This generalization may provide an answer to
the question of expansion that the previous view did not solve. This fits the
mythical representation of YHWH in the Divine Warrior Hymn (see above).

Some commentators have argued that the "coastlands" (איים) in 59:18b
were urged to receive the message of the Servant of DI in 42:1 and 49:1 as
the objects of the salvation of YHWH.[132] However, whether they are the
objects of deliverance only is not certain (cf. Skinner). 59:18 may have a
literary connection to 51:5, because it has a salvation/righteousness hendiadys (cf. 59:16, 17), the divine arm motif (cf. 59:16) and the איים (cf. 59:18)
in parallel. There, the divine arm shall judge the nations (וזרעי עמים ישפטו)
and the coastlands will wait for the arm of YHWH. If the 'coastlands' is
understood as a synecdoche to present 'the nations' as they are in parallel,
then the nations/coastlands are said to be judged as well as waiting for the
divine arm. This would imply the salvific work of YHWH, as the words קוה
and יחל intimate (see 4.3).[133] Therefore, even though the coastlands have
been invited to enjoy the salvation of YHWH, they are also to confront the
divine judgment, whether this judgment implies positive or negative consequences for them. According to 59:18, the coastlands will be judged and
(some of them) saved as recompense in accordance with their deeds, just
like the Israelites.

---

130. The enemy sin may be confused and interchanged with the enemy sinner.

131. In that the locus of theological interest of the text, as the author intends, changes from what is to be seen ("the natural") to what is not to be seen ("the spiritual"),
it would also be termed as "spritualization." See ch 4, for the 'spiritual' and 'spiritual
division' of the people.

132. Kissane 1943:250; Muilenburg 1954:695.

133. According to Gilchrist (1980:373–74) and Hartley (1980:791–92), these two
words are shaded in the positive sense of expectation for a hope.

In brief, the judgment of the coming YHWH is retributive not only for Israel but also for the nations, as suggested in "coastlands." The enemies that YHWH fights against are universal.

19 So they shall fear the name of YHWH from the west,	וייראו ממערב את־שם יהוה
and His glory from the rising of the sun;	וממזרח־שמש את־כבודו
for an envoy will come as light,	כי־יבוא כנהר צר
the Spirit of YHWH will lift a standard for him.	רוח יהוה נססה בו:

This verse describes the aftermath of theophanic judgment in 59:18—the manifestation of the name and glory of YHWH around the world (59:19a). The second half-verse is difficult and has been disputed, but is understood as a promise to send an envoy, who is involved in the theophany.

Does the fear of the nations for the name and glory of YHWH imply that the nations will be saved?[134] The nations will join the eschatological salvation of the coming YHWH as they come to fear YHWH (59:19). The west/east (מזרח/מערב) pair in 59:19 forms a *merismus* to mean the nations of all the earth (including Israel), as in 43:5 and 45:6.[135] However, as Lau pointed out, the order of the words is singular here in that the order is reversed and different from those of all the other six occurrences of the same pair (i.e., usually, the east—the west).[136] For Lau, this is a quotation from 45:6 and the reversed order is a deliberate manipulation of the author to represent the light-metaphor (cf. 59:9–10), and so not a *merismus* signifying "everywhere": the מערב symbolizes the community as darkness (59:1–15a); the מזרח as light symbolizes the Temple as is described in 59:19b. The coming of YHWH caused the fear of God in the community of darkness, and then (as the word order intimates the "temporal sequence," according to him), in the Temple.[137] However, even though the noting of the reversed order and its

---

134. The word וייראו is easily exchanged in confusion with ויראו. Even though some scholars may prefer the latter because the thought is similar to that of 66:18 ("וראו את־כבודי," and they will see My glory), according to Whybray, to "see the name of YHWH" is not natural, as well as the amendment violates the MT pointing for Alexander (1846b:375). Kissane 1943:251; Muilenburg 1954:696; Whybray 1981:228; and Oswalt 1998:526.

135. Whybray 1981:227; Kissane 1943:250.

136. Lau 1994:224. The occurrences of the pair מזרח/מערב are: 1 Chr 7:28; 12:15; Pss 103:12; 107:3; Isa 43:5; 45:6; cf. 59:19 (order reversed). As for the occurrences other than מזרח/מערב, the pair of ים/קדם appears in Gen 12:8; 28:14 (order reversed); Num 35:5; Isa 11:14 (order reversed); Ez 45:7 (2x, order reversed); 48:1, 2, 3, 4, 5, 6, 8 (2x), 10 (order reversed), 16, 17, 21, 23, 24, 25, 26, 27. The pair of ים/מזרח appears in Jos 11:3; 1 Kgs 7:25 (order reversed); 1 Chr 9:24; 2 Chr 4:4 (order reversed); Zech 14:4. Other occurrences include: Ps. 75:6 (מוצא, מערב); Zech. 8:7 (מזרח, מבוא).

137. "Die Gottesfurcht der Gemeinde nimmt ihren Anfang in der Finsternis ("vom Untergang") und mündet ein in die Verehrung der Herrlichkeit, die nach V.19b in

interpretation as a light-metaphor are very plausible, his inferences are not entirely persuasive. (1) Did the author intend to nullify the *merismus* here in the quotation of 45:6, because he did not accept the worldwide implication of theophany either there or here? The reversed word order does not seem to do this. The author must have acknowledged the *merismus* as in 45:6, in which YHWH declares that He is the only one God "from the rising to the setting of the sun," because 59:18 mentions "islands" and ch 60 also portrays the international effect of the coming of YHWH. The purport of the exclusive glorification of YHWH is maintained. Thus, the author must have wanted just to add a new nuance to the *merismus*. (2) Did the author want to suggest that the final consequence of theophany will be achieved in the Temple service? Ch 60 emphasizes the glory of Zion rather than the Temple, although the Temple is part of it as in 60:7, 9. What then would be the intention in reversing the order, if it is not haphazard? As in 58:10 and 60:2, it may signify the dramatic character that the theophany will change darkness to light, which is longed for in 59:9–10 (in this respect, Lau is correct). In conclusion, the reversed מזרח/מערב pair, still referring to the nations of the world as a *merismus*, joins the light-metaphor to describe the striking theophanic effect, in the judgment of the coming YHWH.

However, how does the fear of the name and glory of YHWH in the nations signify their salvation, not just their recognition? This verse [59:19a] may have some literary connection with 40:5 (cf. 52:10) and Ps 102:16[15], and the glory of YHWH may be thematically related to 60:1–2 and 66:18–19, and to 6:3 as well.[138] In 60:1–2, the glory of YHWH brings the glory of Zion, which attracts the nations and the kings (60:3). Because of the contrast between darkness and light in chs 58–59 and 60, the gathering of the nations to the light (60:3–9) signifies their participation in salvation (see 4.3). In 40:5, "the glory of YHWH will be revealed and all flesh will see it together." 40:5b is rendered in LXX as ". . . and all flesh shall see the salvation of God." According to Weinfeld, כבוד, like God's righteousness, is synonymous with salvation in Isa 40–66 as for example in 62:1–2.[139] 59:19a is the fulfilment of 40:5 as well as 6:3. In these two verses, the glory of YHWH fills

---

unmittelbarer Zukunft wieder in den Tempel einziehen wird." ("The fear of God of the community takes her beginning in the darkness ['from the setting'] and flows into the admiration of the magnificence which will enter v. 19b in the immediate future again in the temple.") Lau 1994:224. For Lau (1994:225), v. 19b has a literary influence from Ezek 43, in which the divine glory appears in the temple; so 59:19b represents the divine manifestation in the temple service, which had not been experienced before owing to the partitioned wall in 59:2.

138. Whybray 1981:228; Kissane 1943:250; Muilenburg 1954:695; and Lau 1994:223; Muilenburg 1954:695.

139. Weinfeld 1995:35.

the whole earth, which, according to Weinfeld, is understood as universal salvation.[140] Besides, the contexts of 66:18–19 and Ps 102:16[15] report that the nations will worship YHWH (66:23; Ps 102:23[22]). This signifies that they join the people of YHWH as they are saved.

YHWH's coming results in the fear of the divine name and glory in 59:19a. However, 59:19b, "כי־יבוא כנהר צר רוח יהוה נססה בו," has been considered difficult to interpret, but I hold that it is to be understood Messianically.[141] Mauer (and KJV) suggested, "when the enemy shall come in like a flood, the Spirit of YHWH shall lift a standard against him."[142] It follows the MT accents to interpret צר as the subject,[143] and understands נססה as a derivative from נס. The standard (נס) has been a key concept for the eschatological expectation of PI as well as DI (see below). But, the coming of the enemy is very strange in the context, because the verse belongs to the literary genre of theophany, in which not the enemy, but YHWH comes.[144] For Delitzsch, too, so soon after the divine wrath has been poured out on the

---

140. Weinfeld 1995:36. The idea is developed also in 11:9 and Hab 2:14.

141. Of the modern English translations, two may be typical: KJV ("when the enemy shall come in like a flood, the Spirit of the LORD shall lift up a standard against him.") and NRSV ("for he will come like a pent-up stream that the wind of the LORD drives on."). KJV adopts 'the enemy' as the subject; NRSV adopts 'he' (referring to YHWH) as subject. The interpretation may differ according to the understandings of (Alexander 1846b:375; Koenen 1990:70): (1) What is the subject of the verb יבוא—He (as the verb contains the third person m.sg.; NRSV), צר (as the MT punctuation indicates; KJV, Rofé), or "it" (His glory, as is introduced in the previous colon; Koenen)? (2) What does the word צר mean in here—narrow or tight as adjective (the BDB adopts this meaning for v19b); as noun, straits or distress (as in 63:9, for BDB), adversary or foe (as in 1:24, 26:11, 59:18, 64:1), or, following 1QIsᵃ which adopts צור instead of צר, en envoy (Beuken 1989a:148; Rofé 1989:408)? (3) What is the meaning of the word נססה—to flee, escape; or, drive at/out as the polel form of נוס (BDB), or to wave, raise a standard (KJV, Rofé) as a derivative from נס (a flag, standard)? Minor issues may be added: כי—when or for? רוח—breath (wind) or the Spirit? יהוה—strong or YHWH? בו—for him/it or against him/it; כנהר, צר, or YHWH?

142. Alexander 1846b:376.

143. If we adopt צר as the subject as MT suggests, because the *pashta* comes on כנהר, it can signify adversary or distress. According to Motyer (1993:492), however, צר cannot mean anything than enemy because the same word signified it as plural (צרים) in the previous verse. For Delitzsch (1873:406), it is possible that צר as the subject may mean 'distress' because peace, an antithesis to distress, is coming "like a river" in 48:18 and 66:12. However, in the context, for Koenen (1990:69), the distress cannot come because the world is full of the fear and glory of YHWH. Thus, what is coming should be YHWH or something (someone) that belongs to Him.

144. Beuken 1990:148; Koenen 1990:69.

enemies, they cannot come as human instruments of the divine judgment.[145] Moreover, the number change of צר may be difficult to explain.[146]

Alexander, following Cocceius, interpreted the phrase as "when he will come as their enemy like a stream, the Spirit of YHWH raises a banner in it."[147] This interpretation, as Alexander contended, may fit the context, which "does not lead us to expect an allusion to the coming of God's enemies against Him, but rather to His coming against them, as the preceding clause declares that all the ends of the earth shall fear His name and His glory."[148] This interpretation follows MT pointing, which understands צר as the subject. However, it seems very strained to interpret צר as YHWH being the enemy (of the enemies of YHWH), because the same word צר (as plural) referred to the enemy(-ies) of YHWH in the preceding verse.

Delitzsch (and NRSV) suggests, "He [=YHWH] will come like a stream, a stream hemmed up in, which a wind of YHWH, i.e., a strong tempestuous wind, sweeps away." This interpretation may fit the theophanic context, as in Alexander. But, it needlessly violates the MT pointing, which "forbids the intimate conjunction of נהר and צר as noun and adjective."[149] It is improbable that צר has a different sense from that (as plural) in 59:18.[150] Moreover, "YHWH cannot be swept by himself," which is the main objection to this usual interpretation (Beuken).[151] Although it has been often considered that 59:19b has a literary link with 30:28, in which the theophany is in the image of the overflowing stream, it seems dubious because נהר or צר cannot be found in 30:28 (where נחל is adopted instead of נהר).[152] Furthermore, 59:19–20 is a depiction of salvation just after the retributory judgment in 59:18, so the image of a pent-up stream does not fit the context. For Koenen, the context suggests the theological nuance of רוח יהוה, rather than physical—so, the Spirit of YHWH. Furthermore, the assumed polel form of נוס is used only here as a causative.[153] Koenen modified this interpretation, understanding the subject of יבא as the glory of YHWH in the preceding verse,

145. Delitzsch 1873:406.

146. Koenen 1990:69.

147. Alexander 1846b:374, 376.

148. Alexander 1846b:376.

149. Alexander 1846b:376.

150. Alexander 1846b:376; Motyer 1993:492.

151. Beuken 1989a:148.

152. Delitzsch 1873:407; Whybray 1981:228; Kissane 1943:250; Muilenburg 1954:695; Skinner 1960:194; and Lau 1994:223. כנהר צר occurs in 59:19b, while כנחל שוטף in 30:28.

153. Alexander 1846b:376. According to Rofé (1989:407–9), בו נססה is not natural, and "נססתהו" should come, as a causative polel takes a direct object.

and changing the wind of YHWH into the Spirit of YHWH.[154] Although he maintained the contextual continuity, he could not help violating the MT punctuation. Furthermore, according to Rofé, the נססה cannot be considered as the polel form of נוס, but as the third person feminine perfect of נסס, a derivative from נס, denoting "to wave as a flag," because נססתהו should come instead of נססה בו to signify "drive on/along."[155]

Beuken suggests, "[B]ecause an envoy will come like a river, the Spirit of YHWH will lift a banner for him."[156] This interpretation fits the theophanic context and follows the MT reading, although it adopts 1QIs^a text, in which צור, instead of צר, occurs. The subject "an envoy" may be justified, because צור is not known to us and thus we may assume that צור signifies ציר since ו and י are easily confused.[157] This interpretation neither violates the MT punctuation, nor conflicts with the theophanic context. Although Beuken opines, "But we do not see well how an envoy functions in the context," the envoy also fits the following context as we shall see below. However, we may go a little further. According to Rofé, נהר can be interpreted as "light," because in the late Biblical Hebrew the Aramaic root נהר ("shine, light") is accepted as in Ps 34:6 and Job 3:4.[158] In fact, the same root is adopted in 60:6, albeit as the verbal form in figurative sense. So my interpretation is "for an envoy will come as light, the Spirit of YHWH will lift a standard for him."[159] This may bring another connection with the light metaphor between chs 58–59 and 60.

If we accept this interpretation (Beuken, Rofé, myself), the promise of the coming of an envoy is included in, or presented by, the coming of YHWH, and the envoy will receive a standard for the nations. Because there is no man and no intercessor, YHWH relies on His own arm (59:16) and is going to send an envoy. (The situation is exactly the same as that in 52:10 and 53:1—the arm of YHWH is revealed in the Servant, as YHWH decided to redeem the people because there is no man to answer in 50:2.) This 'Messianic' interpretation is also reinforced by the fact that 'flag' (נס) has been used in the Messianic and eschatological context in the earlier part of the book of Isaiah. In 11:10 and 12, it signifies the Davidic Messiah, towards

154. Koenen (1990:69) interprets, "it [=the glory of YH] will come like a pressing stream, the spirit of YH drives it."

155. Rofé 1989:407–8.

156. Beuken 1989a:148.

157. Rofé 1989:408.

158. Rofé 1989:408–9. Take notice of the Aramic noun נהיר (G-K no. 10466; Strong, 5094), signifying light.

159. Rofé's suggested reading is: "for an envoy will come as light; the spirit of the Lord waves him as a flag."

whom the remnant of His people and the nations will return and gather.[160]
In 13:2 and 18:3, and in 49:22 in DI, it is used in the eschatological context,
which is fulfilled in 62:10 in the gathering of the nations for salvation. The
envoy is coming, possibly, as light, which is a metaphor of salvation, as the
light-metaphor is already familiar to us in 58:8, 10, 59:9–10 and 60:1–3.
Thus, 59:19b is also a theophanic text, not as a simple coming of YHWH,
but as a coming of the envoy of YHWH, who may be going to take the place
of the 'no man' in 59:16. The interpretation of 59:19b is also closely related
to that of 59:20 and 21 (see below). Although Beuken admits the possibility
of interpretation as 'envoy' in 59:19b, he fails to grasp the function of the
envoy in the context.[161]

In conclusion, due to the theophany of YHWH (59:15b–18), the name
and glory of YHWH is revealed and feared by the nations (59:19a), which
implies that they join the eschatological salvation. YHWH is going to send
an envoy like a light, with whom the eschatological expectation of the gathering of the nations will be achieved (59:19b).

20 And a Redeemer will come to Zion,	ובא לציון גואל
to those in Jacob who turn from transgression,	ולשבי פשע ביעקב
declares YHWH.	נאם יהוה:

This verse sets out the aim of the theophany, or rather of the envoy's
coming.[162] It promises that *a* (rather than *the*) Redeemer will come to Zion,
to those who turn from transgression in Jacob.

The term גואל is applied only to YHWH in DI (41:14; 43:14; 44:24;
49:26) as well as in TI (60:16 and 63:16). This may suggest that גואל here
also refers to YHWH. But, the immediate context may suggest a different
or, rather, deeper understanding of the divine figure. Because an envoy is
promised to come in 59:19b and YHWH mentions the Redeemer as a third
person here in 59:20, it is more probable that the Redeemer signifies the
envoy, although it is still possible that YHWH referred to Himself with such
a third-person appellation.[163] If this is the case, it signifies that the divine
appellation "Redeemer" is transferred to someone other than YHWH and
that he is as divine as YHWH and taking the task of redemption of YHWH.
I have already seen this phenomenon in the arm of YHWH, which is identified with the Servant figure as a mediator (see above on 59:16). This may
also be evidenced because in 63:9, redemption of Israel is related to the

160. See 5.3 on 65:25, for the intratextual connection to 11:6–9.
161. Beuken 1989a:149.
162. Beuken 1989a:149.
163. Lau 1994:225. Redeemer as referred to YHWH: Isa. 41:14; 43:14; 44:6, 24; 47:4;
48:17; 49:7, 26; 54:5, and 8. Isa 59:20 is the first occurrence of גואל in TI.

"angel of his presence" (מלאך פניו), who is the second self of YHWH, i.e., both identified with Him and, sometimes, distinguished from Him.[164] The envoy as well as the angel (of YHWH) is a different person from YHWH, but they are called by His name. After all, the coming of YHWH is replaced by the coming of the envoy in the passage. Therefore, although the entire passage relates to the coming of YHWH, in the description of the coming, it is the envoy of YHWH who is promised. This is reinforced by the fact that the envoy, as the second self of YHWH, recurs in the following verse, too, forming a coherent situation. 59:20 continues to describe the theophanic situation of 59:19b—the theophanic verb "בוא" of 59:19b, which must be a presentation of theophany of 59:19a, is repeated in 59:20.

Does the fact that a Redeemer will come to Zion signify that all are saved in Zion? 59:20 also presents the nature of the redeemed community. According to Westermann, there is a tension between 59:20a and 59:20b in that theophany is "for Israel in her entirety" in 59:20a, while in 59:20b salvation is only for the devout as a result of the theophany.[165] Therefore, as a result of the coming of either YHWH or the envoy, a division happens in Jacob's house by which only the converts from Jacob will be restored.[166] "God's redemptive action effects a separation."[167] "The mighty act of redemption works morally through repentance," to those who repent of their sins (1:27–28; 57:18–19a; 59:12–13).[168] This is an eschatological process cleansing the community "as an act of eschatological drama" (57:20–21),[169] the division having started in 56:1–2 (see 2.3). So every member of the redeemed community becomes righteous (60:21). The phrase "turn from transgression" is a deuteronomistic concept, so the redemption is the restoration of the covenantal relationship.

If my interpretation is correct, the envoy of YHWH will come to Zion as a Redeemer. But only those who repent and turn from their sins will

---

164. Childs 2001:523; Seitz 2001:526; Knight 1985:75. See 6.2.3. "The angel of His presence" or "the angel of YHWH" has been sometimes identified with YHWH Himself (Exod 3:2–3) and sometimes distinguished from YHWH, although he/it is certainly of divine origin (Exod 33:2 and 14–15). For Childs, "the angel of his presence" is the extended form of the presence of God, mediated by the "visible agents of the selfsame divine essence," while for Seitz, the "angel of his presence" is YHWH's stand-in.

165. Westermann 1969:352.

166. Ruszukowski 2000:73. We may see the distinction between true Israel, agent of the divine promises, and 'sociological [or, empirical] Israel,' from which a part remains obstinately rebellious against YHWH. Vermeylen 1978:468. See 5.2.

167. Westermann 1969:351.

168. Motyer 1993:492.

169. Pauritsch 1971:92.

be saved, which causes an internal split in the community. Through this process, sociological Israel will be cleansed to form a true Israel.

21 "And as for me, this is my covenant with them,"	ואני זאת בריתי אותם
says YHWH:	אמר יהוה
"My Spirit that is upon you,	רוחי אשר עליך
and My words that I have put in your mouth,	ודברי אשר־שמתי בפיך
shall not depart out of your mouth,	לא־ימושו מפיך
or out of the mouth of your offspring,	ומפפי זרעך
or out of the mouth of your children's offspring,"	ומפי זרע זרעך
says YHWH,	אמר יהוה
"from this time forth and forevermore."	מעתה ועד־עולם:

This verse (re-)establishes the covenant, as an ultimate goal of the theophany in 59:15b–21. The Spirit and the word of YHWH are given to 'you' (masc. sg.), the envoy of YHWH, who is pre-presented in 59:19–20, and to his offspring and their offspring for ever.

Is the Messianic interpretation of 59:20–21 justified?[170] We assume that the two verses as well as 59:19 form a consistent situation, due to the narrative continuity.[171] Even though the formula "אמר יהוה" appears in the sentence twice, the preceding and the following utterances form a continuation. While 'with them' (59:21) has been generally agreed to refer to "those who turn from transgression in Jacob" which is parallel to Zion in 59:20,[172] the identification of the 'you' (masc. sg.) has been debated among scholars. The possible understandings of the 'you' may be: (1) Zion; (2) the prophet; (3) the redeemer. (1) Above all, it is not convincing that the 'you' and the 'them' are identified and considered to refer to the same Zion (i.e., Israel/Jacob), because the 'you' and the 'them' occur in the same context as YH-WH.[173] It could be assumed that 'them' refers to the 'offspring' and the 'you' to Zion. However, Zion is third person (fem.) in 59:20. Furthermore, the

170. Although the verses are quoted in Romans 11:26–27 by Paul, the relation between the verses and Romans is beyond our purview.

171. Some scholars have argued that 59:21 is later addition as prose and thus this may justify the verse being interpreted without connection to the preceding context, as some versions suggest that while 58:1—59:20 are poetry, 59:21 is prose. However, the canonical reading that we adopt may suggest (1) that 59:21 is just a part of the passage (59:15b–21) or chs 58–59 and thus (2) the narrative continuity of 59:21 with the preceding context. This is reinforced by the fact that 'them' in 59:21 refers to 'those who turn from transgression in Jacob' in 59:20 as is widely accepted by the scholars (see below).

172. According to Motyer (1993:493), the world people who fear the name of YHWH in 59:19a cannot be excluded from the "with them," because they are coming to Zion in ch 60, in which glory of Zion is achieved by the work of the redeemer and YHWH in 59:15b–21. See chapter 4.

173. Skinner 1960:195; Whybray 1981:229; Odeberg 1931:197; Knight 1985:40.

fact that the 'you' is masculine singular makes it more difficult. Thus, the first alternative is unlikely. (2) With respect to the second alternative that sees the prophet as 'you,' even though the voice of the prophet appears in 58:1 and resumes in 59:1 (and in particular, as first person plural, at 59:9ff.), it is uncertain whether at this point the historical prophet is being involved in the prophetic narrative.[174] If the 'you' is the historical prophet, another problem is that 'offspring' should be also interpreted historically, but the prophetic office is not hereditary.[175] Although we further assume that the 'offspring' may signify symbolically the relation of discipleship, the 'covenant with the prophets' is peculiar. (3) Therefore, the 'you' is most likely the 'redeemer' in 59:20 who has already been introduced by the narrator as an envoy in 59:19b, if we accept the narrative continuity between 59:19 and 59:20–21. The third person masculine singular 'redeemer' is a title given to the envoy who is coming as light, and is called "you" by YHWH. Thus, the envoy, i.e., the 'you' must be divine as the divine title is given to him, and thus Messianic as well.[176]

The intertextual references may support this interpretation, as the 'you' is endowed with the "spirit" and "word." According to Beuken, the 'you' is identified with the offspring of the Servant in DI. For him, 59:21 has a connection with both 44:3 (as concerns My Spirit) and 51:16 (as concerns My words).[177] The Spirit of YHWH will be poured out on the offspring of the Servant in 44:2–3 and the words of YHWH are given to Zion in 51:16,[178] while My Spirit and My words are granted to 'you and your offspring and the offspring of your offspring' in 59:21. Thus, for him, "your offspring" in 59:21, ch 59 being an introduction of chs 60–62, is identified with the "I"

174. For Smith (1995:126), following Steck, 59:21 has a reference back to 58:1 and the 'you' is a prophetic figure who was referred to in 58:1. He does not consider it appropriate that the 'you' in 59:21 is the prophet of 61:1, because the two texts are intervened by chapter 60.

175. See Emmerson 1992:74. She argues, against such an objection, that the focus is not on the individual prophet but on the prophecy itself which is given to all God's people. Then, her view turns unintentionally to the 'Zion' view.

176. Redeemer has referred only to YHWH in DI: Isa. 41:14; 43:14; 44:6, 24; 47:4; 48:17; 49:7, 26; 54:5, and 8. Isa 59:20 is the first occurrence of גואל in TI. The DI passages do not seem to contradict our inference, but our interpretation clarifies them, as the appearance of the angel/messenger of YHWH has often been considered as that of YHWH Himself in the canonical tradition.

177. Beuken 1989c:416.

178. While for Delitzsch (1873:290), the addressee in 51:16 is Israel, Alexander (1977:269) considers that it is the Messiah, i.e., the Servant, because Zion is spoken of in the third person in 51:16b. This is supported by the fact that "to cover you by the shade of my hand" has a verbal link with 49:2 and "to put my words in your mouth" alludes to 50:4, both of which are the Servant Songs.

in 61:1, who is empowered by the Spirit of YHWH. Eventually, for him, the 'you' in 59:21 as well as the "I" in 61:1 refer to the "offspring of the Servant of YHWH" in DI, because the Servant of YHWH in DI has been promised to be given the offspring in 53:10 and 54:3,[179] as the result of his work in 52:13—53:12.[180]

However, the 'you' seems to succeed to the status of the Servant, rather than that of the *offspring* of the Servant. For Seitz, the reference of Spirit endowment recalls not only 42:1 and 44:3 but also 48:16c.[181] In 42:1, the Spirit of YHWH is put upon the Servant, which contextually seems to refer to Israel.[182] In 44:3, the Spirit is put also upon the offspring of the Servant. However, in 48:16c, the unknown speaker 'me' is sent with the Spirit. According to Seitz, the role of Israel is obviously transferred to the 'me,' God's individual speaker, as confirmed in 49:1–6 (the second Servant Song), in which the anonymous speaker in 48:16c reappears as the Servant of YH-WH.[183] For him, the movement of 59:21 to 61:1 is parallel to that of 48:16c to 49:1, in that both are commissioning narratives in which an unknown figure is given the Spirit, and later reappears as the spokesman of YHWH.

Meanwhile, the covenant in 59:21 has a literary connection with 61:8–9 as well, because the "covenant with them" is parallel (בריתי אותם, 59:21// ברית—להם, 61:8); "as for me" (אני) is parallel (59:21//61:8); the seed (זרע) or descendants (צאצא) are associated with the covenant; and additionally, justice is related to the covenant in 61:8 and 56:1–8, which is parallel to 59:21; and the covenant is everlasting in both texts (עד-עולם, 59:21; עולם, 61:8). According to Gosse, in 59:21, the covenant is with 'you' (masc. sg.) and 'your seed,' while in 61:8–9, the prophetic "I" in 61:1 and the offspring in 61:9 form the covenant. These two covenants thus are parallel, because: (1) the Spirit of YHWH that is on you/me is parallel in 59:21 and 61:1, and (2) their offspring are covenanted and blessed as a result of the mission of the anointed one in 61:1 while they are so because of the 'you' in 59:21.[184] Therefore, it is not difficult to recognize the parallel position of the

179. The "offspring" appears again in 57:3. But, it is offspring of prostitute, a false offspring of Zion, which is compared with the true descendents of Zion as the two offspring can be distinguished by fearing God and taking refuge in YHWH in 57:11 and 13.

180. Motyer 1993:493; Seitz 2001:502.

181. Seitz 2001:502.

182. Whether the Servant is an individual or the corporate Israel may be arguable.

183. Seitz 2001:502 and 423.

184. This discussion naturally leads to the theme of the anointed one, i.e., the Messianic figure, which is reserved for a little while. Gosse 1989:116–18; Seitz 2001:502.

Servant in both places.[185] The Servant-offspring scheme of DI is repeated by the scheme of envoy-offspring [i.e., the anointed one-the servants] in TI. The Messianic figure comes as the covenant mediator (or, to restore the covenant).

In sum, with the intertextual connections to 42:1, 44:2–3, and 48:16 as well as 61:1 and 8, 59:21 implicates the 'you' as in the position of the Servant in DI in that he is granted the Spirit and the words to be commissioned. (This is the role as a spokesman of YHWH.) He is also promised the covenant, and will have offspring in union with him. Therefore, the redeemer in 59:20, as well as the 'you' in 59:21, is beginning to have the tone of a Messianic figure. Having said that, if we remember the discussion about the 'no man' and 'intercessor' (59:16), then it is reasonable to conclude that the passage identifies these figures with those of the 'envoy,' 'redeemer,' and the anonymous 'you,' recapitulating the portrait of the Servant of YHWH (and מבשר as well) of DI.

Conclusion

In conclusion, 59:15b–21 is a theophanic passage, in which, with the decisive coming of YHWH, the injustice of the community, which signifies the breach of the covenant, is overcome, and the eschatological salvation is achieved. The motive of the coming of YHWH is twofold: YHWH's realization that there is no justice, which makes Him furious (this reflects YHWH as Judge), and His character that responds to the lowly and the penitent. He recognized that there was 'no man,' which not only reflects the mythical idea of the monotheistic creation in view of the connections to DI, but also refers to the Servant in DI. Not only the arm of YHWH but also the armor (breastplate, helmet, garments, clothing, and mantle) that YHWH wears present Him as a Divine Warrior. The Divine Warrior imagery originates from the exodus tradition. The judgment by the coming YHWH is retributive as the terms vengeance, recompense, and repayment suggest—judgment is exerted on both the wicked and the righteous. The enemies on whom YHWH's punishment falls are within the community as well as outside Israel—so, the wicked or the sin become(s) His enemy/-ies. As a result of the divine intervention, the whole world will fear the name of YHWH, which signifies that they enjoy salvation. YHWH promises an envoy to come like a light. The envoy is called a Redeemer, which was originally in DI an appellation given

---

185. This is because actually the covenant has been given to the Servant in 42:6 and 49:8, and reconfirmed in 54:10 and because the Servant has been promised to have the offspring as the covenant.

solely to YHWH. When the Redeemer comes to Zion, only the repentant will be redeemed, so there will be a division within the community of Jacob. YHWH promises to the 'you' (the restoration of) the covenant: the Spirit and the word of YHWH will be upon 'you' and 'your offspring' in eternal generations. So, the 'you' is the covenant mediator. The 'you' to whom the covenant is given is identified not only with the envoy like a light and the Redeemer in the context but also with the anointed speaker 'I' in 61:1. This individual (the 'you') who is granted the Spirit and the word is parallel to the Servant in DI. So, the Messianic figure is presented as an envoy to come.

3.4 Excursus: Identification of the Anointed Figure in 61:1–3

I have shown that an envoy is promised to come as a redeemer in the previous section (59:15b–21). I also have suggested that the Messianic figure in 59:19b–21 recurs in 61:1–3. Then, is it justified by 61:1–3 on its own that the first person speaker of 61:1–3 is Messianic? I am going to investigate the identity of the anointed figure in 61:1–3.[186] Who is this?

The Prophet or the Servant Figure?

The anointed figure, i.e., the first person speaker in 61:1–3 has been sometimes identified as the prophet who has the authorial voice, whoever the prophet is—First, Second, or Third Isaiah.[187] This identification arises mainly from the assumption that the Spirit coming upon "me" (this is associated with anointing in 2 Sam 23:1–7), and the verbs "שלח" and "בשר" reflect the commissioning of the prophet, and the mission of the anointed figure represents that of the prophet.[188] Scholars have considered that this

---

186. The relation between 61:1–3 and Luke 4:18–19, in which the Christ himself quotes 61:1–3, is beyond our purview.

187. Targums may be one of the earliest traditions that interpret the anointed figure as the authorial prophet (Childs 2001:502; Delitzsch 1873:424). As Targums assumes the unity of the book of Isaiah, it may understand that the prophet is Isaiah of the eighth century Jerusalem. As Zimmerli considers chs 60–62 (and the Servant Songs as well) are written by Second Isaiah, he sees the anointed figure as taken shape by the prophet's self-description of his mission. Modern scholars usually tend to see the anointed speaker as the prophet TI (Muilenburg 1954:709; Whybray 1981:239–40).

188. Westermann 1969:365–66. For Emmerson (1992:76), the prophetic consciousness of the divine call is "no less authentic" than Amos or First Isaiah—the aim of the prophetic role is expressed as the well-being of the community and the glory of YHWH.

view is supported by the presence of the prophetic figure in other places in TI such as 57:21; 58:1; 59:21; 62:1 and 6; and 56:1.[189] In these texts, there are (implicit) references to a historical prophet.[190] The first-person speaker is assumed to take the prophetic functions and duties,[191] and the prophetic formulae may display the presence of the prophetic figure.[192]

However, although this view and its arguments may have some validity, there are several objections to it. First, it is highly questionable whether the text is presented with a view to showing a personal experience of the prophet. The personal portrait of the historical figure is extremely limited. Childs comments, "The frequent attempt to attribute a personality to the speaker arises not from the text itself, but is a projection from a prior, critical assumption regarding authorship."[193] This is why even Emmerson comments, "Consequently it comes as no surprise to find that the figure of the prophet is *elusive* also in chs. 56–66."[194] Thus, because the text itself (and the narrative) does not focus on the personal experience of the divine calling, it seems of less use to try to reconstruct the personal history of the author.

189. Emmerson 1992:71–79.

190. 57:21 and 58:1 are the most obvious disclosure of the presence of the prophet although the reference is implicit, because the prophet speaks in 57:21 and is addressed by YHWH in 58:1. "My God" (אלהי) implies a prophet being present. To "cry out loudly" (קרא בגרון), "raise your voice like a trumpet" (כשופר הרם קולך), and "declare" (הגד) indicate the prophetic function of proclamation. Emmerson 1992:73. The "do not hold back" (אל־תחשך), in parallel with קרא, encourages the prophetic proclamation. In addition, the "spirit" and "words" in 59:21 also suggest the prophetic figure behind the text. Whybray 1981:229; Emmerson 1992:74. Against the objection that prophetic office is not hereditary, they argue that the succession to the future generation is not as an individual prophet but as a prophetic duty or function.

191. In 61:10 and 63:7, for Emmerson (1992:76–77), the first-person speaker is a spokesman of the community, as a prophetic function, for thanksgiving and intercession, respectively. The latter representative role of the prophet continues in the lamenting prayer in 63:7—64:11[12] as expressed obviously in "we, our" (63:16, 17; 64:5, 6, 7, 8, 11, 12). The intercessory function may also be found in 62:1, in which there appears the prophet's determined commitment to the prayer on behalf of the community. Although sometimes the "חשה" is considered as the divine action as in 42:14; 57:11; 64:11[12]; and 65:6 (Delitzsch 1873:434), it cannot be solely divine because the verb is applied to the non-divine subject "watchmen" in 62:6 (see the main text below). The function of watchmen, as paralleled with remembrancers, is to remind YHWH, which is the very goal of intercession. Thus, the חשה and שקט (as they are parallel) in 62:1 and 6 are better suggestive for the prophetic intercession, which may be found in Gen 20:7; Ps 137; and Zech 1:12.

192. The prophetic formulae such as "thus says YHWH" (56:1, 4; 65:8, 13; 66:1, 12), "says YHWH/your God" (59:21; 65:7, 25; 66:9), and "oracle of YHWH" (56:8; 66:2, 17, 22) may convince the existence of the authorial prophet behind the text.

193. Childs 2001:503.

194. Emmerson 1992:73. Italics mine.

This view may be too much influenced by historical presumption that the text reflects the divine calling of the prophet.[195]

Second, proof of the presence of the historical (prophetic and authorial) figure *behind* the texts (58:1; 59:21; 62:1, 6; and 56:1 as well as 61:1) does not necessarily mean that he is being presented consistently in the prophetic narrative and that the interpretation of the figure in every text should be limited to, and governed by, the historical and personal view. In 58:1 and 63:7 (and 63:7—64:11[12]), it is undeniable that the texts are anchored to a historical situation and thus need to be understood accordingly. The presence of the self-consciousness of a prophet in 58:1 does not seem to provide evidence that the speaker in 61:1–3 refers to himself because the prophets too often speak on behalf of other persons such as YHWH, the Servant (especially in DI), and sometimes Israel (usually as a plural form). Identifying the first person speaker unconditionally with the prophet may be too naïve. The voice is of course primarily of the prophet (as an authorial or narrative voice) but he is speaking in the garb of another person as he so often does in prophecies. In 59:21; 61:1, 10; and 62:1, 6, the texts seem to relate primarily to the discourse situation rather than the historical situation, and in these texts the discourse level appears to be more dominant than the historical level in interpretation. 59:21 is also within the context of the (futuristic) eschatological coming (59:15b–21). Chs 60–62 are a unity and also present the eschatological fulfillment of salvation which may be brought by the coming of YHWH (59:15b–21; 63:1–6).

Third, although the mission of the anointed figure in 61:1–3 initially *takes after* that of a prophet, it is entirely uncertain whether it is limited to the historical prophet as actually portrayed by the text. The function and mission of the figure sometimes goes far beyond the historical personage, especially if the unity and coherence of the text are assumed. In particular, his mission involves eventually the strangers and foreigners (61:5), the nations and the peoples (61:6, 9, 11) as well as Zion (61:4). Furthermore, the year of favor of YHWH and the day of vengeance of our God extend to the eschatological horizon. Thus the anointed speaker has a mission reaching beyond the nation. A historical understanding of the mission in the passage cannot do justice to the full range of the message of the text.

---

195. For Skinner (1960:204), the self-consciousness of the prophet is presented in 58:1 and 62:1. For Whybray (1981:240), "there can be no doubt that the speaker's experiences and convictions are genuine and personal," and thus it must be a prophet that speaks. Also for Westermann (1969:353), the formulae in 61:1–3 and 62:1 suggest a self-introduction of a prophet. For Emmerson (1992:75–76), the sense of conviction of a personal call is so real that he has self-consciousness as the spokesman of the divine word.

In summary, although the mission or role of the anointed figure is somewhat prophetic, not only the text but also the narrative of TI as a whole does not seem to aim at presenting a historical prophet. Instead, there is another way of understanding.

Cannon considered the text 61:1–3 as *a* (fragment of the) Servant Song. This is because the passage has many parallels in the first three Servant Songs—such as the Spirit of YHWH (42:1//61:1) and the prophetic (or teaching; 50:4//61:1) and comforting tasks (42:3//61:1; 42:7; 49:9//61:1).[196] For him, chs 60–62 are also the work of DI as there are so many parallels in these chapters to DI (e.g., chs 42; 49; 54).[197] Thus, 61:1–3 is written as a Servant Song later than the main text of DI (chs 40–55 and 60–62) and inserted afterwards into the present place by DI himself, being the same process as experienced by the Servant Songs.[198] As far as the text can be said to be part of the Servant Songs, the anointed speaker in 61:1 is the Servant of the Servant Songs in DI.

Sometimes, the connection to the Servant Songs has been challenged, mainly due to alleged theological discrepancies. There is no word 'Servant' in the passage (61:1–3); 61:1–3 lacks the universalism of DI; and the passage lacks the Servant's characters such as humility, sense of failure and suffering. There is no echo of anointing in the Servant Songs.[199] However, none of these seems to be so crucial that it may rule out the connection.[200] So, the

---

196. Cannon 1929:284–88. For him (1929:287), the parallel points between the anointed figure and the Servant are as follows: (a) The two figures receive the Spirit of YHWH (42:1//61:1); (b) The Servant is inspired to sustain the weary with the tongue (50:4) while for the anointed figure the anointing is to bring good tidings to the afflicted and to bind up the brokenhearted (61:1); (c) The Servant does not break the bruised reed and not extinguish the dimly burning (כהה) wick while the anointed figure comforts those who mourn and gives the fainting (כהה) a praise (42:3 //61:3); (d) The Servant has the mission to open (פקח) the blind eyes, to bring out prisoners from the dungeon and those who dwell in darkness from the prison (42:7) and he says to those who are bound 'Go forth' and to those who are in darkness 'Show yourself' (49:9) while the anointed figure has been sent to proclaim liberty to captives and opening of the prison to those who are bound (פקח) (61:1); (e) In an acceptable time YHWH heard the Servant and in a day of salvation He helped the Servant (49:8) while the anointed figure is sent to proclaim the acceptable year of YHWH, and the day of vengeance of our God (61:2); (f) The two figures refer to God as אדני יהוה (50:4, 9//61:1). These parallel points are very persuasive though he could not present the follow-up analysis of the broader and deeper level and thus did not suggest the precise character of the Servant.

197. Cannon 1929:285–86. While, for Duhm (1892:xviii), chs 60–62 are part of TI, he argues that such a glorious vision as that in chs 60–62 cannot have been written by the ruined community which just returned from Babylon to Jerusalem.

198. In this he follows Duhm (1892:xx).

199. Muilenburg 1954:709; Whybray 1981:239–40; Skinner 1960:204–5.

200. Skinner (1960:204–5) summarizes why the anointed speaker cannot be the

anointed figure is identified with the Servant figure (his specific tasks are reserved here).

However, while Cannon's view highlights the continuity of the text with the Servant Songs, his view has fatal weaknesses in that not only is this view based on the unproven historical reconstruction, but also it separates the text (and the Servant Songs as well) from the present context(s) and sees the Servant texts as independent, as Duhm did.[201] This is also why Cannon argues that this text does not add anything new about the character or career of the Servant other than what is to be found in the Servant Songs.[202] However, just as the identity and ministry of the Servant become dynamic when the Songs are considered within their contexts, if 61:1–3 is investigated in the context, we may be able to understand the anointed figure more precisely as well as to establish a richer theology.

As a conclusion, although we may find several indications of the presence of the prophet behind the text of TI and although the functions and missions of the prophet may be similar with those of the anointed figure (or, the first-person speakers), the discourse does not suggest that the historical prophetic figure is exegetically presented in 61:1–3. The presentation of the historical prophet is very limited and is probably not intended by the narrative. However, it is also undeniable that sometimes the portrait of the Servant/Messianic figure has been anchored in, or modeled by, the historical or biographical mission of the prophet(s), which may be why the anointed figure (or, the Servant, in DI) has been often too narrowly identified with the prophet.[203] Consequently, we may conclude that behind the mission

---

Servant: (a) The Servant title does not appear in the text of 61:1–3. However, the third Servant Song (50:4–9) does not contain the title, either (cf. 50:10, the voice of the Servant); (b) the prophet's consciousness appears in 58:1, and probably in 62:1. However, the portrait of the Servant may be modeled by the prophetic mission and experiences (cf. 40:9; 41:27; 49:4; 50:4, 5–6); (c) the function of the speaker is just a herald of salvation, which lacks the universalism, being not beyond that of the prophet, while that of the Servant is a mediator of universal salvation. However, the mission of the anointed figure is universal as the year of the favor of YHWH and the day of vengeance may imply in connection with 63:4 and 6; (d) it is difficult to believe "that after the climax in chapter 53 the same personage should again appear in what must be considered a subordinate character." However, the description of the Servant's mission may not be necessarily chronological. The repetition is one of the literary strategy to present theology (the Davidic messiah, the Servant, and the Anointed One) in the book of Isaiah, as Motyer (1993:13–16) observed; (e) a much later prophet than Second Isaiah wrote this chapter. However, the dating is uncertain as we have already seen.

201. It has been argued that the Servant Songs cannot be separated from the context because they are closely intertwined with it. Also see North 1948:138.

202. Cannon 1929:288.

203. So does in DI as well, because of: (1) the proclaiming function (as in the herald

and function of the anointed figure in 61:1–3, who is identified with the Servant figure, there may lie prophetic functions, which provide the basis to describe the mission of the anointed figure, but they are extrapolated to the (future) eschatological dimension.

If we detect a Servant figure in the portrait of the anointed figure, we may be confronted with another issue: is the Servant (figure) a group of people or an individual, or both?

Fluid, Collective, or Individual Servant?

A fluid view of the Servant figure in 61:1–3 attempts to understand both Israel and the prophet himself. For Smart, the prophet DI describes his own ministry in 61:1–3,[204] which is identical with that of the Servant Israel in DI. Since true Israel is embodied in a prophet as a true son of the covenant, on whom the destiny of the chosen people of God is dependent, "when the prophet speaks with the voice of the Servant, he simultaneously speaks most personally and passionately for himself." Therefore, the prophet speaks of a mission, which is both Israel's and his own at the same time.[205] However, because, for Smart, the first person refers to Israel in 61:10–11, and 61:4–9 describes the mediating role of Israel between YHWH and the nations, he tends to see the anointed one in 61:1–3 as the Servant Israel/Zion rather than the prophet himself.[206]

This view of the Servant-Israel coincides with the understanding of the mission of the covenant community of the exodus tradition, and thus the covenantal tradition. In these traditions, Israel functions as the priestly people (or kingdom) among the nations, as found in the mission(s) in ch

---

of good news) and teaching function (41:27, cf. 42:1; 42:2; 48:16; 49:1, 2; 50:4–5; 53:11); (2) personal carriers and sufferings including death (49:4; 50:6–9; 52:13—53:12; cf. 41:11); (3) the narrative voices (40:1, 45:14, or 52:3—the narrative voice is hidden in the sentences such as "God/YHWH speaks . . ."; 53:1—"we"). However, the manifestation of the historical portrait of the prophet is very limited in DI.

204. For Smart, chs 40–66 and 34–35 belong to DI.

205. Smart 1967:260.

206. Smart 1967:259–60. Knight (1985:50) may hold the same view when he says the 'me' refers both TI and Israel at once because the language describing the mission of the anointed figure was the same one of the "calling of God's Servant people, Israel." However, he does not suggest any hermeneutical explanation why the 'me' can signify both TI, an individual, and Israel, a community. Rather, his understanding eventually seems to converge on Israel, because he (1985:59) simply says that the speaker in 61:10 is Zion. For Herbert (1975:163), too, the 'me' is Zion. For Leske (1994:898), too, the Servant (i.e., the Servant-Israel) is identified also with the people-covenant and the light to the nations.

61. In this understanding of the mission of the Servant, there are two chains of relation for the mediating roles of the Servant, i.e., (a) God—the Servant Israel—nations and (b) God—individual Servant—the corporate Servant Israel. However, Smart's understanding does not consider properly the shift of the roles of the Servant from corporate to individual level in DI texts, which is due to the failure of the nation Israel, and the relational tension between the two in the text (see 3.3 on 59:21).[207] Smart seems to have missed the relational tension between the individual Servant figure and the corporate Servant (i.e., the servants), as found in my interpretation of 59:21 and 61:1–3 and 4–9 (especially v. 9). In ch 61, the individual speaker has a mission for the people of Israel (61:1–3) and those people are called priests of YHWH (61:6) and covenanted with YHWH (61:8).

There has been another view for the Servant figure in 61:1–3. For Beuken, the anointed speaker uses the language of the Servant in DI in the presentation of himself to justify the entitlement of his mission.[208] In describing the tasks, the anointed figure is considered to be an echo of the combined figure of the Servant and the Herald in DI because the tasks of the anointed speaker adopt those of the first three Servant Songs,[209] and because the Herald and his mission are quoted in 61:1b–3a from 40:1–2 (to comfort, to proclaim) and 40:9 (herald of good tidings). According to Beuken, the Servant and the Herald of good tidings are actually identified in DI, not only because "the end of ch. 41 and the beginning of ch. 42 are strongly united semantically" (41:27–29; 42:1), but also because the two places are referred to here in the same verse.[210]

However, for Beuken, it is not the Servant, but the offspring of the Servant that takes shape in the speaker of 61:1–3. Of course 61:1 refers to 42:1 and 48:16, but it also refers to 44:2–3 ("I will pour out My Spirit on *your offspring* and My blessing on your descendants"). Even 59:21 ("*My Spirit*

---

207. He also may have been mistaken in his understanding of the Servant in DI, because it is not that the individual Servant and corporate Servant are mixed in DI, but that there is a clear transference of the role of the Servant from Israel (up to ch 48) to individual (after ch 49) in DI as we have seen before. It lacks the consideration of the entrance of the individual Servant on the stage because of the failure of the Servant Israel, and that of his role in the failed Israel (49:5, 6).

208. Anoint and spirit (61:1); cf. having been endowed with the spirit (42:1) and sent with the spirit (49:16).

209. In the first Servant Song (42:7, to open the blind eyes and to bring out prisoners from the dungeon), the second Song (49:5–6, to raise up the tribes of Jacob and to restore the preserved ones of Israel; 49:8–9, to restore the land, to make them inherit the desolate heritages, to say to those who are bound, 'Go forth'), and the third Servant Song (50:4, to sustain the weary one with a word).

210. Beuken 1989:415–18.

which is upon you, and *My words* which I have put in your mouth, shall not depart from your mouth, nor from the mouth of your offspring, nor from the mouth of your offspring's offspring from now and forever") refers to 44:3 with regard to "My Spirit" as well as 51:16 ("I have put My words in your mouth") with respect to "My Words." Thus, for him, the anointed speaker is to be identified with the offspring of the Servant, though the speaker can be (both) an individual and a collective body as well.[211]

However, some questions remain on the interpretive elaboration of Beuken. Although we can agree that 59:21 refers to 44:3 (Spirit upon offspring) and 51:16 (words on you) as well as 42:1 (Spirit on the Servant) and 48:16 (Spirit on the Servant), what is the warrant for his link between the "me" in 61:1 and "your offspring" in 59:21? Beuken does not explain the existence of the singular 'you' (upon you, your mouth) in 59:21. However, if this is kept in mind, it seems more probable to link the anointed speaker with the "you" rather than "your offspring" in 59:21, because the pattern of the relation between 59:21 and 61:1 seems to be parallel to that of the relation between 48:16 and 49:1, that is, a sudden entrance of the individual Servant (see 3.3 on 59:21),[212] and because while the Spirit and the word are granted to the "you," only the words are focused with respect to the offspring in that they shall not depart from the *mouth* of you, your offspring, and the offspring's offspring.

Beuken's view pursues an understanding of the mission and status of the anointed figure in the canonical form of the texts, considering the intertextual link between the text of 61:1–3 and other parts of the book of Isaiah. However, this view does not pay due regard to the tension between the corporate Zion and the individual, by identifying the anointed figure with the "offspring" of the Servant rather than with the Servant. It seems to lack the eschatological understanding of the mission of the anointed figure (see below) in the broader context and in relation to other themes of TI. In sum, this view has a deeper intertextual understanding of the texts of DI and chapter 61, but it neglects the emergence of the individual figure on the stage.

211. Beuken 1989:416. Childs (2001:504–5) and Seitz (1996:237–38) are of the same view. Although Seitz (2001:514) says that the prophet's [the anointed speaker's] mission is coordinated with that of the Servant and he calls the speaker as the Servant, in another article (1996:237–38) he argues that the Servant in DI and the Servant in TI have a genetic relationship, which implies that the Servant in 61:1 is the offspring of the Servant in DI. Seitz does not seem to fully realize the importance of his observation about the emergence of individual figure, which may be incorporated in the following section "Messianic figure."

212. Seitz 2001:419 and 502.

Our last alternative is the view of individual Servant figure. Delitzsch sees that the anointed speaker is the Servant for all the characteristics are found in the portrait of the Servant, who is the same person as the Messiah.[213] This view may be mainly because the anointed figure identifies himself with the Servant and herald in DI because of parallels to DI. A prophetic portrait has not been put forward by the narrative, and the mission of the anointed figure goes beyond the historical horizon. This is because it lies in the eschatological context due to the year of YHWH's favour and the day of vengeance of our God, and also because the consequence of the task of the anointed figure influences not only the people of Israel but also the nations. In 61:1–3, the anointed figure has been in view as the representative of the corporate Zion. Thus, the anointed figure is understood as the Servant figure, i.e., a Messianic figure.

3.5 Summary and Conclusion

According to our study of 59:15b–21, the coming of YHWH is a decisive event that initiates a new era in the historical arena. The coming of YHWH achieves the salvation expectation of the previous parts of TI (and the book of Isaiah), particularly 56:1–8, in which the covenant is understood as the incorporation of salvation as well as eschatological admonition. So the coming is with a view to the restoration of the covenant, opening a new salvific era.

The coming of YHWH is necessitated by the sin of the people and the consequent breach of the covenant, as YHWH sees the injustice of the

---

213. Delitzsch 1873:424–26. This is because, for him: (a) There have not been examples that the prophet speaks of himself in such a length as he has usually hidden himself under the surface; (b) it is always the Servant that has presented his own calling (49:1f.; 50:4f.; 42:1f.; 52:13—53:12); (c) every description of the anointed figure himself has its parallel counterpart in the Servant Songs in DI; (d) it is unexpected that the prophet has put himself to the foreground in ch 61 after he has prophesied the Servant of YHWH as coming forward in 49:1 and 50:4. Here, Delitzsch seems to use the word "the Messiah" as one who prefigures the portrait of Jesus, as the Suffering Servant in Isa 53. As Childs (2001:505) comments that this interpretation "has to be greatly refined," we may well reserve the intertestamental link because the full analysis of this is beyond our task in this dissertation (the NT sense of the Messiah), but we can pursue the theological analysis of the link between the anointed and the Messianic figure in PI and DI (the OT sense of the Messiah) and investigate the roles and missions of the two figures. We mention this sense of Messiah or Messianic figure. Torrey (1928:452) also considers chapter 61 as a Servant poem that takes shape of the Servant who is Messianically conceived. For Motyer (1993:500), too, the anointed figure in 61:1 is the Messianic figure that prefigures the second coming of the Lord Jesus.

people. But the coming is also understood as a response to the repentant people for their sins, so the coming is with a view to salvation.

The portrait of the coming YHWH is as King, i.e., Judge and Warrior. He equips himself with armor to undertake the eschatological task, which is related to both the punishment of the sinners and the salvation of the repentant. So the judgment of the coming YHWH is retributive.

The enemies that YHWH fights against are not only the nations but also the Israelites—YHWH is against the sinners wherever they are (within the community or outside Israel), or rather sin, since the report of the coming YHWH is mythical or apocalyptic and the traditional language applied to the external enemies is generalized to cover the sinners of the community as well. So the enemies of the coming YHWH are universal. Since the glory of YHWH is revealed to the whole world, the nations are understood to be saved.

The coming of YHWH includes, or is accompanied by, a Messianic figure, if my interpretation is right. An envoy is promised to come like a light. He will come to Zion as Redeemer. The language of the coming of YHWH is related to the task of the Servant in DI—He comes since there is no intercessor. The envoy is entrusted with the Spirit and the word of YHWH. With the envoy, the covenant is promised, and so the breached covenant is restored. The envoy is identified with the Anointed One in 61:1–3, who succeeds to the characteristics of the Servant in DI. This confirms that the envoy is also the Messianic figure.

Chapter 4

Zion the Eschatological Temple-City-Paradise (60:1–22)

4.1 Introduction

In chapter 2, I have argued that the covenant concept is the pivotal element of the eschatology of TI. The present situation is understood as a consequence of the breach of the covenant and eschatological salvation achieves the restoration of the covenant. The people are requested to keep justice and do righteousness, which is understood as walking within the frame of the covenant. Even foreigners can participate in eschatological salvation if, and only if, they meet the covenantal requirements to commit themselves to the covenantal bond to YHWH. In chapter 3, we have seen that the coming of YHWH is the decisive event that inaugurates the eschatological era. The purpose of the coming is to exact judgment on Israel as well as the nations, and to save some of them. The eschatological judgment is universal—it includes both Israel and the nations—and purificatory because only those who repent will form a new community, enjoying the eschatological salvation. The coming YHWH is portrayed as the Divine Warrior, and the theophanic tradition is in line with the Day of YHWH tradition. In the portrayal of the coming of YHWH, the future coming of an envoy is promised, who is understood as a Messianic figure. He, together with his descendants, is promised the Spirit and the word of YHWH.

This chapter seeks to show that Zion is also central to the eschatological schema, and incorporates the concepts of both Temple and city. Zion is the center of the world in the eschatological era: the kings and the nations, as well as the children of Zion, are coming to Zion, carrying their wealth and sacrifices. The concept of the new Zion is apocalyptic, not only in relation to the divine light replacing the heavenly bodies in the new Zion, but also because of the use of language describing Zion and other concepts. To this end, Isa 60 is chosen for detailed exposition because it is the best expression of the glory of Zion, lying structurally and thematically at the heart of TI. The glory of Zion (chapter 4) is achieved through the coming of YHWH (chapter 3), realizing the covenantal purpose of YHWH (chapter 2). In this chapter, I will discuss the importance of Isa 60 in TI, especially in chs 60–62 and in relation to the previous context (4.2). And I will also discuss the theological interpretation of the text (4.3).

4.2 Isa 60 in TI

This section argues that there is a literary and theological continuity between Isaiah 60 and the rest of TI. Some have proposed that ch 60 is a self-contained unit, discontinuous with its context, especially with chs 59 and 61.

A sharp break between chs 60 and 61 has been observed mainly due to the difference of the subject matter. While Zion is the subject matter in ch 60, ch 61 concerns a prophetic figure (61:1; Beuken) or "those who mourn in Zion" (61:3; Seitz).[1] Some theological discrepancies have also been detected. For Volz, ch 61 does not belong with chs 60–62, although ch 61 and chs 60 and 62 have some external resemblances:[2]

First, Volz assumes, allusions to DI in ch 61 usually keep the original senses, but those in chs 60 and 62 have only superficial links.[3] However, theological differences from DI in chs 60 and 62 seem to be overestimated. We give only three examples.

(1) For Volz, איים יקוו (the coastlands will wait for Me) in 60:9 signifies that the servants of YHWH wait for YHWH's command to bring the children of Zion home. In 51:5, the source text of 60:9, the nations (i.e., coastlands) wait for the instruction and salvation of YHWH. However, it is

---

1. Beuken 1989a:157; Whybray 1981:230; Cheyne 1895:337; Seitz 2001:505; Bonnard 1972:400; Lau 1994:22.

2. Volz 1932:255. For Cheyne (1895:337), too, ch 60 does not naturally follow chs 58–59, because the contents of the two sections are different.

3. Volz (1932:240) considers that literal quotations in chs 60 and 62 are used in different senses from the *Vorlage*: 60:9 ~ 51:5; 62:11 ~ 40:9; 62:11b ~ 40:10b; 62:10b ~ 40:3; 60:9b ~ 55:5; 60:16b ~ 49:26; 60:13 ~ 41:19.

not certain why the subject of יקוו is understood as the servants in 60:9, not as the coastlands (איים) as specified. Furthermore, the description for the coastlands does not change, either, although there is a slight difference between the descriptions in the two passages. The coastlands wait for YHWH to "give respect/worship to YHWH" in 60:9 while they "listen to the instruction of YHWH" and "enjoy the salvation of YHWH" in 51:4–5. But because ch 60 describes the eschatological salvation of Zion, and the nations/kings (60:3) as well as children of Zion (60:4) are approaching Zion in the chapter, "giving respect/worship to YHWH" also implies "joining the eschatological salvation" and vice versa. The phrase is therefore consistent in having wider meaning at the two places (see 4.3).

(2) As for 62:11 (Behold, your salvation comes) // 40:9 (Behold, your God), in which Volz finds a difference, we have already discussed that the coming of God and the coming of salvation are both eschatological realizations of divine salvation, both phrases being theophanic language (see 3.2).

(3) For Volz, 60:13 has a literary connection to 41:19, but with a new, different use, because the grandeur of the trees in DI serves the miraculous way home, i.e., "the real eschatological feat of YHWH," while the trees in TI are used as timbers to adorn the Temple. So for him, a complete change from the glory of YHWH to the glory of the Temple is reflected in TI.[4] But his interpretation of 60:13 and 41:19 depends on his assumption of the historical situation of the Temple reconstruction in the post-exilic community,[5] which may not be involved in the verse, and it lacks the understanding of a wider theology. Rather the exodus imagery in 41:19 is understood as the change of nature into the paradise in the eschatological era, which is also assumed in 60:13 (see 4.3).[6] In brief, within a fuller theology, quotations in chs 60 and 62 do not show differences in *theological* meanings from the source texts in DI.[7]

Secondly, for Volz, ch 61 divides the community, and only the faithful group is the receiver of salvation, while in chs 60 and 62 the community is not divided.[8] If unity is assumed, the splitting and holistic perspectives of the community do not conflict with each other but present an integrated and coherent theology at a higher level. Division of the community in ch

4. Volz 1932:239. See also Zimmerli 1963/1950:232.

5. Volz 1932:200, 241.

6. Muilenburg 1954:459.

7. 'Same meanings' in the two places that are linked in DI and TI signify that the same (theological) purport of the verses may be applied to the different (literary) contexts.

8. Smith (1995:26) also argues that chs 60–62 are addressed to the entire Jewish community, rather than to a group of oppressed or faithful people within the community.

61 is already present in 59:15b–21 and in chs 56–57 as well as in chs 65–66 (see 2.3 on 56:1–2, and 5.2), so forming one of the important eschatological messages of TI. Isaiah 60 and 62 focus on the saved people, i.e., the servants or the children of Zion. So, there is no theological discrepancy between ch 61 and chs 60 and 62, but only different aspects of a wider theology.

Thirdly, for Volz, ch 61 is YHWH-centered, while chs 60 and 62 are Jerusalem-centered. But the glorification of YHWH and that of Zion are different sides of the same eschatological realization, and not a contradiction. In the bigger picture of the eschatology of TI, the one implies the other and vice versa. In conclusion, Volz's argument for a radical discontinuity between chs 60 and 61 reflects the application of too rigid criteria of consistency.

While Cheyne considers that ch 60 does not naturally follow chs 58–59, precisely because there is a stark contrast,[9] for Muilenburg, ch 60 is related to ch 59 (see also 3.2). While ch(s) (58–)59 emphasize(s) judgment, darkness, and unrighteousness, ch 60 stresses redemption, light, and righteousness.[10] Chs 60 and 59 share the themes such as darkness, justice and salvation, coming, and redemption.[11] The light-darkness contrast in 60:1–2 is related to that in 59:9–10 and 58:8, 10 (see 4.3). The salvific age expected in chs 58–59 has come in ch 60. YHWH is coming to work salvation in 59:16–17; the wall of Zion is called salvation in 60:18. YHWH brings righteousness in 59:16; righteousness becomes the ruler in Zion in 60:17. Violence in the community in 59:6 is gone in the land of Zion in 60:18. The coming of YHWH in 59:15b–21 is repeated in 60:1–2 as the coming of the glory of YHWH. The Redeemer is promised to come in 59:20; YHWH is revealed to Zion as the Redeemer (60:16). So, an extensive theological continuity between chs 58–59 and 60 is evident, although the two parts may have different emphases—darkness and light, respectively. For Childs, while ch 59 presents the confession of the sins of the faithful and the consequent promise of the covenant, this promise is realized in chs 60–62; especially the future glorification of Zion in ch 60.[12] Between the two sections, there lies the theophanic intervention (59:15b–21).

Smith seeks to prove the unity and coherence of chs 60–62 in view of the redactional critical history.[13] He concludes that chs 60–62 as a whole is a unity, presenting the salvation of Zion and her people, especially due to sev-

---

9. Cheyne 1895:337.

10. Muilenburg 1954:697.

11. Bonnard 1972:400.

12. Childs 2001:494.

13. Smith 1995:26–38.

eral thematic links: the wealth of the nations flows into Zion in 60:5–7, 16, while it is supplied to those who mourn in Zion in 61:6. Zion is rebuilt and glorified in 60:10, 13, and 17 as well as in 61:4 and 62:2, 7. YHWH is glorified, being recognized as Saviour and Redeemer in 60:16, 21, while those who mourn in Zion will glorify him in 61:3. Shame turns into joy in the eschatological salvation in 60:5, while gladness and praise replace mourning and despair in 61:3, 7–8. The foreigners will serve Zion in 60:10, while they will work in the fields and vineyards in 61:5. YHWH will accept (רצון) the sacrifices and labors of the nations in 60:7, 10, while 61:2 presents the year of YHWH's favour (רצון). Jerusalem and her people will be renamed in the eschatological era in 60:14, 18 as well as in 61:3, 6; 62:4, 12.[14]

In conclusion, ch 60 is part of the core (chs 60–62) of TI and is related also to the preceding context (chs 58–59). Darkness due to the sins of the people in chs 58–59 turns into light of salvation because of the glory of the coming YHWH in ch 60.

4.3 Theological Interpretation of the Text

Having seen ch 60 in its context, this section argues that Zion is the eschatological city and Temple—the international cosmopolitan hub created by the coming of YHWH as light. The kings and the nations as well as the children of Zion flow into Zion with their wealth and sacrifices. Zion will be rebuilt and even foreign kings will participate in the reconstruction. Zion will be the heavenly Temple-city, in which nature changes into paradise and YHWH becomes their light. The portrait of Zion incorporates OT traditions related to creation, exodus, and the patriarchs. Deuteronomistic as well as Isaianic (PI, DI) traditions are also taken up in order to highlight the fulfilment of eschatological expectations.

1 Arise, shine, for your light has come,	קומי אורי כי בא אורך
and the glory of YHWH has risen upon you.	וכבוד יהוה עליך זרח:
2 For behold, darkness shall cover the earth,	כי־הנה החשך יכסה־ארץ
and thick darkness the peoples;	וערפל לאמים
but YHWH will arise upon you,	ועליך יזרח יהוה
and His glory will be seen upon you.	וכבודו עליך יראה:
3 And nations shall come to your light,	והלכו גוים לאורך
and kings to the brightness of your rising.	ומלכים לנגה זרחך:

14. Smith 1995:37–38.

This strophe presents the dawning of a new eschatological age, as the glory (of YHWH and of Zion) is the keyword of the chapter.[15] Zion is commanded to reflect or become light in the dark world as the glory of YHWH comes to her and the light of the glory of YHWH is shed upon her. As Zion sheds light as a secondary source, the kings and nations are drawing near to her light.[16] In this strophe, creation and exodus traditions as well as theophanic and Isaianic traditions are incorporated and integrated to indicate the fulfilment of eschatological expectation.

Some have interpreted this strophe as well as the whole poem from the historical point of view. For Delitzsch, the verbs 'arise' and 'shine' (60:1) refer to the "redemption from banishment" and the darkness in 60:2 to the night of seventy years' exile.[17] For Lau, too, the state of Zion being prostrate in darkness is in connection with the destruction of the city in 587 BC. Lau considers that the double imperative of ch 60 has a deliberate literary and stylistic connection to 51:17 and 52:1–2.[18]

The call to rise up in 52:2 (and 51:17 as well) is the request of the freeing from the captivity, since the exodus language is employed in 52:11–12.[19] The request is also linked with the command of departure from 'there,' which usually refers to the physical departure from Babylon. However, although the language of the request may at first glance refer to the physical return of the exiles from Babylon, it is also associated with the freeing from the bondage of sin that made her prostrate. The uncircumcised and defiled will not enter the awakened Zion in 52:1. The call is also accompanied by the command to separate from the unclean thing and to be pure in 52:11–12. Thus, the call for rising, as well as the exodus language, in the source text has a dual significance—a physical and a spiritual/covenantal return.[20] The Fourth Servant Song (52:13—53:12) at the climax of DI, however, may suggest that the spiritual return becomes more significant towards the close of DI to present an overall picture of theology, because the Servant carries the sins of the people.

15. For the glory of YHWH, see 6.3.

16. Muilenburg 1954:697, 698.

17. Delitzsch 1873:409.

18. Lau 1994:25–26.

19. Lau 1994:26. For Muilenburg (1954:602, 606), 51:17 and 52:1–2 belong to a unit and the call to awake Zion in 52:2 is taken from 51:17, so the two imperatives in the two places are understood at the same way.

20. Muilenburg (1954:607) comments, "the uncircumscised and the unclean" (52:1) is "[N]ot merely a reference to freedom from foreign oppression . . . , but to the cultically unclean, revealing the inveterate syncretism which had corrupted Israel's faith . . . ."

Although "your light has come" (and the double imperative as well) may still refer to both physical and spiritual meanings, the historical realization of the physical return seems suspended. There is no reference to the specific historical event in the context, so the second sense of 'arising' fits the context better. The light/darkness metaphor is linked to 59:9–15a, in which Zion was plunged into darkness and hoped for light (59:9–10). The darkness signifies the *Unheil*, which is expressed as the lack of justice and righteousness in the covenantal order (see 3.2).[21] Although the poem adopts the language of the 'returning' of the children of Zion and the pilgrimage of the nations (60:4–9), this is primarily metaphorical since there is no evidence for its historical realization even though its ultimate historical anchorage is unavoidable. Thus, although there may well be a literary connection,[22] a direct historical reference in the verses is unlikely. The language in this poem tends to be apocalypticized. It does not remain physical but rather tends to suggest a symbolic and spiritual sense.[23] This is why a historical interpretation of the chapter has been rejected by Beuken, who comments that political, social, and economic terms in ch 60 are based on DI, but are now understood metaphorically.[24] Westermann also considers that the theophanic language in 60:1–3 is very much "spiritualized," because TI "does not link YHWH's coming to Israel with a definite historical event."[25] So, the two imperatives indicate the eschatological fulfilment of the salvation expectation of DI and TI.

In fact, the light/darkness metaphor in 60:1–3 is the fulfilment of a metaphor that has been frequently used in the book of Isaiah.[26] In particular,

21. Clements 1997b:453; Seitz 2001:505; Koenen 1990:153; Beuken 1989a:164.

22. Cheyne 1895:339; Beuken 1989a:163; Childs 2001:496; Whybray 1981:230; Muilenburg 1954:698.

23. Muilenburg 1954:698.

24. Beuken 1989a:158; Volz 1932:241; Cheyne 1895:337–38; Whybray 1981:229; Lau 1994:24. Scholars have identified the post-exilic situation of the poem, especially because of the references to the temple and the building of the city wall in 60:7, 13, 17 and in 60:10. Other factors were also included such as: the holy city being cut-off (v. 15), the poverty-stricken, ill-governed and ill-defended city (vv. 16–18), and small population (v. 21) (Cheyne 1895:337–38). For Lau (1994:24), the date is between the inauguration of the second temple (515 BC) and the construction by Nehemiah (445 BC). However, for Childs (2001:497), the language that refers to the temple and wall is "too elusive to reconstruct chronology."

25. Westermann 1969:357.

26. Motyer 1993:494; Beuken 1989a:164. The contrast between light and darkness occurs: In PI: 5:20, 30; 8:22–9:1, 13:10. In DI: 42:6–7, 16, 45:7, 50:10. Darkness as the counter-sign of salvation alone appears: 45:3, 19, 47:5, 49:9. Light alone occurs: 2:5, 4:5, 10:17, 26:19, 30:26, 49:6, 51:4.

for Clements, 60:1–3 is parallel to 49:6 (and 42:6) and 9:1[2].[27] In DI, the Servant, whether he is corporate or individual, is "the light of the nations" (49:6; 42:6) and "the covenant of the people" (49:8; 42:6).[28] The former title may indicate the gathering of the children of Zion and the nations as suggested in 49:12, 17–18(21) and 22–23, which is realized in 60:1–5. This link suggests that Zion's role in the world fulfils the Servant's function among the nations. This transference of role is also evidenced by the fact that Zion coalesces the various themes in the discourse of the Servant: not only light (42:6; 49:6; 60:1–3), but also being high and lifted up (52:13; 60:1–3, 10, 14), acknowledgement by the kings/nations (52:15; 60:3, 14), and the promises given to the Servant to gain the righteous (53:11; 60:21).[29] The link of 60:1–3 to DI's metaphoric system is also reinforced by the fact that the theophanic revelation of "the glory of YHWH" (60:1) echoes 40:5, in which the glory of YHWH will be revealed to all flesh.[30] In 40:1–11, it is promised that YHWH comes and the eschatological salvation is available to all the nations (see 60:4–5).[31] So the eschatological expectation of DI is fulfilled ultimately in 60:1–3.

Lau rejects the direct connection of the light/darkness metaphor to 9:1[2], because light is bound up with an imminent historical event there. It signifies release from judgment of YHWH without any eschatological implications such as the coming of YHWH, the appearing glory of Zion, and the pilgrimage of the nations to Zion in 9:1[2].[32] However, even he admits an indirect thematic link, because the metaphor might be given an eschatological force through the 'Day of YHWH' tradition or the 'Servant of YHWH' tradition.[33] The (indirect) link may be reinforced by the fact that the former time of darkness and distress (8:22–8:23[9:1]) is in contrast to the latter time of light (9:1[2]), which is parallel to the contrast of light and darkness in 60:1–3.[34] It seems appropriate to judge that, contra Lau, the light in 9:1 is eschatological as it is associated with the Messianic expectation in the future (9:6[7]). By the link of light-metaphor, the eschatological ex-

27. Clements 1997b:453; Lau 1994:30.

28. Lau (1994:30) considers that the Servant in both 42:6 and 49:6 is corporate—in the former, Israel; in the latter, community of Zion. But, as I have discussed in chapter 3, the latter Servant is individual as commissioned in 48:16b, while the former is corporate. Seitz 2001:502.

29. Seitz 2001:508.

30. Cheyne 1895:339; Childs 2001:496; Lau 1994:30.

31. Seitz 2001:508; Volz 1932:244; Beuken 1989a:164–65.

32. Lau 1994:30.

33. Lau 1994:30.

34. Seitz 2001:508; Whybray 1981:230; Westermann 1969:358.

pectation is shared between PI (8:23—9:6[9:1–7]) and TI (ch 60), although ch 60 does not include explicitly the Davidic Messianic expectation of 9:5–6[6–7].[35] The link may suggest that the eschatological vision of Zion in ch 60 is associated with the Messianic era (see 5.3 on 65:25).[36]

Although the contrast between light and darkness in 60:2 is shared with Gen 1:4, 18, Lau rejects the possible literary or thematic link, because creation tradition is not explicit in 60:1–3.[37] However, some scholars have detected it.[38] First, contrary to Lau, 'the' darkness (החשך; with a definite article) may be an indication of the literary link, because it is the only oc-currence of החשך + (ה)אור) elsewhere in the OT (apart from Eccl 2:13). As Muilenburg comments, "it is not impossible that the poet has in mind the deep darkness before the Creation" (Gen 1:2–3).[39] Second, the light/darkness contrast in 60:1–3 may also be related to Exod 10:22–23, in which Israelites have light, while darkness spreads over Egypt, or to Exod 14:20, in which the pillar of the cloud/fire separates between the armies of Israel and Egypt.[40] This may support the creational relation of the passage because the creation and the exodus are often associated in the mythical thought in the book of Isaiah and the OT (Isa 51:9–16; Ps 74:12–17; Hab 3:3–7).[41] Third, the creational link of 60:1–3 may be reinforced by 60:19–20, which is parallel to 60:1–3 in the structure of the chapter, because 60:19–20 may have creational involvement (see below).[42] Fourth, the theophany in 60:1–3 is related to the 'final' and universal judgment of 59:15b–21 and 63:1–6 (see ch 3), so it may justify a creational involvement, as "the end of time is then a repetition of the beginning of time."[43] Besides, the eschatological portrait of ch 60 (and TI as well) tends to incorporate eschatological expectations in Isaiah—the Day of YHWH, exodus theophany, the Servant of YHWH, and Messianic traditions. For Seitz, darkness in 60:2 is "hardly one amenable to 'the confines of this world and of history.'" So it is an apocalyptic term.[44] For

35. Seitz 2001:509.

36. Lau considers that 9:1 (and Mica 7:8ff and Jer 13:16, too) is theme-historical matrix of the eschatology of the day of YHWH or the Servant of YHWH tradition.

37. Lau 1994:29.

38. Volz 1932:244; Bonnard 1972:404.

39. Muilenburg 1954:698.

40. Whybray 1981:230; Beuken 1989a:192. According to Beuken, Jewish tradition has connected ch 60 with the nineth plague of the exodus (Exod 10:21–29) more than with the pillar of cloud/fire (Exod 13:20—14:24).

41. Beuken 1989a:251. See 3.3 on 59:16.

42. Polan 2001:54–55; Whybray 1981:237; Seitz 2001:509; Koenen 1990:142.

43. Muilenburg 1954:698.

44. Seitz 2001:510.

Volz, the phrase "your light has come" reflects the New Year's Festival (Tabernacle feast), which is a light feast, so 60:1–3 portrays the eschatological new year, which symbolizes the new creation as a repetition of the creation.[45] Therefore, although the immediate context does not directly refer to creation, it may be in the background of 60:1–3 as ch 60 presents the ultimate (eschatological) portrait of Zion. This fits the general theology of TI (see 5.3 on 65:17–25), theological unity of TI being assumed.

60:3 combines the themes of light and the coming of the nations to Zion and may involve Torah instruction as well.[46] The coming of the nations/kings to Zion is reminiscent of 2:2–5, so that 60:1–3 may include the fulfilment of 2:2–5.[47] According to 2:3, it is because Torah comes forth from Zion that the nations flow into Zion. According to Volz, the coming of the nations to Zion is different in the two passages, because they come with a view to the instruction of YHWH in 2:2–5, while they bring the children of Zion and their own wealth in ch 60.[48] For Lau, too, YHWH supports above all his people rather than delivers instruction to the nations and, while 2:2–5 refers to an imminent historical event, which is not eschatological, 60:1–3 presents a strong eschatological connection between Zion and YHWH.[49] However, Lau's observation of the old mythological imagery of God's mountain Zion as a seat of divinity in 2:2–5 suggests that the passage is eschatological.[50] Having instruction of YHWH (2:5) and sacrificing at the Temple, and giving tribute to YHWH (60:7, 9), are all crucial elements of the covenantal bond with YHWH. The salvation state of the people is associated with the Torah instruction and walking in accordance with the law, as evidenced in 66:2 ('tremble at my word') and 56:1–8 (see 2.3).[51] So, the seemingly different purposes of the two passages are coherent in the wider context of theology. A canonical perspective on the book of Isaiah suggests a promise-fulfilment relation between the two passages, which may suggest Torah involvement of the passage, although it is not explicit.

---

45. Volz 1932:244. For him, Jesus' saying "I am the light of the world" in John 8:12 reflects the light feast, which is Tabernacle feast as expressed in 7:12. For him, the day of YHWH in Amos 5:18 is also light feast (cf. 5:21). Volz's suggestion of the link of 60:1–3 with the New Year Feast is accepted by Muilenburg (1954:698), while rejected by Whybray (1981:231).

46. Whybray 1981:231.

47. Childs 2001:496; Beuken 1989:164; Lau 1994:29.

48. Volz 1932:245.

49. Lau 1994:32.

50. This cannot be a metaphorical presentation of the present, because 2:2–5 describes the future expectation.

51. Beuken 1989:164–65.

Meanwhile, theophany in 60:1–3 may have another suggestion for the Torah instruction. As Lau observed, the theophanic verb זרח has a literary connection to Deut 33:2, since this is the only other place in the OT that the verb has YHWH as subject.[52] The purpose of the coming of YHWH in Deut 33:2 is to instruct the multitude of the holy people (רבבת קדש) with the Torah of Moses, as He is coming to the assembly of the holy people Israel (Deut 33:2–5). If the theophany itself is associated with the Torah instruction in 60:1–3 as in the *Vorlage* (Deut 33:2–5), the holy people from the nations as well as Israel participate in the salvation of YHWH as they are taught the Torah.[53] DI tradition may also suggest that the passage implies Torah instruction (also see vv. 8–9). 40:1–11 is also linked with 60:1–3 in that כבוד יהוה and ראה in 40:5 as theophanic terms are parallel with those in 60:1–2. The unfailing word of YHWH in 40:8 forms the pivotal message of DI, as it reappears in 55:8–10 forming a macroscopic *inclusio* in DI. The coming of the nations/kings is the fulfilment of the universal call in 55:1. 60:9b is a literal quotation of 55:5 (see below), in which the nations are summoned and will hasten to Zion. Thus, to teach the Torah to the nations becomes one of the missions of the Servant, which is one of the pivotal elements in the eschatology of DI (42:4; 51:4, 7; cf. 50:4, 5, 10). Therefore, 60:1–3 may involve Torah instruction as the achievement of the eschatological expectation of DI in 40:1–11. This would be achieved by the teaching work of the Servant. In conclusion, seeing the literary and thematic connection with Deut 33:2–5 as well as 2:2–5 and 40:1–11, we see that the theophanic experience of the assembly of Israel in Deut 33:2–5 is transformed to the eschatological vision in 2:2–4 and 60:1–3. Thus nations will be included with the holy people. They will be taught the Torah, and the eschatological expectation in 2:2–4 and 40:1–11 is fulfilled in 60:1–3.

The coming of the nations/kings to Zion also fulfils the work of the Servant according to 49:7 (the Servant is the light for the Gentiles in 49:6) and 52:15, in which the kings of the nations give obeisance to the Servant and understand what they have not heard.[54] This fulfilment is evidenced by the fact that 60:4 quotes 49:14–26 (especially vv. 22–23; see below), which is the salvific promise given to the Servant. In it the nations flow to the standard (נס) with the children of Zion carried in their arms or on their shoulder (49:22).[55] Although the Servant is not explicit in ch 60, his identity and

---

52. Lau 1994:28. Ringgren (1980, TDOT [4]:זרח, 141) has already observed that the verb is used in the theophanic description in both texts.

53. Volz 1932:245.

54. Motyer 1993:494; Cheyne 1895:339.

55. Childs 2001:496; Beuken 1989a:166; Lau 1994:34. See note below.

mission are detected in TI (59:19–21; 61:1–3; 61:10—62:1; 62:6–7; 63:1–6; see 3.4 and 6.3).

In summary, the glory of YHWH comes to Zion, shedding light upon her, so Zion becomes a light, by which the nations/kings, who were in darkness, are attracted to Zion. This is not only the fulfilment of the eschatological expectations of DI and PI, but also a re-realization of the creational work and exodus theophany. The nations as saved will be taught the Torah in Zion according to earlier expectations. Although TI has also not taken up explicitly certain themes from the tradition(s) he uses (e.g., the Servant) in order to highlight others, e.g., Zion, it does not signify that he is rejecting or is unaware of those themes, but he affirms their fulfilment in a circuitous way.

4 Lift up your eyes all around, and see;	שאי־סביב עיניך וראי
they all gather together, they come to you;	כלם נקבצו באו־לך
your sons shall come from afar,	בניך מרחוק יבאו
and your daughters shall be carried on the hip.	ובנתיך על־צד תאמנה:
5 Then you shall see and be radiant;	אז תראי ונהרת
your heart shall thrill and exult,	ופחד ורחב לבבך
because the abundance of the sea shall be turned to you,	כי־יהפך עליך המון ים
the wealth of the nations shall come to you.	חיל גוים יבאו לך:

60:4–9 continues the theme of the coming of the nations/kings in 60:3. In 60:4–5, they bring the children of Zion and the wealth of the nations to Zion. When Zion sees the nations coming (60:3), she realizes that they carry her children and bring their wealth. The passage builds on the message of DI. The coming of the nations achieves the prior eschatological expectation of the book.

Who are the "all" (כלם) that Zion sees when she lifts up her eyes in 60:4a? Koenen suggests nations/kings in view of 60:3.[56] For Beuken, while 60:3 suggests the nations/kings, it is the children of Zion from 60:4b.[57] The best answer is 'both'—when Zion looks at the nations/kings coming, she realizes that her children are also coming, carried by them. 60:4a quotes 49:18a, and 60:4b is taken from 49:12 and 22–23.[58] In ch 49, which is the

---

56. Koenen 1990:137. Whybray (1981:231) follows it.

57. Beuken 1989a:165; Lau 1994:35. For Lau, although v. 3 suggests the nations/kings, it is "the descendents of the exiles" from 49:14–26, the background of v. 4a.

58. Muilenburg 1954:699; Childs 2001:496; Westermann 1969:358; Seitz 2001:509; Whybray 1981:231; Lau 1994:35. There is sufficient evidence that whole chapter 49 is in the background of ch 60. Childs 2001:496; Beuken 1989a:166; Lau 1994:34. The verb פאר in 49:3 is a key word in ch 60 (vv. 7, 9, 13, 21) (Beuken 1989a:169). We have already seen that 49:6 is reminded in 60:1–3. 49:12 is quoted in 60:4b (Childs 2001:495; Whybray 1981:231). 49:18a is literally repeated in 60:4a (Muilenburg 1954:699; Childs 2001:496; Westermann 1969:358; Seitz 2001:509; Whybray 1981:231). 49:22b is taken in 60:4b (Muilenburg 1954:699; Childs 2001:495; Cheyne 1895:339). 49:23 is reminded in

background to ch 60, the Servant is promised not only that he will "bring Jacob back to him and gather Israel to himself" in 49:5, but also that he will be "a light of the Gentiles" to bring salvation to the ends of the earth. In 49:12, the children of Zion come back to her; in 49:17–18, while the devastators will depart from Zion, the children of Zion will come back (49:18a; this is quoted in 60:4a). However, in 49:22–23, YHWH will lift up his standard (נס) to the nations, and they will bring Zion's children to her. So, if ch 49 is the background to 60:4, the coming "all" signifies, as 60:3–4 suggests, both the nations/kings and the children of Zion, as is the work of the Servant according to the source text.

The theme of gathering (קבץ), which involves the nations as well as Israel, has developed throughout the book. קבץ (60:4) has a link with 40:10–11, because the glory of YHWH (60:1–2) is related to 40:5, in which all flesh together will see it (see 60:1–3 above).[59] The theophanic promise of 40:5 is repeated in 40:10–11, in which YHWH as shepherd is gathering his people like lambs. קבץ also has a connection with 11:12, in which YHWH will lift a standard (נס), i.e., the Davidic Messiah (11:11), for the nations (גוים), and gather (קבץ) the scattered of Israel.[60] This is supported by the fact that YHWH promises again to lift a banner in 49:22 (נס) to the peoples (עמים). In 55:1–5, whoever is thirsty, either in Israel or in the nations, is invited, and (even) the nations will hasten to Zion (or, the Davidic Messiah). In the light of the 'gathering' theme, 60:1–4 is related to 11:12, 40:10–11(1–11) and 55:5(1–5), the theme having been reaffirmed and developed, all keeping the purport that YHWH will gather the scattered Israel and the nations through his envoys (Davidic Messiah, Servant, or the Anointed One; see 3.3 on 59:19–21). In the gathering of the nations, the mission given to the Davidic Messiah in PI is passed to the Servant in DI and fulfilled in Zion in TI.

Because the nations gather, are they saved? The gathering motif in 60:4 is related to 66:18–21, in which YHWH declares that He will gather all nations and tongues so that they may see His glory (66:18), although the nations are subject to the divine judgment (punishment) of the coming YHWH as seen in chapter 3. The salvation of the nations is exhibited by their experiences of the same fortune as the new people of Zion.

First of all, the nations are saved because they share the concept of the remnant (66:18–19b). The word group of פלט (and מלט), together with

---

60:14 (Whybray 1981:235; Seitz 2001:509; Zimmerli 1963:222; Westermann 1969:362). 49:23b is also quoted in 60:16 (Cheyne 1895:339; Zimmerli 1963:222; Lau 1994:57). 49:26 is quoted in 60:16b (Whybray 1981:236; Bonnard 1972:410; Lau 1994:57; Volz 1932:240; Zimmerli 1963:222; Cheyne 1895:339).

59. Beuken 1989a:165.

60. Delitzsch 1873:410.

שאר, indicates the 'remnant of Israel' concept in PI and DI (and in the OT as well).[61] The people of Israel are subject to divine judgment, but the survivors (פלט) of the judgment will be saved (10:20–21; 46:3–4) to form the remnant. Meanwhile, 66:19b ("sending those who escaped") seems to explain 66:18. It is those who escape that YHWH will gather from all nations and tongues.

Who then are the escapees (פליטים)? Only the intertextual connection to DI may suggest a clue.[62] Above all, the "escapees (of the nations)" has a resonance with 45:20–25, in which the survivors of the nations are urged to draw near to YHWH (45:20) and called to be saved by turning to Him (45:22).[63] In this passage, the escape is from the world-wide conquest by Cyrus which includes the defeat of Babylonia.[64]

However, for Whybray, following Snaith, 45:20–25 cannot function as an invitation to the universal salvation, even though he understands the phrase as (the survivors of) the "nations."[65] For Snaith, the "escaped of the nations" in 45:20 refers to the "descendants of Israel (i.e., of the exile)" in 45:25 and the "ends of the earth" denotes the exiled Israelites in 45:22. The "ends of the earth" is a lyric exaggeration signifying the place where *the Israelites* are as in 43:6 and 41:9.[66] Hollenberg suggests the same view. He interprets פליטי הגוים as "the survivors *among* the nations," which implies the "*foster children*" of Israel or "crypto-Israelites," that is, the Israelites who are scattered in the nations and lose their identity so as to be swallowed up by them (italics his). Thus, for him, "the nations" in DI as well as "the ends of the earth" in 45:22 refers to this group of people.[67]

---

61. Ruprecht 1997:990; Hasel 2001:562–64. For פלט, 4:2; 5:29; 10:20; 15:9; 37:31–32 (cf. 45:20; 66:19); and for מלט, 20:6; 31:5; 34:15; 37:38; 46:2, 4; 49:24–25; 66:7. According to Ruprecht (1997:986), פלט and מלט are virtually identified because they are so similar in meaning and construction.

62. The following discussion is not about TI text, but about DI text. But the discussion may be justified as the legitimate part of "theology of TI" because the canonical reading and the assumption of unity of the book of Isaiah (see the historical survey and methodology paper) justifies that DI (and PI as well) provides the literary background of TI. There seems no interpretational clue for the term in TI and DI provides an intertextual link to the phrase. Thus, the intertextual link in DI may suggest the interpretational clue.

63. Westermann 1969:425; Whybray 1981:290.

64. Whybray 1981:111. Although Cyrus is called my shepherd (44:28) and his anointed (45:1), he is not considered to be a Messianic figure, but rather a second Pharaoh, who sent the people of YHWH. See Seitz 1996:219–240.

65. Whybray 1981:111–12. He even contends that the "ends of the earth" refers to the whole created world, not only the human inhabitants in it. This view seems strained.

66. Snaith 1967:185–86 and 160.

67. Hollenberg 1969:31–32 and 25–26.

However, as Winkle rightly notes, Hollenberg's approach is highly questionable in that, because of his methodological presumption, he always (mis)interprets "the nations" as the "foster children of Israel in the nations" and thus the "nations" are identified with Israel even in cases where the nations are obviously intended in the texts.[68] Although the "ends of the earth" may be poetic (as in Snaith), the phrase should refer to nations beyond Israel. This is because the phrase is expressed in the context of creation in 40:28 and is parallel with both the coastlands in 41:5 and the nations in 52:10. Even though we cannot entirely deny the possibility of interpreting פליטי הגוים as a reference to the Israelite survivors among the nations, the fugitives are here understood to be international survivors including the Babylonians. This is because 45:14, in the context of the passage (45:20–25), tells of the foreigners joining Zion and, according to Seitz, the following reference to the idolaters being ashamed in 45:16 continues in 46:1 with a mention of the fall of Babylonian gods.[69] Consequently, as Hasel also opines, the "survivors of the nations" in 45:20 does not refer to the Israelite survivors, but to "an eschatological remnant of the pagan nations that worship idols, who have escaped YHWH's judgment."[70]

Therefore, if we accept the connection with 45:20–25, the escapees in 66:19 are the people of the nations who survived the divine judgment of the coming YHWH, as is evidenced in 66:15–16 and in 66:18 (באה).[71] This implies that the nations join the remnant of Israel. In fact, the "servants" (66:14) are linked also to 56:6, in which the Gentiles are given the promise that they will be the servants if they keep the Sabbath and stick to the covenant. Therefore, the nations undergo the same fate as Israel in that they are subject to the divine judgment, receive salvation as survivors, and join the eschatological covenant.

In brief, because the nations go through the experience of Israel and join the remnant, they are considered saved. In addition to that, the nations take after Israel in several other ways. First, they take part in the mission to the world which was originally given to Israel (66:19).[72] In 66:19, the survivors of the nations are sent to the nations and coastlands to reveal the

---

68. Winkle 1985:454. The passages Hollenberg interprets "the nations" in such a way include: 45:20–25; 42:1–7; 42:10–13; 44:1–5; 49:1–7; 49:8–26; 51:4–6; 52:13—53:12; and chs 54–55. Hollenberg 1969:31–36.

69. Seitz 2001:401.

70. Hasel 2001:565.

71. According to Motyer (1993:526), the imagery of 65:8–9 is reminiscent of that in 63:1–6, which implies that the judgment of YHWH to produces the servants in 65:8–9 may be exerted over the nations as well.

72. Westermann 1969:425.

glory of YHWH, which was originally a mission of Israel (42:6).[73] Second, the nations commit themselves to the worship of YHWH (66:20). This is a deliberate contrast to the condemnation of the idolaters of Israel in 66:17, 3; 65:3–4, and 11. While the old Israel has sinned by idolatry, the nations will worship YHWH, which implies that they will be in the covenantal relation with YHWH, joining the servants. Thus the worship of the nations fulfils 56:7. Third, they are selected even as priests and Levites (66:21).[74] In short, the gathering motif linked to 66:18–21 suggests the salvation of the nations, because their experiences are the same as those of the servants from Israel.

However, there is still a difference between the Jewish servants and the servants from the nations in that the nations/kings bring the "abundance of the sea" (המון ים)/the "wealth of the nations" (חיל גוים) to Zion (60:5).[75] The 'wealth of the nations' is related to 61:6, in which the native people of Israel will be called the priests of YHWH and the ministers of our God, feeding on the wealth of the nations. For Whybray, the 'priests of YHWH' in 61:6 is to be understood as metaphorical, denoting a privileged status of the Jews.[76] For Kissane, too, the 'priests/ministers' indicates that Israel is considered as the first-born with respect to the nations, "like the sons of Aaron in relation to the rest of Israel."[77]

In short, the nations share the salvation of the new people of Zion as they have a stake in their experience of the transformation. Some of them become the remnant through the divine judgment, are entrusted with the

---

73. The world mission is entrusted to Israel in DI. In the First Servant Song, the servant Israel is appointed to become the covenant of the people and the light of the nations (42:6) so that the coastlands wait for the Torah (42:4) and only YHWH will be glorified (in the world) (42:8). Because of the failure of the Servant Israel (42:18–21), however, the role of the servant is transferred to the individual servant in the Second Servant Song (cf. 48:16). In the Second Servant Song, the titles of the servant are confirmed (49:6, 8), the light of the nations bringing salvation to the ends of the earth, but the servant being the individual servant. As we have taken notice before, after the death of the Suffering Servant, the role of the Servant is shifted to the servants in TI (as called democratization).

74. The 'priests' and 'Levites' do not signify blood family here, but only their duties. As it were, some of the Gentiles will be in charge of the duties similar to those of the priests and Levites in the temple worship. As Whybray (1981:291) concedes, although "among them" (מהם) may refer by the syntax to the nations who brought Israelites or the Israelites, the former is preferable because the nations have been focused throughout the passage.

75. The two phrases may be synonymous or hendiadyc in broader meaning, if the 'sea' represents the nations or the world (Beuken 1989a:167). The abundance of the sea may signify "the sea-borne wealth of the nations" (Muilenburg 1954:700).

76. Whybray 1981:243.

77. Kissane 1943:275.

original mission of the servant Israel, worship YHWH, and serve Him even as priests and Levites, in addition they gather to Zion like the servants from Israel. In these experiences, they stand on the same footing with the servants, i.e., the remnant Israel before YHWH.

In summary, the nations come to Zion together with Zion's children. They also bring their wealth to Zion. This pleases her. The motif of the coming of the nations fulfils the eschatological expectation of PI and DI, as displayed in קבץ and נס as well as in the exodus imagery. While the nations were the enemy of Israel in PI and DI, they are now foster children of Zion, the people of Israel being the first-born son.

6 A multitude of camels shall cover you,	שפעת גמלים תכסך
the young camels of Midian and Ephah;	בכרי מדין ועיפה
all those from Sheba shall come.	כלם משבא יבאו
They shall bring gold and frankincense,	זהב ולבונה ישאו
and shall bring good news, the praises of YHWH.	ותהלת יהוה יבשרו:
7 All the flocks of Kedar shall be gathered to you;	כל־צאן קדר יקבצו לך
the rams of Nebaioth shall minister to you;	אילי נביות ישרתונך
they shall come up with acceptance on My altar,	יעלו על־רצון מזבחי
and I will beautify My beautiful house.	ובית תפארתי אפאר:

This strophe forms part of the previous pilgrimage of the nations, focusing on the transport by land from the East.[78] The camels and flocks come to Zion, carrying gifts to (YHWH in) the Temple and offering themselves on the altar of YHWH.[79]

For Whybray, (religious) nationalism is "unmistakable" in 60:4–9.[80] For Volz, too, the material splendor of Zion is the sign of the crude postexilic nationalism.[81] However, Childs argues that YHWH's supremacy and Zion's exaltation do not imply that the nations will be destroyed. They are coming to Zion to be incorporated in Zion. They are coexistent, although there may be a difference in rank or status (see above on 60:4–5).

The names of tribes in these verses stand for all the nations in the world, referring to Gen 25. Midian, Ephah, and Sheba are from the lineage of Abraham and Ketura (Gen 25:2–4); Kedar and Nebaioth are sons of Ishmael (Gen 25:13).[82] In Gen 17:5, Abraham is the father of a multitude of the

78. Whybray 1981:232.

79. Muilenburg 1954:701.

80. Whybray 1981:231.

81. Childs 2001:497.

82. Beuken 1989a:168; Lau 1994:41. Epha is the first son of Midian. For Lau, the nations are of the east and the west, i.e., from everywhere, as an eschatological concept.

nations, so the tribes represent all the nations of the world.[83] This implies the universality of salvation, as do a number of other indications.

"To bring good news" (60:6) may display the salvation of the nations. For Lau, the subject of בשר is the prophetic author (61:1), because the title "praise" (תהלה) is given to (the gates of) Zion by YHWH in 60:18, 61:11, and 62:7 (cf. 61:3).[84] However, the phrase "to proclaim praise of YHWH" is resonant (rather) with 66:19 (והגידו את־כבודי בגוים), in which the nations are the subject. So, here, too, the subject is probably (the people of) the nations, as represented by "all from Sheba," although Lau was hesitant to accept it because he thought the praise they proclaim is unclear. The "praise of YHWH" (תהלת יהוה) is related to 63:7, in which it signifies the praiseworthy works of YHWH.[85] In 63:7, it is the salvation and redemption (including protection and guidance) of Israel as the people of YHWH in the covenantal relationship. The "praise" is linked often to the restoration of Zion and the universal participation of the nations in the restoration (60:6, 18, 61:3, 11, 62:7).[86] According to Cheyne, 60:6 (ותהלת יהוה יבשרו) is linked to 42:10–12 (ותהלתו באיים יגידו), in which the nations are asked to announce (נגד) YHWH's praise (תהלתו; vv. 10, 12) on the coastlands, and Kedar (60:7) is related to 42:11, in which Kedar is invited to praise.[87] The nations participate in the task of the מבשר (40:9; 41:27). Motyer comments that the subject of בשר in 60:6 is the nations functioning as evangelists, which implies participation in salvation.[88]

The phrase "acceptable on my altar" (60:7) is resonant with 56:7.[89] According to Lau, however, there is no suggestion of universal salvation in 60:7 as in 56:7 and Jer 6:20, the source texts of 60:7. The sacrificial animals just signify in the motif of the pilgrimage of the nations the foreigners' living in the country [Israel] without any eschatological prospect. The context does not indicate universal salvation.[90] However, as we have seen in chapter 2, foreigners are associated with the salvation community in 56:1–8. Furthermore, 60:7 neither necessarily implies that "the Temple had already been rebuilt," nor suggests the historical realization of Temple worship.[91]

---

83. Beuken 1989a:168.

84. Lau 1994:42.

85. It is the only occurrence in the OT apart from Ps 145:21 and 78:4 (cf. 102:22[21]).

86. Beuken 1989a:168.

87. Cheyne 1895:339; Lau 1994:43. For Lau (1994:42), literary connection to 42:10–12 is not proved.

88. Motyer 1993:495.

89. Seitz 2001:509; Koenen 1990:146.

90. Lau 1994:45.

91. Muilenburg 1954:701.

Delitzsch rejects the idea that "animal sacrifice will be revived again," because "[T]he house of God in Jerusalem . . . [56:7] will be a house of prayer for all nations."[92] Because a historical realization cannot be envisaged, the language appears to be apocalyptic, i.e., the strophe is to be understood as metaphorical (rather than historical): The nations/kings (as well as the people of Kedar) will worship YHWH in "the dwelling place of God's glory" (or, Temple as a non-eschatological term) in the new era, which is salvific.[93]

"To beautify My beautiful house" is neither rebuilding of the Temple nor the adornment of the rebuilt Temple.[94] The gifts are not for Zion's adornment (52:1, 54:11–12), but for the glorifying of God's house (60:7, and also 60:13).[95] This may signify that the Temple will be restored to its right function to worship YHWH and to beautify Him.[96] The beauty/beautify (פאר) has often been associated with salvation. In 44:23, YHWH will glorify Himself in Israel through his redemption of Jacob (44:22); in 49:3, YHWH will be beaufied by the work of the Servant; in 55:5, YHWH will beaufity the Davidic Messiah, so the nations run into him.[97] YHWH will beautify the Temple in 60:7 and 13, and Zion in 60:9, as תפארת becomes an attribute of Zion (52:1; 46:13) in DI.[98] פאר or תפארת is related to salvation also in 60:21, 61:3, 62:3, and 63:12.[99] The link between the beautifying of YHWH and salvation may suggest that the nations are also saved, because the Temple will be beautified due to the sacrifices of the nations.

In brief, the nations come to Zion from everywhere, bringing gifts and sacrifices to YHWH and proclaiming the praise of YHWH. Consequently, the Temple will be beautified and the nations join the salvation.

---

92. Delitzsch 1873:414–15.

93. Muilenburg 1954:701. Muilenburg's comment, "In the new age the temple will be restored as the dewelling place of God's glory," is to be understood carefully because "altar" and "temple" are used metaphorically.

94. Pace Whybray (1981:233).

95. Seitz 2001:509.

96. Although in the ancient world 'worship' means sacrifice predominantly, but the passage is in the eschatological context, in which historical restoration of the temple worship is not warranted.

97. Snaith 1967:142. Beuken (1989a:169) understands the singular 'you' in 55:5 as Israel, but it is Davidic Messiah as evidenced in 55:3–4. See Motyer 1993:453–55.

98. Beuken 1989a:169.

99. Beuken 1989a:169.

8 Who are these that fly like a cloud,	מי־אלה כעב תעופינה
and like doves to their windows?	וכיונים אל־ארבתיהם:
9 For the coastlands shall hope for me,	כי־לי איים יקוו
the ships of Tarshish first,	ואניות תרשיש בראשנה
to bring your children from afar,	להביא בניך מרחוק
their silver and gold with them,	כספם וזהבם אתם
for the name of YHWH your God,	לשם יהוה אלהיך
and for the Holy One of Israel, because He has made you beautiful.	ולקדוש ישראל כי פארך:

This strophe complements the camel caravan of the previous strophe, shifting the vision from the East (60:6–7) to the West and focusing on the sea route.[100] The eschatological expectations in PI and DI are fulfilled here.

Flying like a cloud and like doves emphasizes the swiftness of the fleet.[101] "For the coastlands shall wait for me" (כי־לי איים יקוו) builds on the Servant tradition. The phrase is related not only to 51:5 (אלי איים יקוו), but also 42:4 (ולתורתו איים ייחילו), because in 51:5, קוה אלי is parallel to אל־זרעי ייחלון.[102] In 42:4, the coastlands (איים) hope for the Torah (תורה) of the Servant, who will establish justice (משפט) on earth. In 51:4–6, they (איים) look to YHWH and wait for the arm of YHWH. In 51:4, the Torah (תורה) goes out from YHWH and his justice (משפט) will become 'a light to the nations.' So, the nations are open to the eschatological salvation, since they listen to the Torah (see 60:1–3 above). In TI, the salvation community takes the role of the Servant of YHWH since Zion/Jerusalem takes the function of the light of the nations in the YHWH's servant tradition (see above).[103] Here, God's Servant tradition is combined with the motif of the pilgrimage of the nations.[104] By referring to DI text, TI outlines the crossing of the coastlands to Zion where the law and YHWH's righteousness will relieve them from oppression according to the *Vorlage* (51:4–5).[105] For Seitz, the streaming of treasure is related to 23:17–18, in which the new transformed Tyre will provide materials for the Temple use.[106]

---

100. Muilenburg 1954:702; Whybray 1981:233; Motyer 1993:496.

101. Although 60:8 may be adapted from Hos 11:11 (Cheyne 1895:339), further thematic connection is not found apart from the figure of 'speed.'

102. Delitzsch 1873:415; Lau 1994:47; Beuken 1989:170; Whybray 1981:233. Whybray considers the phrase out of place, to amend it as: "for me (the) ships will be assembled." But, this is unnecessary. For זרע in the Servant tradition, see chapter 3.

103. Lau 1994:48.

104. Lau 1994:48.

105. Beuken 1989a:170.

106. Seitz 2001:509; Motyer 1993:193; Clements 1980:195–96.

The phrase "for the name . . . made you beautiful" in 60:9c is the quotation of 55:5b.[107] For Zimmerli, followed by Whybray, the language of earlier prophecy becomes a conventional, pious language, and thus not fitting the context.[108] However, the glory of YHWH and the glory of Zion have been closely related to each other, so in this sense, the glorification of Zion does not deviate from the context. On the contrary, the context of 55:1–5 resounds here—a text applied to the Davidic Messiah (55:5) is adopted and addressed to Zion (60:9) and the nations coming to Zion to give tribute to YHWH (60:9) are considered to be saved as Zion is the place where the gift of the covenant is granted without price to anybody (55:1–5).[109] The glory of Zion before the nations has already been displayed in 60:1–3.

In short, the train of the nations/kings with their wealth and tribute carrying the children of Zion approach so swiftly. The coastlands will hope for YHWH (this is a salvific nuance), joining the train, and Zion will be beautified.

10 Foreigners shall build up your walls,	ובנו בני־נכר חמתיך
and their kings shall minister to you;	ומלכיהם ישרתונך
for in My wrath I struck you,	כי בקצפי הכיתיך
but in My favor I have had mercy on you.	וברצוני רחמתיך:
11 Your gates shall be open continually;	ופתחו שעריך תמיד
day and night they shall not be shut,	יומם ולילה לא יסגרו
that people may bring to you the wealth of the nations,	להביא אליך חיל גוים
with their kings led in procession.	ומלכיהם נהוגים:

60:10–16 deals with the reversal of Zion's fortune—Zion will be restored and reconstructed.[110] In 60:10–11, the nations/kings serve as workmen to build the walls of Zion. The gates are also restored to be open continually so that the nations/kings bring their wealth ceaselessly. So the caravan theme continues here.

What does the rebuilding of the walls by the foreigners signify in 60:10a? The walls are certainly of the city, rather than those of the Temple.[111] For Motyer, "your walls" are symbolic, signifying security or strength of the city.[112] In this case, building your walls signifies the reversal of the roles of Israel and the nations—the foreigners who had destroyed the walls of the

---

107. Whybray 1981:234; Beuken 1989:170; Lau 1994:48; Koenen 1990:148.

108. Zimmerli 1950:222; Whybray 1981:234. Volz (1932:240) also considers 60:9b is the theocentric quotation of 55:5, substantially changing the original meaning.

109. Beuken 1989a:170.

110. Childs 2001:497.

111. Volz 1932:246.

112. Motyer 1993:496.

city come to rebuild the walls to ensure the security of the city.[113] However, the key to 60:10a is the fact of the construction itself, not the walls of "security"—walls are the major structural part of the city. This is because 60:10a belongs to the reconstruction of Zion theme.

Thematically, ובנו is related to 58:12 and 61:4 (cf. 65:21), which form the reconstruction theme.[114] In 61:4 and 58:12, Zion will be rebuilt (בנה), raised up (קום), and renewed (חדש) as it had been the ancient ruins (חרבה), the places long devastated (שמם), the waste cities (ערי חרב) and the desolations (שמם) of many generations. Zion will not be the (City)-Forsaken (עזובה) or the Desolate (שממה) (62:4). The devastation in these words does not necessarily signify only the (physical) destruction of the land by the invasion and captivity by the Babylonians.[115] It refers even more to the spiritual desolation of the community, as either a metaphor or synecdoche for the sinful state of the community, and the spiritual reconstruction to the covenantal restoration. The ruin (חרבה; 58:12) has been used before in a literal sense in DI in 44:26 (the physical destruction of Jerusalem).[116] The word 'desolate' ((ה)שממ) initially referred to the physical destruction of Israel, in PI and DI (1:7; 6:11; 17:9; 33:8; 49:19; 54:3), or to Zion/Jerusalem itself which is desolate in 54:1.[117] However, although the concrete sense of physical destruction might still be kept, חרבה and שמם tend to denote a spiritual destruction in 58:12 and 61:4, because salvation in 58:10 has meant the establishment of justice and removal of the social and religious sins as the context has focused on the issue of sins.[118] While the sin and the physical construction of Jerusalem are not thought to have a direct and logical causality in 58:12, and if the destruction is understood to include the ethical and spiritual aspects of the community, then the promise in 58:11–12 looks forward to an eschatological promise. Therefore, the words such as חרבה and פרץ (breach; 58:12) and שד ושבר (devastation and destruction; 59:7) join the destruction metaphor of sin and judgment. The reconstruction lan-

---

113. Whybray 1981:234.

114. Koenen 1990:154.

115. Delitzsch 1873:428; Kissane 1943:275.

116. It refers in 48:21 to the desert which the people passed through after the exodus.

117. In 49:19, חרבה is parallel to שמם.

118. The ruin may be synecdoche for the destructed social and religious order of Israel (or, Jerusalem) as well as for the physical destruction of the nation/city, rather than it may be a metaphor for the social/religious disintegration. The point is that social/religious aspects of Israel come to be more emphasized than physical aspects here. And the work of the Servant does not seem to be directly related to the physical construction. So, we consider it as metaphor.

guage signifies the spiritual reconstruction of the community in 58:12 and 61:4, without losing the potential reference to the physical imagery. In the construction metaphor, the ancient ruins will be rebuilt (בנה), the age-old foundations will be raised (קום), the breach will be repaired (גדר), and the streets will be restored (שוב) (58:12), as בנה, קום, גדר, and שוב form metaphors of restoration in 58:12 and 61:4.

The reconstruction of the wall in 60:10 belongs to the same metaphorical system. In chs 58–59, the reason for the delay of salvation is due to the sins and iniquities of the people. Turning from their sins (58:1–7) will bring the exodus-like theophany (58:8, 10) and restoration from desolation (58:12). The devastation and destruction (59:7) has been caused by the sins of the people (59:1–8), so they "look for light, but all in darkness" (59:9, cf. 59:11).

For Lau, 60:10a is related to 49:16–17, so "behind the eschatological promises in 49:17 and 60:10 a real historical background must be hidden: destroyed Jerusalem."[119] However, how much a historical realization is involved here is questionable, although its ultimate realization in the future is undeniable. The concept of the destruction language (חרבה, שמם, and הריסות) in 49:19 is connected to the work of the Servant in 49:8.[120] Due to the work of the Servant, who comes to be the covenant of the people (ברית עם; 49:8), the people will restore the desolate (שמם) inheritances in the time of YHWH's favor. Then in the day of salvation, his efforts will bring the people back (שוב) to YHWH (49:5, 6). This implies the return of the people to YHWH by the restoration of the covenantal relationship with YHWH. In addition, חרבה symbolically signifies the state of Jerusalem in 51:3 and 52:9. On the other hand, the word 'to build' (בנה) has been the word of eschatological hope for Jerusalem and the cities of Judah in DI (44:26, 28; 45:13), probably signifying the physical reconstruction of the cities, but not limited to it. The word 'to raise up/restore' (קום) has also been a word of eschatological hope in DI as it is associated with the ruins in 44:26 (חרבותיה אקומם), signifying the physical reconstruction. But the word is also used for the covenantal relationship with YHWH even in DI as it refers to the work of the Servant in 49:6, 8 restoring the tribe of Jacob and raising up the land and inheriting the desolate heritages. The restoration from the ruins and desolate places (שמם; חרבה) and crowding with people there in 49:19–21 signify the restoration of the covenantal relation with YHWH, without completely losing the physical image. This is supported by the fact that the

119. Lau 1994:49.

120. The destruction language in 49:19, 17 is addressed to Zion (49:14), so the address is Zion in 60:10a, too.

exodus language and imagery in DI, referring to the physical return of the exiles, signifies the covenantal return of the people.

In DI's eschatology, the focus of the eschatological hope has been shifted from the 'physical' return of the people from Babylonia to Palestine to the 'covenantal' return of the people to YHWH and from the 'physical' reconstruction of the city to the 'covenantal' (or, 'spiritual') reconstruction of the community in DI. This is also supported by the parallel function between the anointed figure in TI and the Servant in DI in the restoration of Zion in TI. The restoration from desolation in 61:4 is linked with the work of the Anointed Figure of 61:1 and with the coming of 'the year of YHWH's favour' and 'the day of vengeance' (61:2), which are connected to the eschatological expectation of the Servant in 49:8. This suggests the connection between the Servant and the Anointed One, as the Servant was involved in the pilgrimage of the nations theme above. In short, destruction and reconstruction language tends to metaphorically designate the sinful state of the people and the restoration from it in DI. And this is the background of the language in TI (60:10). As the Servant is expected to restore Israel in DI, the anointed figure will reconstruct Zion in TI, according to the intratext ch 61.

What is the basis for the change of the fortune of the city? According to 60:10–11, it is the passing of God's anger and the extension of his mercy as in DI and PI (40:1–2, 54:6; 12:1, 30:9).[121] In 60:10b, YHWH changes His attitude to Israel from wrath and judgment (בקצפי הפיתיך) to favour and compassion (ברצוני רחמתיך), which brings the change of the fortune of Israel from desolation to the everlasting pride and joy in 60:15. These verses (10–11) connect with 54:7–8,[122] in which divine compassion and everlasting lovingkindness (חסד עולם) are compared to the promise to Noah and called the everlasting covenant with words reminiscent of the Noachic Deluge (54:9–10). Because the covenant has been broken due to the sins of the people in DI and TI, the initiative for the restoration of the covenant lies with YHWH alone or rather his zeal (קנה, 59:17; see 3.3). The change of fortune of Zion in ch 54 is due to the work of the Suffering Servant in ch 53 as the righteous (54:3) and her many children (54:1) are linked with 53:11.[123] (As we shall see in 5.2, this may support the connection between the servants in TI and the Suffering Servant in DI.)

---

121. Childs 2001:497.

122. Whybray 1981:234, 235; Cheyne 1895:339; Childs 2001:495; Westermann 1969:360; Beuken 1989a:171. 60:10 and 54:7–8 are parallel in רחם and קצף. The verb עזב in 54:6 also is repeated in 60:15, which forms a construction motif. For Lau (1994:50), the literary relation is hard to prove.

123. Seitz 2001:477.

The permanently open gates have been considered to signify the total security and the ceaseless streaming in of the nations.[124] On this basis,
Steck argued for a contradiction between building the walls and open gates.[125]
But, although the ceaseless streaming is admitted as a continuation of the
influx theme, there seems to be no implication of security in 60:10–11. Thus
Childs rejects the idea, but accepts only the implication of construction (see
above).

In summary, (the walls and gates of) Zion will be rebuilt and even the
nations/kings participate in the work. The kings are included in the procession to Zion. As evidenced in the intratexts, the reconstruction is ultimately
the task of the anointed figure, according to the intratext (ch 61), just as that
is up to the Servant in DI.

12 For the nation and kingdom that will not serve you shall perish; those nations shall be utterly laid waste.	כי־הגוי והממלכה אשר לא־יעבדוך יאבדו והגוים חרב יחרבו:

This verse is widely accepted as a prose addition, which is considered
not to fit the mood and thought in the context.[126] For Torrey, the insertion is with a view to explanation of נהוגים in 60:11b, translated as "led into
captivity."[127] However, for Motyer, 60:12 is the pivotal verse of the chapter;
he states that "Zion really is the key to international destiny, the final form
of the Abrahamic system" (see chapter 2).[128]

This verse may suggest the imperialistic relation between (the remnant
of) Israel and (the remnant of) the nations (see above on 60:4–5). This is for
several reasons. Above all, 60:12 is reminiscent of the Abrahamic promise
in Gen 12:1–3. יעבדוך may be related to Gen 27:29 not only because of its
unique occurrence in the OT, but also because השתחוו in 60:14 is related
to ישתחוו in the verse. Gen 27:29 repeats the Abrahamic promise in Gen

124. Motyer 1993:496; Delitzsch 1873:417; Whybray 1981:234.

125. Steck 1991:66–67. Beuken (1989a:172) also observes a contrast. But, rejected
Steck's view.

126. Childs 2001:494; Muilenburg 1954:703; Whybray 1981:235; Beuken 1989a:159;
Lau 1994:52; Westermann 1969:360.

127. Torrey 1928:451; Lau 1994:52. In general, the passive form may signify "led
unwillingly as captives" (MT, Delitzsch), while active sense "their kings leading them"
(HALOT, Whybray, Duhm). For Whybray (1981:234), "the peoples will bring their
own kings (to Jerusalem) as captives" (ומלכיהם נהוגים) makes no sense in 60:11b, so he
amends the verb to the active "with their kings leading them." For Delitzsch (1873:417),
"in procession as prisoners." For Beuken (1989a:172), there is no implication as to the
voluntariness in the verb, but just worldwide movement to Zion, so "kings led in pro-
cession/guided." For Childs (2001:497), "with kings in procession."

128. Motyer 1993:496. Childs (2001:498) comments, "judgment is decreed for
those who oppose God's salvation" in 60:12.

12:1–3. In Gen 12:1–3 and 27:29, YHWH will bless those who bless Abraham and curse whoever curses him—Abraham is the key to the blessing of the nations.[129] 60:12 as well as Gen 27:29 may present the vassal relationship as יעבדוך may suggest (also see 60:4–5 above).[130] Second, according to Ringgren, 'to serve' (עבד) may signify the vassal-suzerain relationship as displayed in Gen 14:4.[131] If this is the case, 'worshipping YHWH' and 'serving Israel' are consistent in the overall view because the nations serving Israel may imply being part of the people of Zion, who worship YHWH. Third with Lau, 60:12 is related to Jer 27:8, because of עבד + ממלכה/גוי. The glossator changed the destiny of the nations threatened by Nebuchadnezzar to dependency on Zion.[132] If we admit this connection, it suggests that Zion is understood as an 'emperor' just as Nebuchadnezzar is.

For Volz, the mood of 60:11–14a is hostile to the nations, so nationalism is unmistakable.[133] However, Childs rejects a sharp polarity between universalism and nationalism, but argues instead for a polarity between those who turn to YHWH and those who resist His will, throughout TI (see vv. 6–7).[134]

In conclusion, 60:12 may reflect the Abrahamic tradition, because the promise of YHWH that the nations' attitude to Abraham will be the key to their fortune is reaffirmed here with Zion. The fortune of the nations is dependent on Abraham, i.e., whether or not they serve the suzerain Israel as vassals.

13 The glory of Lebanon shall come to you,	כבוד הלבנון אליך יבוא
the fir tree, the pine tree, and the box tree together,	ברוש תדהר ותאשור יחדו
to beautify the place of my sanctuary,	לפאר מקום מקדשי
and I will make the place of My feet glorious.	ומקום רגלי אכבד:
14 The sons of those who afflicted you shall come bending low to you,	והלכו אליך שחוח בני מעניך
and all who despised you shall bow down at your feet;	והשתחוו על־כפות רגליך
	כל־מנאציך
they shall call you the City of YHWH,	וקראו לך עיר יהוה
the Zion of the Holy One of Israel.	ציון קדוש ידראל:

This strophe continues the theme of the reconstruction and restoration of Zion, contrary to the general view that thematic change has been

129. Motyer 1993:496.

130. Ringgren 1999, TDOT (10), עבד:384.

131. Ringgren 1999, TDOT (10), עבד:383–84, 390. For Cheyne (1895:337), 60:12 is based on Zech 14:16–19. Whybray (1981:235) disagrees, because the nations are required to worship YHWH there, while in 60:12 they serve Israel.

132. Lau 1994:53.

133. Volz 1932:247; Childs 2001:495.

134. Childs 2001:497.

made in this strophe from building the city (60:10–11) to beautifying the Temple (60:13–14).[135] Forests of Lebanon come to, and are re-realized in, Zion the eschatological Temple(-paradise) and even the former oppressors come to Zion in subjection to realize that Zion is the City of YHWH. So, Zion becomes the eschatological Temple-city-paradise.

For Whybray, the phrase 'glory of Lebanon' is slightly misunderstood here, because the associated three names of trees are simply timber for the Temple.[136] But he does not seem convincing. He relies on the fact that Hiram king of Tyre gave fir trees (ברוש) and cedars (ארז) to Solomon as timbers of the Temple in 1 Kgs 5:20–24[6–10]. However, the connection with 1 Kgs 5 is not compelling. This connection is based on his historical assumption of the Temple building in ch 60, which is unwarranted. But 60:13 is rather linked to 35:2 and 41:19. The 'glory of Lebanon' (כבוד הלבנון) in 60:13 is in all likelihood quoted from 35:2, because it occurs nowhere else in the OT.[137] The three names for trees (תאשור, תדהר, ברוש) also only come elsewhere in 41:19. For Delitzsch, contrary to Whybray, the 'glory of Lebanon,' most probably referring to the trees, is not "trunks as building materials," but the trees will be "dug up with their roots, to ornament the holy place of the Temple."[138] In 35:2, "the glory of Lebanon will be given to it" is in the context of great transformation of the natural order into paradise (35:1). As Clements comments, "[T]he most barren parts of the land would become as rich and covered with luxuriant growth as the forest of Lebanon."[139] In 41:19, too, the trees are in the context of the transformation of nature (41:18) by the Creator God (41:20), which is a characteristic feature of the eschatology of DI (43:18–21; 48:21; 49:9–11; 55:13).[140] So, it is natural to

135. Motyer 1993:496; Whybray 1981:235; Westermann 1969:360.

136. Whybray 1981:235. Whybray follows Volz (1932:240). Cheyne (1895:339) also opines the different purposes of the trees in the two places. Westermann (1969:360) shares Whybray's view.

137. Cheyne 1895:339; Lau 1994:53; Whybray 1981:235; Beuken 1989a:173.

138. Delitzsch 1873:418. Steck (1991:101–5) considers the trees "not for the temple construction, but for the beauty of the temple garden," while Koenen (1990:151) argues for the temple grove rather than temple garden. But the distinction between temple grove and temple garden seems too speculative.

139. Clements 1980:275. According to Beuken (1989a:173), 35:2 is "within the context of flourishing the desert at the appearance of YHWH."

140. Muilenburg 1954:459; Beuken 1989a:173; Whybray 1981:67. Muilenburg considers 41:17–20 needs a literal interpretation because of the "language of myth" used in the eschatological setting of the poem, following Robinson, who writes, "[T]hese pictures are to be taken realistically, not allegorically." Whybray understands it as a ready-made oasis for the desert travelers. 41:18 may initially refer to Moses' action that opened the rock to draw water in the wilderness (Exod 17:1–7; Num 20:1–13), as Whybray observed.

think that the eschatological expectation of the paradisiacal change of the nature in the background(s) of 35:2 and 41:19 is kept in 60:13. This is reinforced by the eschatological setting of the chapter, in which apocalyptic language and ideas come to the fore (60:1–2, 19–20). So, the trees are not for Temple construction, but manifest the paradisiacal change, i.e., "a token of the eschatological salvation time as the illustration of the creative salvific action of YHWH (cf. 41:20)."[141]

As Lau observed, 60:13 is involved with the "holy mountain of Zion tradition," in which the concept of Zion incorporates the concepts of the eschatological city and Temple. The concept of Zion, initially referring to the city or the Temple mount according to the context (see below), is theologically expanded here by TI because she is eschatologically glorified by the coming of YHWH.[142] This may be supported by the fact that 60:14 returns to the theme of Zion the city, whereas Temple-paradise imagery is dominant and eschatologized in 60:13—the two verses deal with the same eschatological Zion. There may be more evidence for this phenomenon. According to Koenen, 60:13a may correspond thematically to 58:11, in which "Israel will be like a luxuriant garden and in Jerusalem many trees will blossom."[143] In 58:10–12, the imagery of oasis (i.e., 'well-watered garden,' referring to the paradise and reminiscent of the garden of Eden) is associated with the reconstruction of Zion theme (58:12) as well as the light-metaphoric theophany (58:10). So, in the eschatological concept of Zion, Temple and city are incorporated, so "not only the Temple but also Jerusalem/Zion becomes holy area."[144] This may be supported by the fact that the place of my footstool (60:13, cf. 66:1) may signify either the ark, Temple, or Jerusalem,[145] and also that the name of YHWH (לשם יהוה) in 60:9 may be related to Jer 3:17, in which Jerusalem is the throne of YHWH.[146]

The "City of YHWH" and "Zion of the Holy One of Israel" (60:14) belong to the new name theme, both denoting the solidarity of eschatological

---

141. Lau 1994:54. Hiram's gift may also be in line with the bigger idea that the nations/kings will contribute to (build) the new Jerusalem.

142. Lau 1994:55. According to Lau, 60:13 is thematically related to Jer 3:17, in which Jerusalem is the throne of YHWH. Contrary to Koenen (1990:149) and Whybray (1981:235), 66:1 and 60:13 do not suggest different authorship or theology, but form a coherent Zion tradition—involvement of sin is different in the two texts: sin is a separating barrier between God and human in 59:2.

143. Koenen 1990:151.

144. Lau 1994:56.

145. Beuken 1989a:174.

146. Koenen 1990:148.

Zion with YHWH.[147] Zion, the Temple Mountain, is identified, i.e., synonymous, with Zion the city Jerusalem (or the inhabitants of Jerusalem),
and also with paradise:[148] (a) every reference of Zion in TI (59:20; 60:14;
61:3; 62:1, 11; 64:9; 66:8) signifies the city Zion, i.e., Jerusalem, not only
in a historical sense (59:20; 62:1, 11; 64:9) but also in the eschatological
sense (60:14; 61:3; 62:1; 66:8). (b) In 65:11 and 56:7, the Holy Mountain
of YHWH is the Temple Mountain, in which YHWH dwells and is worshipped. In 66:20, the Holy Mountain of YHWH is interchangeable with
(the New) Jerusalem as eschatologized. The Holy Mountain of YHWH in
57:13 is a parallel to, and probably synonymous with, the Land of Israel,
which is eschatologized.[149] In 65:25, the Holy Mountain of YHWH is the
eschatological paradise.[150] Thus, in view of the usage of Zion in PI and DI,
in which it refers to both Jerusalem and the Temple Mountain (i.e., the
Mount Zion),[151] Zion refers to the historical Jerusalem and also signifies
the eschatological city or land, or paradise. As Roberts comments, "Israelite
religious poetry moves easily back and forth between a specific reference to
the Temple and a more general reference to the city as a whole."[152]

   In conclusion, Zion is glorified, turning into the Temple-paradise as
the glory of Lebanon comes to her. This is due to the transformation of
nature, according to the source text in DI, which associates the theme with
the exodus imagery. In the eschatological age, Zion is Temple, paradise, and
city at the same time, closely related to YHWH.

---

147. Beuken 1989a:175, 176; Koenen 1990:141, 154. See 58:12; 60:18; 61:3, 6; 62:4,
12. The "Holy One of Israel" is one of the governing motifs that interconnect PI, DI, and
TI (1:4; 5:19; 41:14; 55:5; 60:9, 14).

148. Roberts 1982a:99; Otto 2003:346; Levenson 1985:128.

149. The parallelism in 57:13 may also be understood as seconding/specification, if
it is historical. But the verse seems eschatological.

150. In 11:9, the Holy Mountain of YHWH is paradise, i.e., the land of the eschatological era.

151. Zion refers to Jerusalem in 1:8, 27; 2:3; 3:16f; 4:3, 4; 10:12, 24, 32; 12:6; 16:1;
24:23; 28:16; 29:8; 30:19; 31:9; 33:5, 14, 20; 34:8; 35:10; 37:22, 32; 40:9; 41:27; 46:13;
49:14; 51:3, 11, 16; 52:1–2, 7–8 in PI and DI. Mount Zion appears in 4:5; 8:18; 10:12;
18:7; 24:23; 29:8; 31:4; 37:32. Especially in 2:3, the Mountain of YHWH is parallel to the
house of God of Jacob and Zion is parallel to Jerusalem.

152. Roberts 1982a:99.

15 Whereas you have been forsaken and hated,	תחת היותך עזובה
with no one passing through,	ושנואה ואין עובר
I will make you majestic forever,	ושמתיך לגאון עולם
a joy from age to age.	משוש דור ודור:
16 You shall suck the milk of nations;	וינקת חלב גוים
you shall nurse at the breast of kings;	ושד מלכים תינקי
and you shall know that I, YHWH, am your Savior	וידעת כי אני יהוה מושיעך
and your Redeemer, the Mighty One of Jacob.	וגאלך אביר יעקב:

This strophe revisits the theme of the change of the ages. Once for-saken and rejected, Zion is on the verge of the everlasting pride and joy in the new era. She is going to be provided for by the nations/kings and will realize YHWH as the Saviour, Redeemer, and the Mighty One of Jacob.

As תחת implied, 60:15 presents the change of fortune: from abandon-ment to transformation.[153] The "forsaken" (עזובה) woman may be related to 54:6–7 (and 62:4, 12 in TI), and 49:14–15 (עזבני).[154] The word עזב here refers to the broken covenantal relationship between YHWH and the people. So, here the covenant is restored. "No one passing through" (אין עובר) may be related to 34:10 (אין עבר), as the result of the punitive judgment of Jerusalem in the day of vengeance and year of recompense for Zion's cause (נקם ליהוה שנת שלומים לריב ציון) in 34:8.[155] This is also a covenantal judgment.

The provision of the nations to Zion fulfils the eschatological expecta-tion of DI. 60:16a is clearly modelled on 49:23 and 60:16b is quoted from 49:26b.[156] For Whybray, however, 49:23 is "entirely reinterpreted" here, be-cause foreign nations will be "slaves" to Zion's children in 49:23, whereas here, Zion sucks the foreign wealth.[157] Westermann also considers that the meaning of the model text 49:23 has been changed in 60:14a and 16a—the wet-nurse literally in DI, but figuratively here.[158] However, the foster father and the nursing mother in 49:23a are consistent with the role of the nations/kings who allow Zion to suck (ינק) milk (חלב) and breast (שד), i.e., give energy to Zion, in 60:16.[159] To "bow down before you with their faces to the ground, lick the dust at your feet" (49:23) is not understood as slavery but as extreme humility and obeisance (see 60:13–14 above). The recogni-tion of YHWH is the restoration of the covenantal relation with YHWH,

153. Motyer 1993:497; Beuken 1989a:177; Childs 2001:498; Koenen 1990:155.

154. Muilenburg 1954:704; Beuken 1989a:177. 54:6–7 and 49:14–17 present Zion as triple identity (mother, spouse, and city).

155. Delitzsch 1873:419; Volz 1932:247.

156. Whybray 1981:236; Bonnard 1972:410; Lau 1994:57.

157. Whybray 1981:236.

158. Westermann 1969:362; Zimmerli 1950:222.

159. Delitzsch 1873:419.

as Botterweck comments, "'[T]o know Yahweh' refers to a practical-ethical relationship."[160] Thus, since it has a salvific connotation, the link suggests that not only Israel (60:16b; as promised in 59:20) but also the nations (49:26b) may enter salvation.[161] The nations are "incorporated as a part of its own population of Zion," being understood as her (foster) children in ch 60.[162] Moreover, there is no restriction in the knowledge of YHWH, and the instruction of YHWH is never excluded for the nations.[163]

In short, when it comes to the new age, the once deserted Zion will be restored, having everlasting pride and joy, fully recognizing YHWH (i.e., restoring the covenantal relation) and being supplied by the nations/kings, who will also share the salvific blessing.

17 Instead of bronze I will bring gold,	תחת הנחשת אביא זהב
and instead of iron I will bring silver;	ותחת הברזל אביא כסף
instead of wood, bronze,	ותחת העצים נחשת
instead of stones, iron.	ותחת האבנים ברזל
I will make your overseers peace	ושמתי פקדתך שלום
and your taskmasters righteousness.	ונגשיך צדקה:
18 Violence shall no more be heard in your land,	לא־ישמע עוד חמס בארצך
devastation or destruction within your borders;	שד ושבר בגבוליך
you shall call your walls Salvation,	וקראת ישועה חומתיך
and your gates Praise.	ושעריך תהלה:

This strophe continues the theme of the turnaround of conditions in the eschatological transformation of Zion. It covers materials, external authority, social order, and the spiritual infrastructure of the community.[164]

The precious metals in 60:17ab may represent the material prosperity, i.e., enhanced economic order.[165] They may be materials for the structure of Zion (Delitzsch), for Temple dishes and vessels (Budde), or material for the construction or equipment of the Jerusalem Temple (Lau).[166] However, for Volz, they are not the raw material (of the Temple) but more than that because a Temple cannot be built with metal alone.[167] So, for Whybray, the

---

160. Botterweck 1986:469.

161. Seitz 2001:509.

162. Beuken 1989a:180.

163. Lau 1994:57.

164. Muilenburg 1954:705; Volz 1932:247.

165. Beuken 1989a:180.

166. Delitzsch 1873:419; Lau 1994:58.

167. Volz 1932:247. Whybray (1981:236) and Beuken (1989a:181) follow him.

precious metals "symbolized spiritual as well as material worth."[168] "The whole material order will go through a substantial change because of YHWH."[169]

It has been suggested that 60:17ab alludes to the Solomonic abundance in his golden age (1 Kgs 10:21, 27), and sometimes even to the shameful incident of king Rehoboam (1 Kgs 14:26, 27).[170] This may be supported by the reference to Sheba. The tribute from Sheba (60:6) recalls the queen of Sheba who brought spices and gold to King Solomon in 1 Kgs 10:1–13.[171] If this is the case, the Davidic-Solomonic prosperity may be the background of Zion's glorification.[172]

Sometimes 60:17b has been considered as a secondary addition, because it seems contradictory to the mention of the trees in 60:13.[173] However, Beuken rejects it, because the trees in 60:13 are not for raw materials for the Temple.[174]

For 60:17c, Childs comments, "[T]he reference to overseers and taskmasters as agents of peace and righteousness draws on the oppression during the Egyptian slavery, which has been overturned."[175] For Westermann, it signifies that "foreign overseers and 'drivers,' [who have been oppressing Israel], are to be replaced by peace and righteousness."[176] However, these interpretations need some caution, because they tend to read overseers/taskmasters literally, suggesting that they will continue to (physically) remain, which is not implied in the text. For Volz, the overseers/taskmasters are figurative; for Delitzsch, peace and righteousness in 60:17c are personified as in 32:16, 17; 59:14 or in 45:8.[177] Peace and righteousness become the

168. Whybray 1981:236.

169. Beuken 1989a:181.

170. Delitzsch 1873:420; Whybray 1981:236; Beuken 1989a:181. Rehoboam was obliged to replace the golden shields with those of inferior metals) behind the text in 1 Kgs 14.

171. Whybray 1981:233; Bonnard 1972:406; Childs 2001:496; Lau 1994:42. For Lau (1994:41), the gold and incense from Sheba are also associated with Jer 6:20.

172. Dumbrell 1977:38–40.

173. Duhm 1892:411; Elliger 1928:22; Koenen 1990:143.

174. Beuken 1989a:180–81. The understanding that the glory of Lebanon in 60:13 is timber for rebuilding the Temple should stand on the contradiction between the idea and 60:17.

175. Childs 2001:498.

176. Westermann 1969:363.

177. Volz 1932:247; Delitzsch 1873:420. For Whybray (1981:236), peace and righteousness are the "personified qualities which symbolize the character of the state of perfection of the coming new age." For Beuken (1989a:181), they are personified new order.

features of the eschatological Zion, functioning like overseers/taskmasters of a city. So, as Motyer opined, "government as such will be wholly absorbed in the exercise of peace."[178]

For Koenen, 60:17c has a direct relation to 58:3, which displays the financial exploitation in the community as נגש implies, while righteous finance is expressed in 60:17.[179] However, the direct relation is weak because the language in 60:17–18 is apocalypticized, so although 60:17–18 is not unrelated to the historical reality, a specific reference to the community problem is not evident. As Motyer suggested, a better interpretation may be that 60:17–18 exhibits the abolition of every force of disorder (cf. 59:6–7).[180]

Violence and the devastation and destruction in 60:18a reveal the present situation of the city. Violence (חמס) may be related to 59:6 and 53:9 because these are the only occurrences in the book of Isaiah. The devastation and destruction (שד ושבר) in 60:18, which is more probably related to 59:6–7 and 51:19, present the current state of Israel in a destruction metaphor (see 60:10 above).[181] For Whybray, the present situation reflected in 60:17–18 is destruction and oppression by a foreign ruler.[182] Whybray's historical interpretation is however too strained. There is pervasive sin, transgression, and oppression in the community. In 59:6–7, the phrase refers to mental and religious corruption due to the sins of the people (59:1–8). In 51:19, it is the total destruction of the city and the people, which is related to the wrath of YHWH (51:17, 21–23), probably in the double contexts of physical destruction (52:3–5, 8, 11–12) and religious degradation (52:1, 11). (So, as is often the case, a purely physical interpretation is too narrow.) The spiritual understanding of the phrase is evidenced by the fact that חמס is in the context of total sinfulness of the community in 59:6. If the link to 53:9 is maintained, it suggests that the work of the Servant to remove violence is effective in the eschatological Zion.

For Westermann, "verse 18b does not mean that 'salvation' and 'praise' are to take the place of walls and gates (so Muilenburg etc.), but that the renewed walls and gates mean salvation and praise for Zion."[183] He tends to see the salvation of Zion as realized materialistically in the historical arena in the near future. For Muilenburg, however, the point is that the physical

---

178. Motyer 1993:498. He interprets the first sentence of 60:17c, "I will make peace your governor."

179. Koenen 1990:155.

180. Motyer 1993:498.

181. Beuken 1989a:182; Lau 1994:60; Cheyne 1895:339.

182. Whybray 1981:236. Westermann (1969:362) also considers it reflects the time after the first return.

183. Westermann 1969:363.

imagery of the historical city is transformed into eschatological equivalents.[184] 60:18b may be related to 26:1 (ישועה ישית חומות וחל), in which YHWH makes salvation the walls and ramparts of the city.[185] This view sees that the language primarily refers to the eschatological era. So, for Beuken, the object of the verb קרא may be salvation and praise rather than walls and gates (although the reverse may be true if walls are understood metaphorically).[186] The verb suggests the new name theme of Zion (see 6.4)—salvation and praise will be the features of the eschatological Zion.

In conclusion, the economic, social, and spiritual order will be transformed in the new Zion. The overseers/taskmasters and walls/gates are not to be understood as literal in the historical arena, but metaphorical equivalents in the eschatological era.

19 The Sun shall be no more your light by day,	לא־יהיה־לך עוד השמש לאור יומם
nor for brightness shall the Moon give you light;	ולנגה הירח לא־יאיר לך
but YHWH will be your everlasting light,	והיה־לך יהוה לאור עולם
and your God will be your glory.	ואלהיך לתפארתך:
20 Your Sun shall no more go down,	לא־יבוא עוד שמשך
nor your Moon withdraw itself;	וירחך לא יאסף
for YHWH will be your everlasting light,	כי יהוה יהיה־לך לאור עולם
and your days of mourning shall be ended.	ושלמו ימי אבלך:

This strophe revisits the theme of theophany as presented in the light metaphor, continuously marking the eschatological change of Zion—YHWH will be the everlasting light of Zion, and will shed light instead of the Sun and the Moon.

It has been considered that these verses display an apocalyptic conception. They reflect a radical change in the cosmos and the Sun and Moon will disappear on the literal interpretation.[187] Some propose that these verses are a later addition since the context is not apocalyptic.[188] However, the context seems to support that 60:19–20 is to be understood apocalyptically on the assumption of the theological unity of the chapter.

However, a metaphorical but non-apocalyptic interpretation has been suggested.[189] For Lau, 60:19–20 is the logical continuation of the coming of light in 60:1–3 because they are parallel to each other, forming an envelope structure of the chapter. YHWH comes as the light of Zion in 60:1–3;

184. Muilenburg 1954:705.
185. Beuken 1989a:183; Cheyne 1895:340.
186. Beuken 1989a:183.
187. Whybray 1981:237; Childs 2001:499; Seitz 2001:509.
188. Westermann 1969:364; Whybray 1981:237.
189. Lau 1994:62.

He is the light of Zion in 60:19–20. So 60:19–20 is to be understood as meta-phorical as is the divine light in 60:1–3.[190] For Lau, YHWH arising like a star is not apocalyptic language, but from זרח in 60:2–3, which is metaphorical. The everlasting light (YHWH) thus does not have a physical apocalyptic sense, but signifies the blessing function of YHWH.[191]

Lau's understanding of the (theological) continuity between 60:1–3 and 60:19–20 is to be appreciated.[192] However, there are several indications of an apocalyptic understanding of 60:19–20.

First, 60:19–20 is thematically related to 65:17–25, which is apocalyp-tic (see chapter 5), as the end of mourning (60:20) is related to 65:19.[193]

Second, the connection to 60:1–3 suggests an apocalyptic reading. Lau fails to grasp the possible thematic link of 60:1–3 with the creation and exodus tradition (see above). Because the creation report and exodus tradition are the background to 60:1–3, both 60:1–3 and 60:19–20 may be understood as apocalyptic, suggesting a literal understanding of the light of YHWH's presence.

Third, 60:19–20 may have the exodus tradition as its background, because it may be related to 4:5 and 24:23 as Cheyne suggested.[194] In 4:5, YHWH will create a cloud of smoke and a glow of flaming fire, which is re-realization of the pillar of cloud/fire in the exodus tradition. The flam-ing fire is literal and physical as the pillar of fire/cloud was so in the past, although it may be realized in the heavenly Zion since all are holy there (4:3).[195] 24:23 also reflects the exodus tradition (Exod 24:9–11) and there the Sun and Moon are literally heavenly bodies. However, their brilliance fades before the magnificence of YHWH, which is also literal and physi-cal light.[196] In the exodus tradition, as linked to 60:19–20, YHWH's light is literal and physical.

190. Lau 1994:61–62.

191. Lau 1994:62; cf. Zimmerli 1950:229. Delitzsch (1873:421) also adopts a sym-bolic understanding—"there will still be both sun and moon, but the Holy Place will be illumined without interruption by the manifestation of the presence of God, which outshines all besides."

192. Setiz 2001:509; Koenen 1990:142; Lau 1994:23. The theme of Zion's divine light in 60:1–3 recurs in 60:19–20. Whybray (1981:237) considers that vv. 19–20 are prosaic interpretation of poetic verses 1–3, which the author has misunderstood in an apocalyptic sense. For Koenen, vv. 1–3 are metaphorical, while vv. 19–20 are literal.

193. Seitz 2001:509; Cheyne 1895:339; Beuken 1989a:185.

194. Cheyne 1895:340.

195. Seitz 1993:41.

196. Clements 1980:206.

Fourth, 60:19–20 may have the creation order as its background. For Beuken, the cosmic phenomena in 60:19–20 are thematically related to the change of day/night, i.e., alternation of the sky lights in Gen 8:22 and Isa 5:30; 13:10; and 50:3.[197] They are also related to the creation order (Gen 1:3–5, 14–19), although at the same time they are closely related to moral and religious life. YHWH "directly presents himself as a light source as well as salvation." For him, 60:19a suggests that "the bases of the earth are shaken and the separation of light and darkness is threatened and they no longer fulfil their task (5:30; 13:10; 50:3)."[198] So YHWH's light replaces the celestial bodies, and the darkness is entirely lacking.[199] If the creation order is behind the text, YHWH's light is literal and physical.[200]

Fifth, the everlasting light of YHWH should be literal because it competes with, and overwhelms, the lights of the Sun and Moon in 60:19, which are literal.[201] The Sun never setting again and the Moon waning no more (60:20) refers to the everlasting light of YHWH, implying that the (physical) Sun and Moon as the cosmic bodies are replaced by the glorious light of YHWH.

Sixth, Zion is the heavenly city as the new creation in ch 60 (as evidenced in 60:13–14), incorporating the eschatological Temple and city. This suggests a literal interpretation of the Sun and Moon, because a literal interpretation in the heavenly realm may signify a metaphorical understanding in the physical/earthly world (see chapter 1).[202] 60:19–20 is apocalyptic language, having a potential to be realized in the earth realm. The fact that all mourning will be ended and all will be righteous (60:21) in Zion is beyond the limits of real history.[203] 60:20bβ may be related to 35:10 (and 51:11) as well as 65:18–19 and 66:10.[204] The end of mourning is unrealistic and thus apocalyptic. In ch 35, the redemption of YHWH, which will end the sorrow and sighing, is related to the transformation of nature (35:2, 7–8). In ch 65, the end of mourning is part of the blessings on the servants in the New Heavens and Earth (see 5.3 on 65:18–19). The end of the days of sorrow is related to 61:2–3, which states that it will be achieved by the Anointed

197. Beuken 1989a:184.

198. Beuken 1989a:184–85.

199. Beuken 1989a:183; Koenen 1990:142.

200. Westermann (1969:364) also suggests the link with Gen 8:22.

201. Lau 1994:62. It is literal that the sun and moon are shedding light, as evidenced by Lau's (1994:62) statement, "the sun and moon do not disappear, but are equal with YH in the function."

202. Childs 2001:499.

203. Childs 2001:499; Seitz 2001:510.

204. Muilenburg 1954:706.

Figure in the Day of YHWH.[205] For Motyer, the background of the removal of sorrow may be oppression (60:14ab), scorn (60:15ab), and repentance (57:18; 59:11, 20).[206] For Beuken, the mourning (אבל—cf. 57:18, 61:2–3, 66:10) is related to darkness (אפלה—cf. 8:22, 29:18, 58:10, 59:9, Amos 5:20, Job 10:22, 30:26).[207] The light of YHWH, as an apocalyptic language, is thus understood as 'literal' in the heavenly city, i.e., the apocalyptic realm.

Therefore, in 60:19–20, a literal rather than a metaphorical interpretation is preferred for YHWH's light and the heavenly bodies, so "Zion's exaltation has cosmic, transnational consequences."[208]

In conclusion, YHWH becomes the everlasting light for Zion, replacing the Sun and Moon. This is done in the heavenly realm, as understood as apocalyptic.

21 Your people shall all be righteous;	עמך כלם צדיקים
they shall possess the land forever,	לעולם יירשו ארץ
the shoot of My planting,	נצר מטעו
the work of My hands, that I might be glorified.	מעשה ידי להתפאר:
22 The least one shall become a clan,	הקטן יהיה לאלף
and the smallest one a mighty nation;	והצעיר לגוי עצום
I am YHWH;	אני יהוה
in its time I will hasten it.	בעתה אחישנה: ס

These two verses focus on the people of Zion in the eschatological era.[209] They will all be righteous and possess the land, and be the shoot of My planting and the work of My hands. They will become a clan of a mighty nation. YHWH will hasten it.

For Volz, all being righteous (צדיקים) signifies "participating in salvation," which is affirmed by Muilenburg while it is rejected by Whybray.[210] For Whybray, the "righteous" signifies those who are "united in the sincere service of Yahweh" in the present situation (chs 57, 59) as in 57:1.[211] However, an eschatological context is at work here. Besides, the link between righteousness and salvation is assumed. In 56:1 and 59:17, righteousness becomes the quality of the people of the redeemed community, righteousness and salvation occurring as hendiadys.[212] This does not contradict

205. Koenen 1990:143.

206. Motyer 1993:498.

207. Beuken 1989a:185.

208. Seitz 2001:509. Westermann (1969:364) comments, "Here the change towers up to assume cosmic proportions."

209. Whybray 1981:238.

210. Volz 1932:248; Muilenburg 1954:707; Westermann 1969:363.

211. Whybray 1981:238.

212. Motyer 1993:498.

59:20, in which only a section of the community is redeemed, because ch 60 describes only the people cleansed by the divine fire (see 3.2). In chs 56–59, there has been a confrontation between the righteous and the wicked. In 59:15b–21 and 63:1–6, there is a destruction of "all atheists to limit the promises of Isa 60–62 to the righteous of the people."[213] So the righteous are saved alone.

"To possess the land forever" (60:21) may signify the ultimate fulfilment of eschatological salvation, reflecting covenantal theology, and as eschatological language it may be related to 57:13 and 65:9 as well as 49:8 and 54:3.[214] In 49:8, the people of the covenant will inherit (נחל) the desolate heritages. It will be done in the time of My favour and in the day of salvation. It is the result of the work of the Servant. In 54:3, the offspring of Zion will possess (ירש) the nations, and the place of Zion's tent is enlarged (54:2). The barren lady Zion will be peopled when YHWH restores her as wife with great compassion (54:1–8). In 57:13, he who takes refuge in YHWH without worshipping idols (57:1–13a) will possess (נחל) the land and will inherit (ירש) YHWH's Holy Mountain. In 65:9, the chosen of YHWH, i.e., the servants of YHWH, will possess (ירש) the Holy Mountain of YHWH and the mountains of YHWH as well, and dwell there. The promise of the possession (ירש) of the land is reaffirmed to those who grieve in Zion (61:3) in 61:7.[215] In 61:4–9, it is related to the construction metaphor (61:4) and the covenant (61:8). The land ownership is a Deuteronomistic concept.[216] It may fulfil the Abrahamic Covenant as 60:22a so does (see below).

The "shoot of My planting" (נצר מטעי) in 60:21 is thematically related to 61:3 (מטע יהוה).[217] In both places, it refers to the people of Zion. For Beuken, it is also related to 11:1.[218] Both places share righteousness (11:4–5; 60:17, 21), peace (topic of 11:6–9; 60:17), land (11:9; 60:21), nations (11:10; 60:3, 5, 11), and the knowledge of YHWH (11:9; 60:16). For him, while the shoot in 11:1 is the house of David, it is the people of Zion in 60:21.[219] The Messianic theme is repeated in the Servant figure, i.e., the Anointed One in TI, who is the covenantal representative of the people of Zion (59:21; 61:1,

213. Koenen 1990:145.

214. Beuken 1989a:186; Volz 1932:248; Whybray 1981:238; Koenen 1990:145.

215. Koenen 1990:145.

216. Koenen 1990:145.

217. Whybray 1981:238; Childs 2001:499. Ketib is the "shoot of his planting" (נצר מטעו). There is no actual difference in meaning because the pronouns refer to YHWH in either case. But, Qere is preferred because of the context.

218. Lau 1994:64; Beuken 1989a:188; Motyer 1993:499. A direct connection is rejected by Childs (2001:499).

219. Beuken 1989a:188.

8–9) as we have seen in 3.3. So the quality of the Davidic Messiah is shared by the servants of the Anointed One.

The "least one becoming a clan"/"smallest one becoming a mighty nation" in 60:22a is in the context of a city motif and is ultimately based on the Patriarchal promises (49:8, 19–21; 54:1–3), and may be related to 51:2, in which the Abrahamic promise is recalled.[220] "*Terwijl het hoofdstuk als ge- heel een totaal nieuwe verhouding van Sion tot de volken heeft aangekondigd, zou nu ineens de oude stammenstructuur ter sprake komen.*"[221] Thus, the old promise to develop a powerful people in number and weight is eschato- logically achieved in the picture of Zion in 60:22 by the work of YHWH to His glory.[222] This also confirms the idea that the eschatological restoration/ fulfilment of the covenant is related to the paradisiacal achievement, and that this is also a fulfilment of the Patriarchal promises.

Isaiah 60:22b has a possible reference to 49:8.[223] As we have seen above (60:4–5), ch 60 is the fulfilment of the eschatological expectation of ch 49. Since 49:7–12 is the promise for the servant, 60:22 is inspired by the picture of the Servant.[224] This suggests that the glorified Zion is the fulfilment of the eschatological expectation by the Servant, if ch 49 is assumed to be the source text in ch 60.

Having discussed the text, the covenant is the main theme of ch 60 around which the chapter is organized. Four observations lend support to this. (1) 60:12 may display the theme of the Abrahamic covenant (see above). The concentric thought flow of the chapter suggests that 60:12 is the core of the chapter.[225] It is thus a necessary part, even though some scholars have

220. Motyer 1993:499; Delitzsch 1873:423; Whybray 1981:238; Westermann 1969:363.

221. Beuken 1989a:189. "Whereas the chapter as a whole has announced a totally new relationship between Zion and the nations, now all of a sudden the old interna- tional structure arises as a topic." (My translation).

222. Beuken 1989a:190.

223. Beuken 1989a:190. Five observations support this. (1) עת occurs only in 60:22 in TI; (2) רצון is connected to 60:7, 10 and 61:2; (3) Holy One of Israel is parallel (49:7; 60:9, 14); (4) the theme of light of the nations/darkness is parallel (49:6, 9; 61:1–3, 19–20); (5) there is an agreement between 49:7 and 60:14.

224. Beuken 1989a:191.

225. Motyer 1993:493; Polan 2001:55–56, 70–71. Although we can agree with Mo- tyer's observation of the structure, his suggestion needs some modification, because: (1) v. 7d (I shall glorify My glorious house) is parallel to v. 9f (He has glorified you), and thus these verses seem to come together to the same paragraph. (2) Vv. 4–14 form a unity and picturing specifically Gentiles' participation to Zion. Thus, the structure of chapter 60 in thought flow can be suggested as follows (cont. overpage):

argued for it being a later addition because they understand the verse to present a narrow-minded nationalism. This contradicts the general trend of universalism in Second and Third Isaiah.[226] As Motyer suggested, the verse and the whole chapter may present the theme of Abrahamic covenant tradition (Gen 12:3), signifying that the people of Zion is the key to the fortune of the world.[227] The promise to Abraham in Gen 12:3 is fulfilled in the people of Zion in 60:12, as Abraham (i.e., his descendants) is going to be a great nation in Gen 12:2, and the Abrahamic promise in Gen 12:1–3 as a whole is achieved in ch. 60. (2) It needs to be noted that the theme of returning to Zion involves both the offspring (60:4, 9) and the nations (60:5, 10), which may come from the Abrahamic covenant scheme in Gen 12:1–3 (see above). The reconstruction of Zion, her eschatological transformation, in ch. 60 has been understood as the formation of the new people of YHWH, which is salvific. (3) 60:22a ("the least one shall become a clan, and the smallest one a mighty nation"), the concluding verse of the chapter, also echoes the promises to the patriarchs (Gen 12:2a, 3), so Abrahamic.[228] (4) In the light of this evidence and the structural understanding of the Abrahamic scheme in ch 60, the theme of the possession of the land in 60:21 may also be an element of Abrahamic covenant tradition.[229] In short, the eschatological portrait of Zion in ch 60 shares the general thematic schema of the Abrahamic promise especially in those who will be the people of YHWH.

Furthermore, the covenant tradition of ch 60 is not limited to the Abrahamic promises. (1) According to Beuken, there is a covenant formula in 60:20–21, saying that God is . . . , the people are . . . , as reminiscent of the Mosaic Covenant. So the new people of Zion are set in the new (Mosaic) covenantal relation with YHWH.[230] (2) As Childs observed, the theme

---

A 1–3, The Lord, light of Zion
B 4–5, Zion's response to the gathering of the nations
C 6–9, New status of the nations: accepted to the Lord materially and spiritually
D 10–11, Serving nations: compassion of the Lord on Zion
      X 12, Zion: the key of world fortune
D' 13–14, Submissive nations: recognition of the nations on Zion
C' 15–16, New status of Zion: Acceptance and rich satisfaction
B' 17–18, Self evaluation of Zion on its new order
A' 19–22, The Lord, the glorious light

226. Childs 2001:497.

227. Motyer 1993:496.

228. See 4.3 on 60:21–22. Whybray 1981:238. Also see 49:8, 19–21; 54:1–4.

229. Kissane 1943:270. Childs (2001:499) comments, "The promise of inheriting the land is repeated . . . ," suggesting Abrahamic promise. See Gen 12:7; 13:14–15, 17; 15: 7, 16, 18–21; 17:8.

230. Beuken 1989a:185.

of Israel's fame in 60:9 is covenantal, because 60:9 is parallel to 55:5 (55:3 refers to the Davidic covenant).[231] (3) The new name of "the branch of My planting" in 60:21 is also a covenant theme as the new name is linked with the (Mosaic) covenant in 56:5. Therefore, the eschatological vision of ch 60 may be understood as fulfilment of the integrated covenant tradition, in which the Abrahamic, Mosaic, and Davidic Covenants have developed into an integrated covenant tradition. As this may imply, the eschatological salvation would be the restoration of the covenant, that is, the fulfilment of the Abrahamic promise as well as of the Mosaic and Davidic covenants.

In conclusion, the eschatological portrait of Zion is the fulfilment of the eschatological expectation of DI in ch 49, which is to be achieved by the Servant according to the source text. It is also the fulfilment of the covenant traditions as well as the patriarchal promises. The people of Zion will be righteous and possess the land, forming a mighty nation.

4.4 Summary and Conclusion

Zion becomes alight achieving glory as the light of the glory of YHWH approaches her, while the world is in darkness. Because of the light of Zion, the nations and the kings draw near to her. This is the fulfilment of the eschatological expectations of DI and PI, as the glory of Zion and the consequent gathering of the nations achieve the Messianic era and the function of the Servant as well. It is also a re-realization of the creational work and the exodus theophany.

The nations coming to Zion with their wealth and sacrifices will be saved in Zion as they come to the covenantal bond with YHWH and are taught Torah instruction. The nations take part in a mission to the world and the worship of YHWH and even serve YHWH as priests and Levites. They also share the concept of the remnant. The train of the nations also carries the children of Zion from everywhere in the world.

The nations and the kings will participate in the construction of Zion, which will be reconstructed as a salvation community. This reconstruction of Zion was anticipated as the work of the Servant in DI and is achieved by the Anointed One in TI. The reconstruction is not so much physical as spiritual or covenantal.

The eschatological portrait of Zion does not present an exclusive salvific privilege of Israel, but the fact that the nations are to serve Israel signifies an imperialistic relation with the remnants of Israel. This is an achievement

---

231. Childs 2001:506.

of the Abrahamic covenant that Abraham, or rather Israel, will be the key of the nations.

Zion turns into a paradise since the glory of Lebanon comes to her, which signifies the transformation of nature as displayed in the exodus imagery. In the eschatological era, Zion is an incorporation of the Temple, city and paradise.

The once forsaken and rejected city Zion will have an everlasting joy and pride in the eschatological era. Zion will be supplied by the nations and kings, and eventually YHWH will be realized as the Saviour, Redeemer, and the Might One of Jacob, coming to a covenantal relationship.

The economic and social order will also be transformed in the new Zion. Peace will oversee Zion and righteousness will rule her; salvation becomes the wall of Zion, and praise becomes the gates. Violence as well as devastation or destruction will be no more in Zion.

YHWH will replace the Sun and Moon as the everlasting light of Zion—often this image has been understood as apocalyptic. Zion is understood as the heavenly city. All the people of Zion will be righteous—this is also apocalyptic.

The people of Zion also possess the land forever, achieving the Abrahamic covenant. The blessing of becoming a clan and a mighty nation also reflects the patriarchal covenant. The new people of the glorified Zion restore the covenant with YHWH. Eventually, the eschatological Zion is the fulfilment of the covenant traditions (especially, Abrahamic, Mosaic, and Davidic covenants) as the eschatological salvific community, and the re-realization of the creation and the exodus tradition as the Temple-city-paradise.

Chapter 5

The New Heavens and the New Earth
(65:13–25)

5.1 Introduction

In chapter 3, I have argued that the coming of YHWH is the crucial event that inaugurates the eschatological era. The coming YHWH brings judgment not only upon Israel but also upon the nations. The coming of YHWH has been initiated by the sin of his people, i.e., the breach of the covenant, so the coming YHWH will save some of them, who depart from their sins, and restore the covenant. The coming of YHWH includes the sending (i.e., coming) of a Messianic figure.

In chapter 4, I have shown that Zion is not only the eschatological Temple-city but also a paradise. Zion as a city will be a cosmopolitan hub, to which the nations will flow with their wealth. The children of Zion will return to her accompanied by the nations. Zion as a Temple will be glorified by the sacrifices and tribute of the nations and also by the glorious trees in and around the Temple, which implies a paradisiacal change. In the eschatological Zion, there will be no Sun and Moon, because the glory of YHWH will shed light instead. All the people of Zion will be righteous in that time.

In this chapter, I try to argue that the New Heavens and the New Earth are created in the eschatological era as the ultimate fulfilment of the eschatological vision. In the new era, it is the place in which the New Jerusalem is located. In the eschatological Jerusalem, the servants will be eventually vindicated and given blessings, which are expressed in earthly terms such as longevity and eating and drinking with joy and gladness, as a fulfilment of the covenant. The Messianic figure promised in ch 59 is understood to be in this New Jerusalem, which is a paradise, as expected in the previous traditions of the book. The eschatological Zion of ch 60 is re-portrayed as the New Jerusalem in ch 65. The eschatological portrait has both continuity and discontinuity with the historical Israel and nature. To show this, 65:13–25 is selected because it presents "the New Heaven and the New Earth" as part of the climactic conclusion of TI (and the book as well). I will discuss the significance of the passage in the context of TI (and in the book of Isaiah) as a preliminary study for interpretation (5.2), and then elaborate the theological interpretation of the passage (5.3).

5.2 Isa 65:13–25 in TI

This section seeks to show that 65:13–25 highlights the eschatological portrait of TI as the central part of the concluding chapters (65–66) of the book of Isaiah as well as of TI (chs 56–64). The concluding section responds not only to the preceding lament (63:7—64:11[12]),[1] retrieving some eschatological picture of the core chapters of TI (chs 60–62), but also to the introductory chapter of the book (ch 1).

Scholars usually consider chs 65–66 as a unit and as the climactic conclusion of the whole book of Isaiah.[2] For example, Beuken considers that 65:1—66:14 highlights the theme of the servants of YHWH, which he says forms a conclusion to TI (chs 56–64). 66:15–20a[21] underlines the theme of the theophany of YHWH, and functions as a conclusion to both DI and TI. In connection with this theme, 66:15–20a[21] shares together

---

1. Whybray 1981:255–56; Westermann 1969a:386. 63:7—64:11[12] is widely agreed to be a communal lamentation used in cultic situation. Whybray suggests four elements of a communal lamentation: (1) the account of YHWH's acts of redemption (63:7–14); (2) the appeal to him for help (63:15—64:5a); (3) confession of sin (64:5b–7); (4) the final renewed appeal (64:8–12).

2. Torrey 1928:466; Childs 2001:532. Recently, a new demarcation has been tried for a concluding section. For Park (2003:311), 65:17—66:24 is a conclusion to the book, because "the New Heaven and Earth" in 65:17 forms an inclusio not only with the prologue of the book (1:2), but also with the end of the section (66:22). He excludes 65:1–16 from the concluding section because several themes in 65:1–16 reappear in ch 66 (E.g. foreign cult [65:3–5.7a.11; 66:3f.17], judgment announcement [65:5.7b.12; 66:4.5f.14b–16.24], and separation between the servants and the wicked [65:13–15; 66:2b.5.14b.24]). However, as even he acknowledges, particular themes repeat (even) in the concluding unit that he set up, so repetition of themes may not be crucial to exclude 65:1–16 (e.g., foreign cult and the division between the servants and the rebels). Because ch 65 has been argued as a unity (see below in the main text), there is no need to delete 65:1–16 from the concluding section.

with DI and TI the gathering of the nations and their acknowledgement of YHWH, and the language such as "all flesh," "tongues," "name," and "sign." Besides, 66:22–23(24) is understood as the conclusion to the whole book of Isaiah, since it retrieves important themes from the introduction of PI (or, the book).[3]

However, Beuken might have introduced his own assumptions to suggest the structure of the concluding chapters. The following problems challenge his analysis. First, the theme of the servants does not stop at 66:14, but extends to 66:22, in which the keyword זרע, forming the theme according to him, reoccurs.[4] This suggests that not only 65:1—66:14 but the whole of chs 65–66 concludes TI. Second, the theophanic motif also occurs in 65:1—66:14 (65:8–12, 66:6), and the coming of YHWH "in fire" in 66:15–16, which is related to 40:10 (YHWH comes "with might"), is shared also by PI tradition (9:17–18; 10:16–17; 30:27, 30, 33) as well as by DI (47:14) and TI (64:1[2]). The theophanic theme, being spread throughout chs 65–66, is not unique to DI and TI, but present throughout the book. Furthermore, PI also shares the theme of 'the gathering of the nations' (11:12), which is alleged to be characteristic of DI and TI. So, in terms of the theme of theophany, chs 65–66 should not be divided into three sections each concluding a particular part of the book. Third, the intratextual relation between 65:25 and 11:6–9 (see 5.3 on 65:25) as well as the lexical agreements between 65:17–25 and ch 1 may not be ignored.[5] Furthermore, the theme of cleansing judgment in 1:24–31 is repeated in 65:8–12, vindicating the righteous. The pilgrimage of the nations and the invitation of the people to return in chs 2–4 are concluded in chs 65–66.[6] In support of this view Sweeney notes that themes and texts from the entire book are referred to in chs 65–66.[7] These suggest that 65:1—66:14 does not conclude just TI but PI and DI, too. Therefore, chs 65–66 are a conclusion to the book of Isaiah as well as TI (and DI).

So Beuken's scheme of the concluding chapters may not be convincing. For Seitz, it is too 'artificial' to divide chs 65–66 and to suggest such a strictly systematic framework of 1–2–3 Isaiahs, although Seitz admits Beuken's observation that chs 65–66 are a 'coherent text complex' as a concluding

---

3. Beuken 1991:204–21. Included are the themes such as heaven and earth (1:2), offspring (of evildoer) (1:4), "comes before my face" (1:12), "rebel against me" (1:2, 28), new moon and Sabbath (1:13), and the judgment by fire (1:31).

4. Beuken 1991:214.

5. Beuken 1991:220. The word pair "heaven and earth" (65:17; 1:2), the promise "I will hear" (64:24) vs. "I will not listen" (1:15), and offspring (65:23; 1:4) will be included.

6. Sweeney 1997a:457.

7. Sweeney 1997a:464. Especially, chs 1, 2–4, 6, 11, 13, and 37:30–32 may be included.

section of the book. For Seitz, "sections 2 and 3 [i.e., DI and TI] are them-selves already indebted to Isaiah traditions that lay before them."[8]

The concluding chapters present the divine answer to the preceding lament, in which the prophet implores YHWH's intervention to save the people from the present predicament (63:7, 15; 63:19b—64:1[64:1–2]; 64:11[12]). This view is however not shared by Skinner, for whom, chs 65–66 do not form a response to 63:7—64:11[12], because the community is different in the two sections.[9] While the whole community is in view in the lament, since "we are all thy people" (64:9), in chs 65–66 they are separated into the servants and the idolaters (65:3–5, 8–10; 66:3–4, 17).[10] Further-more, while a lament is expected to be followed (only) by a salvation oracle, chs 65–66 include a judgment word as well as a salvation oracle.[11]

However, Steck has countered Skinner's arguments. For Steck, chs 65–66, composed of 65:1—66:4 and 66:5–24, correspond to the preceding lament, correcting and extending the previous pray-er's view "that Israel as a whole is entitled to God's response" (63:17a; 64:8).[12] The redactor of chs 65–66 replies that only the righteous, a small portion of the people, will be saved, while the sinners are subject to punishment (65:8–10; 66:14).[13] For Steck, the framework of chs 65–66 corresponds to that of the prayer, 65:1–7 and 66:1–4 forming an *inclusio* of ch 65.[14] 65:1–7 responds to 63:(15–)17a, correcting the pray-er's request that YHWH would intervene for their hard-ening of the hearts and lack of fearing YHWH, as דרך is a link (63:17a; 65:2).[15] The act of YHWH to hold out His hands continuously in 65:1–7 also responds to the prophet's complaint on the restraint and silence of YHWH in 64:11, as חשה (65:6; 64:11) links the two passages. The other boundary of ch 65, i.e., 66:1–4, also provides an answer to 64:11.[16] The end of the prayer (64:11) forms an *inclusio* with its beginning (63:15) in terms of אפק. 63:15 and 66:1–4 form an *inclusio* because of the parallel שמים (66:1; 63:15), נבט (66:2; 63:15), and the dwelling of YHWH (66:1; 63:15).[17] The fire judgment

8. Seitz 2001:539.

9. Skinner 1898:230.

10. Skinner 1898:231.

11. Koenen 1990:161.

12. Steck 1991:221, 224; Seitz 2001:541.

13. For Steck (1991:221), 65:8–10 is related to 63:17b in terms of נחלה.

14. Steck 1991:224.

15. Steck 1991:221.

16. Steck 1991:223.

17. Steck 1991:224.

in 66:15 and 66:24, forming an *inclusio* at the second section, corresponds to the theophanic description in 64:1a[2a].[18]

However, Seitz criticizes Steck. Seitz comments that Steck's correspondence is "only through the lens of redactional intentionality, not in the plain sense presentation of the canonical text as such."[19] For Seitz, chs 65–66 "forthrightly" correspond to the lament from the canonical point of view in the present form.[20] Although in 63:15(7)—64:11[12], the prophet identifies himself with the people who sinned and are subject to the judgment of YHWH, and prays for the divine salvific intervention, in chs 65–66 YHWH announces that only some of the people will be saved, the righteous, while others are subject to punishment.[21] It is not the redactor that corrects the prayer's view, but YHWH's judgment as presented in the canonical form.

Another issue is the relationship between chs 65–66 and 60–62. The eschatological portrait of chs 65–66 is also a summary representation of that of chs 60–62. For Ruszukowski, the promises of salvation in chs 60–62 are fulfilled in ch 65, because the sinners are removed, who have hindered the community from realization of salvation.[22] The servants own the land in 65:9b, while the people of Zion in 60:21 and 61:7 will possess it.[23] While the people of Zion are promised that the harvest and the wine will not be consumed by the enemies in 62:8–9 and 61:6, in 65:13–14 the servants eat and drink, and rejoice.[24] In 62:8–9, the promise is for the whole community, while in 65:13 this promise is limited to the servants.[25] (In fact, this link suggests that the saved people in chs 60–62 are identified with the servants in chs 65–66.) New names are promised in 62:2 and 12; the servants are called another name in 65:15b.[26] The seed of the blessed of YHWH in 65:23b is a fulfilment of 61:9.[27]

However, although we admit with Ruszukowski that chs 60(–62) and 65 share the same eschatological portrait, we need to notice that different approaches are working in the portraits of eschatology in chs 60(–62) and

18. Steck 1991:223.

19. Seitz 2001:541.

20. Seitz 2001:541.

21. Muilenburg 1954:744.

22. Ruszukowski 2000:86.

23. Ruszukowski 2000:82.

24. Ruszukowski 2000:82.

25. Ruszukowski 2000:84.

26. Ruszukowski 2000:82. But in Isaiah 65 a negative part is added beside the positive part which corresponds to the salvation promises. Ruszukowski 2000:84.

27. Ruszukowski 2000:83.

65(-66). While the eschatological portrait of ch 60 is describing a scene (only) after the coming of YHWH, that of ch 65 exhibits a transition from the present to the eschatological era through His coming. So, from the chronological point of view, the eschatological perspective of ch 60 is later than that of ch 65, although the latter concludes the former in the canonical form.

Yet another point is made by Hanson. He holds that although chs 65–66 and chs 60–62 share the picture of the New Heavens and Earth, in chs 60–62 the eschatological portrait is anchored to the historical reality as in DI, while in ch 65 it becomes detached from history. However, there remain historical elements belonging to human life in the eschatological portrait of ch 65, too. In fact, in both chs 60–62 and ch 65 the eschatological portrait presents both continuity and discontinuity with history (see 5.3 especially on 65:25).

In summary, as the climactic conclusion of the book of Isaiah, chs 65–66 should not be divided into three, each concluding a particular part of the book. Although the prophet intercedes for the people in trouble (63:7—64:11[12]), YHWH announces that only the servants will be saved in chs 65–66. These chapters re-present the eschatological portrait of chs 60–62, and retrieve themes from the introduction of the book.

Having discussed the concluding chapters (65–66), how is 65:13–25 related to them? 65:13–25 is the climax of the eschatological portrait in the concluding chapters 65–66, in that it presents the ultimate eschatological goal, i.e., the New Heavens and the New Earth (65:17), as well as the vindication of the righteous. But according to Westermann, 65:1–16a is a unity, rather than ch 65. 65:1–7 forms a complete unit as an announcement of doom, while 65:8–16a presents a shift to the divine announcement of salvation and judgment at the same time.[28] While 65:1–16a is concerned about the contrast between the apostates and the servants, 65:16b–25, deals with the contrast between the miseries of the past and the future salvation.[29] So, for him, ch 65 is composed of two different parts 65:1–16a and 65:16b–25.[30]

However, Muilenburg defends the unity of ch 65, because the calling-answering theme in 65:1–2, 12 and 24–25 forms a structural skeleton of the chapter, and the divine speech is presented as first person throughout

---

28. Westermann 1969:399, 403–4.

29. Westermann 1969:407.

30. Westermann 1969:398, 406. For Beuken (1989b:59), too, the primary cut-off of the chapter lies between 65:16b and 17a, because 65:1–6 exhibits the contrast between the servants and the rebels, while 65:17–25 displays the former troubles and the blessings in the New Heavens and the New Earth.

the chapter, involving contrasting repayment.[31] Furthermore, the contrast between the obedient and the rebels forms a coherent thought in the chapter.[32] Thus, the blessings given in 65:17–25 are understood to form part of YHWH's intention rewarding the servants to vindicate them in 65:8–16. The unity may also be supported by the fact that the demonstrative pronoun "they" referring to "the servants" in 65:21–24 suggests the presence of the sinners as audience. So 65:13–25 is understood in the context to be part of the vindication of the servants, as a continuation of the theme in the preceding section 65:8–12. Responding to the prayer for the intervention of YHWH for the present predicament due to the enemies in 63:7—64:11[12], 65:13–25 affirms that only the righteous will be vindicated by the eschatological coming of YHWH.

With respect to the following context of 65:13–25, Hitzig has suggested that 66:1–6 is an unnatural sequel to ch 65, because the theme of the Temple is unexpected after the theme of the New Heavens and Earth.[33] However, 66:1–6 continues the themes of the coming of YHWH and the vindication of the servants in ch 65, linking chs 65 and 66.

The linkage is shown in the following three arguments. First, the theme of calling/answering in 66:4 is related to 65:12, 24 and 65:1–2. For Beuken, 66:4 (and 65:12 as well) is related to 50:2, because they express the complaint of YHWH against the people who do not listen. However, in contrast, the first half of 50:2 ("Why, when I came, was there no man?") may also be assumed in 66:4 and 65:12, because the vindication of the servants in 65:13–25 is by the judgment of the coming YHWH in 65:8–12 (especially, v. 12). In 66:1–6, too, those who are humble and contrite in spirit and those who tremble at the word of YHWH are vindicated by the theophanic voice in 66:6.[34]

Second, the Heavens and the Earth in 66:1 alludes to the New Heavens and the New Earth in 65:17. YHWH made (עשה) the Heavens and the Earth (66:2) as he creates (ברא) them in 65:17.[35] In 66:1–6, the Heavens are the

31. Muilenburg 1954:745; Beuken 1989b:58; Whybray 1981:267. The theme of the communication between YHWH and His people reoccurs in 66:4, linking the two chapters.

32. Whybray 1981:266, 268.

33. Dim 2005:47.

34. For Beuken (1989d:59), the first half of 50:2 is omitted intentionally in the quotation because it is not important in TI. He comments, "It certainly does not, in a coherent manner, determine the ongoing dynamics of TI's prophecy . . . ." But, this is just the opposite to what we have seen in chapter 3.

35. For Beuken (1989d:54), "all these things" in 66:2 refers to the "heavens and earth" in 66:1. There seems no difference between the two verbs in the two places.

dwelling place of YHWH, in which the throne is situated and from which the governing authority and power is exercised.[36] As we have seen in 4.3, the Holy Mountain in 65:25 is identified with the new Zion in 60:19–20 (65:25), so YHWH is enthroned on the Holy Mountain in the New Heavens and the New Earth.

Third, for Beuken, doing no evil in the Holy Mountain in 65:25 is related to the evildoing of the sinners (66:3) and the presence of YHWH with the servants (66:2) in the Temple (66:1, 6). For him, the rebuilding of the Temple as such is not at issue in 66:1–2, but who are fit to receive God's favour (66:3–5).[37] YHWH favors those who are contrite in spirit and listen to His word (66:2, 4).

Another challenge was made by Volz, who thought that chs 65 and 66 belong to different authorship.[38] They have greater differences in that ch 65 (and 66:3, 4a, 17) has specific enemies among the people and a contrast thereby, while 66:7–24 broadens its perspective into the horizon of the nations beyond Israel/Zion. Thus, for him, the eschatological faith is not presented as an integrated theology in chs 65–66. Rather, inherited diverse eschatological ideas are scattered here and there without forming a unified whole.

However, the division of the community pervades the chapters as well as there are many links between the two chapters. Furthermore, we have seen that the eschatological community includes not only the people of Israel but also those from the nations. Even Volz admits that the two chapters have some common themes such as the centrality of Zion, the servants of YHWH as a faithful group, the New Heavens and the New Earth, and the nations, which form a substantial part of the eschatological theology of TI. Assumption of the theological unity brings a consistent theology at a higher level.

Therefore, these arguments suggest that 65:13–25 is related to the following as well as the preceding contexts, as part of the concluding chapters 65–66, presenting the ultimate eschatological vision and vindication of the servants, who are in trouble in the present time.

One of the issues that concerns commentators is the historical background to this section (or, chs 65–66).[39] As for the reference to the Temple

---

36. Beuken 1989d:55. For Park (2003:347–48) בנה links 66:1 and 65:21, connecting the reconstruction of the houses of Jerusalem at the end in the ch 65 and reconstruction of the house of YHWH at the beginning in the ch 66. But this is unconvincing, because the ideas behind the verses are different.

37. Beuken 1989d:55–57.

38. Volz 1932:296, 281.

39. For the brief summary of discussion, see Muilenburg 1954:758–60; Skinner

in 66:1, Babylonian (Hitzig) and Samaritan Temples (Duhm, Skinner), as well as the Zerubbabel Temple in Jerusalem (Sellin, Elliger), have been suggested without any real evidence in the text, on the presupposition that these verses form a disputatious situation. As for Smart, followed by Mui-lenburg, DI (i.e., TI, for Muilenburg) is the contemporary of Haggai and disputes with him against his appeal to build the Temple and his assurance that the building would bring a new phase of salvation.[40] Hanson develops Smart's view, arguing that the division of the community in 65:13–25 (and in chs 65–66 as well as TI) into the servants and the rebels reflects a real historical situation.

According to Hanson, the conflict in TI reflects the social situation of the post-exilic Jewish community. The sociological conflict between the visionary group (the DI school) and the priestly group (the Zadokites), as reflected in 63:7—64:11 and chs 58–59, continues also in chs 65–66.[41] But, while in other chapters (e.g., ch 58), the conflict has been simple, in chs 65–66 "the schism widens" and the evident controversy over the Temple construction results in the expulsion of one party. The conditionality of chs 58–59 has gone.[42] However, it may be doubted whether such a sociological understanding of the community is backed up by the text.

Firstly, Hanson argues that the cultic vocabulary reflects the Zadokite Temple cult.[43] For him עַל־פָּנַי (65:3; cf. 59:2) is a technical term designating the Temple cult.[44] He also maintains that קרב, נגש, and קדש in 65:5 are "car-dinal" technical terms which exhibit the hierocratic tradition of Zadokite priests, since Ezek 44:13 (נגש), 15 (קרב), and 19 (קדש) show their exclusive rights of access to the Temple.[45] However, it is highly questionable whether 65:3 refers to the cult in the central sanctuary. On the contrary, the verse suggests that the sacrifices are offered "in the gardens."[46] The verse simply

---

1898:244–46.

40. Smart 1934:420–21; 1967:275, 282–86; Muilenburg 1954:760.

41. Chapters 60–62 are the restoration program of the visionary group, for Hanson. 56:9—57:13 come after the chs 65–66 according to his historical reconstruction.

42. Hanson 1979:134–86. As for the summary of his proposal, see Schramm 1995:81–111.

43. Hanson 1979:146–49.

44. Hanson 1979:145–46 and 121. While the בעיניך in Exod 33:16 does not neces-sarily refer to the cultic situation (contrary to Hanson's implication), לפני־יהוה in Exod 28:29–30 and Lev 24:3 does. But, in this case it is especially because the contexts of the verses are already describing a cultic situation. Thus, the phrase may signify the attention of YHWH or the relation with YHWH. Whybray (1981:269) translates the phrase עַל־פָּנַי as "openly."

45. Hanson 1979:148.

46. One may propose that the illegitimate cults are used to heighten the offense of

states that the sacrifices in the gardens offend YHWH. The use of the three other (so-called) technical terms in 65:5 is quite different from that in Ezek 44. In Ezekiel, the accessibility at issue is one towards YHWH, while in 65:5 it is towards the arrogant worshippers themselves. The restraint of holiness in Ezekiel is with a view to the protection of the people, while the claim of holiness in ch 65 is due to their pride. Thus, even if the three words are found in Ezek 44, it is not convincing that 66:5 forms the same situation as Ezek 44 or even that the words exclusively belong to Zadokites. Furthermore, the other technical terms may refer to the official priestly group only when the (pagan) cultic activities in 65:3–4 are accepted as being performed in the central Temple, which is very implausible (see below).

Secondly, Hanson claims that in several places the idolatrous activities refer to attacks on the Zadokite institutional cult. But his interpretations of these passages are very strained. In 65:3–4a, for him, the cultic practices of idolatries, though they are described in the traditional words accusing defilement of worship, should not be taken literally but symbolically, and thus signify an assault on the Temple cult that "*equate*[s] the cult of those attacked with Canaanizing sacrificial practices" (italics mine).[47] In 65:11b, which refers to Gad and Meni, the cultic aberrations of the priestly group are "*symbolized* by pagan abominations" (italics mine).[48] In 66:3 as well, the cultic activities of the opponents are being "equated" with the defiled pagan practices.[49] However, it is not clear why these verses should be read symbolically rather than literally. Hanson is in danger of imposing his theory on the text. Furthermore, it is not certain what is challenged, for Hanson, by the prophets in the Temple cult—whether it is the cultic institution as such or the political opponents who are in charge of the cults. Hanson seems to confuse the two. Thus he suggests that the cults (cultic institution) and prophets are not compatible.[50] Hanson identified the אחיכם in 66:5 with the Zadokite priests, but in the verse, reference to the Zadokites is missing, even though conflict seems evident.

---

the institutional cult, but this is suspicious because sacrifice on the "hill" is brought up not only in this verse but also in 1:29–30 (in fact, these two places are linked in terms of the "hill") and Hanson might have also to suggest that the sociological division also occurs in ch 1 and PI if the reference in 1:29–30 is the same use. Also in 57:7, the lofty and high mountain is displayed as the illegitimate (place of) worship.

47. Hanson 1979:147.

48. Hanson 1979:154.

49. Hanson 1979:179.

50. According to Schramm (1995:177), this kind of understanding of Hanson is revival of the old Torah-prophets contrast schema.

Thirdly, 66:1–4 may not present a polemic situation as Westermann shows.[51] Hanson maintains that there are two different theological stances about the Temple building in 66:1–4, which reflect the two distinct groups of the community. For him, TI (especially ch 66) is contemporary with Haggai and Zechariah. And 66:1–2, one of the theological mottoes of the prophetic visionaries following DI (Chs 60–62 are their program), is a direct repudiation of Haggai's message about the Temple building plan, which developed from the Zadokite orthodoxy in Ezek 40–48.[52] However, Westermann argues that the verses do not present a polemic situation as the terms in 66:1–2 that are adopted from the Psalms are only normal and general. For him, 66:1a and 66:2b is a quotation from Ps 113:5–7 and thus form a normal praise of YHWH. The "all these things" in 66:2a refers to the Heavens and Earth in 66:1a, not to a Temple (e.g., the Samaritan Temple). Furthermore, the subject matter of the passage is parallel to the Psalms such as Ps 50. So, for him, 66:1–2 are too plainly like Psalms to suggest a dispute. Besides, the apparent theological difference does not necessarily suggest the existence of the distinctive 'sociological groups.' Furthermore, the link with Haggai in these verses is doubtful. Rather, these verses are reminiscent of Nathan's oracle to David in 2 Sam 7:1–17 (especially v. 5) and Solomon's prayer for devotion to the Temple in 1 Kgs 8:22–53 (especially v. 27).[53] These two connections may suggest that the main purport of these verses is not concerned with the *new* construction of the Temple (Haggai, etc), but possibly with (the enforcement and the fulfilment of) the covenant of David, because the previous context is the eschatological promise in 65:17–25 and the following is about the sins of Israel. YHWH restores the covenant with those who tremble at the word of YHWH (66:2, 5) and not with those who commit idolatry.[54] Thus, 66:1–2 may not indicate the historical setting that Hanson assumes.

Therefore, the historical allegation of TI (especially 66:1–4) about the Temple is not certain and Hanson's understanding of the conflict in chs 65–66 as a sociological class conflict should be rejected. Hanson's understanding of the situational background of the class struggle may be his presupposition, rather than result of interpretation, which lacks textual evidence. However, some of his observations are useful. These include his observation of the conflicting character of the chapters (but without assumption of the priestly

51. Westermann 1969:412–13.

52. Hanson 1979:172–79.

53. Childs 2001:540; Muilenburg 1954:760.

54. For Beuken (1989d:55–57), as seen above in the main text, the main issue in 66:1–2 is who are favoured by YHWH.

group and the consequent class conflict) and the apocalyptic elements in 65:17–25. His theory emphasizes sociology at the expense of the nuanced theology expounded in this thesis.

What then is the alternative to the understanding of the nature of the distinction of the people in 65:13–25 (or chs 65–66) in the context of TI? First, the division of the community in 65:13–25 (or, chs 65–66) responds to the preceding lament 63:7—64:11[12], in which the prophet refers to the covenantal relationship to appeal to YHWH (63:7–14, [especially 8], 16; 64:7[8], 8[9]). Although the prophet prayed for the whole community, identifying himself with the sinning people, YHWH replies that only the righteous are saved—so the community is to be divided. According to 65:8–12, the eschatological judgment and retribution of the coming YHWH will cause division. The righteous will be rewarded; the wicked will be punished. In particular 65:12 and 15 depict the removal of the sinners by the sword of YHWH in accordance with the covenantal threat of the Deuteronomic tradition (Deut 32:41–43).[55] Second, the "servants" (65:9, 13–15) refers to 56:4, 6, where the term denotes the covenantal bond with YHWH. In chs 65–66, only those who forsake their sins and seek YHWH, trembling at the word of YHWH, are called "the servants," who form the new people after the coming of YHWH and take part in the eschatological salvation. Third, the connection of the cleansing judgment in 65:8–12 and 1:24–31 also reveals that the sinners, who are removed by the coming YHWH, are those who broke the covenant.[56] This judgment will cleanse the community.[57] Fourth, the servants in 65:17–25 are identified with the people in the (new) Zion in ch 60 because the servants inhabit the New Jerusalem in the New Heavens and the New Earth. Thus, the people are divided into the sinners who break the covenant and the servants who are righteous, committed to the covenant and YHWH, and the division of the community in chs 65–66

---

55. The phrase "to be destined to the sword," as Westermann (1969:405) indicated, is probably originated from the Deuteronomic tradition (Deut 32:41–43) as in the "judgment by the sword" in 66:16 and also as in 66:12b, which is the Deuteronomic language. The "(bow down to) slaughter" (לטבח תכרעו) (65:12), "to be put to death" (65:15), and "sword" (65:12; 66:16) as well as the divine wrath (65:3, 5; 66:14, 15–16), together with 34:1–6 (indignation, wrath, slaughter, sword, blood), are also reminiscent of Deut 32:41–43 (sword, blood, recompense, vengeance), which implies the punishment being one of the covenant sanctions, and may be achieved in the corpses in 66:24.

56. Especially take notice of justice/righteousness in 1:27 (see 2.3 on 56:1). The idea of judgment is included in "I will relieve myself from my enemies and avenge myself on my foes" (1:24).

57. Cleansing is evidenced in '(to) purge away your dross and remove all your impurities' (1:25).

is not 'historical' (in the sense of past or present history) but 'eschatological' and covenantal.

In summary, as part of the concluding chapters 65–66 of the book (as well as TI), 65:13–25 presents the vindication of the righteous and the ultimate eschatological vision of the New Heavens and the New Earth. The division of the community is not sociological but covenantal—rebels and the faithful to the covenant and YHWH.

5.3 Theological Interpretation of the Text

Having discussed the contextual significance of 65:13–25, this section tries to show that the New Heavens and the New Earth is given as the ultimate purpose of the eschatological plan of YHWH together with vindication of the servants, so that they may enjoy it. The new creation signifies the paradisiacal change of nature, so it is apocalyptic, although a more prophetic reading might be still possible, though I do not adopt it in the exegesis. The blessings given to the servants to vindicate them are a continuation of the historical life. The rewards for the servants and the punishment of the sinners are in accordance with the covenant, so YHWH's plan of salvation in the covenant is fully realized in the eschatological era.

13 Therefore thus says the Lord YHWH:
"Behold, My servants shall eat, but you shall be hungry;
behold, My servants shall drink, but you shall be thirsty;
behold, My servants shall rejoice, but you shall be put to shame;
14 behold, My servants shall sing for gladness of heart,
but you shall cry out for pain of heart
and shall wail for breaking of spirit.

לכן כה־אמר אדני יהוה
הנה עבדי יאכלו ואתם תרעבו
הנה עבדי ישתו ואתם תצמאו
הנה עבדי ישמחו ואתם תבשו:
הנה עבדי ירנו מטוב לב
ואתם תצעקו מכאב לב
ומשבר רוח תילילו:

This strophe highlights the contrast between the reward to the servants and the shameful punishment of the apostates, as evidenced in the four-fold "behold" (הנה) and the deliberate contrast of "My servants" with "but you" (ואתם).[58] The contrast between the blessing given to the servants and the curse given to the apostates is based on the covenantal tradition. The vindication of the servants and the punishment of the sinners are seen as the eschatological fulfilment of the covenantal enforcement as related to previous traditions such as the remnants (PI) and the Servant (DI).

The blessings (65:13–14) are the vindication of the servants in accordance with the covenant. According to Beuken, the contrasts (eat vs. starve,

58. Childs 2001:537; Skinner 1898:238; Muilenburg 1954:753; Westermann 1969:406.

drink vs. thirsty, delight vs. shame) are from the genre of the covenantal curses and blessings seen in Deut 28:1–26, 48.[59] Joy of heart (טוב לב) may be related to Deut 28:47, which is a covenant warning.[60] Eating and drinking in 65:13 are related to 62:8–9, so for Lau 65:13 is an interpolation of the previous promise.[61] In the light of intertextual reference to Deut 28:33, 62:8–9 signifies the withdrawal of judgment (or curse) of the covenant, i.e., the restoration of the covenant.[62] Not only eating and drinking but also joy and delight, suggesting a banquet, may also be related to 55:1–2, and possibly 25:6 also.[63] The eating and drinking with joy may imply a covenant meal after the eschatological (re-)conclusion of the covenant, i.e., the eschatological banquet.

The vindication of the servants fulfils the eschatological expectations of the previous parts of the book. According to Lau, 65:13 is the fulfilment of the promise of no suffering from hunger (רעב) and thirst (מצא) in 49:10 and, possibly, 41:17.[64] If this is the case, the blessings to the servants are related to the task of the Servant. The promise of deliverance from hunger and thirst as well as from the danger of sunlight in 49:10 was given to the Servant, and will be fulfilled in the "time of My favour" and the "day of salvation" (49:8), which is realized in 61:2 and 63:4 in TI. So the work of the Servant has been effected and transferred to the servants, and in the light of 61:1–3, this is the work of the Anointed One, who takes over the role of the Servant. (The deliverance is expressed in exodus imagery [49:9, 11].) In 41:17–20, too, the promise of deliverance from hunger and thirst is related to the exodus imagery, which is presented as the paradisiacal change of nature (cf. 65:17, 25). In addition, ירנו may be related to 61:7 due to the unique form.[65] The joy in 61:7 is due to the task of the Anointed One proclaiming the "year of YHWH's favour" and the "day of vengeance of our God" (61:2). So, the Anointed One takes over the role of the Servant in the blessings for the servants that vindicate them, fulfilling the promise of DI. The vindication is achieved in the paradise.

The eschatological expectation of PI is also achieved here. The word "sorrow/pain" (כאב) (of heart) (65:14) may link to 17:11 (the only other

59. Beuken 1989b:76.
60. Skinner 1898:239; Duhm 1892:434.
61. Lau 1994:199.
62. The background of 62:8–9 may be the feast of the tabernacle in Deut 16:13–15. See Muilenburg 1954:722; Volz 1932:252; Whybray 1981:250.
63. Seitz 2001:543; Motyer 1993:528.
64. Lau 1994:199.
65. Lau 1994:199.

occurrence in the book of Isaiah), in which the day of sorrow is another expression for the Day of YHWH (ביום נחלה וכאב אנוש; cf. 17:4, 7, 9). In that day the people of Jacob will be exposed to the grief and painful sorrow while there will be just a few remnants (17:4–6). Thus, the warning prophecy in ch 17, which incurs an eschatological division of the community, is thus achieved (or, re-applied) here to the wicked, while the remnant concept is identified with the servants.[66]

In brief, the servants will receive the covenantal blessings and enjoy the eschatological covenantal meal as a token of their vindication, while the wicked will be subject to the covenantal punishment and curse. They will rejoice in the eschatological era as the result of the work of the Anointed One, who takes over the role of the Servant. The eschatological enforcement of the covenant is the fulfilment of PI's and DI's expectations.

15 You shall leave your name to My chosen for a curse,	והנחתם שמכם לשבועה לבחירי
and the Lord YHWH will put you to death,	והמיתך אדני יהוה
but His servants He will call by another name.	ולעבדיו יקרא שם אחר:
16 So that he who blesses himself in the land	אשר המתברך בארץ
shall bless himself by the God of faithfulness,	יתברך באלהי אמן
and he who takes an oath in the land	והנשבע בארץ
shall swear by the God of faithfulness;	אשבע באלהי אמן
because the former troubles are forgotten	כי נשכחו הצרות הראשנות
and are hidden from My eyes.	וכי נסתרו מעיני:

This strophe continues the covenantal division of the people, presenting the ultimate sentence of vindication and punishment as fulfilment of covenantal tradition. While the name of sinners will be delivered to a curse and they will be eventually put to death, the servants will be called another name. This will certainly be made to occur by the God of faithfulness. The servants will fully commit themselves to YHWH, swearing by Him. The afflictions of the past will be forgotten.

As generally agreed, שבועה in 65:15a is an imprecatory formula as in Jer 29:22.[67] The name of sinners will be used as a curse, just as the names of the patriarchs may be used as a benedictory formula (Gen 22:18, 48:20; see below), while the servants are called another name.[68] However, here, the formula functions as an announcement of YHWH to remove the sinners from the new community. Due to this removal the people of the new community will be all righteous (60:21). As we have seen already (5.2), 65:15b ("put to

---

66. We have already noted another connection to the Day of YHWH tradition in 66:15–16.

67. Skinner 1898:239; Whybray 1981:274.

68. Alexander 1846b:449.

death") as well as 65:12 ("destine for sword") are covenantal enforcements of Deut 32:41–42. So, the sinners are removed at last, in the eschatological era.

The giving of a new name (to the servants) in 65:15c recalls Gen 17:5, in which Abram is called a new name Abraham by YHWH who enters a covenant with him, making him the father of the nations.[69] So it may be a new covenantal order in 65:15. "To invoke a blessing" (המתברך) in 65:16 also has an Abrahamic link.[70] So the Abrahamic promise is fulfilled here.

The 'names' such as "My chosen," "My servants," and "My people" refer to the essential qualities of the people of YHWH in the eschatological salvation.[71] The "seed" also refers to the new people. All of these names referred to the people of (the old) Israel before, but now to the new people of YHWH. In this sense, they form the "new name" theme. They are distinct from the whole of (old) Israel, as obedient and entitled to the blessings alone. For Koenen, בחיר and עמי in 65:16b–24 have a different sense from those in 65:8–16a.[72] The "people" in 65:18–19 is a comprehensive description of the whole people as in 65:1–7, while they are part of the community in 65:8–16a. But, his view is not convincing. Although the divine charge is against the people as a whole in 65:1–7, from 65:8 onwards a splitting of the people is in view and only the obedient to YHWH are called My servants (65:9, 13, 14, 15), My selected (65:9, 15, 22) and My people (65:10, [18], 19, 22) and the seed (65:9, 23). In 65:9–10[12], only the remnants, i.e., the obedient of 65:1–7 are the seed, My chosen, and My servants. In 65:13–16, too, they are My servants and My chosen. "My chosen" and "My servants" (65:15) in parallel are related to 65:9. In 65:17–25, those who are blessed are her people (65:18), My people (65:19, 22), My chosen (65:22), and the seed (65:23). The "My chosen" and "My people" in 65:22 are equivalent to "My servants" and the seed in 65:9.[73] The "her people" in 65:18 and "My people" in 65:19 are identified with the "My people" in 65:10,[74] and also with the seed, My selected and My servants in 65:9. They are the servants who possess the eschatological land in 65:9–10. They are different from the rebellious and provoking "people" in 65:2–3, in which the people of the old Israel as a whole are in view. Due to the cleansing judgment of 65:8, the titles

69. Motyer 1993:528.

70. Motyer 1993:529; Cheyne 1895:371; Skinner 1898:239; Duhm 1892:435. Hithpael of ברך, Gen 22:18; 26:4; cf. niphal of ברך: 12:3; 18:18; 28:14.

71. The servants whom YHWH favours are humble and contrite in spirit, and tremble at the word of YHWH, according to 66:2, 5.

72. Koenen 1990:179.

73. Beuken 1989b:87; Koenen 1990:179.

74. The change from "her people" to "my people" seems to have no substantial significance. See Motyer 1993:530.

are applied (only) to the new people of YHWH afterwards. The seed as well as "My people," "My servants," and "My chosen" form the eschatological people of YHWH, belonging to the new name theme.

The (new) titles, as well as "another name," thematically relate to 56:5 and 62:2, as a "new name."[75] In 62:2, the people of Zion are promised a new name that YHWH bestows. According to 62:12, they are called the Holy People, the Redeemed of YHWH, Sought-Out, and the City-Not-Forsaken as the new names. These titles are relational terms, so signify the covenantal restoration.[76] In 56:5, the new (everlasting) name is given as a reward for restoring the covenantal relation (56:5–6). So the "new name" characterizes the quality of the new, eschatological people of YHWH.

The people with "new name(s)" are related to the Servant, for two reasons: (1) The "seed" (65:9) are promised to the Servant in 53:10.[77] (2) The "My chosen" and "My people" in 65:22 also have a connection to 42:1, in which they refer to the Servant Israel (the phrases are singular, while plural in 65:9 and 15). So, the (old) people of Israel are now replaced by the servants. The "seed of the servant are the servant children, borne to Zion (cf. ch 54 and 65:17–25), 'the offspring (זרע) blessed of YHWH' (65:23)."[78]

The total commitment of the people to YHWH is restored in 65:15–16, as thematically related to 56:6. "Swearing by God of faithfulness" may be a reapplication from 48:1 ("to swear by the name of YHWH . . . to invoke the God of Israel") and, possibly, 45:23–24 ("by Me every tongue will swear").[79] In 48:1 "swearing by (the name of) God" signifies a commitment of the people to YHWH; in 45:23–24 it is related to the subjection and obedience to YHWH that is required of the nations. Because the faithfulness of the people has failed in DI, it is required of the new people in TI.

The faithfulness of YHWH is in contrast to that of men. The "God of faithfulness" (65:15) signifies "the God of the faithfully fulfilled promise, the God who turns what He promises into Yea and Amen," fulfilling "both threatening and promises of YHWH."[80] The divine faithfulness is one of the common motifs throughout DI and TI, since the theme forms a framework of both, as it is presented in the *inclusio* of DI in 40:7–8 and 55:10–11.

What are the "former troubles" (הצרות הראשנות)? For Delitzsch, the "former troubles" "*include* the mixed condition of Israel in exile and the

---

75. Childs 2001:537; Lau 1994:200; Cheyne 1895:371.

76. Oswalt 1998:590.

77. Beuken 1990:89; Seitz 2001:543.

78. Seitz 2001:543.

79. Skinner 1898:240; Ruszukowski 2000:91; Beuken 1989b:78.

80. Delitzsch 1873:487; Skinner 1898:240.

persecution of the worshippers of YHWH by the despisers of YHWH."[81] For Whybray, too, the former things are "the former troubles of God's people from 587 BC onwards."[82] However, dating of the text can never be certain, and rather the meaning of the phrase needs be found primarily in the literary rather than historical context.

The phrase "former troubles" may be related to the "former devastations" (שממות ראשנים) in 61:4, the only previous place of the use of the adjective ראשון in TI. If this is the case the former troubles refer to the afflictions of the people due to the sins and the breached relationship with YHWH of the people (see 4.3 on 60:10–11).[83] This is also evidenced by the context. The immediate context may suggest that the former troubles refer to hunger, thirst, shame, mourning and curse that had presumably befallen the servants, which are the covenantal curses.[84] Furthermore, the 'troubles' may be related to 63:9, the only other occurrence in TI, in which צר signifies the affliction of the people from Egypt to Canaan, although this may be a different context. There, YHWH identified himself with the people in their affliction owing to the covenantal bond. (The afflictions are from within as well as from outside.) For Beuken, the "troubles" may also be related to Deut 31:17 and 21 due to the peculiar plural form.[85] In those places, the troubles refer to the disasters due to the punishment of the people who breached the covenant. So, the "(former) troubles" are understood as the afflictions from which the people had suffered so far due to their sins and the covenantal curses.[86]

In brief, the sinners are ultimately removed by enforcing the covenant, while the servants have another name as a reward of the covenantal restoration. The servants will also be blessed by the faithful YHWH, to whom the

---

81. Delitzsch 1873:487. Italics mine.

82. Whybray 1981:275–76. For Whybray, both the "former troubles" and the "former things" in 65:17 refer to the DI's eschatological scheme of former things/new things especially in 43:18–19. But, the "former troubles" may be more related to the previous context than to DI although it is also related to the former things in v. 17 (see below on 65:17 in the main text).

83. Beuken 1989b:80. In 60:9 and 65:7, of the adjective form but adverbial use.

84. Beuken 1989b:80.

85. Beuken 1989b:80.

86. Who will forget the former troubles? According to Koenen (1990:171), the subject of שכח is YHWH in 65:16b, while the subject of זכר in 65:17b is the people. However, for Knobel, forgetting concerns people, while hiding concerns YHWH (Alexander 1846b:452). The second view seems plausible, because the phrase refers to the afflictions that the people suffer from due to their sins. For Alexander (1846b:453), "their former distresses shall be forgotten by them, and for ever hidden from his [YHWH] eyes."

total commitment of the people is made. The afflictions of the people due to
the covenantal curses because of their sins are entirely forgotten.

17 "For behold, I create New Heavens and a New Earth,	כי־הנני בורא שמים הדשים וארץ חדשה
and the former things shall not be remembered or come into mind.	ולא תזכרנה הראשנות ולא תעלינה על־לב:

In this verse, YHWH creates New Heavens and a New Earth, so the
former things will be forgotten. Here the phrase the New Heavens and the
New Earth may be literal rather than metaphorical—which could suggest an
apocalyptic understanding. YHWH's ultimate purpose is not limited to the
historical vindication of the servants.[87]

What the New Heavens and the New Earth refer to is to be found in
the sentence first of all dependent on the meaning of the "former things,"
which may be illuminated or affirmed by the context. For Alexander, 65:17
is hardly a literal prediction of New Heavens and a New Earth, because the
exaltation of the chosen people is *expressed* "as a revolution in the frame
of nature." For him, the "former things" (ראשנות) refers to the "former
troubles" (הצרות הראשנות) in 65:16. Thus, the verse is "a promise or prediction of entire change in the existing state of things, the precise nature of the
change and of the means by which it shall be brought about forming no part
of the revelation here."[88] The New Heavens and the New Earth that YHWH
creates in 65:17 is not different from what YHWH creates in 65:18. 65:17
declares that creation should take place; 65:18 speaks of what the creation
is—making Jerusalem a joy and Israel a rejoicing.[89] So, 65:17 is understood
as follows: "as soon as the exiles return to Jerusalem, it and the whole earth
are renewed," because the literal Jerusalem and the restored Jews are meant
in 65:18.[90] However, the historical interpretation is not convincing because
the (post-exilic) dating lacks textual evidence. The former things are understood primarily in contrast to the New Heavens and the New Earth, so
most probably they refer to the (old) Heavens and Earth in the sentence,[91]
although they may be related secondarily to the former troubles in 65:16.
Alexander tends to emphasize too much the context rather than the sentence itself, which consequently neglects the intratextual reference to the

87. For the sense of 'literal' as reference to the heavenly realm, see 1.3.

88. For Alexander (1846b:452), the phrase may be applied to a moral and spiritual
nature as in the New Testament. See 2 Cor 5:17; Gal 6:15; 2 Pet 3:13.

89. Alexander 1846b:452.

90. Alexander 1846b:452.

91. Delitzsch 1873:488.

"former things" in DI (see below). Moreover, he does not seem to appreciate the fact that Jerusalem has an eschatological sense here.

Westermann develops the view of Alexander. For Westermann, "either v. 17a is figurative, i.e., exaggerative, or doesn't fit the context," although he admits that the verse in itself signifies what later apocalyptic understood.[92] The new creation refers to the creation of Jerusalem and the people in 65:18–19—"Jerusalem and Judah are the only subjects concerned in the renewal of the world."[93] For Westermann, 65:18a, calling the servants to rejoice, should be transferred before 65:16b, because the word 'because' in 65:16b should require the command to rejoice, or the causal conjunction cannot connect with what precedes.[94] Then, 65:18b follows directly on 65:17 and what 65:17a signifies is repeated in 65:18b. But, this rearrangement is unnecessary in an apocalyptic reading that makes sense of the canonical text.[95] For Westermann, the background of 65:17b is in 43:18a, in which "the former saving acts of God will be forgotten in view of the tremendous new saving act."[96] But, forgetting the former things in 65:17b has a different sense from 43:18a because of its different context, although it builds on DI.[97] For Westermann, 65:17b (the former things shall not be remembered or come into mind) has the same meaning as 65:16b (the former troubles are forgotten and are hidden from My eyes).[98] However, for Beuken, 65:16b and 65:17b are different: "65:17 contains a reference to DI, while 65:16b reflects the language and interest of TI."[99] For Westermann, 65:17 is not apocalyptic in that it does not imply that the Heavens and Earth are to be destroyed and in their place New Heavens and a New Earth are created, but that the world, designated as 'Heavens and Earth,' is to be miraculously renewed.[100] However, if the New Heavens and the New Earth are intended here literally, the destruction of the old may be implied. Although a metaphorical understanding may fit the immediate contexts, 65:13–16 and 65:18–24, it

92. Westermann 1969:408.

93. Westermann 1969:408. For Park (2003:343, 249), too, the creation of the New Heavens and the New Earth refers to the creation of Jerusalem and his people in vv. 18–19, as a freeing report for the socially disadvantaged. Similarly, Beuken (1989b:82) considers that "the new cosmos must be understood concerning the release of the servants."

94. Westermann 1969:407.

95. See Oswalt 1998:655, footnote 81.

96. Westermann 1969:408.

97. Westermann 1969:408.

98. Westermann 1969:408.

99. Beuken 1989b:80.

100. Westermann 1969:408.

does not seem to do justice to the verse itself, in which the New Heavens and the New Earth and the former things contrast. This contrast displays the continuation of the eschatological scheme of DI.[101] His understanding does not consider rightly the intra- or inter-textual connections to DI and other sources in the OT.

For Childs, however, the New Heavens and the New Earth is a "radically new vision of the future."[102] The words expressing this new world order are a direct extension of DI. God as the creator of the Heavens and Earth is based on DI (42:5; 45:7, 12, 18, etc.), as the verb ברא refers to God's first creation and its maintenance and preservation in 42:5–6. For him, 65:17b "intentionally" repeats the theme of former things in 43:18.[103] As Motyer opined, the Heavens and Earth signify "the totality of things as in Gen 1:1," so literally a new creation.[104] Childs follows Hanson in the view of the nature of eschatology at work here in ch 65—the new order is entirely different from that of the past, because it is radicalized in TI. The huge gap makes TI apocalyptic.[105]

This literal interpretation pays appropriate attention to the internal evidence (i.e., the schematic contrast) of the sentence and consequently to the intratextual connection to DI to which the contrast in the sentence refers.[106] Childs' interpretation may be supported by several pieces of evidence, appropriately explaining the relation of the verse to the context.

First, the verse itself demands an understanding primarily against the context of DI's eschatological vision, rather than against the immediate context of the passage (although this immediate context should be a secondary consideration). This is above all because of the strong reference to DI by the strategic contrast between the new and the old, which is characteristic of DI (42:9; 43:18–19; cf. 41:4, 22–23; 43:9; 44:6–7; 46:9–10; 48:3–7). The reference to DI is also indicated by the adoption of the typical technical term of DI "former things" and the verb ברא, which relates to the "new" things as well as the initial creation in DI.[107] Westermann argues that the connection to DI texts is just an 'echo' as the frames of reference are different here and in DI. But he does not seem to do justice to the understanding of

101. See 6.5, for the relation between DI's and TI's eschatology.

102. Childs 2001:537.

103. Childs 2001:537.

104. For the literal interpretation of the verse, also see Seitz 2001:544; Motyer 1993:529; Delitzsch 1873:488.

105. Childs 2001:537.

106. Westermann 1969:408; Beuken 1989b:81.

107. Beuken 1989b:81; Lau 1994:136; Whybray 1981:275; Westermann 1969:408; Hanson 1979:156; Berges 2002:13.

the continuity between TI's eschatology in the passage (and in the whole TI) and the message of DI, especially because he assumes that 65:17 and 25 are later additions to give 65:18–24 an apocalyptic tone.[108] But, for Beuken, the link of the contrast between the old and the new suggests that the eschatological scheme in DI, i.e., the contrast between the former things and the new things is in view here in 65:17, also.[109] Canonically viewed, 65:17 (and 25) is a deliberate device to incorporate the eschatological expectations of DI (and PI; see below on 65:25) as well as TI into one here in 65:17–25.

Especially, 65:17 is related to 43:18–19 as generally agreed, because 65:17b is related to 43:18, and because the term "former things" and the contrast between the old and the new are in parallel in the two places. The scheme of "the former things"/"the new things" in DI is replaced by "the former things"/"the New Heavens and Earth" in 65:17. In 43:18–19, the former things (ראשנות) are salvific actions of YHWH in the earlier stages of the nation including the exodus (43:16–17); the new thing (חדש) is the new exodus (43:19–20).[110]

However, the former things/the new things are not limited to the historical exodus/new exodus in DI. The new exodus sometimes refers to the return from Babylon (48:20–21) inaugurated by Cyrus (44:24–45:7), but extends to the work of the Suffering Servant (52:11–12), who completes his work by his death to remove the iniquity (53:6, 11) and transgressions (53:5, 8, 12) of the people. In 43:20, the new exodus, as the re-realization of the first exodus, might be understood metaphorically as being realized in this worldly ambit, but the exodus imagery in 41:18–19 in all probability refers to the new creation (cf. 41:20) turning the wilderness into a paradise (see 4.3 on 60:13).[111] The exodus is sometimes associated with the creation in mythological language (51:9–11).[112] The sharp break between the former things and the new things becomes more evident even in DI, so that the eschatological vision becomes detached from the historical reality to gain certainty of realization. Furthermore, not only the new things but also the former things are related to the creative power of YHWH (or, the creation) in DI, suggesting an ultimate (i.e., apocalyptic) realization.[113] The verb "cre-

108. Westermann 1969:408–11.

109. Beuken 1989b:94.

110. Anderson 1962:177–95. For Beuken (1989b:81), the "former things" are interpreted as the oppression by the Egyptians (cf. 43:17, carriage and horses/armed forces).

111. Westermann 1969:408.

112. For 51:9–11, Muilenburg (1954:596) comments that "the prophet is combining cosmological and historical elements as he does elsewhere in order to give scope and depth to the meaning of history."

113. For Seitz (2001:542), the former things in DI are extended even to the creation.

ate" (ברא) in DI signified not only the creation of the Heavens and Earth by YHWH (40:26, 28; 42:5; 43:1, 7, 15; 45:7, 12, 18) but also the new creation (41:20; [43:7, 15]; 45:8; 48:7) in DI.[114] In 42:9, the first occurrence of the contrast between ראשנות and חדשות in DI, the new things are declared by YHWH, the Creator of the Heavens and the Earth (42:5).[115] In 48:6–7, too, which is also referred to by 65:17 for Beuken,[116] the new things are what YHWH "creates," in contrast to the old creation.[117] The verb "create" (ברא) in 65:17–18 is also the reapplication of the thought of DI.[118] For Volz, as displayed in the triple repetition of ברא, "over and over again our view is being directed towards the Creator YHWH, the Creator of the coming eternal world age."[119] So the former things and the new things may extensively refer to the creation and the new creation in DI.[120]

Meanwhile, although Beuken acknowledges that in DI YHWH is the Creator of Heavens and Earth (40:26, 28; 42:5; 45:18; with the other verbs: 40:12, 22; 44:24; 45:12; 48:13; 51:13, 16), he considers that this theme of creation is not frequent in TI, so he concludes that TI is not interested in the creation of the cosmos (contrary to Hanson).[121] While "create" is pivotal in DI, it has "no binding role" in TI.[122] So, for Beuken, TI interpreted the new things of DI (43:18; 48:6) as "something new," that is, for TI the New Heavens and a New Earth are understood as a metaphorical sense, while for DI they are literal.[123] However, TI also displays elsewhere the idea of the new creation (60:1–2, 19–20; 66:22), suggesting a literal interpretation here, too.

In brief, the first reason for literal understanding of the New Heavens and Earth is the connection to DI.

Second, the fact that 65:17 forms an inclusio in the unit 65:17–25 with 65:25, which is understood to refer to the paradisiacal vision (see below on 65:25), strongly suggests that cosmic vision is in view in 65:17, too. For

114. Whybray 1981:276; Westermann 1969:408. As before, in my usage, DI may signify the author of chs 40–55 without inevitable assumption of independent personage from PI or TI.

115. Beuken 1989b:94.

116. Beuken 1989b:82. Also take notice that ch 48:1–2 has been referred to by 65:9, 15–16.

117. The former things in 48:3 are what YHWH had declared and are realized; the new things are to be created now in 48:7.

118. Whybray 1981:276; Westermann 1969:408.

119. Volz 1932:286.

120. Seitz 2001:542.

121. Beuken 1989b:82; Hanson 1979:155–61.

122. Beuken 1989b:81.

123. Beuken 1989b:82.

Whybray, as for the creation of New Heavens and a New Earth, "this impression of a radical cosmic transformation is strengthened by the final verse (25)."[124]

Third, the (new) "Heavens and Earth" in 65:17 may allude also to 51:6, in which they will be subject to immediate destruction because of their impermanent quality in comparison with the eternity of salvation,[125] and to 51:16, in which the creation of the Heavens and the Earth is related to the future salvation of Zion.[126] But, for Cheyne, in 51:16 "the language is metaphorical and not, as here, semi-dogmatic."[127] Whybray intimates that the author/redactor of 65:17, using 51:6 and the verb ברא, made an erroneous inference, commenting that because "he [TI] *supposed* that he [DI] was speaking of a new creation" in 41:20; 42:5–9; 43:7, 15; and 45:8, "he [TI] has *concluded* that there is in fact to be a completely new beginning."[128] However, for Muilenburg, the references to the Heavens and the Earth are "cosmic in character" in 51:16, which signifies that "God is about to create a new world of righteousness, a new Heaven and a new Earth in the place of the old which will vanish and wear out (vs. 6; cf. 65:17; 66:22)."[129] The literal understanding of the new creation in 51:16 is supported by the fact that the new creation (51:16) is based on the assumption of the destruction of the old (51:6), the two possibly being related and compared to each other.

Finally, the link to Jer 3:16 may suggest a new creation. For Delitzsch, 65:17b has a parallel in Jer 3:16, "which stands in by no means an accidental relation to this passage."[130] In Jer 3:17, all Jerusalem will be the throne of YHWH, implying the dwelling of YHWH in the eschatological Temple as portrayed in ch 60 (see 4.3 on 60:13, 19–20), which is more apocalyptic.

In brief, because of the strong connection to DI and other texts, 65:17 signifies the literal re-creation of the universe. Having discussed 65:17, how does 65:17 relate to the immediate context? This question poses two other questions: How do the former things in 65:17 relate to the former troubles

---

124. Whybray 1981:275.

125. Whybray 1981:276. Also Skinner 1898:240.

126. Cheyne 1895:370; Delitzsch 1873:291. For Cheyne, the creation of the New Heaven and Earth has a "foregleam" in 51:16.

127. Cheyne.

128. Whybray 1981:276. Italics mine.

129. Muilenburg 1954:601; Delitzsch 1873:291. For Delitzsch, "the prophecy speaks of a new heaven and a new earth, in something more than a figurative sense, as a new creation of God (ch. lxv. 17)."

130. Delitzsch 1873:488; Muilenburg 1954:755. Due to "not remembered, not come to mind."

in 65:16? And what is the relation between the creation of the New Heavens and the New Earth in 65:17 and the creation of Jerusalem in 65:18?

Delitzsch obscures the distinction between the former troubles in 65:16 and the former things in 65:17.[131] For Motyer, however, the "former things" is related to the "former troubles" (v. 16), but expresses a greater concept—not only its sorrows but everything about the old order will be gone in this total renewal (cf. Beuken above).[132] In 65:17, the "former things" refer to the Heavens and the Earth; in 65:16, the "former troubles" refers to the troubles of the former times as the context suggests. They are not identified, but the former includes the latter. The connection between the two phrases suggests that the historical vindication of the servants in the eschatological portrait of TI is closely related to the eschatological expectation of DI as expressed in the former-new scheme.[133] The former things/the new things, which *could* signify the old/new creation in DI, *really* do signify them here in 65:17.

The metaphorical interpretation of the creation of "the New Heavens and the New Earth" has understood that it is identified with the creation of Jerusalem (Alexander, Westermann). For example, Beuken considers that the creative action of YHWH lies with the inversion of the life circumstances of the servants in the historical Jerusalem. Thus, for him, "In short, the joy of God's servants is not from the creation of a new cosmos, but God's intervention for the benefit of his servants becomes the new cosmos for them."[134] For Koenen, too, the new creation signifies that YHWH will renew Jerusalem because 65:19b–25 displays a portrayal of the concrete consequences of the intervention. For Koenen, the parallelism of 65:17a and 65:18b shows that 65:17a does not refer to any cosmic changes.[135]

However, in the same way as the former things and the former troubles are related to each other, the new creation and the creation of the New Jerusalem are related to each other because the former things refer to the Heavens and Earth in 65:17. They are not identified when relation to historical reality is in view. For Volz, "In the center of the new creation, the new Jerusalem lies."[136] For Muilenburg, "Against the background of the creation of new heavens and a new earth the life of the community is described."[137]

131. Delitzsch 1873:488. So is Whybray.

132. Motyer 1993:529.

133. This is the way by which TI develops DI (see 3.3 on 59:16).

134. Beuken 1989b:83.

135. Koenen 1990:171.

136. Volz 1932:286.

137. Muilenburg 1954:754.

However, when cosmic vision is in view, the New Jerusalem begins to be identified with the New Heavens and the New Earth, because YHWH dwells there in the heavenly city replacing the Sun and Moon since the New Jerusalem is identified with Zion in ch 60 (see 4.3 on 60:19–20). As a result, there is both continuity and discontinuity between the New Jerusalem and the New Heavens and the New Earth. As far as the material blessings (cf. 65:18–23) are concerned they are distinct, but in view of ultimate vision of Zion the heavenly city, where YHWH dwells and the animals and nature are restored, they are identified.

In brief, the New Heavens and the New Earth refer to the new universe due to the connection to the DI and other texts, as required by 65:17. In DI, both metaphorical and apocalyptic understandings of the new creation and the new exodus may be suggested; TI tends to emphasize the latter. The things in the old world-order will be forgotten.

18 But be glad and rejoice forever	כי־אם־שישו וגילו עדי־עד
in that which I create;	אשר אני בורא
for behold, I create Jerusalem to be a joy,	כי הנני בורא את־ירושלם גילה
and her people to be a gladness.	ועמה משוש:
19 I will rejoice in Jerusalem and be glad in My people;	וגלתי בירושלם וששתי בעמי
no more shall be heard in it the sound of weeping	ולא־ישמע בה עוד קול בכי
and the cry of distress.	וקול זעקה:

This strophe displays the creation of the New Jerusalem and the (new) people of YHWH, creation implying the start of salvation. Because of what is created, the servants are urged to rejoice; the New Jerusalem becomes a city of joy. YHWH also rejoices in Jerusalem together with His people. No more the sound of weeping and crying is heard.

The creation of Jerusalem is not identified with the new creation in 65:17 as we have discussed already (see 65:17 above), but the New Jerusalem is paradisiacal as the city of joy. "That which I created" in 65:18a may refer to both the new creation in 65:17 and the creation in 65:18. So the charge to rejoice does not support that the two creations are identified as in Westermann.

The creation/establishment of Jerusalem as a city of joy in 65:18b signifies (the start of) her salvation, as, for Whybray, "I create Jerusalem" is thematically related to 62:7, in which YHWH establishes (שים) Jerusalem.[138] This initiation of salvation brings the joy of the people and YHWH. The joy of YHWH over Jerusalem is related to 62:5, since this is the only other occurrence of YHWH as the subject of gladness (שוש) in TI.[139] In 62:4–5,

138. Whybray 1981:276.
139. Koenen 1990:176.

YHWH rejoices over Zion as she is no more Deserted, but restored to her husband. For Koenen, the rejoicing Jerusalem in 65:18 is related to the happy people in 60:15.[140] In both places, the joy is due to salvation. The joy is related to the restoration of Zion (60:15; 62:5; 66:10, 14) and to the work of the anointed figure in 61:10 (cf. 61:3).[141] Jerusalem is "either an object in which one may rejoice (65:19; 60:15) or an abode of joy (51:3; 61:7)" in 65:18b (בורא את־ירושלם גילה).[142] The subject of rejoicing in 65:18b is more probably YHWH, although the people are also still possible as the subject, because the phrase "create Jerusalem to be a joy, and her people to be a gladness" (65:18b) may be parallel to 65:19a, since 65:18a, 18b, 19a, and 19b form a chiastic structure. So, in 65:18–19, "God shall rejoice in his people, and they shall rejoice with him,"[143] due to the salvation of Jerusalem. The eschatological city of joy is paradisiacal. Because both gladness (משוש) and rejoicing (גיל) are in parallel uniquely in 65:18b and 35:1, 65:18b may fulfil the eschatological expectation of 35:1, in which the gladness and rejoicing is related to the turning of the wilderness and dry land into the paradise, as displayed in the exodus imagery (35:6–8). This may suggest that the eschatologically created Jerusalem is a paradise, as displayed in 35:2, which is referred to in 65:25 (see below) and 60:13 (see 4.3).

The creation of Jerusalem has both continuity and discontinuity with historical life. For Beuken, the parallel occurrence of Jerusalem and My people forms an envelope structure of the "actual drama" of DI (chs 40–52) in 40:1 and 52:9.[144] So, for him, the parallel Jerusalem and My people may show that the joy (over them) is related to the covenant, implying that the creation of Jerusalem fulfils the eschatological expectation of DI. This shows continuity.

But discontinuity is also involved due to the cessation of weeping and crying. For Muilenburg, the rejoicing and gladness of/in Jerusalem is in contrast to "the sorrow of the former age, the subject of the preceding poem (see 64:10; cf. 51:3; 60:15; 61:2–3)."[145] "No existence of weeping and crying any more in Jerusalem" in 65:19b is thematically parallel to 51:11 (and 35:10), in which the (covenantal as well as physical) return is intended, while a permanent condition is described in 65:19b.[146] For Westermann,

---

140. Koenen 1990:176; Duhm 1892:435.

141. Beuken 1989b:83.

142. Skinner 1898:241.

143. Alexander 1846b:453.

144. Beuken 1989b:84.

145. Muilenburg 1954:755.

146. Westermann 1969:409.

it is a deliberate reversal of the judgment on Jerusalem in Jer 7:34; 16:9; and 25:10.[147] The end of weeping and crying signifies that "[T]he time of mourning is over," which is apocalyptic, since it cannot be realized in the historical arena.[148] Although the "end of weeping" might be hyperbole in the sentence on its own, the intertexts as well as the context (see 65:25 and 19–24 below) cumulatively suggest apocalyptic reading. For Lau, לא־ישמע לא־יבוא, לא־יהיה־לך עוד (בה) is related to 60:18 (לא־ישמע עוד), 19–20 (עוד), and 62:4 (לא־יאמר יוד, לא־יאמר לך שוד).[149] In 60:18 the phrase denotes the change of the fortune of Zion in the eschatological era; in 60:19–20 the change of the cosmic bodies. These changes are apocalyptic. In 62:4, too, the phrase refers to the drastic change of the fortune of Zion.

In sum, Jerusalem is recreated as joy and gladness—YHWH rejoices in her; the people rejoice in His re-creation. The covenant is restored in the New Jerusalem, which is continuous with the old Israel. But the paradisiacal implication of the New Jerusalem is discontinuous. Weeping and mourning will cease in the New Jerusalem, which is apocalyptic.

20 No more shall there be in it	לא־יהיה משם עוד
an infant who lives but a few days,	עול ימים
or an old man who does not fill out	וזקן אשר לא־ימלא
his days,	את־ימיו
for the young man shall die a hundred years old,	כי הנער בן־מאה שנה ימות
and the sinner a hundred years old shall be accursed.	והחוטא בן־מאה שנה יקלל:
21 They shall build houses and inhabit them;	ובנו בתים וישבו
they shall plant vineyards and eat their fruit.	ונטעו כרמים ואכלו פרים:
22 They shall not build and another inhabit;	לא יבנו ואחר ישב
they shall not plant and another eat;	לא יטעו ואחר יאכל
for like the days of a tree shall the days of My people be,	כי־כימי העת ימי עמי
and My chosen shall long enjoy the work of their hands.	ומעשה ידיהם יבלו בחירי:
23 They shall not labor in vain	לא יגעו לריק
or bear children for calamity,	ולא ילדו לבהלה
for they shall be the offspring of the blessed of YHWH,	כי זרע ברוכי יהוה המה
and their descendants with them.	וצאצאיהם אתם:

This strophe presents blessings for the servants in the New Jerusalem—longevity and security of tenure, as examples of reasons for the cessation of the weeping and mourning in 65:19. There no one will die as an infant; every old man will fulfil his days; the young man dies a hundred years old; those who do not reach 100 years old will be accursed. The people will enjoy the long life like a tree. My chosen will enjoy the work of their hands in building

147. Whybray 1981:277; Westermann 1969:409.

148. Muilenburg 1954:755; Whybray 1981:277; Westermann 1969:409.

149. Lau 1994:137.

houses or planting vineyards, or bearing progeny. They are the offspring of the blessed of YHWH, being together with their descendents. These blessings signify the covenantal restoration, possibly suggesting a return to the patriarchal paradise.

In the New Jerusalem, there will be no premature death (65:20). As for the infant of a few days (עוּל יָמִים), Whybray considers that יָמִים is a mistake for יְמוֹת, so there is no "infant who dies."[150] However, this emendation is not compelling. For Hitzig, עוּל יָמִים as well as זָקֵן are connected to the following words, without amendment, so there will be "neither infant (of days) nor old man who shall not fulfil their days."[151] For Volz, "to fulfil the number of days" may be related to Exod 23:26.[152] So the full enjoyment of one's lifetime is a reward for his faithfulness to the covenant.[153]

For Alexander, 65:20b returns to the contrast between the rebellious and the servants in 65:13–15.[154] So, among the servants, "he who dies a hundred years old shall die a child; among you [the sinners], he who dies at the same age shall die accursed."[155] However, such a contrast is not convincing after the final judgment has been exacted and the sinners are removed to create the New Jerusalem as well as the new creation (65:15). For Delitzsch, 65:20b is a synonymous parallelism.[156] Motyer, following Delitzsch, translates וְהַחוֹטֶא בֶּן־מֵאָה שָׁנָה יְקֻלָּל as "but the sinner, a hundred years old, will be accursed" as in RSV.[157] He signifies that "even if a sinner were to escape detection for a century the curse would still search him out and destroy him."[158] However, the presence of a sinner for a hundred years may not be acceptable because there is no sinner in the eschatological New Jerusalem (65:6–7, 12, and 15). For Westermann, on the contrary, הַחוֹטֶא signifies "the one who does not reach," so, the line (65:20b) is understood as "if a person

150. Whybray 1981:277.

151. Alexander 1846b:453. According to Beuken (1989b:85), MT accent suggests only one subject in 65:20a.

152. Volz 1932:286.

153. For Sehmsdorf (1972:527), אֵת מְלֹא יָמָיו (65:20) has a Deuteronomistic connection for the lifetime of a person (Exod 23:26; 2 Sam 7:12; 1 Chr 17:11; Jer 25:34; Lam 4:18), although Koenen (1990:178) doubts it.

154. Alexander 1846b:453.

155. Alexander 1846b:454.

156. Delitzsch 1873:489–490. "He who dies as a youth, or is regarded as having died young, will not die before the hundredth year of his life; the sinner . . . upon whom the curse of God falls, and who is overwhelmed by the punishment, will not be swept away before the hundredth year of his life."

157. For him, it is still possible to translate as "He who fails to reach a hundred will be considered accursed."

158. Motyer 1993:530.

happens not to attain to a hundred years, there must be some exceptional reason for this."[159] However, this interpretation does not assume such a person, but rather emphatically affirms non-existence of such a person, because no curse will be there.

The longevity fulfils the eschatological expectations of PI and DI and suggests a return to the primordial age. For Lau, 65:20 signifies that "anyone, whether young or old, has no untimely death" and is thematically related to 46:3–4, in which YHWH promises protection of the people until their old age or grey hairs, as part of the salvation of the people, i.e., the new things of DI.[160] The issue of longevity or death may also be related to 25:8.[161] For Delitzsch, while in 25:8 the power of death is ultimately destroyed, in 65:20 and 22 the power is just limited.[162] For Hoffmann, however, there is no real difference between the two places and in ch 65 "less is affirmed than in 25:8," which is reasonable if only the longevity in 65:20 and 65:22 signifies the same thing.[163] The "lifetime of a tree" (ימי העץ; 65:22) may allude to the "tree of life" (עץ החיים) in Gen 2:9 and the "hundred years old" (65:20) may recall "the days of one hundred and twenty years" in Gen 6:3.[164] If this is the case, the lifetime is restored in the New Jerusalem as those of the patriarchs who lived before the Deluge (65:20) or even as that promised before the Fall in Eden (65:22).[165] There will be no premature death or death at all, if the problem of sin is resolved, the original sin distinguishing between life before and after the Fall.

The security of tenure in 65:21–22 and that of labor and childbirth in 65:23 may suggest the restoration of the covenant as they are covenantal blessings, as supported by four observations: (1) 65:21–22 may be thematically related to 62:8–9, which is reminiscent of Deut 28:30 and 39–40 as well as Lev 26:16.[166] For Koenen, inhabiting houses, planting vineyards, and eat-

159. Westermann 1969:409. Similarly, for Whybray (1981:277), "any one who dies without attaining the age of 100 may be assumed to have been cursed for some fault."

160. Lau 1994:137–38.

161. Motyer 1993:530.

162. Delitzsch 1873:490; Westermann 1969:409; Skinner 1898:241. For Whybray (1981:277), due to the theological difference, 25:8 belongs to much later period.

163. Delitzsch 1873:490. For Motyer (1993:530), too, the power of death will be destroyed here as well as in 25:8.

164. Seitz 2001:545.

165. Seitz 2001:544; Duhm 1892:435. For Whybray (1981:277), a death of hundred years old is premature, so "return to the legendary longevity of age before the Flood in Genesis."

166. Whybray 1981:277; Cheyne 1895:372; Volz 1932:286; Alexander 1846b:454; Delitzsch 1873:490. For Lau (1994:138), there is a change of situation between v. 21 (blessing situation) and 62:8–9 (curse situation). But this is not evidenced by the text.

ing fruits of the blessed of YHWH belong to a Deuteronomistic theology.[167] According to the covenantal curses (Deut 28:30, 39), "if Israel does not obey the covenant, numerous forms of human labor will be unfruitful—house and vintage here."[168] So 65:21–22(23) may be a deliberate reversal of the covenantal woes. The people themselves will enjoy what they have worked for—"without some one else stepping in, whether a countryman by violence or inheritance, or a foreigner by plunder or conquest (62:8), for their lifetime is as long as that of trees."[169] (2) For Lau, the "work of their hands" in 65:22 may be Deuteronomic (Deut 2:7, 14:29, 15:10, 16:15, 24:19), as YHWH blesses them in the framework of the covenant.[170] (3) According to Sehmsdorf, "shall not labor in vain" (לא ייגעו לריק) in 65:23a is based on the Deuteronomistic theology, since it may be related to Deut 28:33.[171] So, it may be a removal of a covenantal curse. The phrase may also have a resonance thematically in reverse to the curse on the labor of man and the ground in Gen 3:17–18, in which the thorns (קוץ) and thistles (דרדר) are the typical impediments of the productivity of the labor and the ground. Here, the impediments due to the disobedience are removed.[172] So, here the curses of the original sin as well as of the covenantal breach of Israel are removed. (4) For Lau, 65:23 refers to Lev 26:16 (and 20), the covenantal curses, since בהלה and לריק are in parallel.[173] The "child-birth without trouble" (לא ילדו לבהלה) in 65:23 may have an allusion to Deut 28:32, 41, in which by the covenant curse the children will be captives.[174] In addition, the phrase may be the reversal of curse given to the first woman in Gen 3:16 (בעצב תלדי בנים).[175] Thus, the phrase may signify the removal of the curses of the first disobedience as well as the covenant breach of Israel. It may also be related to 66:7–8 and 54:1. Zion as a woman once bereaved and un-impregnated comes to bring forth without pain and be peopled, as bearing children (20, 23) may be related to bringing forth seed in 65:9.[176] Therefore, the vindication of the

---

167. Koenen 1990:178. See Deut 28:30, Jos 24:13, Jer 29:5, 28, and 35:9.

168. Beuken 1989b:86.

169. Delitzsch 1873:490.

170. Lau 1994:138.

171. Sehmsdorf 1972:526. For him, Jos 24:13 is also related, but this may not be the case, because in this verse "a land you did not toil" is given as a blessing, while in 65:23 "you will not toil (in vain)" is (the removal of) a curse.

172. Seitz 2001:544.

173. Lau 1994:139.

174. Beuken 1989b:88.

175. Seitz 2001:544.

176. Beuken 1989b:89.

servants may present the restored covenantal relation with YHWH in view of secured tenure, labor, and progeny.

This vindication of the servants fulfils the eschatological expectation(s) of PI and DI. Three observations support this: (1) The "work of their hands" in 65:22 may be related to Isa 3:10(–11), in which the righteous will enjoy the fruit of their deeds, while the wicked deserve woe and disaster.[177] In TI, the "work of the hands of My chosen" (65:22b) stands against those of the sinners (57:12, 59:6).[178] In 57:12–13, their works will not benefit them, as their reliance on idols is not effective, while he who finds a refuge in YHWH will inherit the land and possess the Holy Mountain of YHWH. (2) For Childs, it is "fully evident" that 65:23 is linked with the promise given to the Suffering Servant in 53:10–11, because of the "seed."[179] The "offspring of the blessed of YHWH" is a realization of the servant promise. As Seitz comments, "the 'seed' that the servant is to see becomes, in this new heaven and earth, a new creation altogether."[180] (3) The offspring of the blessed of YHWH (זרע ברוכי יהוה) is related to 61:9 (זרע ברך יהוה).[181] For Beuken, the words 'seed,' 'blessed,' and 'descendants' are key words of the core theme of TI—"how do the descendants of the servant come about?" The promise of blessing to the servants is very similar to what God said about "the oppressed" in ch 61. So, the oppressed are identified with the servants.[182] Contrary to Beuken, who considers the 'seed of the blessed of YHWH' is identified with the messenger in ch 61,[183] the seed are the followers of the Servant figure (the anointed one) in 61:1 (see 3.3 on 59:21). The seed (זרע) of the blessed by YHWH in 65:23 may also be related to Gen 17:7.[184] So the Abrahamic promise may be fulfilled here. In conclusion, the vindication by the covenantal blessings fulfils the eschatology of PI and DI, separating the servants from the wicked. The ordinary life in 65:20–23 displays that "the era of salvation as here envisaged is in no sense thought of as lying beyond space and time."[185] So, it presents continuity with history or the present life in the eschatology of TI.

---

177. Lau 1994:139.
178. Beuken 1989b:87.
179. Childs 2001:538; Beuken 1989b:89.
180. Beuken 1989b:88, 89; Seitz 2001:544.
181. Lau 1994:139; Whybray 1981:278; Volz 1932:287; Duhm 1892:437.
182. Beuken 1989b:89.
183. Beuken 1989b:89.
184. Motyer 1993:531.
185. Westermann 1969:409.

In brief, the servants will be blessed in longevity and livelihood as well as in the tenure, returning to the pristine paradise. This implies that the traditional promises and covenant(s) are realized as the curses are removed.

24 Before they call I will answer;	והיה טרם־יקראו ואני אענה
while they are yet speaking I will hear.	עוד הם מדברים ואני אשמע:
25 The wolf and the lamb shall graze together;	זאב וטלה ירעו כאחד
the lion shall eat straw like the ox,	ואריה כבקר יאכל־תבן
and dust shall be the serpent's food.	ונחש עפר לחמו
They shall not hurt or destroy	לא־ירעו ולא־ישחיתו
in all My Holy Mountain," says YHWH.	בכל־הר קדשי אמר יהוה: ס

This strophe continues the theme of blessing to the servants—the instant communication between YHWH and the people in the New Jerusalem, and presents the "peace and harmony in the animal world" as the "picture of new cosmos."[186] Before they call, YHWH will answer. The carnivore and the herbivore coexist on the grass, fulfilling the command of YHWH in Eden, and the serpent has dust as food. There is no hurt and destruction in the Holy Mountain of YHWH.

The perfect communication is a reversal of the perennial refusal of Israel to hear YHWH, i.e., the covenant restored. The response of YHWH for the call of the people in 65:24 is the reversal of 65:1–2, 12 and 66:4, in which the people obstinately did not respond to YHWH, who continuously called and spoke to them. This exhibits a perfect harmony of will between YHWH and the people as well as the people's accessibility to God.[187] This verse fulfils the promise of YHWH in 58:9 that He will make an immediate response to all requests of the people, when they practice justice and righteousness in the community.[188] The people make complaints for their *Unheil* caused by their formalistic piety and sinful behavior in chs 58–59. Thus, the peace between YHWH and the people signifies the restored covenantal relationship between them.

The disruption and restoration of communication, an important expression of the covenantal relation between YHWH and Israel, fulfils Isaiah's prophecy about lack of listening and comprehension by the people in 6:9–10 as well as the promise in 30:19 in PI, in which the promise of response is associated with the cessation of mourning. The relational breach is evidenced in DI, too. Israel, the deaf and blind, has eyes to see and ears to hear but is unable to hear God's word (43:8). In 41:17 and 49:8, the promise of divine response is granted in the exodus imagery, and will be achieved at

186. Delitzsch 1873:491; Beuken 1989b:90.
187. Beuken 1989b:90. For Delitzsch (1873:491), all prayers will be heard.
188. Koenen 1990:177.

the time of My favour and the day of salvation.[189] The theme continues also in TI in those who refuse to see and listen (65:1–2), and thus are subject to death (65:15).[190] The harmony of will fundamentally restores the broken relationship between YHWH and His people. The instant communication (65:24) may also be an inversion of the communication lost in the garden because of the disobedience of the first humans in Gen 3. Seitz comments, "In the ruptured existence after disobedience, God must call to humankind, who is hiding."[191] The communication is fully restored by the removal of the distance between YHWH and His people in the New Covenant (Jer 31:33).[192]

The interpretation of 65:25 is one of the hottest issues. For Westermann, 65:25 does not fit the context as it is a later addition. "In vv. 19b–24 the conditions of life are those of present historical existence, and they are only transcended in v. 17a and v. 25." For him, 65:25, a quotation from 11:6–9, is a description of a transformed world.[193] 65:17 and 25, encouraging the "impression of a radical cosmic transformation" to each other, give a quasi-apocalyptic overtone to 65:18–23, which originally had no cosmic reference.[194] This is a reasonable observation, but he does not seem to recognize and appropriately maintain the tension in the crevasse between 65:25 and 65:18–24 due to his unnecessary assumption of the 'later addition'—discontinuity is too much emphasized. He takes note of the close relation between 65:17 and 25 as well as the intratextual connection to PI, which is useful to interpret the whole text.

Contrary to Westermann, Beuken tries to interpret 65:25 in the context of ch 65—continuity is too much emphasized. For Beuken, the harmony of the animal world (65:25) is related to the harmoniously perfect communication between YHWH and the servants in 65:24.[195] In addition, 65:25a is well connected to the 'eating' motif, an important idea in the chapter, because the harmony in the animal kingdom is described in the peaceful aspect of their eating "together."[196] In 65:4, the idolatrous meal offends YHWH; YHWH provides his servants with a meal as a blessing (65:13, 21–22). The phrase "the serpent will have dust for food" concerns the theme of 'eating.'[197]

189. Lau 1994:140.

190. Seitz 2001:543.

191. Seitz 2001:545.

192. Seitz 2001:545.

193. Westermann 1969:410–11.

194. Whybray 1981:275.

195. Beuken 1989b:91.

196. Beuken 1989b:91.

197. Beuken 1989b:91.

For Beuken, the lamb in 65:25 stands for the weak party of the community, representing the servants of YHWH.[198] For him, 65:25 does not concern the expectation of a paradise, although 65:25 refers to 11:6–9.[199] In 65:17–25, the reference to Gen 1–3 is extremely weak. Furthermore, 11:6–9 does not refer to a paradise, but forms a "thought pattern determined by tradition." "In the ancient Near East, the harmony of the animal kingdom is a motif to portray the legitimate monarch, as the legal governor of the deity, and thus maintains peace, which is the state of the cosmos that salvation achieves." However, this messianism of the ancient Near East is lacking in ch 65 (as well as in 11:6–9). Then, how does TI link his prophecy about the salvation of God's servants to the vision of the prince of peace from the tribe of Jesse? He suggests that for TI in 65:25 the harmony of the animals was connected with the tribunal between "the lowly and the oppressed of the land" and "the wicked" (11:4), which is the main topic of TI (56:9—59:20; 61–62). TI has then exploited the vision of PI in a free manner. TI entirely overlooks the Davidic Messianic vision of ch 11, only picks up the theme of justice, as displayed in the connection between אמונה/צדק in 11:5 and אלהי אמן in 65:16.[200]

Beuken's view is developed and clarified in Ruiten, who stands in line with the view that 65:25 is "embedded very well in the literary context of Isa 65."[201] For Ruiten, although 65:25 and 11:6–9 have differences,[202] the former is a recapitulative quotation of the latter.[203] Contrary to Beuken, 11:1–9 centers on the theme of the Davidic Messiah as a future ruler who brings a time

198. For Park (2003:351), too, the animal kingdom is a symbol for freeing the oppressed from the injustice and exploitation by the power of the stronger, as in 11:6–9.

199. For him, the latter is original, because the latter is more detail.

200. Beuken 1989b:92.

201. First, 65:25 is related to 65:24, as the harmonious animals reflect the instant communication between YHWH and the servants. Second, 65:24–25 has a connection to 65:12, since 65:24 reverses the unresponsive relation in 65:12b, and 65:25c is contrast to 65:12c in that evil and displeasure in 65:12 are gone in v. 25. Third, the Holy Mountain of YHWH in 65:25 is related to the mountains of YHWH in 65:9. Last but not least, the eating motif in 65:25 is perfectly fitting with ch 65. For him (1992:31–32), Eating motif includes not only 65:4 and 65:13, 21–22, but also 65:10, due to the 'pasture for flocks.'

202. Ruiten (1992:36) identifies a threefold difference between the two passages: different literary context, shortening of the text, and different utterances about the serpent.

203. It is generally agreed that 65:25 is a recapitulative quotation of 11:6–9. Seitz 2001:544; Childs 2001:538; Ruiten 1992:34. In the process of recapitulating 11:6–9, wolf represents the predatory animals such as wolf, leopard, lion and bear, and lamb (טלה) stands for the non-predatory such as young ram (כבש), child, calf, fatling and cow in 65:25.

of peace and justice. For Ruiten, "after the animal intermezzo [i.e., 11:6–8] the text returns in v. 9 to the theme of vv. 1–5," because "a righteous rule means that no evil will be done on God's holy mountain."[204] For him, the contexts of the two passages, too, have a thematic connection. The Davidic Messiah judges the needy and the poor with justice and righteousness while he will strike the earth and kill the wicked by the rod of his mouth and the breath of his lips, in 11:4. Isaiah 65:1–16 also describes reward and vengeance on the servants and the wicked in accordance with their deeds. For him, however, the connection between the righteous ruler and the harmony in the paradisiacal animal world in 11:1–9 is not taken up in 65:25, because there is no other occurrence of such a link elsewhere in the OT.

For Ruiten, the verb "graze" (רעה) in 65:25a not only represents the verbs in 11:6–9 (dwell, lie down, graze)—through רעה, the motif of 'eating' is the primary link between the two passages.[205] But it is also linked to an important theme in TI and DI.[206] The wicked shepherds (רעים) neglect the righteous in 56:11. In 40:11, YHWH as a shepherd (כרעה) feeds (ירעה) His lambs, leading them back to Zion. (For him, 40:11 is also alluded to by טלה, which does not occur in 11:6–9 but in 65:25a.) However, the connotation of רעה in Isa 40:11 is rather different from that in Isa 11:7 and 65:25.[207]

For Ruiten, 11:8 continues the antithesis between the two classes of animals—between the serpent and a nursing child, which is lacking in 65:25.[208] The semantic connection between 65:25c and 65:25ab is very strong in that the 'predatory animals' with the 'eating' motif is common to both. So, "in spite of the resemblances between 11:8 and 65:25c, the tenor seems to be different. In 11:8, the (once) dangerous serpent is now keeping company with the little child without harming it. The text of 65:25c does not say that the serpent is now harmless, but it only mentions that dust is the serpent's food."[209] So, for him, "the point of 65:25c is not 'being together in harmony' of predatory and tame animal, but 'eating' dust,"[210] the sense of which is determined by the intertextual connections to Gen 3:14, Micah

204. Ruiten 1992:36.

205. Ruiten 1992:37–38.

206. Beuken 1989b:92.

207. For Ruiten (1992:38), the primary connotation of רעה in 40:11 is "leading" or "tending" the flock, while it is "feeding" them in 11:7 and 65:25.

208. There is a connection between the serpent (נחש) in 65:25 and the asp (פתן) and the adder (צפע) in 11:8, in addition to the connections in the preceding and the following verses.

209. Ruiten 1992:39–40.

210. Ruiten 1992:39.

7:17, Ps 72:9, and Isa 49:22.[211] For him, "licking dust" refers to "an attitude of humility of rulers and the nations with regard to YHWH and his people." Thus it contains the elements of both cursing for the oppressors and blessing for the oppressed. This meaning of 65:25c is also applied to 65:25ab. Therefore, 65:25 presents both blessings of the servants and the downfall of the wicked, as the original sense of 11:6–9 does not continue here because only the "eating theme" is adopted in the recapitulation.[212] The grazing of the predatory animals signifies curse; that of the herbivore signifies blessings. Therefore, 65:25 metaphorically signifies the blessings/vindication of the servants (65:17–24) and the curses/downfall of the wicked (65:1–16).[213] However, although Beuken and Ruiten have tried in their interpretation of 65:25 to consider the context as well as the intertextual connections, their view needs to be challenged.

First, contrary to Beuken and Ruiten, it may be suggested that the connection between the Messianic figure and the paradisiacal world or the Davidic Messianic vision in 11:6–9 is *assumed* in 65:25, although it is not explicitly mentioned. This is especially because a Messianic figure has been suggested to come in 59:19[15b]–21 (see 3.3) and 61:1–3 (see 3.4).[214] While Beuken, following the majority of scholars, rejects the Messianic interpretation of 65:25, for Childs the question is how the intratextual link is understood by the readers of *the book*. For Childs, TI adopts the Messianic vision of ch 11 to describe the conclusion of his eschatological portrait. "Intertextuality serves to identify the new creation of ch 65 with the Messianic hope of PI."[215]

In connection with this, Ruiten's view seems to be based on an unnecessarily restricted interpretation of 11:6–9. It is not certain why 11:9 cannot be related primarily to 11:6–8, as well as 11:1–5. If 11:9 is taken together with 11:6–8, the message of 11:6–9 is the universal peace and harmony without animosity in the (natural and human) world brought about by the

---

211. For Ruiten, the phrase 'and dust shall be the serpent's food' may be related to Gen 3:14, "the source for the alteration in Isa 65:25c," to Micah 7:17 due to the occurrences of נחש and עפר, and to Ps 72:9 and 49:22–23 due to "licking dust." In Gen 3:14, the serpent's eating dust is in the context of a curse. In Micah 7:17, the nations lick dust like a serpent, signifying an attitude of humility. In Ps 72:9, the enemies' "licking dust" indicates awe for the righteous king, showing an attitude of humility. In 49:22–23, the nations lick dust, showing homage to Israel.

212. Ruiten 1992:31–42.

213. Ruiten 1992:39–41.

214. According to Motyer (1993:13–16), 61:1–3, 10–11 and 62:1–7 and 63:1–6 suggest the presence of the figure in TI.

215. Childs 2001:538–39.

rule of the Messianic Davidic king.[216] Delitzsch considers that in 65:25 as well as in ch 11, the description of the new age ends with "the peace of the world of nature," rejecting the view that 65:25 is "only attached quite loosely to what precedes."[217]

Second, it is not certain whether Beuken and Ruiten have rightly reflected the wider theme of chs 65–66. For Ruiten, the 'eating' motif is pivotal in the interpretation of not only 65:25 but also 11:6–9 and ch 65. However, 'eating' in ch 65 (or, in fact TI) is related to the celebration or the blessing/cursing of the covenant (in 65:4, a celebration of the [anti-]covenant and idol worship; in 65:13 and 21–22, a restoration of the covenant). In ch 11, the eating is a symbol of coexistence and peace (as 11:9a summarizes 11:6–8 with "harming" and "destroying," and it is quoted in 65:25), which is realized by the Messianic rule, as based on the Davidic covenant (55:3–5). Viewing the wider theme, i.e., the covenant, the Messianic vision (11:6–9 and 11:1–5) of the Davidic covenant is realized in 65:25, as the judgment with justice and righteousness is part of the Messianic rule.

This may be supported by the concept of the Holy Mountain of YHWH. According to Beuken, My Holy Mountain is the place where salvation of the servants of YHWH is realized (57:13; 58:14; 60:18, 21; 61:7; 62:4).[218] It is also "the place where YHWH in holiness dwells in the midst of his people, and now, they with him."[219] My Holy Mountain is uniquely in 11:9 in PI and DI. In 11:9, in the Holy Mountain of YHWH, the radical transformation of nature (a characteristic of apocalyptic) is achieved due to the Messianic king.[220] The "My Holy Mountain" "incorporate[s] into the portrayal of ch 11 also the transformation of Jerusalem into the heavenly Zion."[221]

Third, contrary to Beuken, there are many allusions to Gen 1–3 in 65:18–24, as we have seen above (on 65:19–24). This may suggest that 65:25 is a reapplication or restoration of the paradisiacal portrait of the early part of Genesis. Furthermore, the (carnivore and herbivore) animals grazing on the grass may have an allusion to Gen 1:30, in which YHWH grants every green plant as food to "all the beasts of the earth." If this is the case, 65:25 is a restoration of the paradise of the creation.

In brief, as evidenced in several places in TI, the intertextual connection to 11:6–9 may suggest the presence of the Messianic figure also in TI,

216. Clements 1980:122, 124.
217. Delitzsch 1873:491.
218. Beuken 1989b:78.
219. Motyer 1993:531.
220. Whybray 1981:278.
221. Childs 2001:539.

which is underscored by the intratextual connections in view of overall theology. Several allusions to Genesis in the context may suggest the paradisiacal realization in 65:25. This restoration of the paradisiacal portrait in Genesis is also suggested by the intertextual connection to Gen 3. Ruiten (and Beuken, too) has not fully considered the intertextual link with Gen 3:14, which forms the difference between 11:6–9 and 65:25.

What then is the purport of the simultaneous quotation of Gen 3:14 about the serpent, dropping the accounts about the adder and viper in 11:8? There are several interpretations:

First, Michaelis suggests that "the serpent shall continue to eat dust" (Gesenius).[222] For some, the reference to the serpent has no connection with the context except the eating habit of animals.[223] However, intentional connection with Gen 3:14 displays an additional point. For Alexander, this view is "too small a promise for the context, since a very small part of the evils which men suffer can arise from this cause."[224]

Second, Alexander suggests that "even the serpent will be *innocuous*" (Volz, Park).[225] For Alexander, in accordance with the ancient doom, the serpent "shall be rendered harmless, robbed of his favourite nutriment, and made to bite the dust at the feet of his conqueror."[226] This understanding has been applied metaphorically. For Ruiten, the quotation signifies the curse or humiliation of the oppressive nations (as in Mich 7:17; Ps 72:9; and Isa 49:22–23) and a blessing to Israel, which seemingly fits the scheme of division in the previous passages.[227] For Park, too, the reference to the serpent is not about the curse on the serpent itself, but functions merely as a *symbol* for the animals that live on the lowest earth, referring metaphorically to humans. So, for Park, the power of the nations is pressed down like the serpent.[228] However, this (as well as the first) view tends to depend on the intratextual connection to Isa 11:6–9 rather than appropriately considering the intertextual connection to Gen 3:14. Contrary to Ruiten, the "serpent eating dust" (נחש עפר לחמו) is a deliberate connection with the creation narrative (Gen 3:14, אל־הנחש—ועפר תאכל), in which the phrase is a curse

222. Alexander 1846b:455.

223. Whybray 1981:279; Cheyne 1895:372.

224. Alexander 1846b:455.

225. Volz 1932:287. Italics mine.

226. Alexander 1846b:456.

227. Ruiten 1992:41.

228. Park 2003:357.

of disobedience. Delitzsch rejects as allegory the interpretation of animals as men. Rather 65:25 concerns the state of peace in nature in paradise.[229]

Third, Motyer may consider that the quotation of the serpent signifies the only unchanged point in the new creation i.e., a curse on sin (Beuken).[230] This is because the act of eating dust is a curse now and in primitive time. However, sin is already removed by the judgment (or, punishment) before the new creation (65:12, 15).

Fourth, for Vitringa, "the original curse upon the serpent who deceived Eve (Gen 3:14) shall be fully executed—the serpent should henceforth prey only upon low and earthly men."[231] This last view seems plausible, because it presents the characteristic of the new creation as the recapitulation of the creation, due to the deliberate connection with Gen 3. For Seitz, "To speak of a new heaven and a new earth is to return to the creation and the curses that followed upon the very first act of disobedience." Gen 3:14 belongs to the former things and God must begin all over again, going back to "the very point of rupture . . . beyond the rebellions of Isaiah's generation." The serpent cannot coexist with other creatures except as a parasite. "Mentions of the curse over evil as embodied in the serpent . . . makes clear that Genesis language and context are pivotal in the construction of this unit."[232]

In summary, the people and YHWH will be in perfect communication. A paradise of the peace and harmony of even the animal kingdom is achieved in the Holy Mountain of YHWH, the New Jerusalem. The covenant is restored in the Holy Mountain. The transformation of nature is both continuous and discontinuous with the history and nature. The animals will be there, too, a continuity; the nature of the animals needs to be entirely changed to restore the paradise, a discontinuity.

5.4 Summary and Conclusion

65:13–25 highlights the eschatological message of TI, since it is an essential part of the concluding chapters 65–66 of the book as well as of TI, responding to the preceding lament (63:7—64:11[12]) as well as the introductory

---

229. Delitzsch 1873:491–92. For Cheyne (1895:370), 65:25 describes a "purely physical miracle, without any human connection." For him, "just as, according to 32:15, the moral regeneration will be produced by a special divine influence, so by creative energy a corresponding physical scenery for this will be provided, viz. 'the new heavens and the new earth,' which, unlike the old (51:16), will stand as perpetual before YHWH (66:22)."

230. Motyer 1993:531; Beuken 1989b:91.

231. Alexander 1846b:455.

232. Seitz 2001:544.

section (chs 1–4) of the book. It presents the vindication of the servants, however it is not limited to it but extends to the portrait of the New Heavens and the New Earth and the New Jerusalem as well.

The vindication of the servants is presented as blessings such as eating and drinking with joy, which are understood as a covenantal meal, suggesting an eschatological covenantal restoration. The punishment of the wicked is also covenantal, as achieving the eschatological expectation of the earlier parts of the book.

Ultimately sinners will be put to death, while the servants will be given another name and all be righteous in the New Jerusalem. Total commitment to YHWH is achieved at that time and the former troubles due to covenantal breach are forgotten.

The New Heavens and the New Earth that YHWH creates in the eschatological era are understood as literal, because the verse should be understood primarily in the context of DI due to the strong connection to DI. Not only the contrast of the former-the new but also the "former things" and the verb "to create" (ברא) are based on the eschatological vision of DI, in which the former things and the new things extend to the creation and the new creation. Although the New Heavens and the New Earth are related to the context, they are a new revelation that cannot be absorbed entirely into the context.

The New Jerusalem is paradisiacal, being situated in the New Heavens and the New Earth. It is a city of joy and gladness, since there will be no more weeping and mourning. The servants (i.e., the eschatological people in the New Jerusalem) are blessed with longevity, security of tenure, and effective labor, which are understood as the removal of the curses of the covenantal breach as well as the primitive disobedience—so the return to the patriarchal paradise.

In the eschatological era, the relational breach between YHWH and the people will be removed as well. In addition, as suggested by the intertextual link to the eschatological expectation to PI, the animal world is also restored to peace and harmony, another sign of cosmic change. This is also supported by the patriarchal return in the preceding context.

The eschatology in the passage is both apocalyptic, in that the new creation replaces the old one, and prophetic, in that the reward/punishment scheme is continuous, and in accordance, with the covenantal framework.[233] From the prophetic viewpoint, the New Jerusalem is located in the New Heavens and the New Earth; form the apocalyptic sense, they converge to

233. For Childs (2001:538), "The promise in ch 65 is not an apocalyptic flight into an imaginative world of fantasy, but the fulfilment of God's will taking shape throughout the entire book of Isaiah."

be identified, as the Temple Mountain and Zion become to be identified in the eschaton.

Chapter 6

Conclusion

Eschatological Theology of Third Isaiah

6.1 Introduction

According to the historical survey (chapter 1), the Reformers did not doubt the theological and authorial unity of the book of Isaiah. They saw TI in the context of the whole Bible, and did not recognize its distinctive features. The assumption of the theological unity of the book of Isaiah, and of TI, was fundamentally challenged by the development of historical criticism. Source critics observed different literary units and diverse theological themes and concepts even in a single unit. Theological interests were subordinated to a complex source-critical analysis, so it was impossible to build a coherent theology of TI. Through Duhm's work a sharp break was made between DI and TI, because of the alleged contrasts between Babylonian and Jerusalem settings, between exile and the return of the people. A redactional approach has focused on the historical development of the final form of TI. It tries to find how diverse materials came to comprise the present form of the text. But there is no agreed reconstruction of the process, because TI provides insufficient historical evidence. A comprehensive theology is difficult to discern because theology can only be developed after such a reconstruction, and the theological concerns become secondary and fragmented according to the alleged redactors and authors. A canonical approach pays attention to the theological enterprise of the canonical texts, since the authoritative function of the text within a faith community is central. The entire book of Isaiah can thus be treated as one corpus. Although the text has a historical dimension, the canonical context is primary. The canonical approach subordinates the conventional distinct historical settings and theological tensions to a coherent theology of TI.

In this connection, I have sought to construct a coherent theology of TI, leaning on the canonical approach. As in the canonical approach, I consider that the assumption of theological unity enables a richer understanding of the theology of TI. Nevertheless, I still need to consider the theological diversity of TI materials. So it is important to identify categories to present the coherent but complex theology of TI. To this end, I also assume that eschatology is at the heart of the theology of TI.

Because the theology of TI is proposed as eschatology, I have also tried to define several important terminologies and set basic assumptions for the investigation of the eschatology of TI. By eschatology, I indicate an idea of a general future hope of Israel. Apocalyptic is defined as heavenly language (i.e., language referring to the heavenly realm) or mythical patterns that reveal eternal realities, including a cataclysmic vision. I have highlighted three features of apocalyptic: apocalyptic representation, eschatological duality, and cosmic scope. Apocalyptic literally refers to the heavenly realm in its representation. Here, 'literal' signifies a straightforward description of reality (in the heavenly realm). While metaphor describes something (A) in the historical world by something else (B) in the historical world (so, earthly language), apocalyptic is heavenly language, which refers to the heavenly realm, although apocalyptic language is also eventually metaphorical in that it is ultimately applied to this world. So apocalyptic is mythical, because myth is defined as protological and thus timeless events, i.e., events in the heavenly realm, which may be applied to the earthly world at multiple times. Myth is legitimate, theological language or God-talk. Mythical thinking, which is defined as thought that takes into consideration realities and activities in the heavenly realm based on the two-tier-world picture, is required to understand mythical or apocalyptic language. The view that myth is understood as earthly words that refer directly to the earthly world and as metaphor is not warranted by the Biblical portrayal of the two-tier-world picture. Eschatological duality refers to the distinction between this world and the world to come. It facilitates discontinuity with the historical world. I understand that apocalyptic is a particular type of the broader view of eschatology as it addresses Israel's future hope in a specific way. The widely-held views of dualism and a pessimistic view of history in apocalyptic may be too rigid.

As I have shown in 1.3, because eschatological and apocalyptic issues are closely related to each other, a fragmented approach to a particular issue may not be successful. A holistic approach is needed to solve the eschatological issues of TI in relation to the wider framework of the theology of TI. A paradigm of either prophetic or apocalyptic eschatology does not do justice to the complex text of TI, which is open to a wide range of eschatological interpretations.

My exposition in this book has shown that the full eschatological implications of TI have both continuous and discontinuous aspects, including apocalyptic language and a cosmic dimension. I have discussed four major themes for the eschatological theology of TI: the covenant (56:1–8), the coming of YHWH (59:15b–21), Zion (60:1–22), and the New Heavens and the New Earth (65:13–25). Other important themes of TI are included in these categories. This concluding chapter will summarize my studies on the key themes in the main chapters to present the eschatology of TI.

6.2 The Eschatology of Third Isaiah

This book has sought to show that the heart of TI's theology is eschatology. Eschatology is created by the actions of YHWH, who is dealing with His people. When He called Israel and made them His people through entering into the covenant relationship, eschatology begins as a story of YHWH's activities that looked towards an end, fulfilling his purposes. The need for YHWH to take initiatives to achieve his purpose becomes clearer and clearer as the story continues. When the people sin and are under judgment and are urged to return to YHWH, the divine purpose is manifested and reaffirmed through his decisive intervention, prompted by the sins of the covenant people. Because the old empirical Israel has failed due to their sins, the new people of YHWH are formed by the coming of YHWH, not only from the old people of Israel but also from the nations. The eschatological people enter and dwell in the new Zion, the eschatological city. They inhabit the New Heavens and the New Earth. Just as YHWH had come to establish His people entering into the (first) covenant, He restores it by coming and entering into a new covenant concluded with the new people, which is the eschatological reapplication of the past. In this way, the original divine purpose is ultimately fulfilled.

So an eschatological reading of the covenant may be considered to be the theological center of the theology of TI, and eschatology is the legitimate and comprehensive summary of the theology of TI. The covenant is a cross-sectional concept, which regulates the relationship between YHWH and the people at a particular point in time. But eschatology is a dynamic concept, which reflects the dynamics of that relationship through time, so it is linear (in that it perceives the divine works through the course of time) or rather multidimensional (because it has vertical as well as horizontal aspects). The covenant functions as a framework to express eschatology. Israel, the people of YHWH, has been formed as the covenantal partner of YHWH. The present judgment (arising from the wrath of YHWH) is based on the covenant tradition. The coming of YHWH is with a view to the implementation of the covenant. The coming YHWH carries out judgment on the nations as well as on Israel to save some of them and to punish others. The eschatological salvation will also involve the restoration of the covenant. With the coming of YHWH an envoy is promised to come as redeemer, who (this dissertation argues) functions as a Messianic figure and a covenant mediator. This vision of the Messianic figure is the fulfilment or re-representation of the Messianic expectations of PI (the Davidic Messiah) and DI (the Servant)—these two traditions also reflect the covenant tradition. Reading TI in the context of PI and DI, TI incorporates the eschatological expectations of the previous parts of the book.

The Eschatological Framework of the Covenant

Some see a sharp break between 56:1–8 and the preceding chapters, but its discontinuity has often been overemphasized. Because a Babylonian background for DI is not assumed (see chapter 1), a geographical shift in ch 56 is also regarded as unproven in this dissertation. Several suggestions for the historical situation of 56:1–8 lack textual evidence, but are rather speculations based on historical assumptions. References to the ritual activities as well as the Temple in 56:1–8 do not indicate a definite *Sitz-im-Leben*, as often assumed by scholars taking a historical perspective. Rather, they are detached from historical specificity and form a coherent narrative and theological continuity with the preceding sections of the book of Isaiah (so an apocalyptic flavor). References to foreigners and eunuchs are insufficient to reconstruct a historical situation in 56:3–7. They are adopted as an illustration of the universal salvation accessible to anyone who returns to YHWH (55:1–5, 7). The inclusion of foreigners and eunuchs reflects the eschatological salvation community rather than a historical Temple community, as the new people of YHWH. An eschatological rather than a historical perspective is dominant in 56:1–8.

As the introductory section of TI, 56:1–8 recapitulates the eschatological messages of DI and PI and reflects the eschatological vision of TI.

The eschatological vision of TI incorporates DI's eschatological vision of covenant restoration, on the one hand, and that of PI, i.e., the expansion of salvation to the nations, on the other hand. This expansion to the nations was also developed in DI.

56:1–8 has clear links to DI, and reiterates the pivotal elements of the eschatological expectation of DI, such as the imminent coming of salvation and the demand to keep justice and do righteousness. 56:1–8 also affirms the important eschatological vision of PI, i.e., the gathering of the nations to Zion. These two eschatological expectations in 56:1 and 8 give an envelope structure to the passage, suggesting that the whole passage is to be read from an eschatological perspective. The alleged theological difference from DI is also rejected, although there is in 56:1–8 a new formal appearance of keywords for the theology of TI. Because there are indications of an envelope structure(s) in chs 56–59 and chs 56–66, 56:1–8 may function as an introduction to TI.[1] However, continuity with the preceding sections of the passage is more significant than discontinuity, when focus is on theology.

According to our exposition of 56:1–8 (chapter 2), the covenant is the overarching theme that incorporates other major themes such as salvation, justice, righteousness, (keeping) the Sabbath, the Temple, and the Holy Mountain. The covenant in TI is a unified or integrated concept that incorporates the various covenantal traditions. The covenant in 56:4, 6 is not only Mosaic, but is also related to the Davidic Covenant as well as the Abrahamic and Noachic Covenants. The covenant in 59:21 also integrates the Noachic, Abrahamic, and Mosaic Covenants. In 61:8, the Davidic and Abrahamic Covenants are closely related. The covenant is thus not a self-obligation of YHWH but a mutual relationship between YHWH and humans. In chs 54–55, which form the background to 56:1–8, the Noachic (54:9–10), Abrahamic (54:1–3), Davidic (55:3–5) and Mosaic (55:6–7) Covenants are integrated. Restoration of the covenant is the goal of eschatological salvation, in which not only Israel but also the nations will participate.

The eschatological expectation transmitted from DI is summarized as the salvation and "righteousness" (צדקה) of YHWH, and accordingly the passage demands that the people keep justice and to righteousness (56:1). The justice and righteousness of the people of YHWH are pivotal elements of the covenant order, so the command is understood as an admonition for the restoration of the covenantal relation with YHWH. Obedience to the command and the consequent restoration of the covenant is understood as participation in salvation. The relation between the offer and announcement

1. This does not exclude the possibility that a broader section, e.g., chs 54:1—56:8 as in Seitz (2001:485), forms an introduction of TI. Our concern is primarily limited to chs 56–66.

of salvation and the demand for human response emphasizes that divine action and human obedience coincide in the realization of salvation in individuals. Keeping the Sabbath, like keeping justice and doing righteousness, is understood as allegiance to the covenantal order, rather than as an indication of membership in the post-exilic ritual society (56:2). Entering the Holy Mountain and offering burnt offerings and sacrifices (56:7) are also understood as part of the covenantal order in the eschaton.

The eunuchs are required to keep the Sabbath, choose the things that please YHWH, and hold fast to the covenant (56:4). The foreigners are required to join themselves to YHWH, keep the Sabbath, and hold fast to the covenant (56:6). These requirements are all an expression of the covenantal bond to YHWH. To the eunuchs who achieve the covenantal bond to YHWH, eschatological salvation is promised since monument and name (יד ושם) signify a continuation and share in the eschatological blessing (56:5). The foreigners who meet the requirements are entitled to enter the Holy Mountain of YHWH, which signifies inclusion into the eschatological salvation community of Zion (56:7). This is the fulfilment of the eschatological expectations of PI (2:2–4) and DI (55:5). The allusion of the "house of prayer" may suggest that the eschatological vision is modelled on Davidic and Solomonic prosperity.

It is YHWH who gathers the outcasts of Israel and others as well (56:8). The 'gathering of outcasts' theme is Deuteronomistic (Deut 30:4) and Isaianic (11:12). The outcasts banished due to the breach of the covenant (Deut 30:4) return to the Davidic Messiah, together with the nations (Isa 11:10–12). In the context of DI, "those already gathered" and "others" that YHWH will gather refer to the returning children of barren woman Zion (54:7) and the nations summoned to (the New) David (55:5). So 56:8 fulfils the Davidic and Mosaic Covenants as well as both the eschatological visions of PI and DI.

In summary, in the prologue of TI (56:1–8), the two streams of the eschatological expectations of DI and PI are incorporated and extended— the expectation of the imminent salvation of DI and the expectation of the gathering of the nations to the Holy Mountain in PI. The covenant concept is pivotal in the eschatology of TI, in that it is the overarching theme that incorporates the other major themes. The covenant concept is the framework of the eschatology of TI in view of the sequence of eschatology: (broken) covenant → judgment (enforcement) → the restored covenant. The eschatological salvation is characterized by the restoration of the covenant with YHWH. By the covenant we mean the integrated tradition of Noachic, Abrahamic, Mosaic, and Davidic Covenants. Salvation is open to anyone who commits to the covenantal bond with YHWH, even foreigners and

eunuchs. The description of the introductory section lacks historical specificity, but is generalized to present a continuous theology with the contexts
(chs 54–55), and may best be understood as having an apocalyptic flavor.

The Coming of YHWH as the Initiation of the Eschatological Era

The imminent coming of salvation pronounced in 56:1–8 (chapter 2) is realized by the coming of YHWH in 59:15b–21 (chapter 3), which initiates the
eschatological era.

YHWH comes because He sees that there was no justice, which dis-
pleases Him (59:15b). The intervention of YHWH in 59:15b–21 is the enforcement of the covenant, since "no justice" characterizes the breach of the
covenant in 59:1–15a. It is to deal with the present situation of the people
and to respond to their responses. This breach is also evidenced in chs
58–59, which form a single extended unit, transgression (פשע) and Jacob
forming an envelope structure in 59:20 and 58:1, and both chapters being
centered on the sin of the people. There are several other links between the
two chapters, such as justice and righteousness. 59:15b–21 together with
56:1–8 forms an *inclusio* of the section chs 56–59. The demand to observe
justice and do righteousness in 56:1–8 has come to nothing in 56:9—59:15a,
so the covenant is broken. Thus, YHWH comes in order to restore the covenant, together with justice and righteousness, in 59:15b–21, fulfilling the
expectation of salvation (56:1–8). YHWH's coming also responds to the repentant response of the people in 59:9–15a. YHWH dwells with the contrite
and the lowly of spirit and revives their hearts in 57:14–21 as well.

YHWH also sees that there is no one to intercede (59:16a). This may
refer to the absence of a righteous leader in the community, or it may highlight the total corruption of the community as displayed in the preceding
context. However, according to the intratextual links to DI, it may also signify the aloneness and sovereignty of YHWH in the creation of universe
(40:12–14; 41:28; 44:24) and the exodus event (50:2), implying eschatological salvation by YHWH alone. Although there is no reference to the
creation or exodus in 59:15b–21, a connection is implied by the character
of the passage as a mythical Divine Warrior Hymn. Being detached from
the historical arena, it is apocalyptic. Another intertextual connection to
DI is found in the intercession of the Servant (53:12, ולפשעים יפגיע) because
"no man" and "no one to intercede" (מפגיע) are interchangeable in 59:16.
The exodus connection is supported by the "arm" of YHWH (59:16; 53:1;
52:10). The aloneness of YHWH refers to the work of YHWH by Himself
in DI, especially in the work of the Servant worked by the arm of YHWH.

So I consider that the arm of YHWH refers to the Servant. Because there is no man and no one to intercede, YHWH brings salvation by His own arm and relies on His righteousness (59:16b). This connection to the Servant prefigures such a figure (see below).

YHWH comes as the Divine Warrior, putting on armor to engage in the battle (59:17). The Divine Warrior tradition in the book of Isaiah is ultimately based on the exodus tradition and the Sinai theophany. The judgment of the coming YHWH is retributive: reward is given to the righteous; punishment to the sinners, as displayed in vengeance (נקם), recompense (גמולה), and repayment (שלם). The coming of YHWH is on the day of vengeance, i.e., the Day of YHWH, in continuation of the DI and PI traditions. The enemies of YHWH are both within the community and outside Israel (59:18). YHWH always fights against sin/sinners as the enemy. In the Divine Warrior Hymn, the enemies of YHWH become generalized (or, mythical) to signify sin/sinners whether within or outside Israel. So the judgment of the coming YHWH is universal. Universal judgment is also accompanied by universal salvation. YHWH will be feared over the world due to the manifestation of His name and glory (59:19a). Fearing the name and glory of YHWH in the nations signifies their salvation. It fulfils the expectations of PI (6:3) and DI (40:5), in which the glory of YHWH fills the whole of the earth.

In my interpretation, an envoy is promised to come as light (כנהר), and the Spirit of YHWH waves a flag for him (59:19b). This Messianic interpretation is also evidenced by the "standard" (נס) in the eschatological context in PI and DI as well as TI (13:2; 18:3; 49:22; 62:10), which is especially related to the expectation of the gathering of the nations. The envoy coming to Zion is designated a Redeemer, a divine appellation, implying the enigmatic nature of the Messianic figure (59:20): divine but distinguished from YHWH. His redemption will be achieved in those who turn from transgression in Jacob, so the eschatological judgment is purificatory. Due to the coming of YHWH the community is divided and only the righteous will be saved. The covenant is re-concluded between YHWH and those who depart from transgression (59:21). The Spirit and word of YHWH are granted to the Messianic figure and to his offspring forever. The envoy is promised the covenant, so he is a covenant mediator. The breached covenant is restored by the promised envoy. He is identified with the Anointed One (61:1) and succeeds to the role of the Servant in DI. The relationship between the Messianic figure (i.e., the envoy or the Anointed One) and the servants, i.e., the offspring of the Anointed One in TI, is parallel with the relationship between the Servant and his offspring (i.e., the righteous) in DI (48:16c//59:21; 49:1//61:1).

In summary, the coming of YHWH in 59:15b–21 is a fulfilment of the expected imminent coming of salvation and an execution of the eschatological warning to keep justice and do righteousness in 56:1. In 59:15b–21, the injustice of the community is overcome and the breached covenant is restored by the coming of YHWH, who brings eschatological salvation. The coming YHWH is portrayed as a Divine Warrior, based on the exodus/ Sinai tradition. The coming of YHWH is necessitated by the sinful state of the people, who have broken the covenant. It may also be motivated by the repenting and lamenting prayer of the people. It is the Day of YHWH, i.e., the day of the final/eschatological judgment and salvation, fulfilling the Divine Warrior tradition of PI and DI. The purpose of the coming is primarily judgment, which is not limited to punitive actions, but also leads to the salvation of His people. Not only Israel but also the nations are subject to the judgment. The judgment is cleansing as well as retributive and universal. The coming of YHWH entails the eschatological division of the community into the wicked and the righteous, i.e., those who turn from sins will alone be saved. In my interpretation, the coming of YHWH is also accompanied by (or, includes) the coming of a Messianic figure, who is identified with the Anointed One and succeeds to the role of the Servant as the covenant mediator. The eschatological vision of the Divine Warrior is apocalyptic, since the language of the Hymn is detached from historical reality and is connected to the mythical idea of creation and exodus.

Zion the Eschatological Temple-City-Paradise

Through the coming of YHWH in 59:15b–21 (chapter 3), the eschatological salvation is achieved in Zion (chapter 4). In this eschatological community the expectation of imminent salvation (chapter 2) is realized and the breached covenant is restored (chapter 3). An apocalyptic and not a historical interpretation is argued for since the text does not have a specific historical event as its reference.

I have argued in chapter 3 that from a literary and theological point of view ch 60 is continuous with the preceding section 59:15b–21 (see 3.2). Because the coming of (the glory of) YHWH in 59:15b–21 is repeated in 60:1–3, and the light/darkness metaphoric system links chs 58–59 and ch 60, the glorification of Zion in ch(s) 60(–62) is understood as the consequence of the coming of YHWH in 59:15b–21. Darkness due to the sins of the people in chs 58–59 turns into the light of salvation due to the glory of the coming YHWH in ch 60. The darkness in the present community is banished in the new Zion (violence and destruction, 59:7//60:18; peace,

59:8//60:17). Consequently, as the result of the coming of YHWH (59:15b–21), the glorification of Zion and the salvation of the people are achieved in chs 60–62. Only those who depart sins and come to the covenant (59:20–21; 56:4–7) enter Zion.

The new eschatological era dawns as Zion is lit up and glorified since the light of the glory of YHWH approaches her (60:1), while the world is in darkness (60:2). Because of the light of Zion, the nations and the kings draw near to her (60:3). The charge to Zion to arise and shine is a deliberate connection with DI (51:17; 52:1–2), but TI does not understand it as the realization of the physical return of the people but as the decisive turning from sins. The text is distanced from historical reality through its apocalyptic language. The contrast between darkness and light displays the eschatological contrast between *Unheil* and salvation in TI. It fulfils the eschatological expectations of DI (49:6; 42:6) and PI (9:1[2]). The function of the Servant as the light of the nations is achieved here in Zion because Zion, like the Servant, is lifted up high and acknowledged by nations and kings. In a metaphoric link with PI, the eschatological glory of Zion implies an achievement of the Davidic Messianic era as expected in PI (9:5–6[6–7]). The contrast also realizes afresh the creation of the cosmos in Genesis as light is created in 'the' darkness (Gen 1:4). It is also related to the exodus event (Exod 10:22–23; 14:20), which is itself often related to creation.

The eschatological Zion is an international hub. The nations/kings come to Zion, carrying the children of Zion (60:4) as well as the wealth of the nations and the abundance of the sea (60:5). The gathering of the nations in the eschatological Zion fulfils the eschatological expectations of PI (2:2–5; 11:12) and DI (40:10–11; 49:6, 7, 22–23; 52:15; 55:4–5). It was expected that YHWH would gather the nations and the scattered of Israel to the standard, i.e., the Davidic Messiah (11:10, 12). The Servant of DI was promised so that the nations would flow to the standard (נס) carrying the children of Zion (49:22), and this is fulfilled here. The gathering theme also fulfils 40:10–11, in which the shepherd YHWH will gather the lambs, his people. The coming of the nations is also a fulfilment of the promise given to the Davidic Messiah in 55:4–5, the source for the literal quotation of 60:9b. It also fulfils the expectation of the introductory section of TI (56:7–8; see above and 3.3). This gathering of the nations is eventually achieved in 66:18–21, where they see the glory of YHWH and thus enjoy salvation. The coming of the nations (60:3, 4–5) is with a view to receiving the instruction of the Torah in PI (2:2–5), signifying the covenantal bond with YHWH and thus salvation. The nations that will not serve Zion will perish (60:12), which is the fulfilment of the Abrahamic covenant (Gen 12:1–3). The link of "will serve you" (יעבדוך) to Gen 27:29 may suggest the same. This does not exclude the nations from salvation, because the concept of the remnant is applied to the nations as they join the eschatological community. The link suggests an imperialist relationship between the people of Israel and the nations in Zion (cf. Jer 27:8). Israel is the first born son, while the nations are the foster children in Zion.

The wealth of the nations comes from everywhere in the world, as implied by the names of the city referring to lineages of Abraham in Gen 25 (60:6–7). It comes not only from the East by land (60:6–7), but also from the West by sea (60:8–9). The nations also bring good news (60:6; cf. 42:10–12), so they participate in the task of the herald (מבשר) of DI as well (40:9; 41:27). The flocks of the nations acceptable to the altar of YHWH fulfil the eschatological promise given to the foreigners who participate in the covenantal bond with YHWH in 56:7 (see 2.3). Because the right function of worship is restored, the Temple will be glorified. The swiftness of the caravans of the nations is due to their anticipation of salvation, as implied by the link with DI (51:5; 42:4). The nations look forward to the Torah of the Servant (42:4) and the arm of YHWH (51:5). The glorification of Zion (60:9c) is achieved in relation to the promise of the glorification of the Davidic Messiah (55:5b) in DI, since the two glorifications are closely related to each other. Zion will receive provision from the nations and the kings (60:16), who feed her with milk as foster father and nursing mother. This fulfils the eschatological expectation of DI (49:23).

Zion will be reconstructed and restored as the eschatological city (60:10). The nations and kings will participate in the reconstruction of Zion as workmen. As the links suggest (58:12; 61:4), the reconstruction of Zion refers to the spiritual or covenantal rather than physical reconstruction, because the sin and injustice of the community is the cause of the desolation of the community in TI. In the links to DI (49:16–17), the destruction language (49:19) is related to the work of the Servant (49:8), who will bring the people back to YHWH (49:5, 6) and will thus achieve the restoration of the covenantal relationship. The construction language (קום, בנה) in DI sometimes has the physical meaning (44:26, 28; 45:13) but often refers to the covenantal relationship (49:6, 8), as does the exodus imagery. But, the metaphorical use of the language is in view in TI, as the work of the Anointed One succeeds that of the Servant (the year of YHWH's favour, the day of vengeance; 61:1//49:8). The reconstruction is the work of the Anointed One in TI. The change in fortune of the city is because YHWH changes his attitude towards His people from wrath to favor (60:10b) due to His compassion and everlasting loving kindness (חסד עולם) (54:7–8). If we dare to incorporate one of DI's distinctive, it is also due to the death of the Servant (ch 53) that Zion is promised prosperity and salvation in chs 54–55.

Zion is also the eschatological Temple, and even paradise. The forests of Lebanon will adorn the Temple, which will thus be glorified (60:13). The trees associated with the glory of Lebanon are not timbers. Rather the clear links to 35:2 and 41:19 suggest that it signifies the transformation of nature into paradise (35:1; 41:18–20). So the eschatological expectation of the paradisiacal change in PI and DI is realized in TI. As a result, Zion is the incorporation of the city and the Temple and turns into paradise, as is often indicated in the Zion tradition. This is also evidenced by the fact that in 58:10–12, the "well-watered garden," referring to paradise, is realized after the reconstruction of Zion. As the "City of YHWH" and "Zion of the Holy One of Israel" imply, the eschatological Zion is closely related to YHWH, and thus indicates a restored relationship with Him; in fact Zion as the Temple is the place where YHWH dwells and is worshipped (60:14). The once forsaken and deserted Zion will have an everlasting pride and joy in the eschatological era (60:15), due to the restoration of the covenant with YHWH ("forsaken" refers to the broken covenant in DI; 54:6–7; 49:14–15).

The material prosperity of the people and the economic order of the nation will also be transformed in Zion (60:17). The glorification of Zion may be based on the Davidic-Solomonic prosperity (so the Zion tradition), as suggested by the precious metals (1 Kgs 10:21, 27) and the reference to Sheba (1 Kgs 10:1–13). The social order will also be transformed since peace and righteousness function as their overseers and taskmasters (60:17c), and since violence as well as devastation and destruction will entirely disappear in Zion (60:18a). In the context of DI, it may be that violence has been dealt with by the Servant (53:9). As a result, salvation and praise will be the nature of the eschatological Zion, as salvation will be the wall of Zion and praise will be her gates (60:18b).

In the eschatological Zion, the heavenly city, YHWH will be the everlasting light replacing the Sun and Moon (60:19–20). This might be a metaphor, since in the parallel passage in the chapter (60:1–3) YHWH is metaphorically the light of Zion, which signifies the blessing of YHWH. However, 60:1–3 suggests an apocalyptic reading of both texts since it is related to the creation and the exodus tradition (see above). Furthermore, the thematic link with 65:17–25 supports an apocalyptic understanding of the passage. 60:19–20 may also be related to the exodus tradition (4:5; 24:23), in which YHWH functions as a light. The everlasting light of YHWH competes with the physical light of the Sun and Moon, which may also suggest a literal understanding. Many of the apocalyptic indications in the chapter and in TI make such a reading more plausible.

The people of Zion will be all righteous, possessing the land in the eschatological age by the work of the hands of YHWH (60:21). The righteousness of the people indicates their salvation, as it is often related to salvation in TI (56:1; 59:17). "Possessing the land forever" may signify the ultimate fulfilment of eschatological salvation (57:13; 65:9; 49:8; 54:3), which is Abrahamic. It may fulfil the Abrahamic Covenant, as is suggested by the announcement "a little one becomes a clan, the smallest one becomes a strong nation" (60:22a; Gen 12:2; 17:20; cf. Isa 49:8, 19–21; 54:1–3). This implies that the eschatological salvation is the fulfilment of the Patriarchal promises. The glorification of Zion is also the fulfilment of the promises given to the people of YHWH in the covenantal traditions (Davidic and Mosaic as well as Abrahamic). The eschatological salvation in ch 60 is portrayed as the result of the work of the Servant of DI in the eschatological expectation of ch 49 (60:22b refers to 49:8).

In summary, Zion is glorified due to the coming of the glory of YHWH and achieves eschatological salvation (ch 60). The eschatological Zion also fulfils the expectation of the gathering of the nations and that of the imminent salvation in 56:1–8. Zion will be transformed into an international center to which the nations/kings will flow to present homage to YHWH as a result of becoming the new people of YHWH and joining salvation. The gathering of the nations as foster children fulfils the eschatological vision of PI and DI. The nations have a subordinate status in comparison to Israel in Zion, Israel being the first-born son, while the nations are the foster children. The eschatological Zion incorporates a transformed Temple and city; in fact it turns into paradise. It is a reconstructed city—the covenantal order is restored. Salvation and praise will be fundamental elements of the city and all the people will be righteous. The eschatological Zion will be established by the work of the Servant, i.e., the Anointed One. It represents the climactic fulfilment of the covenantal traditions. As the everlasting light, YHWH will replace the Sun and Moon. Chapter 60 is also apocalyptic, not only because of the apocalyptic vision of the YHWH in Zion (60:19–20), the cosmic significance of the glorification of Zion (60:1–2), and the transformation of Zion (60:13), but also because the language of the eschatological vision in ch 60 is detached from historical reality and forms a continuity at the theological and literary level.

The New Heavens and the New Earth the Eschatological Goal

The New Heavens and the New Earth become the ultimate goal of the eschatological vision of TI (chapter 5), which will be achieved by the coming of YHWH (chapter 3). It will eventually fulfil the eschatological expectations in the introductory section of TI (chapter 2), so the covenant will be restored and the nations will gather on the Holy Mountain. The New Heavens and the New Earth will provide a new environment for the people of Zion, in which the New Jerusalem, i.e., the eschatological Zion will be situated (chapter 4).

The New Heavens and the New Earth in 65:13–25 highlight the eschatological vision of TI as the pivotal section of the climactic conclusion of the book and TI (chs 65–66). A historical approach to those chapters and 65:13–25 based on the assumption of the post-exilic Jewish society is misleading, not only because it lacks evidence but also because it distorts the theological understanding of TI as well as the book of Isaiah. The theory of sociological division of the community in chs 65–66 (as well as TI) is rejected because it is based on a number of doubtful assumptions. Rather the division of the community arises because the covenantal commitment to YHWH of the people is tested by the eschatological judgment of YHWH.

The coming of YHWH brings vengeance (נקם), recompense (גמולה), and repayment (שלם) to the people: reward to the righteous and punishment to the wicked (chapter 3). As a result, the servants will be blessed by eating, drinking, rejoicing, and singing with gladness of heart, while the apostate "you" will be subject to shame, crying out in pain of heart (65:13–14). These different repayments are based on the covenantal blessings and curses (Deut 28:1–26, 48; 62:8–9//Deut 28:33). The food is understood as a covenant meal celebrating the eschatological re-establishment of the covenant, as well as the enjoyment of salvation (55:1–2; 25:6). The servants, those who abide by the covenant, are vindicated. This vindication fulfils the eschatological expectations of DI and PI. The blessings are awarded to the servants due to the task of the Servant (49:10; 41:17), since deliverance from hunger and thirst will be fulfilled at the "time of my favour"/"the day of salvation" (49:8). This (in my reading) is realized by the Anointed One in 61:2 and 63:4 in TI. Thus (the work of) the Anointed One brings the blessings (61:2) as well as the punishment (63:4) in TI. The vengeance and retribution in TI (61:2; 63:4) also fulfil the expectation of PI (34:8). Sorrow (כאב; 65:14) is the achievement of the Day of YHWH in 17:11.

The apostates will be ashamed, an outworking of the curses of the covenant, and ultimately put to death (65:15, 12), which is the sanction of the covenant (Deut 32:41–42). The Abrahamic promise is fulfilled in giving a new name to the servants (Gen 17:5) and in invoking a blessing (Gen 22:18; 12:3). The eschatological vengeance will come true as an expression of the God of faithfulness, who requires of His servants a total commitment to YHWH (65:16), which fulfils 56:6 (see 3.3). The servants are the offspring (65:9) of the Anointed One, i.e., the offspring of the Servant in DI (53:10), forming the new people of YHWH in the eschatological Zion

(65:22) as the chosen of YHWH (65:15). The former troubles that will be forgotten (65:16c) in the new era refer to the former devastations (61:4), signifying the troubles or afflictions of the people under divine judgment for the breach of the covenant (Deut 31:17, 21).

YHWH creates the New Heavens and the New Earth, which is the ultimate purpose of the coming of YHWH (65:17a). Due to the new creation, the former things are entirely forgotten (65:17b). To those who have a historical approach to this verse, the new creation is understood as a metaphor referring to the change of living condition in the historical ambit, but several elements suggest an apocalyptic understanding. The strong contrast between "the *New* Heavens and the *New* Earth" and the *former* things and the adoption of the typical technical term "the former things" (הרשנות), together with the verb "to create," suggest that the verse needs to be understood primarily in the context of the eschatological expectations of DI (43:18–19; 42:9) rather than in the immediate context. According to 43:18–19, the new things refer to the new exodus, which may refer both to physical return from Babylon and to covenantal restoration from a sinful state. However, the sharp break between the former things and the new things grows, since the physical aspect becomes less emphasized and the covenantal/spiritual aspect more. So the metaphoric and mythological language of the new exodus, referring to the new creation, becomes detached from the note of historical continuity even in DI. This suggests a non-metaphorical understanding of the new creation. 65:25, the parallel verse of the new creation in 65:17 forming an *inclusio* in 65:17–25, strongly suggests an apocalyptic reading of 65:17. The new creation may allude to the cosmic Heavens and Earth in 51:6 and 16. An apocalyptic understanding may also be supported by the apocalyptic atmosphere in TI (especially, 60:1–2, 19–20; 66:22; cf. 63:1–6; see 5.3). The former things (65:17) are also understood primarily in the context of the eschatology of DI, while the former troubles (65:16) are understood primarily in the immediate context of the verse. So the former things refer to the first creation (i.e., the Heavens and the Earth). Due to the new creation, the things belonging to the old world-order will be forgotten. Although some scholars understand the creation of the New Heavens and the New Earth metaphorically and identify it with the creation of the New Jerusalem, an apocalyptic understanding maintains a difference between the two creations. However, when eternal reality is in view (in the heavenly realm), they begin to become one, as YHWH dwells in the New Jerusalem (Zion).

The New Jerusalem is the city of joy, in which both YHWH and the people rejoice together (65:18–19). Judging by the gladness and rejoicing, the New Jerusalem fulfils the eschatological vision of the paradisiacal change of nature in PI (35:1–2, 6–8). The emphatic expression of the end of weeping in the New Jerusalem is best understood apocalyptically (65:19b).

The blessings of the servants in the New Jerusalem suggest that the New Jerusalem is a return to the primordial paradise and that the curses due to the original sin as well as the covenantal breach are removed. The blessings fulfil the eschatological expectations of PI and DI. The longevity in the New Jerusalem prevents premature death (65:20), and extends to the "hundred years old" (65:20), which may be reminiscent of the "days of one hundred and twenty years" in Gen 6:3, while the lifetime of a tree (65:22) may allude to the "tree of life" in Gen 2:9. The blessing of longevity fulfils the eschatological expectations of DI (46:3–4) and PI (25:8). In 25:8, linked thematically to 65:20, the power of death is destroyed, which arose due to the original sin (Gen 2:17). Blessings such as inhabiting houses, planting vineyards, and eating fruit signify restoration from the covenantal curses (Deut 28:30, 39–40). The "work of their hands" may be Deuteronomic and covenantal (Deut 2:7; 14:29). The phrase "shall not labor in vain" may also be Deuteronomic (Deut 28:33), and be resonant with the curse on the labor and the ground in Gen 3:17–18. The "child-birth without trouble" (65:23) removes the covenantal curse on the people (Deut 28:32, 41) as well as on the first woman (Gen 3:16). The effectiveness of the "work of their hands" (65:22) is promised to the righteous (3:10). The "offspring of the blessed of YHWH" (65:23) fulfils the promise given to the Servant (53:10–11).

In the eschatological Jerusalem, a perfect communication is realized between YHWH and the people (65:24). This also signifies the covenant restoration in terms of the reversal of the chronic disobedience of the people to listen to YHWH (65:1–2, 12; 66:4), which is stated as endemic in PI (6:9–10; cf. 30:19) and DI (43:8). Thematically, it also reverses the communication lost due to the original disobedience in Gen 3, achieving the New Covenant (Jer 31:33).

Nature is also restored. In the New Jerusalem, the eschatological Zion and the Temple-city-paradise, the carnivore and the herbivore animals coexist and eat grass, fulfilling the command of YHWH in Eden (Gen 1:30), and even the serpent has dust as food (65:25a). There will be no hurt or destruction on the Holy Mountain of YHWH (65:25b). Sometimes the continuity between 65:25 and 65:18–24 has been overemphasized, sometimes the discontinuity. The former view tends to interpret the picture of the animals as a metaphor portraying humans. It considers that justice is realized between the oppressed (the herbivore) and the oppressors (the carnivore) through the blessing of the servants and the downfall of the wicked. The latter view considers the picture as apocalyptic and a later insertion. The metaphoric understanding tends to emphasize the immediate context and does not do justice to the intertextual connections; the apocalyptic interpretation tends to emphasize the theological discrepancy with the context. But a nuanced balance is needed here: apocalyptic understanding and consistency with the immediate context at a higher level of theology.

There are several indications of an apocalyptic understanding of the picture of the animals. The parallel verse 65:17 suggests an apocalyptic reading (see above). The intertextual link to 11:6–9 suggests that the Davidic Messianic vision and the paradisiacal world are fulfilled here in 65:25. Several allusions to Gen 1–3 have suggested a return to the primordial age (see above). The reference to the serpent is a deliberate link to Gen 3:14, signifying that not only the original curse on the serpent but also the curses on any evil will be fully executed, so the serpent coexists with other animals without poison. There will be no more harm and destruction not only in the human world (city) but also in the animal world (paradise), in which YHWH rules and is worshipped in his garden (Temple).

In summary, the New Heavens and the New Earth are eventually created by the coming YHWH to fulfil the ultimate goal of the eschatological plan of YHWH in TI (65:13–25). The concept of the New Heavens and the New Earth is apocalyptic, referring to a dramatic change of the universe. The new creation, together with the New Jerusalem, fulfils all the eschatological expectations of TI as well as those of PI and DI. The intertextual connection to DI shows that the 'new' creation reflects a heightening of the discontinuity of the old-new eschatological contrast in DI. The purpose of the new creation is in line with that of the restoration of the covenant and that of the vindication of the servants. To create the New Heavens and the New Earth, repayment is effected: blessings to the servants and punishment to the wicked. The blessings on the servants are due to the work of the Servant and accordingly due to that of the Anointed One, who takes over the role of the Servant. The Holy Mountain of YHWH (i.e., paradise) even includes the natural world and is filled with peace and harmony. The blessings of the covenant also suggest the reversal of the covenantal curses. The concept of the new creation builds on the Messianic paradise of the eschatological vision of PI (11:6–9), in which the Davidic Messiah rules over the cosmic world and the nations gather to him. It also fulfils the initial curse on the serpent, so evil will be entirely removed. The covenantal and the original curses are overcome. This paradise is a return to, or rather the re-application of, the primordial paradise in the early chapters of Genesis, as several allusions to Genesis also imply. Several allusions to Genesis 1–3 in 65:17–25 suggest the restoration from the curses of the Fall narrative. The power of sin will be eventually eliminated. The New Heavens and the New Earth (65:17), the

New Jerusalem (65:18), and the paradisiacal portrait (65:25) are understood to be apocalyptic.

Nature of the Eschatology of TI

The theology of TI is understood as eschatology. The eschatology of TI is the development and fulfilment of the eschatology of PI and DI, reaffirming the theological unity of the book of Isaiah. This fulfilment includes the vision of a Messiah, the gathering of the nations, provision by the nations, the worship of the nations, the glorification of Zion, the realization of justice and righteousness, the restoration of the covenant, the coming of YHWH in terms of the Divine Warrior tradition, and the paradisiacal change of the universe—the substantial key components of the eschatology of PI, DI and TI. While this is a more contested affirmation, I have argued that the Davidic Messianic vision of PI and the Messianic vision for the Servant in DI are fulfilled in the portrait of the Anointed One in TI. The Anointed One in TI is the agent of YHWH for the eschatological enterprise. He is promised to come by the coming YHWH. The mission of the Day of YHWH is entrusted to him. The blessings are based on his work. He is the covenant mediator between YHWH and the servants. Although there is no explicit reference to the Messianic figure in TI, it is assumed in TI, as is suggested by the intertextual references to PI and DI as well as by the fulfillments of the covenant tradition including the Davidic Covenant.

The eschatology of TI is also the fulfilment and reapplication of past traditions: not only the covenant traditions but also the creation and exodus traditions. The covenant is understood as the integrated tradition of the Noachic, Abrahamic, Mosaic, and Davidic Covenants. By forming the new people of YHWH, the foundation of the nation in the Mosaic Covenant tradition is fulfilled. In the portrait of the Messianic figure and the gathering of the nations, the Davidic covenant is fulfilled. In the portrait of Zion, the Abrahamic promises and the Mosaic covenant are realized. In the eschatological vision of TI, YHWH's work in the creation and the exodus is also reapplied.

The nature of the eschatology of TI is both prophetic and apocalyptic and both continuous and discontinuous. This is often detected in relation to the fact that the eschatology of TI is understood in the framework of the covenant. In that the eschatological salvation is the restoration of the covenant, the eschatology of TI is continuous with history. The covenant will be restored in the arena of history, so the eschatology is prophetic. In that the blessings of the previous covenantal order of Israel are granted to the servants as described in realistic terms, in that the prophetic eschatological expectations of PI and DI are incorporated to form a coherent eschatological theology in TI, and in that traditional themes are projected into the future to form the eschatology of the coming of YHWH, the eschatology of TI is prophetic and continuous with the historical reality.

However, the eschatology of TI is also apocalyptic. The language of 56:1–8, 59:15b–21, 60:1–22, and 65:13–25 is apocalyptic. In that all the people of the old Israel are judged and are to be destroyed (because the covenant is broken and there is no justice at all), the eschatological community is discontinuous with the historical community, and thus the eschatology of TI is discontinuous with history. The present evil due to the sins that caused the breach of the covenant will be judged and exterminated by the coming YHWH and sinners are to be destined to the sword, and so the eschatology of TI is discontinuous with the present and history. In that the old universe is destroyed and the New Heavens and the New Earth (the new creation) are created, the eschatology of TI is ultimately apocalyptic.

In the description of the eschatological community, the eschatology of TI integrates both the prophetic and apocalyptic elements of eschatology. The description of the eschatological community is realistic, so the eschatological community is formed in the framework of history (so continuous with history). But the community is also presented as located in the New Heavens and the New Earth, which have to be created and replace the old ones (so discontinuity between history and eschatology). Although the portrait of the New Heavens and the New Earth and that of the new Zion are apocalyptic, their ultimate anchorage in the historical arena is not denied. Therefore, in the description of the eschatological community, prophetic eschatology and apocalyptic eschatology are integrated because historical community is located in the apocalyptic cosmos. The eschatology of TI is therefore both prophetic and apocalyptic.

6.3 A Concluding Remark

This research is a new quest to integrate the theology of TI. It reaffirms that TI is organically related to the rest of the book of Isaiah, and the theology of TI is the conclusion to the theology of the book, integrating the theologies of DI and PI. A canonical approach that this study adopts is one of the features of this dissertation.

This study shows that the covenant is the main theme, i.e., the possible theological center of TI (as well as probably the book of Isaiah). It has also argued that the covenant is an integrated concept of various covenant traditions. It shows that the Messianic expectations of PI and DI are implicitly present in TI. The coming of YHWH is the crucial event that initiates the eschatological era, distinguishing the eschatological community from the empirical community of the old Israel. Fulfilling the covenant traditions, Zion is the eschatological community in which YHWH as well as the nations and Israel dwell. A distinctive emphasis is also that the eschatological Zion is the incorporation of Temple, city, and paradise. In this study the New Heavens and the New Earth are understood in an apocalyptic sense.

This study also clarifies several important terms of TI eschatology such as apocalyptic, myth, eschatology, and mythical thinking and language. It solves some eschatological/apocalyptic issues, such as the source and nature of eschatology and apocalyptic. The covenant traditions and the mythical thinking are the fundamental momentum and matrix by which eschatology has developed.

However, this book raises several issues worth studying further. Although a Messianic figure is a very important theme in TI, its study is limited in this volume. The Messianic theme in the book of Isaiah is worthy of another scholarly elaboration. A more balanced study of the theology of the book of Isaiah and the relation(s) between First, Second, and Third Isaiah, are significant topics for further study. The nature of eschatology, especially apocalyptic eschatology, needs further attention, especially in the book of Isaiah.

Bibliography

Ackroyd, Peter R. 1978. "Isaiah I–XII: Presentation of a Prophet." In *Congress Volume 1977*, edited by J. A. Emerton, 16–48. VTSup. vol. 29. Leiden: Brill.

———. 1982. "Theological Reflections on the Book of Isaiah: Three Interrelated Studies." *King's Theological Review* 5: 43–48.

Alexander, Joseph Addison. 1846a. *Commentary on the Prophecies of Isaiah: 2 Volumes Complete and Unabridged in 1. Vol. 1 (Chs 1–31)*. Reprint. Grand Rapids: Zondervan, 1977.

———. 1846b. *Commentary on the Prophecies of Isaiah: 2 Volumes Complete and Unabridged in 1. Vol. 2 (Chs 32–66)*. Reprint. Grand Rapids: Zondervan, 1977.

Allen, Leslie C. 1990. "Some Prophetic Antecedents of Apocalyptic Eschatology and Their Hermeneutical Value." *Ex Auditu* 6: 15–28.

Anderson, Bernhard W. 1962. "Exodus Typology in Second Isaiah." In *Israel's Prophetic Heritage*, edited by Bernhard W. Anderson and Walter Harrelson, 177–95. London: SCM.

———. 1980. "Exodus and Covenant in Second Isaiah and Prophetic Tradition." In *Magnalia Dei: The Mighty Acts of God. Essays on the Bible and Archaeology in Memory of G. E. Wright*, edited by F. M. Cross, et al., 339–60. Garden City, NY: Doubleday.

———. 1988. "The Apocalyptic Rendering of the Isaiah Tradition." In *The Social World of Formative Christianity and Judaism*, edited by J. Neusner et al., 17–38. Philadelphia: Fortress.

Anderson, T. David. 1986. "Renaming and Wedding Imagery in Isaiah 62." *Biblica* 67: 75–80.

Archer, Gleason L. 1982. *An Encyclopaedia of Bible Difficulties*. Grand Rapids: Zondervan.

Aune, D. E. 1992. "Eschatology: Early Christian Eschatology." In *ABD Vol. 2 (D–G)*: 594–609.

Aune, D. E., et al. 2000. "Apocalypticism." In DNTB: 45–58.

Barton, John. 1984. *Reading the Old Testament: Method in Biblical Study*. London: Dalton Longman and Todd.

Berges, Ulrich. 2002. "Der Neue Himmel und die Neue Erde im Jesajabuch: Eine Auslegung zu Jesaja 65:17 und 66:22." In *The New Things: Eschatology in Old Testament Prophecy—Festschrift for Henk Leene*, edited by F. Postma et al., 9–15. Maastricht: Uitgeverij Shaker.

Beuken, W. A. M. 1972. "Mishpat: The First Servant Song and its Context." *VT* 22: 21–30.

———. 1986. "Isa 56:9—57:13—An Example of the Isaianic Legacy of Trito-Isaiah." In *Tradition and Re-Interpretation in Jewish and Early Christian Literature: Essays in Honour of Jürgen C. H. Lebram,* edited by J. W. Van Henten et al., 48–64, Leiden: Brill.

———. 1989a. *Jesaja deel IIIA: De Prediking van het Oude Testament.* Nijkerk: Callenbach.

———. 1989b. *Jesaja deel IIIB: De Prediking van het Oude Testament.* Nijkerk: Callenbach.

———. 1989c. "Servant and Herald of Good Tidings: Isaiah 61 as an Interpretation of Isaiah 40–55." In *The Book of Isaiah,* edited by Jacques Vermeylen, 411–42. Leuven: Leuven University Press.

———. 1989d. "Does Trito-Isaiah Reject the Temple? An Intertextual Inquiry into Isa 66:1–6." In *Intertextuality in Biblical Writings: Essays in Honour of Bas van Iersel,* edited by S. Draisma, 53–66. Kampen: Spika Draisma.

———. 1990. "The Main Theme of Trito-Isaiah: 'The Servants of YHWH.'" *JSOT* 47: 67–87.

———. 1991. "Isaiah Chapters LXV–LXVI: Trito-Isaiah and the Closure of the Book of Isaiah." In *Congress Volume Leuven 1989,* edited by J. A. Emerton, 204–21. Leiden: Brill.

———. 2004. "The Emergence of the Shoot of Jesse: An Eschatological or a Now Event?" *CTJ* 39: 88–108.

Blenkinsopp, Joseph. 1995. "The 'Servants of the Lord' in Third Isaiah: Profile of a Piestic Group in the Persian Epoch." In *The Place is Too Small for Us: The Israelite Prophets in Recent Scholarship,* edited by Robert P. Gordon, 392–412. Winona Lake, IN: Eisenbrauns.

———. 1997. "The Servant and the Servants in Isaiah and the Formation of the Book." In *Writing and Reading the Scroll of Isaiah: Studies of an Interpretive Tradition,* edited by Craig C. Broyles and Craig A. Evans, 155–76. Leiden: Brill.

———. 2003. *Isaiah 56–66: A New Translation with Introduction and Commentary.* New York: Doubleday.

Bonnard, P.-E. 1972. *Le Second Isaïe: Son Disciple et Leurs Editeurs Isaïe 40–66.* Paris: Librairie Lecoffre.

———. 1974. «Le Second Isaïe: Bücherschau.» *ZAW* 86: 246.

Botterweck, G. J. 1986. "ידע." In *TDOT* vol. 5:448–81.

Box, G. H. 1908. *The Book of Isaiah: Translated from a Text Revised in Accordance with the Results of Recent Criticism with Introductions, Critical Notes and Explanations, and Two Maps.* London: Pitman and Sons.

Brettler, Marc Zvi. 1989. *God is King: Understanding an Israelite Metaphor.* Sheffield, UK: Sheffield Academic Press.

Brown, Michael L. 1997. "אשר." In *NIDOTTE vol. 1.* 570–72.

Caird, G. B. 1980. *The Language and Imagery of the Bible.* London: Duckworth.

Calvin, John. 1550. *Calvin's Commentaries Series No. 3: Isaiah.* Reprint. Grand Rapids: Associated Publishers and Authors, n.d.

Cannon, W. W. 1929. "Isaiah 61,1–3 an Ebed-Jahweh poem." *ZAW* 47: 284–88.

Carpenter, Eugene. 1997a. "גמל." In *NIDOTTE vol. 1.* 871–73.

Carr, David. 1996. "Reaching for Unity in Isaiah." In *The Prophets: The Biblical Seminar 42*, edited by Philip R. Davies, 164–83. Sheffield, UK: Sheffield Academic Press.

Carroll, Robert P. 1978. "Second Isaiah and the Failure of Prophecy." *Studia Theologia* 32: 119–31.

————. 1982. "Eschatological Delay in the Prophetic Tradition?" *ZAW* 94: 47–58.

Cathcart, K. J. 1992. "Day of YHWH." In *ABD Vol. 2 (D–G)*, 84–85.

Cerny, Ladislav. 1948. *The Day of Yahweh and Some Relevant Problems*. Prague: Nakladem Filosoficke Fakulty University Karlovy.

Cheyne, Thomas Kelly. 1895. *Introduction of the Book of Isaiah*. London: Black.

Childs, Brevard S. 1960. *Myth and Reality in the Old Testament: Studies in Biblical Theology*. London: SCM.

————. 1976. *A Century of the Old Testament Study*. London: Lutterworth.

————. 1979. *Introduction to the Old Testament as Scripture*. Philadelphia: Fortress.

————. 1980. "Isaiah and the Zion Tradition." In *Isaiah and the Deliverance of Jerusalem: A Study of the Interpretation of Prophecy in the Old Testament*, 72–89. JSOTSup 13. Sheffield, UK: JSOT.

————. 1982. "The Unity of the Book of Isaiah." *Interpretation* 36: 117–29.

————. 1985. "Beyond Tradition-History: Deutero-Isaianic Development of First Isaiah's Themes." *JSOT* 31: 95–113.

————. 1997a. "Zion as Symbol and Political Reality: A Central Isaianic Quest." In *Studies in the Book of Isaiah: Festschrift Willem A. M. Beuken*, edited by J. Van Ruiten and M. Vervenne, 3–18. Bibliotheca Ephemeridum Theologicarum Lovaniensium CXXXII. Leuven: Leuven University Press.

————. 1997b. "'Arise, shine; for your light has come': A Basic Theme of the Isaianic Tradition." In *Writing and Reading the Scroll of Isaiah: Studies of an Interpretive Tradition*, edited by Craig C. Broyles and Craig A. Evans, 441–54. Leiden: Brill.

————. 2001. *Isaiah*. OTL. Louisville: Westminster John Knox.

————. 2004. *The Struggle to Understand Isaiah as Christian Scripture*. Grand Rapids: Eerdmans.

Clements, Ronald E. 1965. "Prophecy and Eschatology." In *Prophecy and Covenant*, 103–18. London: SCM.

————. 1980. *Isaiah 1–39*. The New Century Bible Commentary. Grand Rapids: Eerdmans.

Clifford, Richard J., S.J. 1993. "The Unity of the Book of Isaiah and Its Cosmogonic Language." *CBQ* 55: 1–17.

Collins, J. J. 2000a. "Apocalyptic Literature." In DNTB: 41–45.

Conrad, Edgar W. 1991. *Reading Isaiah*. Minneapolis: Fortress.

Craigie, P. C. 1976. *The Book of Deuteronomy: NICOT*. London: Hodder and Stoughton.

Cross, F. M. 1953. "The Council of Yahweh in Second Isaiah." *JNES* 12: 274–77.

————. 1966. "The Divine Warrior in Israel's Early Cult." In *Studies and Texts: Biblical Motifs—Origins and Transformations*, edited by A. Altman et al., 11–30. Cambridge: Harvard University Press.

Crüsemann, F. 1994. "»Ihnen gehören. die Bundesschlüsse« (Röm 9,4). Die alttestamentliche Bundestheologie und der christlich-jüdische Dialog." *KuI* 9: 21–34.

Darr, Katheryn Pfisterer. 1994. "Isaiah 60." In *Isaiah's Vision and the Family of God*, 190–97. Louisville: Westminster John Knox.

Davies, G. I. 1989. "The Destiny of the Nations in the Book of Isaiah." In *The Book of Isaiah,* edited by Jacques Vermeylen, 93–120. Leuven: Leuven University Press.

de Gruchy, John W. 1999. "Bible Study: A New Heaven and a New Earth—An Exposition of Isaiah 65:17–25." *Journal of Theology for Southern Africa* 105: 65–74.

Delitzsch, Franz. 1873. *Biblical Commentary on the Prophecies of Isaiah. Vol. II.* Edinburgh: T. & T. Clark.

Dim, Emmanuel Uchenna. 2005. *The Eschatological Implications of Isa 65 and 66 as the Conclusion of the Book of Isaiah.* Bible in History. New York: Lang.

Döderlein, J. C. 1789. *Esaias.* Norimbergaeet, Bavaria: Monarth.

Donner, H. 1985. "Jesaja LVI 1–7: Ein Abrogationsfall innerhalb des Kanons—Implikationen und Konsequenzen." In *Congress Volume Salamenca,* edited by J. A. Emerton, 81–95. VT Sup 37. Leiden: Brill.

Driver, S. R. 1913. *Introduction to the Literature of the Old Testament.* Edinburgh: T. & T. Clark.

Duhm, Bernhard. 1892. *Das Buch Jesaia: übersetz und erklärt.* Göttingen: Vandenhoeck & Ruprecht.

Dumbrell, William J. 1977. "Some Observations on Political Origins of Israel's Eschatology." *The Reformed Theological Review* 36: 33–41.

———. 1985. "The Purpose of the Book of Isaiah." *Tyndale Bulletin* 36: 111–28.

———. 1988. "The Prospect of Unconditionality in the Sinaitic Covenant." In *Israels Apostasy and Restoration: Essays in Honor of R. K. Harrison,* edited by Avraham Gileadi, 142–55. Grand Rapids: Baker.

———. 1994. *The Search for Order: Biblical Eschatology in Focus.* Reprint. Eugene, OR: Wipf and Stock, 2001.

Eissfeldt, Otto. 1962. "The Promises of Grace to David in Isaiah 55:1–5." In *Israel's Prophetic Heritage,* edited by Bernhard W. Anderson and Walter Harrelson, 196–207. London: SCM.

Elliger, K. 1928. *Die Einheit des Tritojesaja (Jes 56–66).* BWANT 45. Stuttgart: Kohlhammer.

Emmerson, Grace I. 1992. *Isaiah 56–66.* OT Guide. Sheffield, UK: Sheffield Academic Press.

Engnell, Ivan. 1948. "The 'Ebed Yahweh Songs and the Suffering Messiah in 'Deutero-Isaiah.'" *Bulletin of the John Rylands Library* 31: 54–93.

Enns, Peter. 1997. "משפט." In *NIDOTTE vol. 2:* 1142–44.

Everson, A. Joseph. 1974. "The Days of Yahweh." *JBL* 93: 329–37.

Farrar, Frederic W. 1886. *History of Interpretation: Eight Lectures.* London: Macmillan.

Fensham, F. C. 1966. "A Possible Origin of the Concept of the Day of the Lord." In *Biblical Essays: Proceedings of the 9th Meeting of "Die Ou-Testamentiese Werkgemeenskap in Suid-Afrika" held at the University of Stellenbosch, 26th–29th July 1966; and proceedings of the 2nd meeting of "Die Nuwe-Testamentiese Werkgemeenskap van Suid-Afrika" held at the University of Stellenbosch, 22nd–25th July 1966,* 90–97. Bepeck: Potschefstrom Herald.

Fiorenza, E. Schuessler. 1984. "Eschatology of the NT." In *IDBSup.* 271–77.

Fisher, J. 1939. *Das Buch Jesaias.* Bonn: Hanstein.

Fitzgerald, Curtis W. 2003. *A Rhetorical Analysis of Isaiah 56–66: A Dissertation Presented to the Faculty of the Department of Old Testament Studies Dallas Theological Seminary.* Ann Arbor, MI: Proquest Information and Learning Company.

Fowler, Mervyn D. 1987. "The Meaning of LIPNE YHWH in the Old Testament." *ZAW* 99: 384–90.

Freedman, David N. 1960. "History and Eschatology: The Nature of Biblical Religion and Prophetic Faith." *Interpretation* 14: 143–54.

Gilchrist, Paul R. 1980. "יחל, wait, hope." In *TWOT vol. 1*: 373–74.

Gosse, Bernard. 1989. "L'alliance d'Isaïe 59,21." *ZAW* 101: 116–18.

Gowan, Donald E. 1986. *Eschatology in the Old Testament*. Edinburgh: T. & T. Clark.

Grant, Robert M. 1984. *A Short History of the Interpretation of the Bible*. London: SCM.

Greenberg, Moshe. 1983. *Ezekiel 1–20: A New Translation with Introduction and Commentary*. New York: Doubleday.

Gressmann, H. 1905. *Der Ursprung der israelitisch-jüdischen Eschatologie*. Göttingen: Vandenhoeck & Ruprecht.

Hanson, P. D. 1971a. "Old Testament Apocalyptic Re-examined." *Interpretation* 25: 454–79.

———. 1971b. "Jewish Apocalyptic against its Near Eastern Environment." *Revue Biblique* 78: 31–58.

———. 1975. *The Dawn of Apocalyptic*. Philadelphia: Fortress.

———. 1984. "Apocalypticism." In *IDBSup*: 28–34.

———. 1987. "Israelite Religion in the Early Postexilic Period." In *Ancient Israelite Religion*, edited by Patrick D. Miller, Jr. et al., 485–508. Philadelphia: Fortress.

———. 1988. "Third Isaiah: The Theological Legacy of a Struggling Community." In *Reading and Preaching the Book of Isaiah*, edited by Christopher R. Seitz, 91–104. Philadelphia: Fortress.

Harrison, R. K. 1969. *Introduction to the Old Testament*. London: Tyndale.

Hartley, John E. 1980. "קוה, wait, look for, hope." In *TWOT vol. 2*: 791–92.

Hasel, G. 2001. "פלט." In *TDOT vol. 11*: 551–67.

Hasel, Gehard F. 1989. *Old Testament Theology: Basic Issues in the Current Debate*. Grand Rapids: Eerdmans.

———. 1992. "Sabbath." In *ABD vol. 5*: 849–56.

Herbert, A. S. 1975. *The Book of the Prophet: Isaiah Chs. 40–66*. Cambridge: Cambridge University Press.

Hermisson, Hans-Juergen. 2002. "'Deuterojesaja' und 'Eschatologie.'" In *The New Things: Eschatology in Old Testament Prophecy—Festschrift for Henk Leene*, edited by F. Postma, et al., 89–105. Maastricht: Uitgeverij Shaker.

Hollenberg, D. E. 1969. "Nationalism and 'the Nations' in Isaiah 40–55." *VT* 19: 23–36.

Holmgren, Fredrick. 1974. "Yahweh the Avenger: Isaiah 63:1–6." In *Rhetorical Criticism: Essays in Honor of James Muilenburg*, edited by Jared J. Jackson and Martin Kessler, 133–48. Pittsburgh: Pickwick.

Hugenberger, G. P. 1995. "The Servant of the Lord in the 'Servant Songs' of Isaiah: A Second Moses Figure." In *The Lord's Anointed: Interpretation of Old Testament Messianic Texts*, edited by Philip E. Satterthwaite et al., 105–40. Carlisle, UK: Paternoster.

Jenni, E. 1982. "Eschatology of the OT." In *IDB vol. 2*: 126–33.

Jeremias, J. 1984. "Theophany in the OT." In *IDBSup*: 896–98.

Johnson, B. 1998. "משפט." In *TDOT vol. 9*: 86–98.

———. 2003. "צדק." In *TDOT vol. 12*: 239–64.

Jones, D. R. 1964. *Isaiah 55–66 and Joel*. Torch Bible Commentaries. London: SCM.

Kellermann, U. 1991. "Tritojesaja und das Geheimnis des Gottesknechtes: Erwaegung zu Jes 59,21; 61,1–3; 66,18–24." *Biblische Notizen* 58: 46–81.

Kendall, Daniel, S.J. 1984. "The Use of Mishpat in Isaiah 59." *ZAW* 96: 391–405.

Kessler, Werner. 1956. "Zur Auslegung von Jesaja 56–66." *Theologische Literaturzeitung* 81: 335–38.

————. 1960. *Gott Geht Es Um Das Ganze: Jesaja 56–66 und 24–27*. Stuttgart: Calwer.

Kissane, Edward J. 1941. *The Book of Isaiah: Translated from a Critically Revised Hebrew Text with Commentary (vol 1: ch. 1–39)*. Dublin: Browne and Nolan.

————. 1943. *The Book of Isaiah: Translated from a Critically Revised Hebrew Text with Commentary (vol 2: ch. 40–66)*. Vol. II (XL–LXVI); Dublin: Browne and Nolan.

Knight, George A. F. 1978. "Eschatologie im Alten Testament (1951)." In *Eschatologie im Alten Testament*, edited by H. D. Preuss, 22–30. Darmstadt: Wissenschaftliche Buchgesellschaft.

————. 1985. *The New Israel: A Commentary on the Book of Isaiah 56–66*. Edinburgh: Handsel.

Koenen, Klaus. *Ethik und Eschatologie im Tritojesajabuch: Eine Literarkritische und redaktrionsgeschichtliche Studie*. Tübingen: Neukirchener, 1990.

Kraus, Hans-Joachim. 1966. "Die ausgebiebene Endtheophanie. Eine Studie in Jes 56–66." *ZAW* 78: 317–32.

————. 1992. *Theology of the Psalms*. Philadelphia: Fortress.

Kutsch, E. 1994. "ברית." In *TLOT* vol. 1: 256–66.

Laato, Antti. 1998. *"About Zion I will not be silent": The Book of Isaiah as an Ideological Unity*. Coniectanea Biblica Old Testament Series 44. Stockholm: Almqvist & Wiksell.

Lau, Wolfgang. 1994. *Schriftgelehrte Prophetie in Jes 56–66: Eine Untersuchung zu den literarischen Bezügen in den letzten elf Kapiteln des Jesajabuches*. BZAW 225. Berlin: de Gruyter.

Leene, H. 1997. "History and Eschatology in Deutero-Isaiah." In *Studies in the Book of Isaiah: Festschrift Willem A. M. Beuken*, edited by J. Van Ruiten and M. Vervenne, 223–50. Bibliotheca Ephemeridum Theologicarum Lovaniensium CXXXII. Leuven: Leuven University Press.

Leske, Adrian M. 1994. "The Influence of Isaiah 40–66 on Christology in Matthew and Luke: A Comparison." In *SBL 1994 Seminar Papers*, 897–916. Atlanta: SBL.

Levenson, Jon D. 1985. *Sinai and Zion: An Entry into the Jewish Bible*. Minneapolis: Winston.

Liebreich, Leon J. 1956. "The Compilation of the Book of Isaiah (1)." *JQR* 46: 259–77.

————. 1957. "The Compilation of the Book of Isaiah (2)." *JQR* 47: 114–38.

Liedke, G. 1997. "שפט, to judge." In *TLOT* vol. 3: 1392–99.

Lindblom, J. 1962. "Judgment and Salvation: Eschatology." In *Prophecy in Ancient Israel*, 360–75. Oxford: Blackwell.

Lohfink, N. 1967. "Eschatologie im Alten Testament." In *Bibelauslegung im Wandel*, 158–84. Frankfurt: Knecht.

Luther, Martin. 1972. *Luther's Works Vol. 17: Lectures on Isaiah Chapters 40–66*. 1527–30. Reprint. Saint Louis: Concordia.

Maass, Von Fritz. 1967. "Tritojesaja?." In *Das Ferne und Nahe Wort: Festschrift Leonhard Rost Zur Vollendung Seines 70. Lebensjahres Am 30. November 1966 Gewidmet*, edited by L. Rost, 153–63. Berlin: Töpelmann.

Martens, Elmer A. 1996. "Accessing Theological Readings of a Biblical Book." *Andrews University Seminary Studies* 34: 233–49.

Mathews, Clare R. 1995. *Defending Zion: Edom's Desolation and Jacob's Restoration (Isaiah 34–35) in Context.* Beifefte zur Zeitschrift fuer die alttestamentliche Wissenschaft, Bund 236. Berlin: de Gruyter.

McCarthy, D. J., S.J. 1965. "Notes on the Love of God in Deuteronomy and the Father-Son Relationship between YAHWEH and Israel." *CBQ* 27: 144–47.

McConville, J. Gordon. 1997. "ברית." In *NIDOTTE vol 1*: 747–55.

McCullough, W. S. 1948. "A Re-Examination of Isaiah 56–66." *JBL* 67: 27–36.

McKenzie, John L. 1946. "The Divine Sonship of Israel and the Covenant." *CBQ* 8: 320–31.

———. 1967. *Second Isaiah: A New Translation with Introduction and Commentary.* The Anchor Bible, Vol. 20. New York: Doubleday.

———. 1971. "Die neue Gemeinde: Gott Sammelt Ausgestossene und Arme (Jes 56–66), by Karl Pauritsch." *JBL* 90: 488–89.

Melugin, Roy F. 1976. *The Formation of Isaiah 40–55*. Berlin: de Gruyter.

Mendenhall, G. E., and Gary A. Herrion. 1992. "Covenant." In *ABD Vol 1 (A–C)*: 1179–1202.

Michel, D. 1966. "Zur Eigenart Tritojesajas." *Theologia Viatorum* 10: 213–30.

Miller, P. D., Jr. 1968. "The Divine Council and the Prophetic Call to War." *VT* 18: 100–107.

———. 2000. "Cosmology and World Order in the Old Testament: The Divine Council as Cosmic-Political Symbol." In *Israelite Religion and Biblical Theology: Collected Essays*, 422–44. JSOTSS 267. Sheffield, UK: Sheffield Academic Press.

Moberly, R. W. L. 2001. "Whose Justice? Which Righteousness? The Interpretation of Isaiah 5:16." *VT* 51: 55–68.

Motyer, J. Alec. 1993. *The Prophecy of Isaiah*. Leicester, UK: InterVarsity.

Mowinckel, Sigmund. 1922. *Psalmen Studien II: Das Throngesteigungsfest Jahwes und der Ursprung der Eschatologie.* Oslo: SNVAO.

———. 1958. "Jahves Dag." *Norsk Teologisk Tidsskrift* 59: 1–56.

———. 1959. *He That Cometh*. 1951. Reprint. Oxford: Blackwell.

Müller, Hans-Peter. 1964. "Zur Frage Nach Dem Ursprung Der Biblischen Eschatologie." *VT* 14: 276–93.

———. 1969. *Ursprünge und Structuren Alttestamenticher Eschatologie.* Beihefte zur Zeitschrift für die alttestamentliche Wissenschaft 109. Berlin: Töpelmann.

Muilenberg, James. 1954. "Isaiah 40–66." In *The Interpreter's Bible*, 381–773.

Nel, Philip J. 1997. "שלם." In *NIDOTTE vol. 4*: 130–35.

Neufeld, Thomas R. Yoder. 1997. "The Divine Warrior in Isaiah 59." In '*Put on the Armour of God': The Divine Warrior from Isaiah to Ephesians*, 15–47. JSNTSup 140. Sheffield: Sheffield Academic Press.

Nicholson, Ernest W. 1986a. "Covenant as a Theological Idea." In *God and His People: Covenant and Theology in the Old Testament*, 83–117. Oxford: Clarendon.

———. 1986b. "The Covenant and the Distinctiveness of Israel's Faith." In *God and His People: Covenant and Theology in the Old Testament*, 191–217. Oxford: Clarendon.

———. 1995. "Prophecy and Covenant." In *The Place is Too Small for Us: The Israelite Prophets in Recent Scholarship*, edited by Robert P. Gordon, 345–53. Winona Lake, IN: Eisenbrauns.

Nickelsburg, George W. E. 1992. "Eschatology: Early Jewish Literature." In *ABD Vol. 2 (D–G)*: 579–94.

Niehaus, Jeffrey J. 1997. "Theophany, Theology of." In *NIDOTTE vol 4*: 1247–50.

Niskanen, Paul. 2006. "YHWH as Father, Redeemer, and Potter in Isaiah 63:7—64:11." *CBQ* 68: 397–407.

O'Connell, Robert H. 1994. *Concentricity and Continuity: The Literary Structure of Isaiah*. JSOTSS 188. Sheffield, UK: Sheffield Academic Press.

Odeberg, Hugo. 1931. *Trito-Isaiah (Isaiah 56–66): A Literary and Linguistic Analysis*. Uppsala Universitets Arsskrift 1931. Uppsala: Hakan Ohlsson.

Ollenburger, Ben C. 1987. *Zion: The City of the Great King—A Theological Symbol of the Jerusalem Cult*. JSOTSS 41. Sheffield, UK: Sheffield Academic Press.

Oswalt, John N. 1981. "Recent Studies in Old Testament Eschatology and Apocalyptic." *JETS* 24: 289–301.

———. 1997. "Righteousness in Isaiah: A Study of the Formation of Chapters 56–66 in the Present Structure of the Book." In *Writing and Reading the Scroll of Isaiah: Studies of an Interpretive Tradition*, edited by Craig C. Broyles and Craig A. Evans, 177–92. Leiden: Brill.

———. 1998. *The Book of Isaiah: Chs. 40–66*. Grand Rapids: Eerdmans.

———. 2004. "The Book of Isaiah: A Short Course on Biblical Theology." *CTJ* 39: 54–71.

———. 2005. "Isaiah 60–62: The Glory of the Lord." *CTJ* 40: 95–103.

Otto, E. 2003. "ציון." In *TDOT vol. 12*: 333–65.

Otzen. 2004. "שבה." In *TDOT vol 14*: 286–94.

Park, Kyung-Chul. 2003. *Die Gerechtigkeit Israels und das Heil der Völker: Kultus, Tempel, Eschatologie und Gerechtigkeit in der Endgestalt des Jesajabuches (Jes 56,1–8; 58,1–14; 65,17—66,24)*. Frankfurt : Lang.

Pauritsch, K. 1971. *Die neue Gemeinde: Gott Sammelt Ausgestossene und Arme (Jesaia 56–66)*. AnBib vol. 47. Rome: Biblical Institute.

Payne, J. Barton. 1967a. "Eighth Century Israelitish Background of Isaiah 40–66 (1)." *WTJ* 29: 179–90.

———. 1967b. "Eighth Century Israelitish Background of Isaiah 40–66 (2)." *WTJ* 30: 50–58.

Peels, H. G. L. 1995. *The Vengeance of God: The Meaning of the Root NQM and the Function of the NQM-texts in the Context of Divine Revelation in the Old Testament*. Leiden: Brill.

———. 1997a . "נקם." In *NIDOTTE vol. 3*. 154–56.

———. 1997b. "קנאה." In *NIDOTTE vol. 3*. 937–40.

———. 2003a. "The Jealousy of God in the Old Testament." In *Shadow Sides: God in the Old Testament*, 41–56. Carlisle, UK: Paternoster.

———. 2003b. "The Vengeance of God in the Old Testament." In *Shadow Sides: God in the Old Testament*, 72–86. Carlisle, UK: Paternoster.

Perlitt, L. 1986. "Bund." In *EKL vol. 1*: 567.

Petersen, David L. 1992. "Eschatology: Old Testament." In *ABD Vol. 2 (D–G)*: 575–79.

Pfeiffer, Robert H. 1966. *Introduction to the Old Testament*. 1941. Reprint. London: Black.

Polan, Gregory J., OSB. 1997. "Still More Signs of Unity in the Book of Isaiah: The Significance of Third Isaiah." In *SBL 1997 Seminar Papers*, 224–33. Atlanta: Scholars'.

Polan, Gregory J., OSB. 1986. *In the Ways of Justice toward Salvation: A Rhetorical Analysis of Isaiah 56–59*. Frankfurt: Lang.

———. 2001. "Zion, the Glory of the Holy One of Israel: A Literary Analysis of Isaiah 60." In *Imagery and Imagination in Biblical Literature: Essays in Honor of Aloysius Fitzgerald, F.S.C*, edited by Lawrence Boadt and Mark S. Smith, 50–71. CBQ Monograph Series no. 32. South Bend, IN: Catholic Biblical Association of America.

Polaski, Donald C. 1998. "Reflections on a Mosaic Covenant: The Eternal Covenant (Isaiah 24.5) and Intertextuality." JSOT 77: 55–73.

Preuss, Horst Dietrich, edited by. 1978. *Eschatologie im Alten Testament*. Wege der Forschung 480. Darmstadt: Wissenschaftliche Buchgesellschaft.

Preuss, Horst Dietrich. 1996. "The Chosen People of God and the Nations." In *Old Testament Theology Vol 2*, 284–307. Edinburgh: T. & T. Clark.

Rendtorff, Rolff. 1985. "Isaiah 56–66 (Trito-Isaiah)." In *The OT: An Introduction*, 196–200. London: SCM.

———. 1993a. "The Composition of the Book of Isaiah." In *Canon and Theology: Overtures to an Old Testament Theology*, 146–69. Minneapolis: Fortress.

———. 1993b. "Isaiah 56.1 as a Key to the Formation of the Book of Isaiah." In *Canon and Theology: Overtures to an Old Testament Theology*, 181–99. Minneapolis: Fortress.

———. 1997. "Approaches to Old Testament Theology." In *Problems in Biblical Theology*, 13–26.

———. 1998. *The Covenant Formula: An Exegetical and Theological Investigation*. Edinburgh: T. & T. Clark.

Reventlow, Henning Graf. 1997. "The Eschatologization of the Prophetic Books: A Comparative Study." In *Eschatology in the Bible and in Jewish and Christian Tradition*, edited by Henning Graf Reventlow, 169–88. JSOTSS 243. Sheffield, UK: Sheffield Academic Press.

Ringgren, Helmer. 1961. *The Messiah in the Old Testament*. London: SCM.

———. 1980. "זרח." In *TDOT vol 4*: 141–43.

Ringgren, Helmer et al. 1999. "עבד." In *TDOT vol. 10*: 376–405.

Roberts, J. J. M. 1973. "The Davidic Origin of the Zion Tradition." *JBL* 92: 329–44.

———. 1982a. "Zion in the Theology of the Davidic Solomonic Empire." In *Studies in the Period of David and Solomon and Other Essays*, edited by Tomoo Ishida, 93–108. Tokyo: Yamakawa-Shuppansha.

———. 1982b. "Isaiah in Old Testament Theology." *Interpretation* 36: 130–43.

———. 1992. "The Old Testament's Contribution to Messianic Expectations." In *The Messiah: Judaism and Christianity Origins-Developments Earliest Judaism and Christianity*, edited by James H. Charlesworth, 39–51. Minneapolis: Fortress.

Robinson, Gnana. 1975. "The Meaning of יד in Isaiah 56.5." In *ZAW* 87: 282–84.

Robinson, H. Wheeler. 1981. *Corporate Personality in Ancient Israel*. Edinburgh: T. & T. Clark.

Rofé, A. 1989. "Isaiah 59:19 and Trito-Isaiah's Vision of Redemption." In *The Book of Isaiah*, edited by Jacques Vermeylen, 407–10. Leuven: Leuven University Press.

———. 1997. "Prophecy and Apocalyptic." In *Introduction to the Prophetic Literature*, 98–105. Sheffield, UK: Sheffield Academic Press.

Rowland, Christopher. 2005. "Apocalyptic." In TDIB: 51–53.

Ruiten, J. T. A. G. M. van. 1992. "The Intertextual Relationship between Isaiah 65:25 and Isaiah 11:6–9." In *The Scriptures and the Scrolls,* edited by A. S. van der Woude, 31–42. VT Sup 49. Leiden: Brill.

Ruprecht, E. 1997. "פלט (to save); מלט (to deliver)." In *TLOT vol.* 2: 986–90.

Russell, David Syme. 1964. *The Method and Message of Jewish Apocalyptic: 200 BC–AD 100.* London: SCM.

Ruszkowski, Leszek. 2000. *Volk und Gemeinde im Wandel: Eine Untersuchung zu Jesaja 56–66.* Goettingen: Vandenhoeck & Ruprecht.

Ryken, L., ed. 1998. *Dictionary of Biblical Imagery.* Leicester, UK: InterVarsity.

Sauer, G. 1997a . "גמל, to do, show." In *TLOT vol. 1*: 320–21.

———. 1997b . "נקם, to avenge." In *TLOT vol.* 2: 767–69.

———. 1997c . "קנאה, fervor." In *TLOT vol.* 3: 1145–47.

Schnutenhaus, Von Frank. 1964. "Das Kommen und Erscheinen Gottes im Alten Testament." *ZAW* 76: 1–21.

Schramm, Brooks. 1995. *The Opponents of Third Isaiah: Reconstructing the Cultic History of the Restoration.* JSOTSS 193. Sheffield, UK: Sheffield Academic Press.

Schultz, Richard. 1995. "The King in the Book of Isaiah." In *The Lord's Anointed: Interpretation of Old Testament Messianic Text,* edited by Philip E. Satterthwaite et al., 141–65. Carlisle, UK: Paternoster.

———. 1997. "Justice." In *NIDOTTE vol.* 4. 837–46.

Schunck, Klaus-Dietrich. 1964. "Strukturlinien in der Entwicklung Der Vorstellung vom 'Tag Jahwes.'" *VT* 14: 319–30.

———. 1974. "Die Eschatologie der Propheten des Alten Testaments und Ihre Wandlung in Exilisch-Nachexilischer Zeit." In *Studies on Prophecy: A Collection of Twelve Papers,* 116–32. Supplements to Vetus Testamentum. Leiden: Brill.

Sehmsdorf, E. 1972. "Studien zur Redaktionsgeschichte von Jesaja 56–66, I und II." *ZAW* 84: 517–62 and 562–76.

Seitz, Christopher R. 1992. "Third Isaiah." In *ABD vol.* 3: 501–7.

———. 1993. *Isaiah 1–39: Interpretation—A Bible Commentary for Teaching and Preaching.* Louisville: John Knox.

———. 1996. "How is the Prophet Isaiah Present in the Latter Half of the Book? The Logic of Chs. 40–66 within the Book of Isaiah." *JBL* 115: 219–40.

———. 1999. "Old Testament Apocalyptic." *Evangel* 17. 74–76.

———. 2001. "The Book of Isaiah 40–66: Introduction, Commentary, and Reflections." In *The New Interpreter's Bible, General Articles & Introduction, Commentary, & Reflections for Each Book of the Bible, Vol. 6*: 307–552. Nashville: Abingdon.

———. 2004. "'You are My Servant, You are the Israel in whom I Will be Glorified': The Servant Songs and the Effect of Literary Context in Isaiah." *CTJ* 39: 117–34.

Sekine, Seizo. 1989. *Die tritojesajanische Sammlung (Jes 56–66) redaktionsgeschichtlich Untersucht.* Berlin: de Gruyter.

Sellin, E. 1912. "Alter, Wesen und Ursprung der alttestamentlichen Eschatologie." In *Der alttestamentliche Prophetismus,* 103–93.

Skinner, J. 1915. *The Book of the Prophet Isaiah Chapters I–XXXIX.* 1896. Reprint. Cambridge: Cambridge University Press.

———. 1917. *The Book of the Prophet Isaiah Chapters XL–LXVI: The Cambridge Bible for Schools and Colleges.* 1898. Reprint. Cambridge: Cambridge University Press.

Smart, James D. 1934–35. "A New Interpretation of Isaiah 66:1–6." *The Expository Times* 46: 420–24.

Smart, James D. 1967. *History and Theology in Second Isaiah: A Commentary on Isaiah 35, 40–66.* London: Epworth.

Smith, P. A. 1995. *Rhetoric and Redaction in Trito-Isaiah: The Structure, Growth and Authorship of Isaiah 56–66.* Leiden: Brill.

Smith, Ralph L. 1993a. "In That Day: National Eschatology." In *Old Testament Theology: Its History, Method, and Message,* 398–435. Nashville: Broadman and Holman.

Snaith, Norman H. 1953. *The Distinctive Ideas of the Old Testament.* London: Epworth.

———. 1967. "Isaiah 40–66: A Study of the Teaching of the Second Isaiah and Its Consequences." In *Studies on the Second Part of the Book of Isaiah,* edited by Harry M. Orlinsky and Norman H. Snaith, 137–262. Leiden: Brill.

Spykerboer, H. C. 1989. "Isaiah 55:1–5: The Climax of Deutero-Isaiah. An Invitation to Come to the New Jerusalem." In *The Book of Isaiah,* edited by Jacques Vermeylen, 357–59. Leuven: Leuven University Press.

Steck, Odil Hannes. 1991. *Studien zu Tritojesaja.* BZAW 203. Berlin: de Gruyter.

———. 1997. "Autor und/oder Redaktor in Jesaja 56–66." In *Writing and Reading the Scroll of Isaiah: Studies of an Interpretive Tradition,* edited by Craig C. Broyles and Craig A. Evans, 219–61. Leiden: Brill.

Steinmetz, David C. 1982. "John Calvin on Isaiah 6: A Problem in the History of Exegesis." *Interpretation* 36: 156–70.

Stigers, Harold G. 1980. "צדק, be just, righteous." In *TWOT vol.* 2: 752–55.

Strong, John T. 1997. "Zion: Theology of." In *NIDOTTE vol.* 4: 1314–21.

Sweeney, Marvin A. 1988. *Isaiah 1–4 and the Post-Exilic Understanding of the Isaianic Tradition.* Berlin: de Gruyter.

———. 1997. "Prophetic Exegesis in Isaiah 65–66." In *Writing and Reading the Scroll of Isaiah: Studies of an Interpretive Tradition,* edited by Craig C. Broyles and Craig A. Evans, 455–74. Leiden: Brill.

Tamerius, Travis. 2002. "Sounding the Alarm: N. T. Wright and Evangelical Theology." *The Reformation & Revival Journal* 11.2. Online: http://www.hornes.org/theologia/travis-tamerius/n-t-wright-evangelical-theology. 2006.

Torrey, Charles Cutler. 1928. *The Second Isaiah: A New Interpretation.* Edinburgh: T. & T. Clark.

Travis, Stephen H. 1979. "The Value of Apocalyptic." *Tyndale Bulletin* 30: 53–76.

Uffenheimer, Benjamin. 1997. "From Prophetic to Apocalyptic Eschatology." In *Eschatology in the Bible and in Jewish and Christian Tradition,* edited by Henning Graf Reventlow, 200–217. JSOTSS 243. Sheffield, UK: Sheffield Academic Press.

VanGemeren, Willem A. 1990a. "The Day of the Lord." In *Interpreting the Prophetic Word,* 214–25. Grand Rapids: Zondervan.

———. 1990b. *Interpreting the Prophetic Word.* Grand Rapids: Zondervan.

Vermeylen, J. 1977/78. *Du Prophete Isaïe a l'apocalyptique. Isaïe I–XXXV, miroir d'un demi-millenaire d'experience religieuse en Israel.* 2 vols. Paris: Wiklander.

Volz, D. P. 1932. *Jesaja II.* KAT, 9. Leipzig: A. Deichertsche Verlagsbuchhandlung D. Werner Scholl.

von Rad, G. 1959. "The Origin of the Concept of the Day of YAHWEH." *Journal of Semitic Studies* 4: 97–108.

———. 1965a. *Old Testament Theology, vol. 2: The Theology of Israel's Prophetic Traditions.* Edinburgh: Oliver & Boyd.

———. 1965b. "The Day of Jahweh." In *Old Testament Theology, vol. 2: The Theology of Israel's Prophetic Traditions,* 119–25. Edinburgh: Oliver & Boyd.

———. 1966a. "The City on the Hill (1949)." In *The Problem of the Hexateuch and Other Essays*, 232–42. London: Oliver & Boyd.

———. 1966b. "The Theological Problem of the Old Testament Doctrine of Creation (1936)." In *The Problem of the Hexateuch and Other Essays*, 131–43. London: Oliver & Boyd.

———. 1975. *Wisdom in Israel*. London: SCM.

Vriezen, Th. C. 1953. "Prophecy and Eschatology." In *Congress Volume: SVT no. 1*, edited by G. W. Anderson et al., 199–229. Leiden: Brill.

———. 1962. "Essentials of the Theology of Isaiah." In *Israel's Prophetic Heritage*, edited by Bernhard W. Anderson and Walter Harrelson, 128–46. London: SCM.

Warfield, B. B. 1916. "The Divine Messiah in the Old Testament." *The Princeton Theological Review* 14: 369–416.

Weinfeld, Moshe. 1992. "'Justice and Righteousness'—mshpt wtsdqh—The Expression and Its Meaning." In *Justice and Righteousness: Biblical Themes and Their Influences*, edited by Henning Graf Reventlow and Yair Hoffman, 228–46. JSOTSS 137. Sheffield, UK: Sheffield Academic Press.

———. 1995. "כבד." In *TDOT vol.7*: 22–38.

Weiss, Meir. 1966. "The Origin of the 'Day of the Lord' Reconsidered." *Hebrew Union College Annual* 37: 29–71.

Wells, Jo Bailey. 2000. "'The Holy One of Israel': The Context of Isaiah." In *God's Holy People: A Theme in Biblical Theology*, 130–59. Sheffield, UK: Sheffield Academic Press.

Wells, Roy D., Jr. 1996. "'Isaiah' as an Exponent of Torah: Isaiah 56.1–8." In *New Visions of Isaiah*, edited by Roy F. Melugin and Marven A. Sweeney, 140–55. Sheffield, UK: Sheffield Academic Press.

Westermann, C. 1969 . *Isaiah 40–66: OTL*. London: SCM.

Whitley, C. F. 1963. "Pre-Exilic Prophecy and Eschatology." In *The Prophetic Achievement*, 199–220. London: Mowbray.

———. 1972. "Deutero-Isaiah's Interpretation of Sedeq." *VT* 22: 469–75.

Whybray, R. N. 1981. *Isaiah 40–66*. The New Century Bible Commentary. Grand Rapids: Eerdmans.

Wildberger, Hans. 1991. *Isaiah 1–12: A Commentary*. Minneapolis: Fortress.

———. 1997. *Isaiah 13–27: A Continental Commentary*. Minneapolis: Fortress.

Williamson, H. G. M. 1990. "Isaiah 63:7—64:11: Exilic Lament or Post-Exilic Protest?" *ZAW* 102: 48–58.

———. 1994. *The Book Called Isaiah: Deutero-Isaiah's Role in Composition and Redaction*. Oxford: Clarendon.

———. 1998. *Variations on a Theme: King, Messiah and Servant in the Book of Isaiah— The Didsbury Lecture 1997*. Carlisle, UK: Paternoster.

———. 2006. *A Critical and Exegetical Commentary on Isaiah 1–27: Volume 1: Commentary on Isaiah 1–5*. London: T. & T. Clark.

Winkle, Dwight W. van. 1985. "The Relationship of the Nations to YAHWEH and to Israel in Isaiah 40–55." *VT* 35: 446–58.

Wright, N. T. 1992. *The New Testament and the People of God: Christian Origins and the Question of God, vol. 1*. London: SPCK.

———. 1999a. "In Grateful Dialogue: A Response." In *Jesus and the Restoration of Israel: A Critical Assessment of N. T. Wright's Jesus and the Victory of God*, edited by Carey C. Newman, 244–77. Carlisle, UK: Paternoster.

———. 1999b. *New Heavens, New Earth. The Biblical Pictures of Christian Hope.* Cambridge: Grove Books.

———. 2007. *Surprised by Hope.* London: SPCK.

———. n.d. New Heavens, New Earth: The Biblical Picture of Christian Hope. http:// www.leithvalley.org.nz/Resources/NewHeavensEarth_Wright.pdf. 1–17.

Zillessen, A. 1906. "'Tritojesaja' und Deuterojesaja." *ZAW* 26: 231–76.

Zimmerli, W. 1963. "Zur Sprache Tritojesajas (1950)." In *Gottes Offenbarung. Gesammelte Aufsätze zum Alten Testament*, 217–33. Theologische Bücherei 19. München: Kaiser.

Scripture Index

Isaiah *(continued)*

Isaiah *(continued)*

Isaiah *(continued)*